Selected Essays by Zhu Yuechun

朱粤椿选集

——论适应主义（上）

On Adaptationism（Vol. 1）

朱粤椿 著　李南哲 译

·广州·

广东省出版集团
新世纪出版社

图书在版编目（CIP）数据

朱粤椿选集：论适应主义. 上、下/朱粤椿著；李南哲译. —
广州：新世纪出版社，2014.1
  ISBN 978 - 7 - 5405 - 4629 - 8

Ⅰ．①朱…　Ⅱ．①朱…②李…　Ⅲ．①散文集—中国—
当代　Ⅳ．①I267

中国版本图书馆 CIP 数据核字（2013）第 313849 号

出 版 人：孙泽军
责任编辑：秦文剑　傅　琨
责任技编：王建慧
装帧设计：张竹媛

出版发行：新世纪出版社
　　　　　（广州市大沙头四马路 10 号）
经　　销：全国新华书店
印　　刷：广州伟龙印刷制版有限公司
　　　　　（地址：广州市从化太平经济开发区创业路 31 号）
规　　格：890mm×1240mm
开　　本：32
印　　张：17
字　　数：440 千
版　　次：2014 年 1 月第 1 版
印　　次：2014 年 1 月第 1 次印刷
定　　价：198.00 元（上、下）
质量监督电话：020 - 83797655　购书咨询电话：020 - 83781537

目录

下

朱·粤·椿·选·集

中文

——论适应主义 上

序

朱粤椿先生将其若干文稿结集付梓,嘱我为序。

我与朱先生深有交情。他为人厚德重义,至仁笃诚,学诚渊博而谦逊随和,堪为良师益友。

朱先生的文集,开宗明义:"献给世界热爱和平的人们。"文集首篇《论适应主义》。

这里的和,不止于人与人个体之间的和,更是包含了宇宙万物的无垠大和。适应,亦即顺乎天理,才是万物生存之道,才能达到大和。

人与人之间要和睦相处,要"容得左右,容得前后,容得自己"。

国家内部要和谐统一。"一个国家,只有民族和解,融合一体,团结一致,这个国家才有希望兴旺发达"。

国与国之间要和平共处。谴责超级大国的"霸权主义和单边主义"。

人与自然要和谐相生。人类要"用最理智的科学方式方法去开发利用自然"。

无限宇宙的运动都必须依照一定的轨迹。"如果地球不适应在宇宙运行,地球也得消亡"。

为了这个大和，万物都必须适应固有法则。作为个人，要以"一生爱自己，爱家，爱事业，爱民族，爱祖国"为根本。作为国家，"国之内政，别国要尊重"。作为人类，"要爱惜自然的一切"。

　　总之，宇宙万物都必须适应固有的规律和法则，也叫天理，决不可倒行逆施，伤天害理，才能和谐相处，生存发展。朱先生的适应主义理论和大和共生的思想，洋溢在他著作的字里行间。

　　我对朱先生的著作理解不深，不敢妄言作序。仅以数语，聊寄愚悟。

赵善祥

2011 年 12 月 27 日

论适应主义（一）

　　浩瀚宇宙，洪荒无止境，沿着既定轨道运行着的渺小的地球是并存着生命体和无生命体的物质大千世界。

　　地球作为有生命体的星球，是宇宙的一个组成部分。如果地球不适应在宇宙间运行，地球也得消亡。其他星球如果适应有生命体存在，也一定会有以不同表现形式出现的已经适应了生长环境的高、低等动物，植物的存在。

　　从地球上存在的物质来看，造物主真是神奇伟大，它所造就的一切物质都可以被人类加以利用、适应。

　　一切的科学都是人类在生存和享受、利用造物主的物质元素过程中归纳发现的结果。人类从中去研究、创造、发现和加以利用。再用化学现象、物理现象、生物现象、数学现象和语言文字等去解释造物主所创造的物质。

　　一切宗教信仰都是人类为弃恶扬善而设定的信念。有人类存在的一天都会有宗教信仰的存在。宗教信仰能平衡人类的思想观念和心态，人类生活于世上生命很短暂，宗教信仰就是心安理得地实惠于人类的学科。人类平衡心态就不会向社会和自然界发泄不良心态，宗教信仰引导人类对善与恶、曲与直、是与非确定界限。宗教信仰是弃恶扬善的学科，是创造和顺人类社会的经典学科。

　　人类是大自然中动物类至高无上的动物，人类有高思维、高智商，随着人类历史进化而进步。人类每时每刻生存的两个环境，首

先是自然环境，其次才是社会环境。

在人类创造的社会中，人创造适应人类生存发展的社会制度，推翻坑害人类的社会制度，人类生存必须遵循和适应社会规律法则，造就一个适应人类生存的社会环境。

人与自然的关系中，人类利用自然界物质越多，环境污染就越严重，自然界有生命群体和无生命群体之间发生巨变，直接影响有生命群体不适应，无生命群体的巨大变化导致个别种类生命体消亡，人类保护好适应人类生存的自然环境，人类才能在适应的环境下生存发展。

1. 人的根本

人甫一出生，今后对他影响最大的是出生地。当然，国家的制度、民族风俗习惯、当地风土人情、宗教信仰对人也有很重要的影响。但人生七彩第一个染缸着色点是——故乡。

任何一个民族，任何一个国家，从人之初开始，首先实行的是家教，再由学校、社会以及国家进行教育。使其初涉人世时能够得到扶正培养。

教育差异是由家庭、国情、民族风俗习惯的不同而产生的，所以人类社会中人生观和世界观、社会科学观点和自然科学观点也就千差万别了。

但有人类存在一天，就有一种认识是人类的共识，那就是人一生爱自己、爱家庭、爱事业、爱民族、爱祖国，这是人的根本。

家是人始终的窝，家是人生命延续点，家是国的单元，家教是国教的基础，家业是国业的顶梁柱，家产是国产的源泉，没有众多的家就没有国的建立。先有家才有国，家宁，国才安。保家卫国、报国为家。人生活在社会上，这是立足处世的基本点。

人类从原始社会群居开始发展至今，跟世上所有动物一样，有

二人以上就必须有头目——即王者，人有人王，兽有兽王，虫有虫王（人类细观蜜蜂会感悟很多学问），人群没有王，就像网没有纲。王者永远都适应单、寡、孤、独，我相信好王一定会带领、教化好民众，好民一定会维护好王。

粤椿语录

廉洁不乱心田

一个清高正直的人，面对金钱、名位、权势、美色等诱惑，皆能自律自重，心意坚若磐石，不贪图、不钻营，所以不会迷乱心智，失去操守。

2. 人祸之我见

人祸——人为的灾难。

战争是人祸中最大灾难。还有矿难、海难、车祸、天灾、恐怖袭击、他杀，或因死罪被他人杀、自杀、打劫、殴斗、械斗、谋杀等各种突发性伤亡事故，夺走了人的生命，使人死于非命。

人生各有各的活法，但死是人类最统一的、最公平的、就是一次的。人类的死千差万别，但可归为两类，死于本命或非命。

有的人一出生几秒钟就死了，所以人类把未成年人的死称为夭折，中年而死的称为早逝，晚年（60 岁后为晚年）而死是人的生老病死（人类规律）有寿，自然死亡，死于本命。

人祸事件，每年每月在世界某角落均有发生。第二次世界大战希特勒下令在集中营实行最残酷的种族灭绝，杀害了 1200 多万犹太人和吉卜赛人。日本侵略中国时，仅南京大屠杀就有 30 多万人死于日本屠刀下，这两大事件被杀的人手无寸铁，有老的、少的、

男的、女的，还有将婴儿抛于空中再用刺刀刺死，多么残酷，多么灭绝人性。这些死于非命的人，跟战场上两军交火、双方真枪实弹拼死的人有根本区别。有人类存在的一天，人都不应该忘记这些悲惨的事件。

人类历史中，一个战场获殊荣的将军，一个推翻旧君主打出江山的皇帝，一个拥有千万、亿万身家的矿山老板（特别是煤矿老板），在他们的脚下有多少人死于非命。

自古以来，有些死于非命的人，永远让人怀念、崇敬，他们永远活在人们心中，这就是用自己生命为国为民牺牲的军人、消防人员、维和部队人员、海事抢救人员、维护公共安全的警察、流行疾病救护人员，等等，这些人为了国家安危，为了人民大众平安环境，为了遭受天灾人祸的人们，挺身而出，献出生命，他们虽然死于非命，但任何时代人们都怀念他们——英雄、烈士。

 粤椿语录

孝悌忠信人之本，礼义廉耻人之根

孝顺父母、友爱兄弟、尽忠职守、诚正信实、循礼守法、行事合宜、廉洁不贪、知耻改过，是我们做人的根本，也是幸福的泉源。

3. 家规族规与法律

人类自身素质问题也是社会的首要问题。

自从造物主造就了人类，也就是男人和女人结合，奇迹般地从一到二、由二到三，于是人生人，生生不息，家生家，生生不止。人类也不断地在进化过程中注重着质量和数量。

到今时今日，地球上共存了不同肤色、不同语言、不同民族、不同文化、不同宗教信仰和风俗习惯的几十亿人口。人有活着的权利，每个人都是平等的。人生活在世上，借时空经过，人生一世，犹如草木一秋。

人类有着贫富之分、贵贱之分、职业之分、国家之别，总的一句就是永远存在差别。没有差别，就没有向往看齐的追求，人的七情六欲时刻在差别中去寻找、比较、争议、争夺。由于欲望有别，物质财富有别，贵贱有别，人的思想有别，就产生行动，行动的错与对就要定法律标准。

人类最早的法律标准是从家规族规而起的，家规族规是原始生活逐步进化成家居与族居而形成的法规。

在这进化过程中，人意识到优生良养必须遵照规范的道德标准。从性开始，人类要优生良养，一代胜一代，对婚嫁的基本要求是不准近亲通婚，不准乱伦；从家规、族规到宗教教义，再从国家安全、维护人生权利，逐步形成今天的与时俱进的法律、法规、宗规、家规。中国历史上就有完善家教家规的训文——朱子家训。

人类社会中，每个国家、每个民族、各宗教、各教派所定的法律、规章、制度等，都是适应他们的条文，是他们的家内之政，国内之政，别国要尊重他们的内政，不能干涉，更不可以将自己的政见强加于别国，或者找个借口，无中生有，强行侵略，加权施压，发动战争。

粤椿语录

正直谦让的美德

老年幸福、子孙昌荣，他们少年、中年时，一定是为人正直，不与人争，懂得"退一步海阔天空"的道理，所以上天赐予福禄寿，获得生活幸福又平安。

4. 大国与冷战

在人类社会中，谁都希望完善自己，完善家庭，完善国家。对于国家兴亡，每个国家中的国民都有责任。为了国家，为了家庭，献身自己，责无旁贷。人的生命是最宝贵的，但仍然舍得献给国家和家庭。

有人类战争史以来，一个大国攻打弱小的国家，犹如大人打小孩那么容易，但小孩要还击大人，只能用万般无奈的鬼点子了。

自从超级大国冷战以来（冷战期是 1947 年至 1991 年，以苏联为首的共产主义阵营和以美国为首的资本主义阵营之间展开在太空、高科技、远程导弹、中程导弹等方面的军备竞赛，并互在势力范围内争夺、渗透），阿富汗、朝鲜、越南、柬埔寨、中东等地区成了霸权试验地。待到 1991 年苏联解体，分裂出 15 个国家时，冷战正式结束。霸权国家为了争夺资源在世界范围内又开始了称霸、夺地盘、设军驻、布控等行为。

这期间，小国、弱国对大霸权国毫无他法，只能以身保家卫国，从完善自身到完结自己。以身去为国作最后的贡献，人肉炸弹就这样诞生了——称之为恐怖主义。

世界上每一个人，用你自己的一双手，压住你自己的胸膛，拍一下，问一声天，再拍一下，问一声地，又拍一下，问一声自己的良心何在。这样做，拿人权、道德标准来衡量怎样对得起自己？怎样对得起家庭、老人、小孩？怎样对得起君王和乡亲父老百姓大众。当王的，拥有高官决策权势的又用这样的方法问一下自己，当你要对敌方作出的决策时，将你自己置于对方位置想一下，你的决定带来的结果你承受得了吗？每个人都这样想，人类祈求和平的起点就有望了。

正规定名恐怖活动、恐怖组织、恐怖头目或恐怖分子的基本事

件是在 1922 年至 1939 年，当时巴勒斯坦只有 8 万多犹太人居住，二战的原因令 45 万多犹太人拥到巴勒斯坦，此后两年间犹太人的人数增加到 100 多万，但阿拉伯人和英国人一下子接受不了这个现实，对犹太人进行诸多刁难。本身就是难民，进而变成烂民的犹太人，不时地组织恐怖袭击，恐怖名词与行动就不断以各种花样出现了。1945—1947 年，大规模恐怖战争在中东点燃了，1947 年联合国投票决定将巴勒斯坦一分为二，新的国家以色列诞生了。应验了圣经上说的"在耶路撒冷的一边必须有犹太国诞生"。

中东问题以"恐怖"二字经历了 60 多年，现在仍然有增无减，这些地方是超级大国霸权主义推销点、试验地，也是杀鸡儆猴的地方。这样造成了中东国家和周边各国没有过一天安宁的日子，可恨又可悲！冤报冤，仇报仇，何日能休？

 粤椿语录

朋友有益，人情有裨

孔子曰："友直，友谅，友多闻"。平日广结善缘，结交正直、诚信而博学的益友，有助于增长德性与见识。发生困难时，益友就会成为贵人，必要时伸出援手，互相扶持。

5. 战争与人祸

战争是人祸，自从有人类，年年月月都有大大小小的战争，任何性质的战争都是由当权者点起的战火，其中军火商成为"渔翁"，平民百姓遭殃。

每次战争，赢者更赢，输家更输。战火到达的地方，生灵涂

几千年以来，战争是为了掠夺土地、资源、金银珠宝，有的甚至是为了一个美女（中国明朝末年吴三桂为了陈圆圆）造成连年恶战。

从性质上说，战争有两种，一种是侵略其他国家或地区的侵略战争；另一种是本国本地区内部的权力之争，或民众反暴政的内战。

侵略之战，随着历史进步，侵略者的借口越来越阴险狡诈。到了现代，超级大国动不动就以武力解决纠纷，暴露出霸权主义和单边主义的霸气。那些小国政治上听它的，资源上由它来摆布垄断，稍有些不听从，就找个借口，启动立体式打击将被侵略国数天之内夷为平地，这是威胁人类至灭顶之灾的现代战争。

西元前每次大的战争都会持续打数年，西元 636—642 年穆斯林侵略占领巴基斯坦、叙利亚、波斯和埃及，1243 年蒙古入侵塞尔柱（塞尔柱人在蒙古入侵前已占领了阿富汗等七国），1592 年日本侵略朝鲜半岛，直接威胁中国（当时明朝国力昌盛），1824—1886 年英国入侵印度期间多次入侵缅甸，1886 年英国将缅甸划为英属印度的一个省。1937 年日本侵略中国，1942 年日本占领缅甸及东南亚六国。

人类历史上没有一年停过战火，近代第一次世界大战损失 500 亿英镑，伤亡人数有近 4000 万。第二次世界大战的损失和伤亡人数比第一次世界大战多了几倍。当权者一念之差，伏尸千万，流血万里，一次战争劫掠了多少生命和财产！

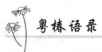

读好书，说好话，行好事，做好人

希望人们以谦和真诚的善念来待人处世，在生活之中积极行善，传布善念，让社会充满祥和的氛围。

6. 不可干涉内政

每一个国家、每一个地区、每一个民族，他们自己的政治制度、法律法规、族规、民约、家规宗条是属于他自己的国政、族政、家政——内政。每个国家、每个宗教、每个家庭都有自己一本难念的经，让他们在独立自主的情况下，用适应解决他们内部问题的办法，自己去选择解决。任何国家将自己的条条框框强加给其他国家是毫无道理的。

但任何国家或地区，如果其国策民生的制度不适应广大民众的生存，肯定会出现造反现象，甚至爆发内部战争——即内战。任何外来政治、经济的干扰对正在内战的国家或地区也是错误的行为。

特别是霸权主义国家，谁的事都要管，喜欢在有内战发生的国家或地区趁火打劫，趁机掠夺，从政治、经济方面培植自己的代理人，其实这样做比自己去攻打该地区还划算。当今世界是冷战时代，冷战同样炮声隆隆，军火商大手收钱，弱国资源照样被强国霸国掠夺。弱小国家出现内战，真是"小国不发癫，霸国断火烟，小国发了癫，霸国冒火，有炒又有煎"。每个国家内战都有霸权国趁机得利，也有公正、公义的国家伸手援助。

战争是人祸，也是人类社会的必然产物，只要有战争的地方，都是失去生命和损失财产的地方。人的意识是社会制度的根本来源，社会制度的一切策略是主持社会秩序的准则。如果出了严重差错，即成为战争的火药包，一旦遇到可以点燃的导火索，战争就爆发了。

 粤椿语录

行藏敦节义，千秋浩气冲霄汉

天地振纲常，一片丹心耀日华。

君子处世，有道则见，无道则隐，行为须重节义；像关圣帝君如此的典范，千载以来，一片浩然正气，充塞天地之间。

宇宙人世间的一切事理，均须讲究纲纪、重视伦常，像关圣帝君的八德全修，一片赤忱丹心。与日月光华，相映成辉。

7. 贪是败坏的根源

贪是人类败坏的根源。

从"贪"字看，点与撇之分就是变成另一种意义了，由"贪"变成"贫"——穷尽的意思。

有人类以来，私欲是本性。私欲是道德、法规、法律的分水岭，正常合法的收入是应得的财产，非法所得就是贪，凡是贪的人没有一个有好结果，都会落得坏的下场，与数量成正比。为了欲望，不择手段去搜刮，贪饮而醉，贪财而亡，贪色而乱至死，贪玩丧志，贪食伤身……所以古人说，人贪财死，鸟贪食亡。

世界各国贪官越多，官场越腐败，买官卖官现象越多。要买到一个肥缺，得花上一笔可观资金，那么贪官在其任期三分之一时间先贪回买官的成本。剩下的时间要继续贪，为连任或再往上爬筹谋本钱。

卖官的，先弄到一笔资金作往上爬的资本（小官献大官，逐级进贡），然后囤积大批金银珠宝，古玩名画，宅可和皇宫媲美，车骑赛过总统，美女、丫鬟成群，挪用公款，有的私立行宫，富甲朝廷。清朝出了个大贪官——和珅，从他家清理出来的财产等于清政府十三年财政收入。

古希腊埃及著名是以科学经济强盛起来的，后因贪官迭出，走

向衰退。缅甸强盛蒲甘王朝也因末期出现大贪官依勒等，将蒲甘王朝推倒灭亡。中国明末大批贪官，导致最勤俭的崇祯帝在景山自尽。

每一个朝代，成事是忠臣清官，败事是奸臣贪官。忠臣清官多人加害，像中国清朝于成龙。奸臣贪官多人护，如中国清朝和珅。人虽然同生于一个国家或地区，其民族、文化、宗教、信仰、社会制度、生活习俗等有差别，但人对自己政府、民众公共事务之心是忠，是奸，是清廉，还是贪污，所采取的态度，是没有差别的。所以每个国家和地区的历史都是人类社会中明君与暴君、忠臣与奸臣、清官与贪官、良民与恶棍、好人与坏人、男人与女人在人生舞台上的一出戏，单演和合演的记录，从粉墨登场到卸装散去，后人认为适宜留作资料供人参考的就是人类历史。

8. 人口问题

一个国家或地区的人口分布密度问题是关系到国计民生的重大问题。

人口数量与品质是决定国民经济收入和国民经济发展的关键问题。人口问题有几方面要素，男女性别比例、国民健康程度、幼儿教育、青少年就读率、成年人就业率、老年人敬仰率、整个社会文化教育、卫生保健、传染疾病的防治、全民体育锻炼、国民身体素质、社会福利等等——这些对国家整体发展是至关重要的。人每时每刻都为衣、食、住、行而劳作。生产需要物质，消费要用物质，生产和消费共同产生污染，这些与人口密度息息相关，人们在人口与社会、人口与自然之间寻找适应天、地、人三者的行之有效的和顺理由，并付之行动。

人生活的空间和时间，就是在有限度的地球表面时空。限制人口增长就成了地球表面分布的国家或地区所面临的实际性问题，人

口密度越大，对国家造成压力越大，社会和自然界危机感就越强，进行社会管理和自然资源利用会产生污染，人口增长会对此过程中每一个环节增加困难。人口是影响社会安定与否的重大因素。

冷战几十年，没有世界大战，只有局部地区小战争，也就让许多国家有生存发展机会。相对的稳定，使农、林、牧、渔、轻重工业配套发展，解决了民众的衣、食、住、行。人能安居，必定乐业，生产上去，人口就飞速发展。温饱思情调，饥寒生盗心，人类就是这样发展过来的。

中国解放初期才4亿多人口，当时中央政府号召多生子女，谁知1965年人口超过7亿多，政府马上采取行之有效的计划生育政策，这才把人口控制到当今的13亿，另一个人口大国印度，目前的计划生育可行办法尚未健全，估计其人口会在本世纪中超过中国。

目前只有俄罗斯人口是负增长，按照持人口合理发展观的人看来，俄罗斯不要鼓励发展人口，应该顺其自然，这可能是俄罗斯的福缘。

人在地球上的数量越来越多。人为了生存，不择手段地向社会和大自然索取，人多食光一方，食穷一方。有句不好听的话，人比毒蛇蝎还毒，人比最猛的野兽还要凶猛，因为这些最凶猛的东西都会被人从口里咽下去，当这些东西在地球上消失的时候，人也就去了。

9. 浅析道德标准

人生处世有人性道德标准——人道，也称德行、德性。

德性有好坏之分，好的是真、诚、实。坏的是假、奸、虚。好坏每时每刻都在人的言、行、举、止中表现出来，每个人的所作所为都属于表现结果——德性。

待人接物，言行举止的德性有尊严之分，人格、国格、家格、族格、党格、帮派等之格，总之归纳一句话，内部之分，敌我之分——原则与非原则之分。这是国际公认的具有广泛普遍意义的人类功德性，好与坏之分，由人群所属性质而定。

但对人类所有物质产品、贸易往来——一切商品、公众利益事业，科学研究成果，新闻报道、历史文献，一切作品，广告媒体等，全世界、全国、各地区、各民族、各帮派、各家庭到每个人一定有真、诚、实与假、奸、虚这样德性之分，有人类存在的一天，人都要遵守公德，否则就会带来不堪设想的人祸事件。

假药、假酒、假医术、假食品等不知坑害了多少人的生命，假技术、假产品、假商品搞得人财两空，假科研专案，虚假广告资讯传媒骗取钱财，危及生命，误导人们上当受骗。这些不单是某人、某家、某地区、某国家的事，是全人类要共同关注的大事，而且是头等大事——人在共同适应倡导公德——真、诚、实。

如果不去倡导这种公德，那么就会人害人，家害家，国害国，最后自己害自己。

人生活着就是最幸福，一切都是为了生，为了活——这就是生活。

生活是靠物质的质量达到人生活标准，人才活得健康、平安，只有健康，平安才能长寿，才能谈到为己、为家、为国有所贡献。

所以人的发现、研究、创造的一切生活物质必须是真实的、有益人生存和健康发展的物质。"真实与虚假"——"利与害"由此及彼，人类全由自己取舍。

10. 宗教信仰

宗教信仰自有人类以来，在人的心目中就是确定终身的信念。

人从哪里来，又到哪里去，天上的日、月、星、辰为什么周期性运行，地上千万种生灵生生息息，天时气候无常变化与有规律变化，在这众多不解中，于是人类相信造物主为了人的福祉，会从天上给人带来神灵庇佑，人才能平安度过一生。人的一切生活与作为，是给自己、来世、子孙万代造就幸福、平安和吉祥。所以人们在进化过程中，常常会确立先知、先觉的神灵概念，神是无处不在、无事不灵的。

宗教信仰，是人能建立和顺生活的精神支柱，是人的一种精神归依、一种稳定寄托。人们可以从寄托的信念中修正、净化自己生活劳作中的污点，所以人类就确立了佛教、基督教和天主教、伊斯兰教、道教、儒教等。有人类一天，宗教信仰就陪伴着人类度过人生历程。

因为科学理论是已知得到证实的理论——现实科学理论，浩瀚宇宙未知的物质永远都比已知的物质多。但未知也是造物主已设定的物质现象，那宗教信仰的经文可以说是现象科学理论。

从几大教派可以看出现象科学的存在。

佛教、基督教和天主教、伊斯兰教的神灵、真主都在天堂上，人从天而降生人间。人在凡间去体验人生的苦与乐，去感受人生七情六欲，从而经历生、老、病、死的磨炼，合格（正果）则升回天堂，未合格（正果）再投胎转世，无限轮回至成正果为止。

2000多年前出于东方中原的儒教主张"天人合一、天人感应"。三纲五常是天授意人，用于人治人的仁政，这样才能长治久安，是人有条不紊的保障，否则人就会犯"天条"，遭"天谴"。这是用人应顺天之理念去使家国繁荣昌盛。

道教则重在"现世"及人自身修行，把自己修炼成健康长生的人，"以人天相应"的原则"教化世人"人要以"审时济世"的方式去"返璞归真"，充分享受人生在世的七情六欲，再以苦修成仙，过神仙般逍遥自在日子。

宗教信仰是统治者和平民百姓的信念，适应这个国家或地区的

民族的教经，让他们为适应而选择，为选择而逐步去应验——这就是宗教信仰。

11. 人的处事

人活在世上，一是成家，二是立业，每天都为家庭生活中大大小小的事、事业上大大小小的事操劳。人就是这样，忙碌到老，最后的结果，才是真正的成绩。鉴定人每一个时期、每一件事情，或人一生的成绩，始终不必分析过程，只用看结果。人的一生在青壮年时期都为非作歹，但晚年积善积德为国为民为家立下了让世人公认的不可磨灭的功勋，可以说此人是坏的花结好的果，放下屠刀，可立地成佛。反之青壮年时期立下汗马功劳，但晚年害国害民害家，是好的花结坏的果，成罪人或千古罪人。所以人生的过程往往不会评论，结果就是一锤定音。

事情好与坏的是非标准，是根据其所发生的国家或地区的法律、法规、宗教信仰、宗族、家规道德范畴来鉴证。涉及跨国的有国际法规来规定，结合国际法规考虑，避免犯错误。

有些突发性的人为错误导致犯法，是人没有预先考虑就去做了。如驾驶机器失误等，不受人为思想指导实施了错误行为导致错误的结果，这种错误，人们应酌情评论和区别对待。

人居天底下，活在人群中，凡立歪心思去做恶劣的事情、伤天害理的缺德事，都会有恶报。触犯法律的，法网恢恢，疏而不漏，这就是恶有恶报的规律。

人生活在天地间，人为家生、为国生，为正大光明的事活，一生所作所为对得起天地良心，过程依法守则行事，结果一定是好的。这种所作所为是适应人在社会中和顺处世，积德行善的基础。这样好的结果是利国、利民、利家、好自己。

孝顺的人最聪明

孝顺父母的人最聪明。因为我们孝顺父母，我们的孩子看见了会有样学样，长大后也会孝顺我们；天地神明看见了，会保佑我们，一家大小平安顺遂。所以，孝顺父母的人最聪明。

12. 大是大非

在一个国家或地区内部，执政党和在野党之间、民族之间、各民族联盟的武装力量之间常常会发生政见争执，甚至引起武装冲突或卷入长期马拉松内战。

但人类自古至今，无论是有条文宪法也好，或无条文口碑也好，在每个人的心中，分裂国家损害民族利益和尊严的人、叛国投敌出卖国家民族利益的人都会失去一个国家公民的公心，都是国家的"奸细败类"，这个是被每个国家或地区的公民列入首条的大是大非的原则。

在遵守这一条大是大非的原则基础上，国家内部的党派斗争、民族之间的斗争、各派势力武装力量的斗争等内战、内斗是内部的战争。

近两百年来，发生内战的国家越来越多，1837—1840年加拿大上下地区内战，1864—1865年美国南北内战，1947—1949年中国内战，1964—1975年越南战争，1963—1975年柬埔寨内战，1967—1970年非洲尼日利亚、卢旺达、扎伊尔等国内乱，缅甸50多年来民族武装冲突从未平息。总之，世界没有一天停止过内战、内乱的。

凡出现这种内战、内乱的国家，都会有第三国多种势力渗透和干预，一种是良性的渗透，希望尽快结束战争，和平统一。另一种是趁火打劫，支持分裂分子，另有图谋。

凡是有内战、内乱之国，各党、各帮、各派、各民族，应首先以国家统一、民族团结为目的，各方共商同议，寻找解决办法，在政见分歧上以妥协来疏导，求大同存小异，以利国大体为重，大是大非为先，大团结为荣，以分裂为耻、内乱为辱。每个国家公民如能做到这一点，国家各民族和顺团结就有希望了。

粤椿语录

克己怀仁，帮助邻朋戚友

怀着仁爱之心，诚恳主动地关怀、帮助身边的朋友与亲人，久而久之，便能获得不可思议的助缘。俗谚有云："百万买宅，千万买邻。"尤其是好邻居的守望相助，更是一大福报。

13. 言行一致

人生活在世上，能够自始至终对自己言行所带来的一切结果负责，这个人的一生就是"讲诚信"。

果敢文中"君子一言既出，驷马难追""君子一言九鼎"都是说人要说话算数，决不食言。讲到就要做到，说话不是放屁。

想要人的言行得出令人满意的效果，必须用负责任的态度对待自己的言行，但万一自己的言行出了差错，无法兑现承诺，甚至触犯了国法、家族之规、宗教信仰之教条，甚至造成灾难人祸，这个时候，不要去回避自己言行所造成的事实，而应正面直对自己言行所造成的结果，负担起依法依理应负的责任，这就是——诚信。

人的语言是表达自己的想法和情意的有声方式（聋哑人用手势来表达），人对自己所讲的话要负责，怎么说你就怎样去做到，做出的结果，无论好坏你都要承担责任——这也是诚信。

人将语言成文的东西，如：合同、契约、承诺、签名的文件、票据等，这些口头或手笔形成文字应承的内容，属于你承担的责任，你做到了——这也是诚信。

人的行为，包括指挥别人行动，出谋划策组织团体行动。在这些行动中，主谋的、参与的、执行的各负其责，按理勇担自己应负的责任，这也是人的——诚信。

人只有你和我双方开始交流才成对话，自言自语是不需对对方负责的。自杀、自暴、自悟、自觉、自醒、自修，益与害全是自己的，言行是对自己的，责任一定是自负、自作、自受的。

诚信有三级体现：

初级个人行为，即人与人或个人与组织、国家的言行。

中级组织行为，即家与家、宗教与宗教、团体与团体的言行。

高级国家行为，即国家与国家，地区与地区的言行。

这三级的言行都做到言必信，行必果、果必承，这才是适应人类建造和顺社会的——诚信。

14. 阶级社会

自从人类有阶级社会，就有人群层次之分。阶级、层次的来源是市井（市场）。有了市井，就有人管人，人管物，人管财，以经济作为基础，管理设了一级又一级，直至中央政府——宫廷、皇上、总统……发展到当今，就形成了现代市场经济。

东方流传这样的说法"未有朝廷，先有市井，未有市井，先有换亭"人与人之交，家与家之往，最初交换物品的地方叫"亭"，

交换多了就成了圩、集、市，全世界城市、圩镇均是水陆交通方便的地方，市井就是这样发展起来的。

市井是经济集散地，必须推选人来管理财物，管理财物的人收管理费——税就开始了，管理市井的人对经营物品的（商人）人进行买卖、加工、仓储等行为实施管理，进而开始设工商管理、市井管理，由宗教、部落的头人来管理市井、管理人，头人随着社会进化，设镇、县、府、省、中央集权等衙门，直至形成今天的人管人上层建筑。

从世界历史上看，早在中国西元前230年秦始皇统一中国，首先统一度量衡，方便了市井中的贸易交流，促进了市场经济的发展。欧洲罗马帝国征服了希腊等地区后，也在西元前146年后在市井中统一了度量衡。缅甸蒲甘王朝自1044年起230多年注重市井经济。1776年美国推翻了英殖民，独立后市井的市场经济快速发展，至当今称霸世界。

人生活的质量，是物质财富提供的，物质财富的多少体现了市场经济的兴衰，一个国家，一个家庭，物质财富不丰富，怎样治理也不会成功的，一个国家或地区从中央政府到民众，要结合自己本国本土的国情、民情，找到适应治理自己市场经济的活路，扎扎实实以科学发展生产力，把经济搞上去，这是目前摆在世界各国人民面前的任务，和顺团结的日子一定要经济的支撑。

15. 本位民族民主

民族问题，是多民族国家的中央政府首要解决的问题。是关系到国家安定团结的大问题。

多民族的国家有两种不同性质的现象。一种是联合政府，国家的组成是多邦国（以单一本位民族为主体的邦国）组成的，如缅甸、美国、伊拉克等，另一种是多民族国家，经过久远历史形成

的，多民族相依相护几千年的国家，也可以说相依为命的国家，如中国、印度。

这两种国家实质性的差别，在于国家的人民民主与民族内部的民主，民族内部的民主与世袭头人的本位民族之间的矛盾。

问题的症结就在本位民族内部民主，联邦政府与各帮派的民主路线，是否能够达成共识，顾大局地适应联邦政府和本位民族邦国生存发展的正道——这就是民族民主。

阻碍民族民主的病灶是本位民族邦国的世袭头人问题，世袭头人这把邦国头等宝座，谁当上了都舍不得退下去，但并不是退去就是好事，不退下去就是坏事。世袭与退让，民主与独裁，首先由本位民族邦国的国民来决定。本位民族内政的事由本位民族内部大多数人决定，这本来就是民族民主。

如果每个邦国都能做到本位民族民主，回过头来要顾联邦政府大局，国家统一，民族团结，才是带领民族民主国家走富裕道路的首要条件。在国家安定的环境下，每个国家公民应有民主的权利和义务，这样人权才能发挥出来，联邦政府要正确对待本位民族邦国的民族民主，在宪法上肯定安邦和民之纲领外，还要针对每时期民族政策和策略的变化做适应调整，民族民主是与时俱进的，千万不可粗心大意。

粤椿语录

宅仁心厚天赐福

体念上天有好生之德、不残害蚂蚁昆虫，不毒鱼、电鱼等，并且要感谢天地之所赐予，敬重字纸、五谷。我们若如此用心好好做人，上天会不断为我们增添福禄寿。

16. 学做人

人生处世，首先学做人，会做人才会做事，会做事才会处世。

做人就像木匠刨方正的木条板材一样。首先在材料上用直角尺准确规矩边角，之后随意去取方圆眼洞，各种形状图案，接合各种框架器材均厘毫不差，构成美观大方器具的整体。

做人就是要先懂做人之规矩、做人之道理、做人之常识，而且做人之立心一定要良。人在每一件事情上，用心要良，做好的事情自然会得到好的结果。

学做人，东方儒理说得很好，"三纲五常""天理、人理、物理"是人一生尊为处世之本的准则。

人类一生中，有一条人理串在天地间，人有上才有下，有左才有右，有前才有后，一个人的一生活在世上的时空，永远是其中，中容亦中庸，容得左右，容得前后，才能容得自己。人才能生存，否则，人将不人。

儒理学说会使人先得悟，悟出人生在世"天理之何在，人理之何在，物理之何在……"。容理走正道，办正事、务正事，正人先正己，治人先治己，正理是做人之纲，做事是人处世之目，纲正目不歪。

人如果不择手段去追求私欲，一定触犯"天理、人理、物理"。失之纲常，就是乱。乱的世界就毁灭人性，伤天害理。

世界是否动荡，国家是否安宁，家庭是否和睦，问题就在能决定国家之间和国家之内的决策者，包括组织、家庭之间和组织、家庭之内的决策者的行为是否符合"天理、人理、物理"。

人永远要有纲常来指导自己的意识，用意识去指导决策和行动，纲常是错误的，那意识决策和行动都是错误的，那错误将会导致罪行。

粤椿语录

心好命就好

命运是可以改变的，就像土地一样，我们若是懒惰，则沃土会变成贫地，作物就生长得不好；我们若勤劳，贫地就会变成沃土，五谷也会长得丰硕。因此，只要我们能够诚心忏悔，而且不断改正内心的错误，心地慈悲、公平，那么必能获得神明的护佑，得到平安。

17. 民族民主

民族团结和民主治国是当今社会主流方向，更是多民族国家中央政府的首要问题。

民族民主首先要适应该国的国情，讲得明显一点，古老文明国和新大陆移民国的民主是不同方式的，互相参考时，借鉴有益，成套方式移植有害。因为每个民族文化习俗、宗教信仰、生活习惯、风土人情是有区别的。

文化表现在文字、语言。习俗重在婚、嫁、礼、仪，红、白（喜、丧）大事有别，这是区分民族的根本。

民族宗教信仰的变迁有两种，一种是本土宗教，一种是外来宗教。

如古老中国，它的本土教是道教、儒教，唐朝前曾有多人到西域取佛经，唐朝初期再派玄奘出使西域（当今印度）才真正取回佛经。

印度是佛教发源地，被英国殖民近百年，其间缅甸被英国划入印度，直至1947年，在这几十年间，英殖民者强行把基督教拖入印度、缅甸。缅甸克钦邦（景颇族）连英语都加注景颇拼音，成为

克钦文。现在印度，缅甸还有部分人信奉基督教。

生活在北美洲、美国、墨西哥、加拿大的土著族人（印第安人）的文化，以及15世纪前密西西比庙宇墩文化等，在15世纪后由于欧洲大批移民侵入后就消亡了。在人类生存发展的社会大环境下，适应的就生存下来，并不断壮大，不适应的就消亡。

民族风土人情是多样化的，既有本民族的特定风土人情，又有相邻周边民族的风土人情，这些在相互渗透，因为人类在生活的社会中友好往来是很正常的事，民族间通婚、通商是必然的，入乡随俗，入水随曲是人之常理。世界每个角落的民族，全封闭的是极少数了。为逐步适应飞速发展的社会，禁闭的民族也得学跳交际舞。

民族团结和民主治国，这是人类社会中最复杂、最无标准的。绝对的集中曾经是人类社会生产力、创造力、凝聚力的来源，推动着社会的发展。而绝对的自由使人类成为一盘散沙。人群不如一群蚂蚁。蚂蚁、蜜蜂的凝聚力体现在集中力量，明细分工，发挥单个自由，大象群、猛狮群、飞禽群也是这样适应自然并生存。人有时骂那些"衣冠禽兽"的人"禽兽不如"。所以人类社会中，民族民主的问题是因每个国家，每个民族的社会制度、生活方式而绝然不同的，因民主与集中的方式而不同。美国、澳大利亚、加拿大这些移民组合国，长期以来为了对付土著民族，养成用大众表决方式去决策立足生存的适应自己民族的条文。今天引以为豪的"民主"，实际上很多地区都不适应。欧洲、亚洲，有两个最为特殊的国家和地区，缅甸在被英国殖民时，是印度一省，从来没有民主，1947年独立以来出现了两个极端，一个是军政府高度集中，一个是帮派高度自由，民主造成联邦政府变成"乱邦政府"；另一个是中国香港，在英国殖民时期当奴仆的各党派没有一个提民主，1997年回归，自己当家做主人时，成天喊叫民主，宁做奴隶不愿做主人的是缅甸少数人和香港少数人。

首先要确立民族团结和民主治国是内政的观点，每个国家或地

区认定确立每个公民自身权益的自由权利是适应他们大家庭的事，简单地说，别家的饭菜不合口味，勉强咽下也会拉肚子，好好地让他们过适应他们的日子。让每个国家每个地区内部各民族去制定适应他们自己生存发展的民主与集中——制度。

18. 亦说天灾

人类常遇天灾，人一听到关于天灾的预报，就心情不安。特别是当人知道或发现流行性传染病时，就更加闻之色变。大的天灾死伤数目惊人，财产损失千万亿计。这是自然界对人类的惩罚。

天灾跟人祸一样，每年都有大大小小的天灾事件发生，165—167 年三年间大瘟疫扫荡了罗马帝国，1347—1351 年五年间一次历史上最凶恶的黑死病瘟疫袭击中东和欧洲地区，造成四分之一的人死亡。1353—1354 年两年间黑死病在中国大爆发，1976 年中国唐山大地震，夺走几十万条生命，2005 年印度洋大海啸，沿海几个国家被卷走了几十万人。

地震、海啸、飓风、龙卷风、山洪泥石流、火山喷发等天灾是闪电式的，一刹那间，夺走数十万人的生命和百千亿财产，人类承受来自自然的突如其来的惩罚，数分钟内人财两空。每当遇到这种事件，真是触目惊心。

更加可怕的还是瘟疫——流行性传染病，这样的灾难时间漫长，区域广泛，死者难找人埋，病者难找人医，生者逃离加快传播，可怕加可悲，人们一听到传染性流行疾病马上色变。

对于预防流行性传染病，一般采取一经发现，立即管、控、防、治的措施，这样可以使疫情得到有效控制和治疗。

对于突发性的地震、海啸、龙卷风、冰雹、雷电、火山喷火等天灾，人们采取的预防措施是提高预报技术，逐步摸索，逐步去设法减少不必要的损失。

但是人类与自然界之间有特定现象，"人最大可为可定千年之计，人最不可为难测一旦之灾祸"这是人为与天然的分水岭，也是造物主设置的自然定律。人类对此绝无解数。人在天灾面前，若有天命，死去也活来。

人类对待天灾，从预防和救灾，要以积极态度对待，而且要将保护自然环境作为人类的首位任务，人类对自然环境破坏越大，自然界对人类惩罚报复就越多。

粤椿语录

积德累功，慈心于物

力行好事，积累道德。心存慈悲，珍惜爱护天地所生的万物。如此努力耕耘心中福田，道德累积多了，自能获得天助、人助，做人做事，必然圆满吉祥。

19. 拯救地球

人生活在世上，利用自然界的物质满足自己生活的需要。自然界中的物质直接利用或加工再使用，最后始终变成垃圾——工业废物和生活废物。这与人的需求用量成正比。这些废物有可降解的或不可能降解的，也有可再加工成再生物质的，但都对自然界造成了污染，使土质、水质、空气均受到不同程度的污染。被污染的环境又反过来污染人类。

人利用物质在衣、食、住、行等方面改善生活，提高生活品质。有些物质的原材料直接对人体就是有害的，有的在加工、生产过程中变成有害物质，排放的废物肯定是污染物，只不过其污染程度有高低之分。

人类利用物质越多，污染就越多。人吃得多，大小便排泄也多；汽车跑得多，排出的尾气、废气就越多；工厂多（特别是化工厂、药厂），排放的废水、毒烟、毒气就越多。总而言之，人多，利用物质多，废物就多，污染就越严重。

人类造成污染，危害了自己，危害着一切有生命的动植物。据科学家初步考查证实，每天有数以十计的物种从地球上永远消亡。如果自然界动植物都消亡得寥寥无几时，人类也可能随之消失。

人类是自然界中的强食者，自然界本是弱肉强食，大食小、恶食善、精食笨、智食愚。人食自然界中可以食的物质。各国都有将大象、犀牛、鳄鱼、狮子、老虎、大蛇、飞鸟、鲸，即天上、地上、水里能提供给人吃的，能赚钱的，人类全部会下手去抢捕——人是自然界最凶残的高等动物。

但话又说回来，创造世界物质财富的是人，破坏自然界物质的也是人，福、祸、功、过自己去想。保护人类唯一的家园——地球刻不容缓。在生产、利用、保护自然环境的问题上，人应该在自娱中去寻找自悟，自迷中去寻找自醒，自救是人真正获救的方法。

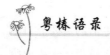

行仁履义，正气塞乎天地

修身立命，大名炳若日星。

实践仁道，大义凛然，关圣帝君的正气，无所不在，充塞天地之间。

修身养性，尽心如命，关圣帝君的大名，如日月星，光明永照人寰。

20．对自然的认识

人类自从有文字，逐步有记事。有记事开始就是人类有历史依据的开始。人类历史对自然的认识，总结物质在自然界中变化的现象，科学地归属物质元素（几十种物元素）物理现象、化学现象、生物、生理现象，并用它们去解释，分析自然界中无奇不有的大千世界。

远古中国人，很早就用易经五行，金、木、水、火、土去解释，分析世界上所有物质的阴阳变化，将宇宙、日、月、星、宿象、景与地球间万物，按五行相属、相生、相克，分析得清清楚楚，还将人的七情六欲与天、地、人、神、灵，如分析自然界物质一样说得明明白白。

人类在生活、生产过程中去观察自然，分析自然，去发现自然物质变化，创造生活物质，在提高生活品质的过程中又破坏自然环境，这就需要人类从利弊中去衡量选择。

适应人类利用而且对环境污染极少的——取！适应人类利用对环境污染极大的——弃！

21．人与自然

人从自然中来，又回到自然中去。人顺其自然即是——缘。人的生命在历史长河的时空中，再长寿也如流星一样，有生就有死，这是造物主更新生命体的自然定律。动物、植物、微生物等有生命存在的物种都逃避不了终去的命运。

人的生命有长短，短的一瞬间，普通的一百或几十岁，几百岁的长寿者也有史记载。死对人真是最大的无可奈何。造物主太偏爱人类了，自然界的一切物质都好像是为人类而设造的，可见人的智慧的力量有多么的伟大。但是，人类会不会用最理智的科学方式、方法去开发利用自然界，爱惜自然界的一切呢？这就是人类需要研究议论的课题。

人类生活最基本是解决衣、食、住、行，物质来源的一种是取之于自然，人类多取一点，这种物质在地球上就消失一点。如石油、煤等矿产资源。这些物质是造物主设造好的，现在的科学家推理考证这些物质是经过亿万年所形成的，这是有依据或无依据的考证。几十年的生命怎能准确考证亿万年前的事情呢？推理罢了。

人类向大自然索取的物质越来越多。这些不再生的物质一去不复返，"枯竭"二字已经近在眼前了，危及人类生存的时代迫近了。

物质来源的另一种是利用物质再生。人类懂得将野兽养成家畜，将海、河、湖泊的水生鱼类引回池塘养殖，将野五谷引种作食粮，这些通过每年周而复始地轮作不断增加的物质，是人类世世代代永不枯竭的物质来源。这是适应人类生存的索取物质途径。

自然界有很多再生的能源，如果人们不利用，它就随着时空白白流失，如太阳能、风能、水能，这又是人类能永远利用的能源，这种再生能源干净，无污染。让那些快要枯竭的自然物质缓慢开采，为子孙万代着想吧。

 粤椿语录

时时行方便，念念积阴功

时时刻刻记得利人方便，就如同一场及时雨；心中不忘随时行善，持之以恒，日积月累勤修道德，必能蒙受天地神明的疼惜。

22. 动植物与环境

宇宙间的一切物质都是造物主造就出来的，这些都随着时间和

空间的改变不时变化，特别是有生命的物种，如果跟不上时空的变化就会自然地消亡。

海边的红树林，它是生长于陆地与海岸交界的滩涂而又扎根海岸淤泥的植物，潮起潮落，飓风巨浪，不时地冲击它，但为了适应繁殖后代，它是植物中明显胎生植物。红树林的果实种子，是先在树上的果实中长成根、茎、叶的小树苗，再脱落到海泥中生长。所以红树林是植物生命体中适应强的代表品种。但随着人类对大海污染程度的不断增加，红树林的命运也面临着严峻考验。据科学家考证，陆地上的植物种类已经有数千种从地球上消失，消失的数量大得惊人。

随着气候不断变化，动物的个体和群体也在不断变化着，特别是海生动物，有由水生逐步变成两栖动物的趋势，可能会有一天，地球上的陆地会被水中的大型动物登陆占领。

因为人类不断地滥用地球上的物质资源，有利用就有破坏，有利用就有污染，有污染就有物种不断地消亡，气候环境从良性变成恶性。人类破坏了自然界的生态平衡，自然界也会报复人类，这样的自然规律，谁都无法改变。唯一的办法是，人们赶快行动起来，从保护环境入手。

从资料来看，每天全球大约有几十余种生物类物种消失，有五十余种植物消亡，人类既然意识到环境问题，就应赶快行动起来，挽救地球一切生物，也就是挽救自己。

 **粤椿语录**

善养天地正气

一个光明磊落的人具有天地正气，可以化解私欲与偏执。我们若行为正当、为国尽忠、孝顺父母，就能吸收正气，做事公正，没有私心，就不会做出伤天害理的

事；而对于怨、恨、苦等意念，也能了悟，自然能有豁然自在的心境。

23. 历史之我见

人类在宇宙中的地球上生活经过的时间和空间就是人类进化的社会历史。

自然界一切物质在宇宙中度过的时间和空间就是自然物质进化的历史。

社会的进化和自然的进化自有文字记载以来就形成两大类知识——自然知识和社会知识。过去的都是历史，用现代的眼光和契约评论历史是错误的，历史是每代人在当时的社会环境和自然环境下的经历，人的思维是适应当时社会环境和自然环境的，在这种情况下人才造就了当时的现实的历史。人类每时每刻都在写自己的历史，共同谱写家庭、民族、国家的历史。一切历史是社会和自然经过时空的记录。

历史是留给后人去承上启下的，免于后人重蹈错误，用于警示后人，教训后人，用于借鉴对照以开拓未来，一代胜过一代。

历史留下两种遗产，一种是物质遗产，另一种是非物质遗产。两种遗产一样重要，传承历史是人类的任务，失传是人类的损失，继往开来是人类永远的宗旨。

历史是个人、家庭、民族、地区、国家经过时空的记录，千差万别。符合天理、人理、物理的历史，引以为荣。违背天理、人理、物理的历史应引以为耻、为鉴。

国与国之间，为了土地、财产违背天理、人理、物理，无道地去发动战争，令生灵涂炭。

人类最可憎可恨的是战争，人类最可悲可怜的也是战争。战争

是人为造成的。不论大小，不论国战、族战、群战、家战，战争是人类最黑色的历史。

不管是外战还是内战，都会造成人的伤亡，财产的损失，家庭支离破碎，人们流离失所。战后新君新政权出现，亦叫改朝换代。各行各业，重新兴起，出现历史新时代。

24. 生于理，活于性

人生活在世上，就是个体生命在社会空间走一趟，人从自然中来，也必然回到自然中去，谁都避免不了。

人是有思维的高级动物，人有智慧能够创造物质和利用物质。人的七情六欲贯穿人生的整个过程，人都有脾气和生活习性。

脾气决定命运，在家庭里、社会上，人的意识形态都是先自我发挥，然后相互发挥，人的发挥以礼、智、仁、义、信等去表现。表现的意识以自己脾气为基础，知识学术是智慧的表现。素质是谦虚谨慎、言行达理，还是持势傲朝、横言无礼都由一个人的脾气决定，所以脾气能决定你自己的命运。

人的生活习性决定人的健康，人活着就得衣、食、住、行、作与息。人自古以来日出而作，日落而息。

人体生命总是自然而成的，人不可追求过分享乐，夜夜笙歌醉天明，日日熟睡梦天黑。作与息是决定身体基元健康的重要因素。衣着打扮，对食物甜、酸、苦、辣、咸的偏好，住宅环境，行动习性，七情六欲变化无常，都影响人的健康。

人活在时空中，人活在性情脾气里，生活就是生于理，活于性。

25. 审时度势

人要善于审时度势。

人出生不能选择的是国家、地区、人群种族、家庭等，这是自

然之妙缘，即前缘所定的。

既然人来到世上，那么在人世走一趟已成定局，但走的时间长短，路途畅直顺利，还是曲折艰难，真是时也，命也，运也——全是缘与份。

人一生，不管你的学识如何，不论你的成功与失败的比例如何，人处世做事，千万不可盲动，要认真审时度势。

势是社会潮流。每个国家或地区，一朝天子一朝臣，一季蔬菜伴一季餐食，某一时期的政策法令规章制度由当权者而定，千变万化，这是策略。

人就应量度自身处境，去适应推行的政策法令。世间的政策法令跟天气一样，说变就变。相对的稳定也有节外生枝的变化，作为个体、家庭、小集团的小单元，就是遇到节外生枝的小气候都可能遭毁灭性打击。

"时"是经过空间（宇）的时间（宙），在每一个人经过的时间中，自然气候和社会气候不时千变万化，故古人云：天有不测之风云，人有旦夕之祸福。几千年来，人面对自然社会变化、人与人之间的变化，常说一句俗语"此一时彼一时"。古语说明，"时"和"势"的把握很重要，对人们的审时度势起着很重要的作用，善于审时度势者成功率高，否则处处碰钉子，寸步难行。

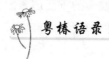 **粤梅语录**

当思守命由天，安贫乐业

每个人都有自己的机缘。处于顺境时，要心存谦卑，感恩，珍惜拥有的一切；遭逢逆境时，则应安分守己，顺天行事，并努力充实自我；贫穷困顿时，要保持乐观，尽心尽力工作，以待时机成熟。

26. 民族主义

世界各国、各地区，基于环境根源、社会根源、自然根源、历史根源以及人类自身进化根源的原因，凡有人类居住的地方，都生活着各式各样的民族，群体的大小千差万别，都有自己的特殊族规和独特文化。我们一般可以从语言、生活习俗去区分民族属性。

世界各国、各地区基本是多民族组成，有土著（原住民）和外来民族。在任何地方，异地先后移居进来的情况也存在，外移民族也有，因历史时空不同，所以各民族的意识观念、宗教信仰也就有极大差异。这种意识观念就是民族主义。

民族主义有两种：狭隘民族主义和广阔民族主义。一般由多民族组成的国家或地区，国家行为对外巩固国家防务特定界限行政范围，对内各族人民在行政范围内共议国策民生大计，各民族平等，各公民平等人权。这些平等是由宪法法律、规章制度去法治完成。而拿本民族利益去触犯国家各民族共同利益的一切行动，都是狭隘民族主义。拿本民族利益去与国家各民族的共同利益相融合的，顾全大局的是广阔民族主义。有些民族举狭隘民族主义之旗，去闹独立、闹分裂，破坏国家统一。有的国家用特定民族政策让民族实行自治，这是对民族的一种政策宽容，有些民族就身在福中不知福，还以无政府主义和狭隘民主主义闹独立、闹分裂，这不管是在哪个国家或地区都是不容许的。

一个国家，只有民族和解，各民族团结一致，这个国家才有希望兴旺发达，才有威望振四海。

粤椿语录

行善之方在于诚

行善之道，不在乎多寡、大小，而贵乎诚心！而所谓的"诚"，若能由衷地发自内心，不为名利、不求回报，真诚无私地奉献，那么善心善行将更加圆满。

27. 习性的舍取

人的七情六欲，刚柔并济。如果正常去发挥，也是适应性的表现，这是正常脾气的运用。如果该容忍的不容忍而去大发脾气，则会大乱。该屈的时候你一定要忍辱负重，待该出手的时候要不失时机地伸展正义和才能。该放下的、该舍弃的一定要放得下，不该舍弃的，如国土、国格、家威、自身人权和天理等，丝毫不能舍弃。

所以能够舍此才能得彼。能够含屈才伸出有力。这是决定性的脾气施展，施展得越好，你的命运就越好。

生活习性是健康之根本，逢喜事时要适度喜庆一番，碰到怒不可遏的事要按量发泄，该忧虑的份内事酌情疏通，该思考的事情谨慎解决，悲伤的事情快速处理走出阴影，从恐惧心境自救出来，惊吓之余净心调养，羸弱之体，适度进补，寒底之躯温辛转阳，结实之身注重阴阳平和。热攻五脏六腑要清火排毒之饮。躁烦之藏内润滑肠胃，火气十足之象，引火近事源从疏排，这一切都是生活习性所引起，也只能从生活习性中去根治、调养。人对甜、酸、苦、辣、咸五味各有所好，但人的口味会受到自己长期生活居住的环境、气候以及自身身体素质的影响。调节自己饮食习惯、作息时间对健康起决定性作用，失衡会使疾病有机可乘。

粤椿语录

　　　　毋谓善小而不为，毋谓恶小而可行。

　　道德的完善必须日积月累，不断做善事，避免犯错，有了过错，要马上改正。在生命终了时，一切钱财都带不走，唯有道德带得走。为了今生的平安，来世也平安，做善事，不可分大小，更不可为自己犯的错找借口，如此持之以恒，身后才能带着道德，返回天庭！

论适应主义（二）

新年的祈盼：

人类社会发展中，在没有敌对的情况下，国家之间、家庭之间、人与人之间，最好以真诚的态度去相处，友好交往，互补物质有无，互相开展经济贸易，共同保护地球自然环境，合理利用物质，归纳一句话就是：和平相处，和睦相待，造就和平人类、和平社会环境，这就是缅甸和平党的理想。

每个一生为和平事业的人，都会有无量的福禄寿。

1. 人处世靠诚信，做事靠自信

人生是苦短的，一百岁才三万六千多天。童年成长，晚年衰退，除开头尾，剩下无多。正所谓，人生有涯，百年转瞬而过。

社会人群汇成各民族、各阶层，有无诚信、自信，生活质量大不一样。青壮年是处世做事的大好时期，需要掌握自己的生活轨迹。每人都要拥有昨天，把握正在运作的今天，期望理想的明天。人的一生，就是周而复始地运作"昨、今、明"三天。

人生经过的时空，处世要诚信。诚信是人的品质，是处世立命之本。人生活交往，就是相互观察言行是否诚实，评估实质的诚意。

诚信程度，众人有目共睹。诚信度高的人内外一致，表里一

致，万事畅通，自己做事，别人放心。诚信度低的人连他自己的人都不放心。对没有诚信的人，所有的人都怕。只有非交往过的、生疏的人，才会吃亏，上没诚信的人的当。

诚信是做人的基础，是人生事业成功的保障，是人应始终坚持的道路。论自信，人连自己都不信自己，将一事无成，因为人先知己，才能知彼，知彼知己才能百战百胜。

自己的体力、自己的智慧，自己最清楚。自己量力而行的事，成功把握才会大。充分发挥自己的智慧，行事自始至终，才有胜利的把握。

人有了诚信，是人生最大资本。人有自信，人才能最大发挥自己的才能。人有诚信，才能走南闯北，一年四季畅通无阻。

人生实现理想抱负，首先要量力而行。自信、现实的行动，要克服战胜困难，走过艰难曲折的过程，目标才会实现。自己对照社会现实、事态发展的详细情况，先知己，然后再知彼，必定百战百胜。对于每一件事，连自己都不相信自己能干，能做好，那就不必去做。人不自信，畏首畏尾。人有自信，才敢想敢干。

有限的生涯中言而无信，无朋友，心想事不成。做事不自信，万事成蹉跎。

2. 人的生活常识比文化知识更重要

生活得好不好，是人生第一课题。人就这样一天天地过，品质的好坏与时间都是同样的，空间则千差万别。青少年就是学习科学文化知识，充实自己，目的是在有生之年生活得有品质。

文化知识是很重要的。无论中国传统文化知识，还是世界文化知识，都很重要。人通过学习和运用知识，不仅使生活品质得以提高，还形成不同人群的传统文化，汇成世界文化。人因为有了文化知识，人生才丰富，人才有修养和品位，才有人类文明。

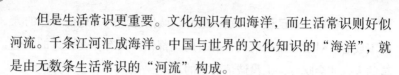

但是生活常识更重要。文化知识有如海洋，而生活常识则好似河流。千条江河汇成海洋。中国与世界的文化知识的"海洋"，就是由无数条生活常识的"河流"构成。

面包在烘烤过程中，面粉中的直链淀粉部分已经老化，这就是面包产生弹性和柔软结构的原因。研究淀粉老化和面包弹性的因果关系，以及柔软的面包逐渐变硬的"变陈"现象，引入"变陈"的时间、速度与温度，就有了烘烤知识。

夏天多喝番茄汤，或者多喝白开水或淡盐水，喝优酪乳能解酒后烦躁，蜂蜜和大葱同吃会引起中毒，鱼不能放太久，等等。诸如此类的生活常识五花八门。很多科学家、文学家就是从各自的生活中观察发现，总结研究常识而得出结果的。

生活常识丰富的人，即使没进过学堂，也不妨碍其成为文化名人。有些人连自己的名字都不会写，照样成名成家，例如禅宗六祖慧能是最有哲学思想的佛教名家。

如果米饭夹生，可用筷子在饭内扎些直通锅底的孔，洒入少许黄酒重焖。炒鸡蛋时将鸡蛋打入碗中，加入少许温水搅拌均匀，倒入油锅里炒，炒时往锅里滴少许酒，炒出的鸡蛋蓬松、鲜嫩，让食客流连忘返。有一门绝技，有一手独门艺术，有一技之长，人生才富有，才活得有滋有味。

人生可以没有文化知识，不可没有生活常识，不可反常，不可失常。

3. 生命无常，心要正常

我们每个人，通常都要经历出生、成长和死亡的过程。这个从生到死的过程，每个人各有不同，有人长命百岁，有人短命夭折，有人活一辈子无一天的计划，有人做事三思后行，谋定而动，很有计划。人生可定千年之计，难定一旦之灾祸。

人要能追溯昨天、明白今天、预算明天，必须升级自己的经验常识，学习所积累的文化知识，这就有了才艺、术数等。做人不会计数，说话做事就要出错。在学校，数学是主课，培养我们的算数能力。

什么数都可以准确计算。人有如一台电脑、一颗星，有预制的程式、固定的轨道，人生有确定的法则，可以计算，甚至可以精确到小数点后若干位。

但人命长短，我们却不能计算。生命是细胞、生物繁衍变化的过程：新陈代谢、生长发育、遗传变异、选择适应的过程。这个过程在造物主、编程者那里是预定的，对于我们被造的人而言，却是不知道的。所以马太福音说：看是看见，却不明白。因其不明白，所以会遭遇天灾人祸。生命选择因此才有了意义：约姓定名，人类有了家族；约定俗成，社会有了习惯；约法三章，国家有了法规。

人生有经历和定数。宿命在天，奋斗在人，人生意义在我。古人把人生的过程比作结冰或烧火的过程。冰化成水，火灭成灰。人生无常，才有意义。

佛教说诸行无常。正如《金刚经》所说："过去心不可得，现在心不可得，未来心不可得。"无常使生灭相续，人生意义由此而生。很多苦难都因无常可变才有希望。所以做人虽可谋划，却因缘分所致，不可强求，也不可懒惰。

人想要随缘勤奋，就要有良好的心态：宽容、平常心、自尊、自信，等等。心态决定命运。心态不好，遇困难就焦躁，做事就越糟。好的心态未必能让人一定获得成功，却可以让人很好地把握现在的生活，享受过程，提高人的幸福指数。

所谓好心态，其实就是正常心态。所谓正常，就是行端立正、心情平常，即平常心。物乱我心，自心不乱，行方不乱。说白了，就是做人要中庸，既不随波逐流，却也不要离经叛道。人的心态失常就会坏事，所以一定要修之正常。

4. 德行之高自在必得

古希腊人有"美德即知识"之名言，中国古人更说出了具体的美德：自强不息、厚德载物、申命行事、恐惧修省、常德习教、明照四方、思不出位、朋友讲习等。能修得这些德行之一，都堪称正人君子，可做大事、成大业。

司马迁的《史记》中记载：黄帝修德振兵，战蚩尤、联炎帝，平天下暴乱。重德行，是中国正人君子的人生正道：天行健，君子以自强不息；地势坤，君子以厚德载物。人生倘若拥有厚德载物之德行，也就拥有了最重要的柔顺美德。

厚德载物之人生德行，是人对大地自然之势的效仿：谁都可以踩地，地都不计较，不偏贫向富，不趋炎附势。这个德行名叫大度，既非积极也非消极。地在为万人踩的同时，呈现的是坚韧不拔的品质，因而成为万人的依托。人是铁，地是磁。没有人能够跳在空中，最后不掉下来的.

人修德正行，如船舶有了指南针，航行于海上就不会迷失方向。人因此能未卜先知，踩踏薄霜便知道即将是寒冰时节，该加衣保暖，该储粮过冬。

地厚磁力强，德高人自在，无为无不为。人如果能够像地一样正直无私、刚正不阿、广大宽阔，静观事变，任何事都不会损害自己。无求则被所有人求。

人之美，贵在内涵，美柔在内才不会红颜薄命、才子折寿，即使生活在和平时代，服务于朝廷，没有建功立业的机会，也能够因为不逞强斗狠而善终。

厚德载物有慧眼，不仅看见，而且明白。厚德之人有知识，更有文化，懂得不以文化知识为光环炫耀，不到可以说的时候，能够缄口不言。缺德必褊狭好斗，最后如同天龙战于郊野，黑血染黄

沙，留下尸首或残身。

黄帝修德振兵成万邦君主，人修德正心成人中龙凤。自强不息、厚德载物，龙凤精神需要永远坚持。时机不到而说话会因言获罪。德行之高人自在，在等待时机之际，饮食宴乐却不玩物丧志，自带的风水必将逐一得到。

5. 人之沉沦与自我升华

每个人一生都面临生活沉沦与人格升华的选择，这是人拥有自由的条件。沉沦，可指人在身体陷入疾病痛苦折磨中，或处于酗酒、吸毒等厄运中，精神不振后出现的自甘堕落、自杀、杀人等人性变异或降级的行为。

比如一些青年在成长期间因情爱不顺意而忧郁成病，而后做出窥浴、野合、宿妓、吸毒等行为，伤人或自戕，最后不珍惜生命，或投河自杀，或杀人犯罪等。动物没有人的理性和自由，一生被天赋的生存本能操控，为生态平衡活着，无堕落更无升华。

自我，指主体存在的独立性、自觉性，即本我的主动性，及每个人的个性、兴趣、观点。说白了，人生主要受着自己形成的观念的支配。张三如果认同"爸爸说我鲁莽"的说法，很有可能因斗殴杀人被判死缓，而没能成为可立功的刑警。李四如果认同"老师说我笨"的说法，很有可能捡垃圾几十年，埋没了其天赋的厨艺。

一般人的自我认识并非就是真正的自我，而是多数教师、家长、同学对他的评价，是大众经验。一个人如能超越大众的社会意识，就有了自我：要么偏执沉沦，要么品格升华。

升华是这样一些现象：湿衣服晒干，白炽灯钨丝变细，蜡烛燃烧成灰，樟脑丸变小，气温升高下冰的融化，等等，升华是水、铁、蜡、樟等不同的物质逐渐变形的现象，哲学上指运动形式从机械运动升级为物理运动、化学运动等。

人能超越众人的个人经验或社会意识，变为与众不同或与人（师、官、父等）不同，就有了自我。人对自己和社会的认识趋于邪恶，就会作恶多端，为非作歹，这就是沉沦堕落；人对自己和社会的认识趋于善良，就会择善而从，从善如流，这就是升华超越。人沉沦，就如泥石流，顺地势而下，越滚夹带的杂物越多，自我如同面孔涂了泥沙，盖了树叶，看不见了。人升华，就如负重上山，越高越与众不同：清风明月，宁静致远，至善如神。

6. 积德行善与为非作歹

积德行善，相对为非作歹而言，积德指不间断地做好事，行善就是做好事，行是行为活动，善是言行利人和由衷为人。

积德行善最早出自《周易·坤》："积善之家，必有余庆。"此处积善与厚德同义，合成四个字就是积德行善：不损人、不害人，并促成别人成就好事，奉行仁、义、礼、智、信五常伦理。德即得，得到的是好的家庭、学校与好的子孙。

"积德行善"是一种人文素质，是个人修行，是一个人言行自律的文化传统。现代社会的公益行为是公民国家的积德行善。

佛家讲积德行善，是通过布施、持戒、忍辱、精进、禅定、般若六种方法，消除心灵的六种污垢：贪欲、毁坏、嗔怒、懈怠、散乱、愚痴，重现个人天赋的德性。

如果说人的贪欲是德行的污垢，太贪了就真的会产生蛇吞象的结果，消除的方法就是布施、持戒、忍辱、精进、禅定、般若，这些方法对应消除贪欲、毁坏、嗔怒、懈怠、散乱、愚痴。真正积德行善关键是提升自己的品格，并非仅仅给乞丐几块钱。

为非作歹，简单地说，是指做种种坏事。为非作歹的人，内心邪念强烈，想人往坏里想，报复心极大，受不得损伤，被骂一句，要还十句。挨人一耳光，要断人一只手。这是因为极度自卑而被妒

火攻心，如没毁掉有教养的人，不解心头嫉恨。

有些人为非作歹，并非出于报复心，而是因为唯利是图，才不择手段，或骗或盗或打或杀。还有人贪欲太强，贪官利用权力和钱财包二奶，违背道德伦理。

为非作歹的人，把邪理当正理，得理不饶人：要么"宜将剩勇追穷寇"，要么"痛打落水狗"。所以能这样做的人，是妄念强到极致，把歪理邪说当成真理，甚至认为放之四海而皆准，于是为非作歹，做坏事理直气壮，甚至拉人一起团体犯罪。

7. 事不如人意，狗不吃牛屎

为非作歹的人最终会穷凶极恶，步入穷途末路，行事全然反规律，什么自然规律与社会规律全都不在心里。然而自然规律与社会规律同时存在，是不以人意为转移的。

自然与社会，千变万化。一朝天子一朝臣，一春秋鱼送一春秋饭。人类每件事情都想称心如意，可结果往往事不如人愿，狗不食牛屎。

天有不测风云，人有旦夕祸福。人之为事，不量力而行的太多，每一件事情都与天时、地利、人和息息相关。哪有人想怎么就能怎么，欲望都达到的？如果那样，天理、人理、物理全没有了，人类几千年章法、规章全没有了。人若随心所欲，自然界和社会就会乱作一团了。

当你事事不称心如意的时候，静下心来禅悟，进而调节自己的心情。

当你经历自然界天灾人祸之难时，要用理智去面对，冷静思考，用有效可行的办法自救……

当你违法违章的时候，最要有勇气理智面对，回避、逃避都会一错再错，甚至走极端，最后发展到无可挽回的地步。

人生所遇的事，不如意的太多太多。人谋事是受社会现实、自然现实的规律限制的。古人言"谋事在人，成事在天"……

8. 顺之自然规律与顺应社会潮流

小学课本中"自然"一词，是指当今物理学所实证研究的自然界，即物质世界、宇宙整体，小至中微子，大至星系，以及通常说的生命。我们如果说某人的打扮不自然，是说他本来面貌或气质特征等被掩没了。自然，很多时候指"自然环境"（天气及地质等），或没有人类介入的"荒野"，如野生动物、岩石、森林、沙滩及地下的矿藏和能源等，特别将其与人造物（园林、商品等）相区分。

与自然相联系，就有了规律的说法，从自然规律，我们又推导出社会规律。规律即规则、律法等所有法则的合称，像人没有被打扮的面貌、没被发现或开采的矿藏一样，是自然界本身带有的属性，不以人的意志为转移。我们不能创造、改变和消灭规律。我们可以抽水上山建造水库，灌溉高地，但水如果不借外力始终是往低处流的。

汉语说自然规律，一个"道"字就说完了。道，即神、法、真理、天地万物。"道"字最早出现在道家的《道德经》的第一章第一句话的第一个字：指所谓"终极真理"，我们可以说，却不可以把说的当成真道；道的本质，人无法说清楚，如同我们说一张桌子，怎么说都只是所了解的一个侧面。

道有神性，衍生万物；又是无处不在的法则，人、地、天都必须遵循。我们这些性情中人，说"道"这个字，只是道路、道理等意思，没有修道以去除七情六欲的意义。古人说"道"常与"德"相联系，就好像是人的德行列车的路轨。

故而自然规律永存，我们必须永远顺应它，不要痴心妄想去改造它。我们可以顺应、引导和改变的只是社会潮流，即流行文化，

尤其是现代文化。现代文化的特色就是水往低处流，裹着泥石流，借助工业技术的影视出版等传媒事业与大众情趣互动所产生的文化，即大众文化，只在特定的时间和地点流行。

现代工商业加速了文化的流行。文化在古代流行百年甚至千年，到现代也就流行几年、十几年。流行文化通常较为肤浅，太深奥就没法流行。顺应社会潮流，但切莫离经叛道。

9. 礼义由心生，罪恶由心起

人之四维中的礼义，并非交际中的礼仪。礼貌和仪容可打扮，礼让和义务却不可伪装。孟子说：礼是辞让之心，义是羞恶之心。人无礼义，空披人皮，为非作歹，禽兽不如。人做事心无礼义，反复无常，折腾社会。官治国心无礼义，管人如禽兽，国无宁日。人不知礼义，男人晃肩，女人扭臀，行走无人样，行事无善心。

传苏轼和佛印禅师开玩笑，苏轼说他看佛印像牛粪。佛印说他看苏轼像如来。两人看法为何不同？因为人心不同。苏轼心存牛粪好斗，就拿牛粪比佛印。佛印心存如来谦让，就拿如来比苏轼。比喻未必恰当，却心存善念，以德报怨。

儒家由仁心引领义、礼、智，共同表现人的善心。礼由心生，守礼行事有分寸。心中有礼，才会真正施礼于人。男人西装革履，存心非礼，不守进退辞让的法则，纷争一起，恶由胆生，左手抽耳光，右手拔手枪。

2012年12月，美国康州发生胡克小学校园枪击案，20名儿童死亡，再次引发"控枪"争论。美国民间拥有约2.5亿支枪，如果发生群体性事件，会发生什么事情？公民持枪成了自卫权利，信奉基督成了礼节习惯，将有多少枪战？

苏轼以牛粪羞辱佛印时，已偏离了君子儒必修的是非之心，不理智，在用言语伤人了。如果他被佛印激怒，遭骂甚至挨耳光，还可能为非作歹。现代社会很多刑事案件皆由口舌是非引起。罪恶由心起，所以非礼作恶犯罪。

是非只因多开口，烦恼皆因强出头。万恶的不是旧社会，是刻意标新立异。居心不良，禁枪禁刀禁不了饮食中投毒。有心犯罪，酒瓶饭碗拳头都能杀人。治安系统再完善，也不能抑制人作恶的罪性。法律越健全爱心越缩小。格子化了爱心，人就成了围棋的棋子。人的罪行由缺德的罪性引发。罪性是"五十步"，罪行是"百步"。

没有善念和信仰的人最危险。辞让、羞恶的礼义之心是人内在的德性，如果没有，礼貌仪容就如同表面光鲜的马粪，会是作恶多端的包装。觉悟成佛难，守住善心是关键。礼让他人，就能当仁不让、义不容辞、义尽仁至，纷争就能大事化小、小事化了了。心是菩提：悟空、舍弃、自在。

10. 天机深藏，不可随便道破

天机，顾名思义，上天的机密，与道家所说的自然神道、佛家所说的如来佛法相关联，是儒家天道、天理、天意的另一种表达。所有兵机、贼机，如同诸葛亮的锦囊妙计——神机妙算之术，都是天机。所有神佛道儒之术都含天机。

天机，还可谓智慧实相的机密，无论哲人的沉思，或者神人、天人的沉冥，凡流传到后世来的经典语录、文章，表面文字多用比喻，为的就是将智慧隐藏其中，让我们在懵懂的感知中有所记忆，随着生活常识的丰富和德行的升华，慢慢有所感悟、理解。领悟天机，需要联想，理智地打开慧眼，不要被私情迷惑。

智慧之精华尽在天机。智慧让人可以深刻地理解人、事、物、社会、宇宙、现状、过去、将来，有能力思考、分析、探求神佛道儒之真理，让人不求成功而自然成功。世人少见天机，沉迷在文化

知识的海洋中，怅寥廓失心智，丢了慧眼。

知识太多皮毛，不多时日就会脱落、老化，但皮毛因为光鲜，而为人所迷。沉迷者可能就成了专家、学者，被办公桌、研究室套牢，囚禁住脑袋瓜，非美德不可解套。精华是最重要、最好的，故而常有"取其精华，去其糟粕"的说法，却很少有人真正做到。

天机中的智慧精华，是神佛道儒之术的光华、光辉所在，如同五脏之精气、日月之精华。故而欲识天机，需去除五脏六腑中的邪气，还需清理神经中枢的恶意，不让邪恶入侵伤害头脑。苏格拉底说美德即知识，儒家讲仁义礼引领智力，意义就在于以高尚品格"扬精华以炫燿兮，芳郁渥而纯美"。

高德之士从所谓封建、民主等政治争执中超脱出来，清风明月相伴，自尊至善如神，在玩物丧志者只见青山翠岛的地方，能慧眼洞见天地精灵与日月精华。

道法感悟，玄奥确定的内容就是天机。天机不可泄露。这就像一个蛋，在壳上扎一个针孔，此蛋就再也孵化不出鸡来了。道破天机必须看时机，聆听天意。

11. 论虚荣和务实

人间多险恶，全在真与假。话假、事假、物假、情假、义假，假的一切让人类险恶不断发生，假的深重导致罪恶的深重，假的漫长导致其影响也漫长，假的广度有多大害的广度就有多大，一切都成正比。假情假意，夫妻朋友反目成仇，最后各奔东西。有甚者血灾之祸，祸害家人或左邻右舍。

虚荣心万事皆空，务实心万事充实。虚荣心是自尊心的过分和扭曲的表现，是一种追求虚表的性格缺陷：为了取得荣誉和引起普遍的注意而表现出来的一种情感——盲目攀比，好大喜功，过分看重别人的评价，自我表现欲太强，有强烈的嫉妒心，等等，这些都

是失常的表现。

虚荣心，俗称要面子，"打肿脸充胖子"是其最感性的解释。古代朝廷官员坐八抬大轿，鸣锣开道，炫耀自己的权势，这就是虚荣心作祟。人为了虚荣，可能撒谎骗人，甚至偷盗，走上犯罪道路；或者攀比富人，请吃大餐，让自己过几个月缺钱的日子；或者借名人的名头去吓人惹祸，引出官司。

人处世靠诚信，做事靠自信。靠自己，所得才牢靠。渴求虚荣，借用外表、学识、财产，表现得妄自尊大，最后失去朋友，被人孤立。渴求表扬或赞美，以虚假的方式保护自己的自尊，最后是虚假被揭穿，万事不成，渴望皆空。

人之所以求表面的荣誉或虚假的荣光，是因为依赖性，人自信心不够，想因人成事，希望走捷径获取成功，渴望天上掉下馅饼。这通常是在孩子时代父母教育不当所致，孩子能力不强而自卑。

然而一个人想做成事情，重要的是要有一颗务实心。务实就是讲究实际、实事求是。李时珍就是务实地在各地收集民间药方并验证，才写成《本草纲目》。

无论农耕或者游牧、工商，大凡这个民族能在文明时代五百年不灭亡，其传统文化就必然有务实心的培育。孔子教育弟子"知之为知之，不知为不知"，传授的就是"一是一、二是二"的务实之道。

儒家教育的精神是：大人不华，君子务实。不图虚名，充实人心的就是务实之心——注重现实，崇尚实干，排斥虚妄，拒绝空想。踏实交朋友，万丈高楼平地起，万事都是一件件积累起来的。务实心是中国的传统美德和五千年文明的基石。

12. 权利、意识与生命

人为财死，鸟为食亡。说的是过了头的恶果。财富可提高生活

品质，人却不能贪财，贪心是不正确、不平常的心态。正确的平常心是：地位再高，与人往来常持平民百姓心态；财富再多，常以穷人美德去生活，不浪费食物、自然物质与有用财物。有德行之人，地位再高，依然平民心态常驻心田，财富再足，处处以勤俭朴实过日子。

人有如电脑，是说人有预制的程式，遗传基因决定了人的个体性状。物种进化永远是臆想和哲学推论。思想可进化，物种不能，就像狗不吃牛屎，猴不能成人一样。

武王伐纣时，率诸侯会盟立誓，说："惟天地万物父母，惟人万物之灵"。这不是人的狂妄，是基于人可管理和制服地球万物的事实。同时武王也说明起兵革命的理由：不是犯上作乱，是顺天应人、应天命，复兴善政。

革命不是暴乱，意义不在于杀人。革命意义在于终止暴政，保护人命。人命，关系极为重大，不可草菅人命。所以元曲《杀狗劝夫》中说："人命关天，分甚么首从。"也就是说，人无罪被杀，杀人者要偿命，要重罚。

历史上分辨正教邪教或正理歪理，不是看自我标榜，而是看其教义、主张。凡教人做好人，除恶扬善，关爱人生，维护人命的，就是正教正理；凡教人做坏人，颠倒是非，混淆黑白，杀人越货，草菅人命的，就是邪教歪理。

邪教歪理，张扬暴力，煽动仇恨和恐怖主义，骗人或逼人作恶人，反天道、反常识，离经叛道。正教正理，教人上敬神灵，下孝父母，教人与人为善、和平共处、同舟共济，引导人顺从天道、天理，按照常识踏踏实实做人，不离经不叛道，正常地面对困难，在劫难逃，就理智承受，大难不死，必有后福。

理智是生命的保护神。哲人视人为政治和理性的动物，引人信神回天做人。圣人视人为天地造化万物之灵，教人以灵性处世，与人为善、择善而从、从善如流。

贾谊以投鼠忌器的故事劝皇帝不要对大臣施加酷刑，以免伤及皇帝的自尊。今天还可用投鼠忌器劝人不要贪财，以免养虎遗患，害了难得的人命。唯利是图，卖假酒谋财，就可能害了人命。

13. 论发展

发展，即演变升级。不论大小，国家、家庭、民族，发展不外两种形式：一是注重政治而昙花一现；二是文明治理而长久治安。

古代巴比伦、埃及、印度、爱琴等地区的政治，走马灯似的旋转，只在神话和考古中有残缺不全的影子。我们现在说的公民政治"保先生"（保尔提克斯，Politics），孙中山解释为"管理众人之事"，引申出民族、民权、民生三大主义，在大陆只实践了20年。而中国古代"天下为公"的政治统治方式，从炎黄传说到清朝，则持续了五千年。

依据《尚书》等古籍的说法，中国君主制的特征是"道洽政治，泽润生民"，君主统率大臣，以"民贵君轻"的政治思想治国，西周以前天子及诸侯要修道，上承天命，施行善政。天子一旦行恶政，就会被承传王道的诸侯以革命的方式替代。

这就是今日说的以德治国，不是口说，而是实实在在地履行，并落实到君臣日常生活的方方面面，治国首先是礼乐教化，从上到下自律，并受舆论监督。这种教育主道的柔性管理，给了自由文明很大的空间：适时地推陈出新，社会才能发展。

文明治理，以武力强盛为后盾，就能统治长久。例如商朝经历17代31个修道君主，据传有510年。而西方文明走的是武力强盛为主道的城市化、公民化的路子，直接以城市公民的生活方式去征服和改造外邦异族，先毁灭原来的文明，后以奴隶制或农奴制重建，先实行贵族、共和、民主、寡头等统治方式，都不行，就实行君主专制。这种"以武力殖民征服后，再用法治主道"的文明，持

续都不过 500 年。

中国传统文明五千年，武力始终是后备，走的是"见龙在田，天下文明""自强不息，群龙无首"的路：文人以正大光明、文采飞扬的文章展示阳刚正气；君主以文德、文教治国，武力备而少用，甚至不用；全民以孝道自律，安居乐业。

14. 人类处世三展示

首先，展示文化教养。

你有文化吗？读书人被这样问及的时候，是理性的自省还是恼羞成怒？你爱国吗？钓鱼岛主权问题的游行示威中出现严重的打、砸、抢等暴力行为，估计很少有人能在家里跟父母探讨其源头，能溯源到五四运动游行时出现的烧房屋、打外交官的事。我们知道了许多事，却在该同情时挖苦，该谴责时喝彩。

如果思想的进化不是进入理性升华的佳境，而是进入人云亦云、以讹传讹的众口一词的"井"里，幸福必然是远在天边，遥不可及。1950 年，全国的识字率只有9%，至少有95%以上的人会乐于助人，笑脸指路，义务引路等。现在识字的人在90%以上，却少有1%的人，被人无意踩了一脚，还能心平气和。高学历者中走路晃肩、随意扭臀、随地下蹲、粗口骂人的人不在少数，有的甚至还是名牌大学的教授，还以名门世家后裔为夸耀。

其次，展示有作为的心态。

当今功利性文化教育离经叛道，不再传君子自强不息、厚德载物之道，把国内生产总值当作硬道理讲，引人思想掉入这样的陷阱：要想不庸庸碌碌，不当官就要钱，否则就是虚度一生。如此成就事业就只争朝夕，为扬名立万悬梁刺股，少有怀道隐身、清风明月的君子了。

孟子曰："人有不为也，而后可以有为。"孟子这样说，也这样做，成了后世儒家尊崇的亚圣。《孟子》流传千古，至今还芬芳如昔，这就是大有作为。如果孟子屈节做了争雄诸侯的相国或大夫，也就没有"民贵君轻"的名言和《孟子》名著传世了。河流入海，暗道归来。当今我们很需要复兴孟子的有为精神。

再次，展示自己的强力。

有李小龙的骨架肌肉，就够健美了。李小龙将散打技艺发挥到极致，也够强力了，却只活了 32 岁，付出了折寿的代价。反暴政的强力不是体格，是不移志、不淫乱、不屈节的心力。这是孟子教诲的。

15.　论强与弱

有篇 2006 年的文章在网上流传，文章是一位 15 岁左右的初中生写的，宣称："这个社会，没有对与错，只有强与弱。"他主要依凭初中校园内外的乱象，以很有限的眼见、听闻和报道推断：做人要明哲保身，偷偷"努力使自己变强！强于一切！"

这位学生眼见的"强"是：50 厘米长的西瓜刀被拿进宿舍，"混混"抢劫敲诈，老师不敢管排队插队现象，校内打架谁狠谁赢……这些现象的确很多，说话夹带着很多臆想。因为没有分析"这个社会"对人心的变异，说"不敢"是偏颇的。

耳听的"强"是：有无权势天壤之别，穿得太拽会死得很早，成名英雄斗不过黑帮枭雄……这些都是道听途说，人云亦云，以讹传讹；是大众话语，谴责恶势力可以，不宜为胆小找理由。司马光、王守仁 10 岁前就有三省吾身、天下为公、仁者爱人、为仁由己、当仁不让、杀身成仁、仁至义尽、义不容辞、先礼后兵、明辨是非等千年正统恒言，这个学生没有，好似太原人脚下煤被掏空了一样。

枪打出头鸟，拔刀相助自找被扁，落难之际好朋友都是睁眼瞎

（是狗屁朋友），鸟尽弓藏（兔死狗烹、谋杀功臣）没用了就杀……对这些红尘警言，囫囵吞枣地接受。学生不学斯文，上学白上。不怀疑成见，没有自我。这才是真的弱，

黑帮和警员黑白相护，唇亡齿寒。"在这个世上，没有（法律）平等这个说法"，只有官官相护，不得不贪。成王败寇，弱肉强食是千古不变的。"这个世上"，这样说话，好似学物理学、化学一样，只是为了考试。15 岁的年龄，原本英雄出少年，却如此孱弱，随"权利气球"西飘，2000 字里不见"仁""义""礼"，断然否定"智"。

权利气球人说弱势话语："即使要做英雄也要做默默无名的英雄，要举报也只能偷偷举报，要学会的不仅是保护自己，还要顾及家人的安危。"做"商人 + 小偷"，这两个心愿会达成吗？

16. 论穷与富

穷与富跟弱与强不等同。无论身体或心志，都是穷未必弱，富未必强。

穷，钱财少，生活窘迫。但这并不可怕，可怕的是因为穷而产生的自卑情结，由此嫉恨富人及其子弟，怨忿老天爷不公平：让有的人天生命好，不用努力就可以轻松取得成功；让自己命苦，出生在市井穷巷或穷乡贫农家里，没钱上大学而终身耕田……因为穷而造反，没逼也上梁山，通常成为刑事罪犯。

有报道说穷人被不公正对待的事：城管打死在街上卖东西的穷老太；同遭车祸丧生，农村穷家少女的赔偿不及城市户口的一半。同人不同命，同伞不同柄。"穷则思变"被曲解，穷人被鼓动起来造反，如今其后代终点回到起点。穷人穷困依旧，过程只是折腾。穷，最怕失志屈节被困，潦倒之后不是被害死，就是饿死。

穷与富，只要户口、职业流动开放，就没有阶级壁垒。穷不失

礼义，不失德性，富裕就有基业，致富只是时间问题。老当益壮，穷当益坚，坚持正道终将获得转机。关键还在于贫穷不移志，反倒穷而后工，诗文技艺越出众。

穷山恶水，是自然环境。人不是穷山恶水。人穷志不穷，穷而不失气节，心志不穷，穷困境地则可以改变。如宋朝欧阳修，穷得无纸笔读书，但他德性升华，有读书志向，用芦苇在沙地上写字、画画，借书抄读，最后，他23岁成进士，时来运转。

穷并非终极状态，而是现在时态，或过去祖辈的遗留。所以穷并非走投无路。宝剑锋从磨砺出，梅花香自苦寒来。天道酬勤，穷有技艺，只等时机。穷人依靠天时、地利、人和的因素致富，才是通途。

有人说，人情就是钱、亿万富翁可以用钱让犯了杀人罪的儿子逍遥法外。这仅仅是以偏概全的激愤之语。穷在一时，富也是。缺德，贵如浮云、流水，转瞬即逝。离道，富贵逼人趋炎附势，富如走马灯，富贵骄人，不可一世，无德贪淫，穷奢极欲，好景不长。穷有志，终成过去时；富有德，富贵才长久。处世行礼义，人生最光辉。

17. 论礼、义、智、信、勇

人的意识形态，首先表现在礼。孟子说的"仁义礼智"四善心，仁、智在心，可以作假。失礼之义僵硬。唯有礼，到处见到。君臣之礼、父母子女之礼、师生之礼、长幼之礼、邻里之礼、职场之礼……有礼人间方有序，有序才不乱，礼是规章、法规的基石、鼻祖，是人情的温床。非礼，仁、义、智一一尽失。

义是人类行为的表现，义气、义务履行了才算。先礼后兵，义才不僵硬，有情有义。礼约定俗成后，情自然发生，孝敬失真通过失礼即可鉴别。义先于行为，礼俗之情的质决定义的品位。好情美

义，情出自心态，义见于举动，义的行动体现行为之高尚。英雄、烈士将义发挥到最高点。

智是日光知识。人的智商是先天的，却要靠后天学唱逐步积累，其实是开发，在实践中不断总结。在人类思想进化中，浩瀚自然的千变万化中，人是在社会和自然的环境中，通过积累生活常识，发展文化知识，接受信仰日光沐浴，思想才升华为智慧。有的智慧光芒四射，有的大智大伟，创造人间奇迹，永远载入史册。

信是人类做人做事的栋梁。信有待人接物、做事的诚信，有自己为人为事的自信。一个人的成功始终要坚持诚信和自信。做人诚信，能广交朋友，再与人为善，就能广结善缘，真正神通广大。做事自信，敢面对磨难，在命运的劫难中坚守正道，除掉魔性，失败有了转机就是成功，同时拥有幸福。

人的勇是礼、义、智、信的总装发射，审视自己面对的人和事，"恨邪恶、爱善良"是原则。有爱自己所爱的勇气，有恨自己所恨的勇猛。这就是人类的勇士，只有勇士方能成为英雄。爱憎分明的仁人志士，有勇气才能择善而从。

礼、义、智、信、勇，是真正的仁者、义士、智者、信徒、勇士的心智资源。

18. 猜忌害人害己

猜忌，由人的猜疑和忌妒两种心态组成，这种心态很不正常，既害人又不利己。

人生无常，心要正常。这是社会定理。人是七情六欲的生灵，七情表现为喜、怒、忧、思、悲、恐、惊七种情绪，六欲指身体湿、寒、实、热、燥、火六种状态。七情因六欲引起，六欲是人体的生理感受，七情六欲适度，则为人身所需要，过度则令人生病。

情欲是人与动物共有的，是感觉状态及其原因。人因为理性而

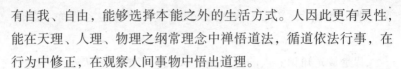

有自我、自由，能够选择本能之外的生活方式。人因此更有灵性，能在天理、人理、物理之纲常理念中禅悟道法，循道依法行事，在行为中修正，在观察人间事物中悟出道理。

讲道理并与人为善，就能以平常心态善待别人的成长进步和发达顺利，并真诚祝贺。若是亲戚朋友，更要庆贺，共用欢乐。如果心态失常，不平不正就会猜忌。人千万不可有猜忌之心态。有猜忌之心的人，成不了大器，很难开创自己的事业。

犯猜忌，会无端怀疑别人对自己不利，见不得他人好，总是心怀不满、心理失衡。自我是需要怀疑的，通过思虑澄清思想中的疑点，以清晰的认知指导自己的言行。但无端怀疑他人，即无凭无据、信马由缰地猜测他人，往坏里想这个人的言行，就是不对的，整人的运动差不多都是由捕风捉影的猜疑和忌妒开始的，借着冠冕堂皇的名义。

专横跋扈或优柔寡断的人往往爱猜忌。礼义廉耻四维缺失的人，心态失常，无论男女老少，都猜忌多心。人生有猜忌之心，必然幸灾乐祸，你猜忌的别人，是因为你犯了"眼红病"，等到他们有了灾祸，你一定会幸灾乐祸，这更是心态不正常。

人心底有了猜疑，必会萌发猜忌。一旦有了猜忌，发展到不可收拾的地步，必然导致不应有的恶果，甚至流血千里，伏命千万。历史由猜忌引起的战争、毒杀、谋害，历朝历代历年案例层出不穷，生存生活之道日渐变异。

19. 生存之道与生活之道

生存之道是人处世交往之道，生活之道是人活着的衣食住行之道。

处世之道，现今多被当作待人接物、与人相处、人际交往的技巧，是可以传授的技术，其实并不是这么表面的事。处世交往之

道，是人的立身之本，是人适应自然环境融入社会之道，展示仁、义、礼、智、信、忠、勇、耻等人的德行，就是人处世的道德。人因此与动物相区别。

处世之道在人类文明早期，主要在贤士、君子身上才有所体现，君子重义，贫穷不移，威武不屈。由此形成礼尚往来、文质彬彬、一诺千金、杀身成仁等德行，能做到这些的才是男子汉大丈夫。越往后世，人活得越来越世故，处世之道逐渐退化为政治社会交往，讲究技巧。例如宋朝苏轼不善于逢迎被贬官，而清朝和珅却因为会讨好乾隆而飞黄腾达。

生活之道，无论君子、小人或贵族、平民，都需要有衣食住行的活着之道，但是自然环境（千差万别的地理环境和气候环境）有所不同，在服饰、美食、住宅、行路等方面，各地区的民族明显有所不同。

生活之道，在现代社会，成为大众成功和幸福之术，跟利益和感觉相联系。随着世袭贵族的消失与不再普遍倡导君子德行，人们越来越少忧虑死亡，尤其在年轻的时候，主要关注生命与活着。这是社会潮流、群众文化影响的结果，较多谈论真诚、爱、两性、时间、愤怒、恐惧、耐心、屈服、宽恕、快乐等生命活着本身的课题。

大丈夫的活法不普遍。所有人却都必须考虑衣食住行等生活问题，这是人类的基本需要，每个人都离不开这些。由于讲究衣食住行之道，社会因而发展，人为折腾出来的布票、粮票、平房、泥土路成了过去。

中国祖祖辈辈就是由圣贤君子立身处世之道，引导大众生活之道，一路走到今天。这成为我们的根源地。我们的生存成为祖宗生存的延伸，绿化美化荒山野岭，蓄水到水库，发展农林牧渔多种事业，成为我们生存与活着的使命。人类生存由此没有被经济困住，活出了生存的质量……

把处世看作艺术和哲学，与西方对比，这更是一种东方尤其是

中国功夫。生活既是生存基础上社会环境的课题，也是国家的政策法令、民族族规、家庭持家之道。善处世、会生活的人，无论顺境逆境，都能逍遥自在，怡然自得。

20. 做人要正直，做官莫贪心

"正"字方形，三横两竖没有曲笔，比喻不可屈节；去一竖合成"上""下"两个字，上下都不出头，"上"字加一竖变为"止"字。这可以理解为做人做官都要适可而止，不可贪婪。在官欲、财欲攀高的物质时代，人利令智昏，小小的一官半职就敢大笔一挥一餐吃掉六口之家两年正常生活费，一件名牌大衣是六口之家三年衣禄，一双鞋或一只手表是一平民百姓七十年衣食住行一辈子的享用……因此有的成了贪官，生活腐化得使身体不受营养重负，最后死于暴食贪享之中……

人有了地位会带来钱，有了钱还想谋地位，有了地位想更高。人类争权夺利的天性，使国与国之间、集团与集团之间、人与人之间，一代又一代、一年又一年，每时每刻都不放松，总是争夺。于是国家为谋求地区霸权而称王。民族部落为了生存而去巩固和扩大势力范围，达到地位权利去影响经济创收。个人、家庭、民族也这样去谋求权位和利益。

社会不断进步，经济飞速发展，贫富日渐悬殊，人的欲望受到差异的影响，人为地想缩小差异，男女老少居心不良、言行不正，就会越走越错。人在悬崖边，一步之差，就可能掉入万丈深渊，粉身碎骨。

在经济快车道上，人穷志短、人富德退，欲望变成无底洞，越富越缺德，越贫越缺志，因而急功近利，为了多得眼前一元，不惜损失日后一间屋。现在解了口渴，将来渴死。人缺志向如同船缺方向，滚在社会泥石流中，不见了人样，必将更缺德。社会靠德行

（礼义智信勇的德纲）维持，人类缺德混同禽兽。

人生存在社会上，应正直做人，正直做事，凡做一件事，要先有想法才去做，思想首先要良。良就是正直。人理跟物理都是同样的道理。物理上，木匠工作比较简单，制造加工木器具，为了对接饱满结实，形状美观大方，加工每一根方条、每一块板子、每一个孔眼，都要用规和矩去测量准确，务必求正。先正，后就不会斜。做人的道理比较复杂，但跟木匠工作的理是一样的，也要先正，端正人心和行为，收敛贪心，修正错误。先正己，后正人。正人正业，才是真正的事业。

21. 好公民学做承前启后人

每个公民身不由己，自己不能选择国家、民族、地区、家庭环境、父母双亲、生命的长短，但自己可以选择做什么样的人：或遵纪守法，或违法乱纪。

好公民先要学做人，第一步要以自己为中轴，学习识别上下左右前后。

上是你的父母、祖父母、曾祖父母，外祖父母、外曾祖父母、兄长、叔伯及外表兄长、叔伯，乃至官长。人对上，要孝字为先，尊敬为重，这是人的天职之责任。对领导、官长、老师，要服从忠心，诚意去完成自己的职责。对上尽孝、尽忠，不能犯上作乱，按天理、人理、物理之法则履行人生的责任。

下是你的子女、弟妹、学生、职员、工人。你自己是他（她）的长辈。养育、教育的是子女、弟妹，对待他们要有爱心、耐心。教育下属如同对待子女、弟妹。

你的左是同事、同学、夫妻，你的右是邻舍、同乡、同宗、同祖、同国、同源。左右之人群要和睦相处，互相帮助。远亲不如近邻，一辈子这几万天都是左右相处而过日子的，要互相尊重、互相

爱护。

前是自己经历过的，是自己的昨天，是历史，是经历过的日子、前事。人不该忘记的不是阶级，是前事。前事不忘，后事之师。人一出生，就是三天一个周期过的：昨天，天天多；明天，天天少；把握今天是至关重要的。务实今天，即承前启后：今天承传昨天，开启明天。人生永远是周而复始的"昨、今、明"三天，人就是这样活到老的。

人在三天的演绎中过日子，时刻要遵循"上下左右前后"六字法则去生活。为人处世，要善懂善用这六字法则。善于做人，一定会善于做事，只是兴趣不同事不同。因而人各有各的理想，但事业成就都是自己一天天积累沉淀的。

22. 实现理想先要脚踏实地

人步入社会，理想是很多的，按天理、人理、物理的科学态度去制定的目标，加上自己不断地向目标努力，就会实现自己的理想。

人的愿望有的太多太多，也有的太少太少。太多不知足的人，私欲膨胀为沼泽，芳草绿油油的，吸引得人想躺上去，后果则是沉陷下去，生命窒息；或者膨胀为气球，越来越大，越飘越高，最后在强气压下炸毁自己。太少而不能修无为或自然道的人，则会怨天尤人，终日愤愤不平；或者志大才疏，眼高手低，不能够脚踏实地地从小事做起，没有累积的经验和人脉，大事又做不了，废了自己。

有些人为了信仰活着，虔敬地相信神会给予一切，所以只是守候，却不尽职责义务做好分内的事。命中有终需有，命中无莫苦求，与世无争，以求安心，但也要脚踏实地做事，要有安身立命的一技或数技。世上大多数人特别是劳苦大众，先得认命，做好现在

的事，不欠现世账，这样才会心安理得，才会得到命理自带的财物或功业。

踏实做人做事而心安理得的人，头上三尺有神灵（神、道、佛祖、天主、玉皇等）照看。请神仙是敬神之心的表示，脚踏实地做事是尽职尽责。平平淡淡对待富贵，平平常常对待穷苦，这就是平常民众正常的思路。平民法则：忍一时风平浪静，退一步海阔天空。在多民族的国家或地区，统治者应奉行信仰自由，给良民充分的自由：自主地信奉各自选择的神灵，祈盼和平，忍无可忍才抗争。

刑法主要制裁思想极端的人。众多平常心态的人，需要的是教化和抚慰。生命无常，心要正常。正常心态的人，可以以禅定后的所得去修正错误，在自我升华中增进智慧，以豁达的胸怀去审时度势，知足常乐，得道觉悟。

23. 国家传统是人思想的根

国家是祖国与家乡的合称。家乡是家庭与故乡的合称。家庭是自己在现住地、出生地等稳定的歇息安居的处所。老祖宗的根源地是故乡。祖国指故乡所在国。人在一生中总是念念不忘故乡。大唐李白有诗说："举头望明月，低头思故乡。"

人到了这个丰富多彩的世界，无论走到哪个国度，一般总会惦记自己的祖国，即故乡国，自己的脑海里不时有祖国的影子。

在海外，华人流传这样一首表达思想情感的歌曲，大意是："天甚清，风甚凉，乡愁阵阵来。故乡人，今如何，常念念不忘，在他乡，一孤客，寂寞又凄凉。我愿意回故乡，再寻旧生活，众亲友聚一堂，重享从前乐。"可见身在异乡异土的华人恋故国、故乡之情。

美国黑人作家亚利克斯·哈利在《根》一书中，把人生的根扎

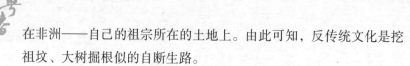

在非洲——自己的祖宗所在的土地上。由此可知，反传统文化是挖祖坟、大树掘根似的自断生路。

根源于何处，源于人的生命记忆的深处，是记忆中刻骨铭心的情绪，例如对天灾人祸的恐惧，对童年趣事的欢悦。

不管哪国公民，何种宗教信仰，在异国他乡终老的平民，或战死异国他乡的将士，都希望魂归故里。英国贵族罗素，中国平民苏轼，活的都是心安理得。

人，世踏世、代踏代地往前走，前有古人是肯定的，后是否有来者，这是根源是否能延续的问题：保守可传宗，激进难接代。不同人民、不同国度、不同个人观念的问题千差万别，各自明白，各自珍重，是别人不应强加指点的善恶问题。

24. 贪，终至贫苦

贪是万罪之首。果敢文中"贪"字中的"今"，上点下移成撇，就成了"贫"字。贪，佛教称为贪毒，与嗔、痴并列为三毒，指世人纠结各种事物、名分的欲望，使人迷醉于眼前的一切所产生的幻境。贪得无厌，不计后果，自毁毁人。

贪是三毒之首，贪饮（贪酒）又是贪毒之始。酒据传有近万年的历史，是能放松人的身心，具有催情、迷神作用，能令人产生快感、增进人的娱乐情绪的饮料。历史不乏帝王饮酒失德而亡国的记载，例如羲和、夏桀、商纣、杨广等。酒池肉林不是好事。

贪色根源于人四季可以发情的性欲本能，人会被色情所困进而神智迷乱而犯罪，贪色与贪饮一样古老。夏桀、商纣、周幽等帝王，都因为女色而失道缺德，最终祸国殃民。

贪财，是贫富分化之后的文明时期出现的罪过。谋财害命，可谓文明死罪。

贪食，指一种超过需求而拼命吃东西的生理病症，造成很多肥

胖病人。我当知青时食欲很大，那是体力支付的需要。后来知道女人生气的时候也会猛吃，才知道心情不好还有与不思饮食相反的情况。人肥胖之后，行动不便，疾病增多。

贪婪这种欲望过度所生的贪饮、贪色、贪食、贪财的罪恶，最难控制，人贪婪进而得寸进尺，永不满足，为贪而贪，不考虑自己是不是真的需要贪的东西，损人利己甚至损人且不利己。好酒贪杯误了做事，失了信誉。特洛伊王子和周幽王好色，惹来亡国之灾。贪食所致的损伤主要是对个人身体，却也危害不轻。

贪婪文化从西方到东方，正危害着全人类。贪酒成祸，贪色成悲剧，贪财丢了命，贪食害了身体。贪欲无止境，人必然自食恶果，终至一贫如洗、苦不堪言。贪财在工商业社会催生出拜物宗教，夺了亿万人的心志。玩物丧志始于贪心无法控制。贪欲成了人的心魔，以魔为神，智力步入歪门邪道，一失足成千古恨。

在天主教的七宗罪里贪色、贪食、贪财（包含在贪婪之中）占了三项，都是贪婪的欲望所致。中国儒教视淫乱为万恶之首，视浪费食物、敛财无节制为罪恶。中国道儒佛认识节制贪欲的意义更早，反贪由舆论到起兵，有步骤，很理智。

25. 英雄、庸人、懒人

人活在世上千姿百态，各有各的活法，各有各的行为，但归纳起来也就是几个层次的人：少数英雄、多数庸人（凡夫俗子）、少数懒人。

英雄胸有国与家，心目中，时常念想家庭成功、国家兴旺。超个人、党派的人民利益才是他个人的行为宗旨。能平常地过日子，也能舍弃个人所得，紧急关头显出英雄本色，为国为民奋不顾身，献出自己的力量乃至生命。这就是英雄。

庸人平凡，其中比较自私的，被儒家视为小人。小人把生活当生意，首先计较的是自己有否利益，利益大小、多少在他心中占第一位，他每时每刻靠算计过日子，认为算计社会、算计别人，自己得到利就是自己的本事，得到就是胜利，失去利益就是失算，他甚至算到父母、兄弟、妻儿子女、亲戚朋友的身上。为自己，无所不为、不顾他人、作恶多端，敢把德、信、义、礼全都抛弃，最后机关算尽，反而害了自己。

懒人是小人中的极端分子，眼高手低，碌碌无为，总想不劳而获，贪图享受。这种人总是打损人利己的主意。偷、抢、骗、斗、吸毒的，多数从这种人中产出。

懒人有社会红眼病，特长是善于拿自己的长处比他人的短处，愤世嫉俗到敌视世间的伦理和良知，没有认命的良心基础，没有竞争的个人勇气，借钱不还，只盼望被给予，没有创造，全是拿来主义，只享用过程。他（她）的反传统思想最强。懒人每个族群中都有不少，是社会治安不稳定的根源。

英雄、小人、懒人，是人类社会的三个类别。英雄少数，小人最多，懒人也不多。多数平民都遵纪守法、循规蹈矩，认命是自我安慰，随缘才顺其自然。做良民是理智的人生选择。是良民养活了自己、达官贵人，还有韭菜一样割了又生的大小贪官，有些时期还养活了无道的昏君奸臣，甚至还包括卖国求荣的极端坏人。

26. 组织与伦理

人类有两大特点：一是组织，人群的组合形式；二是伦理，最初的组合规则。

组织最松散的是人群乌鸦似的临时凑合，所谓乌合之众，没有纪律，一冲就散。组织，最初的紧密形式就是氏族部落，以血缘为纽带；后来出现了血缘不同、姓氏杂居的村社、宗教、城市、军队、监狱、法庭、国家；到现在更是有了用钱财、章程、契约组成

的工厂、公司、政党等集团。社会因组织而扩大，这就是发展。

社会因为有组织而逐渐复杂，由小变大，基本的轨迹是：由血缘群落到杂姓城市，由氏族部落（部族）到酋邦国家（民族）。最初的组合规则就是伦理，即血缘群落的辈分关系，有了母子、兄弟、姐妹等家庭伦理，以及对自然神的崇拜。

原始部族内部很亲密，也很排斥外人，以此来保持组织的稳定性，这样也就有了战争。从历史记载上看，四五千年前，中华黄土地的中原（中土）之地打仗是为了争做君主联邦制的帝君，后来修德振兵、选贤禅让，逐渐有了封建贵族制部族王国，像扑克组合，大小贵族形成纳贡及护卫关系。地中海地区（尼罗河、两河流域）则是具有征服毁灭性质的种族或城邦奴隶制关系，战争激烈，并持续不断，伦理松散的部族昙花一现。

这就形成了东方以中华自然神信仰为传统的天道天命、王道教化的文化，"仁义礼"统帅"智"的组织形式，"和为贵"，贵族和平民一直有债务、德才的流动关系。春秋战国五百年的称霸争雄战乱后，平民和贵族的世袭血统关系被打破，从秦朝到清朝，天、地、君、亲、师五权信仰支撑君主制国家两千年的仁政和暴政的治乱循环。

从欧洲、北非到西亚、中亚、南亚，在中国的西方，一神（耶和华或耶稣、真主）信仰支撑崇尚武力政治的等级制度、神道教化，国家组织跟日本类似。故而在儒家文化圈，脱亚入欧，企业化管理社会的变革中，日本最顺利，中国则最费周折。

27. 实事求是

组织、伦理及其信仰形成传统文化之后，逐渐有了讲道统和务现实的朋党对立，有了实事求是的人理。人在有所作为的过程中，有所事是，也无所事事。求是，是人理之基石。

《汉书》以实事求是之理，说汉景帝之子献王刘德收藏古书。秦始皇焚书后，周朝古文书籍比较少见，用秦朝时期抄写的古书掺杂后人的思想。刘德收藏古书时，很注重鉴别文本的真伪，留传下文献考证，这就是实事求是。

从实事求是的藏书传统发展出儒家古文经学：辨别古典文献真假本义。文天祥就义后，儒生以佛学方法空谈天理。清朝以考据之学重提实事求是，倡导古文经学传统：尊重和依照古书的本义做学问。岳麓书院将"实事求是"作为院训。

天理是宇宙太空、日月、星辰运作中，春夏秋冬、气候变化、山河海潮、自然理动的法则。风雷雨雪来去等天理，是人类可感受的宇宙法则和敬畏自然的理由。

物理是宇宙一切物质本来就存在的物理、化学、生物性质，物种的遗传现象，以及固有元素所能产生的变化定律。这种物质变化的合理性，统称为物理。

人要尊重天理、物理，形成人的伦理。人类生存、生活、发展，如何活出人的品格？人一辈子，怎样活得有模有样、有品有质？生活天天好、日日新之际，如何不失人间正道？人类几千年历史流传下人共同生存之理：家规、族约、国法。人只有自觉遵守天理、物理、伦理，才能自由自在，活得潇洒，使家庭平安幸福，社会治理有序。

国家在三理基础上制定法律，让人类有理有条地生活、劳作，让家规、族约、国法有理可讲，有章可循。社会由此能够治理通顺，国泰民安。人类敬守天理、物理、伦理，人人遵守家规、族约、国法，是天下太平的基本因素。

28. 适可而止，不可过度

灯谜"得意莫再往"，谜底是"适可而止"。适可而止，即人

的言行恰到好处。人在生活和社会活动中，凡事都要适可而止，不可过度、过头，以人体而言，手自然下垂，下不过膝。

人仿效自然物理、宇宙天理形成的伦理，并非社会惯例、宗教信仰和法律，例如八卦"天地雷风水火山泽"喻示着"父母兄弟姐妹"的伦理道德关系。伦理，简单地说，就是人与人以及人与自然的关系和处理这些关系的规则。

中国人以"天地君亲师"为五天伦，规定"忠、孝、悌、忍、信"五规则，作为君臣、父子、兄弟、夫妻、朋友五人伦关系的情理。这好比当今社会经理和职员之间由职业身份自然衍生出来的行为规范。当今的职业伦理侧重利益互补。古代的人际伦理侧重恩情互惠，形成天伦之乐和人伦常理，即通情达理的伦理。

人的行为不可乱来，须有理可循，思维遵循逻辑或人情。逻辑推理能力高低，决定智商。低智商者一分钟、一小时、一天，甚至一年困惑的事情，高智商的人一秒钟就能明白。但是聪明的人，思想千万不可过头。思想过头，反天理、物理，反伦理、法律、逻辑等人理，行为就会过度、过激、过火，失去社会准则和自然法则。聪明的上限是不过头，不反社会准则和自然法则，否则会聪明反被聪明误。

人类中大多数人是中低智商的，甚至是愚蠢的，傻傻的。傻人要笨鸟先飞。中低智商的人，凡事要反复思考，所谓三思而行，多静思自己所定行为方向跟社会、自然法则的误差大小。聪明人一会儿的思考，傻人用一小时反复思考、对照，这样能避免做低三下四的过膝蠢事。低到过膝的蠢事，会令人大失体面和人格的。

大千世界，一样的米养千万种人。人在行为之初，要静思。特殊行为更见证聪明才智。学习知识、积累经验，是人类生存的必备技巧。

29. 智力进化与道德退化

人类经过的时间和空间，在越来越复杂的社会阶层组合中不断进化。这跟自然界的一切物质经过的时间和空间，是自然现象排列组合的复杂进化相类似。

文明社会，在社会实体（家庭、行会、政府等）、目标（由规章确定，排除自发性）、系统（内部要素，及演化规则确定的结构等）、活动（人际交往，以及经济、政治、文化等）的组织要素的复杂排列中进化。

起初由王者和贵族来组织社会，组建城市和国家。神道信仰和世间法律并用，战争主要用于平定内乱和保家卫国，国家道统可长达千年以上，共和制莫过 500 年，民主政府百年辉煌就到了头。

现代社会创造性地转换贵族律法传统，以议会确定规则。

宪法指导律师、法官的职业性司法活动，政府、军队、政党、学校、医院、企业、工会、慈善事业、宗教信仰等组织，都要遵守议会制定或者帝王钦定的法律。道德伦理不如古代重要了。

法律把身份世袭的等级制度中贵族的自由特权，数学运算似的公约或平均化了。工匠、商人的技术，原先受宗教或礼教伦理限定，现在成了可推广的专利。工商阶层原来是勤劳致富，现在革新工业、财经技术，国家文明推进到福利制度出现后，法国人玩物丧志，活得像中国清朝的八旗子弟。希腊人更被中国游客称为"天下第一懒"，懒到 2010 年政府破产。

中国人 20 世纪 80 年代逐渐富裕起来，却没有承传 1949 年以前的礼教伦理教化。摸着石头过河的改革用特区、开发区的地价、免税等优惠政策引资，以出让农民工的福利和牺牲环境的代价发展经济，经济发展了，奸商唯利是图的观念也出现了。

智力进化与道德退化作交易。几千年的文明历史是良民用血

汗、贵族和达官用管理知识成就的。达官贵人自私享乐造成官逼民反，制度复杂化伤了自然元气。

30. 自然元气是社会发展的本原

人类是凭借社会关系与理性智力，获取地球生命的最高地位的。人类社会发展的过程，自然元气是决定潮流盛衰的根源，是社会制度存在的基础。

元气是民生国计。民生是国之本，国计是国之策。民众好似经济基础，是政府、议会、法律等上层建筑的基石。共和制普选的民众选票，全出自万众心田——传统所生的同心同德的元气。美国白人没有新教，就没有慈善基金会。中华民国反礼教，就少了宋江、武松、杨再兴似的英雄，多了西门庆、潘金莲等奸夫淫妇。

良民无法维持生活，过好日子，家国就会崩溃，经济就会衰退。好教化与好日子培育的民众心田，是适合民众生存的社会制度。这种社会制度是民生土壤。信奉上帝和耶稣的美国民心，敬畏天地和父母的中国民心，都是两国国计民生的元气。

自然界靠元气。地球靠宇宙合适的空间、阳光、水分提供生存之源。地面的动物、植物，地藏的矿产元素，相互生存、相互利用、相克相生。平衡的、相克相生的自然环境，空气、土壤、水分，在宇宙运行的规律中是正常的。人类、动物、植物，一切生物都是由于有元气的因素才能在阳光下、土壤中生存。

失去平衡，就破坏了自然源泉。如雨水、空气失衡，河水海水变质、地震、洪水、气候反常、瘟疫流行等天灾就降临。人类、动植物等生命体就遭殃。人类破坏环境而引起的灾难是自作自受。保护地球环境，是保护人类社会生存发展的本原。

中国神农架是目前世界仅存的元气十足的地方之一。地面植被未受破坏，四季分布自然，适合生物体、动物种群生息发展。南北东西气源运动形成的垂直气候，千变万化。西伯利亚与中国南海洋气流在此碰撞，形成奇雨。青藏雪原元气，黄土高原干风在长江、黄河四季流动与气夹流运动中，华北平原疏散回流下，令神农架千姿百态，雨量充沛，云流变化万千，冬天冰雪封山，地藏能源丰富，适应地下一切元素、地上一切植物、动物及生物的繁殖生长。神农架因传说炎帝神农氏在此搭架采药尝百草而得名。神农架元气托起黄帝陵。自然元气藏着炎黄文化的秘密。

论 适 应 主 义（三）

1. 性情与仁义

人，由一撇一捺写成，道，分左右行中庸：文质彬彬有仁义，虽有野性能舍弃。

做人有品性，修行上台阶，不在显耀中沦落。人生最大的失败，在于钻牛角尖，不知道退一步海阔天空。天生我才必有用，精益求精才有彩。人任性必败无疑。

做人要不偏不倚，做事要有始有终。人活在情中，有信仰，情才纯净；无信仰，率性恣情，人被欲控，就浪费了珍贵人体。儿童做事凭兴趣，被快乐的感觉所奴役。人生成年，循道而活：出世，清静无为，逍遥自在；入世，坚守原则，心明眼亮。

钱够用即可，不为名车、豪宅、美女、地位所困，才是真的英雄。人生精彩在于修炼，贫穷不移志，富贵不淫心，威武不屈膝，利刃能斩乱麻，慧剑能断情丝。

造化弄人，专为挑战命运者设置障碍。无论男女老少，重在自然：不要回避苦难，不要陷溺玩耍，不要玩物丧志。因此，应该认真生活，每天都是现场直播不能掉以轻心。

人生是个过程，有人多彩，从1到9；有人单色，不停地从1到2。人有原则，又善待时机，即便不求成功，成功自得。人无原则，以时务为成功而不愿脚踏实地，一生难免失败。山穷水尽道德

在，才有柳暗花明村。

大千世界，无人不冤，有情皆孽。不怕天作孽，最怕自作孽。人生彩虹风雨后，自作孽永陷黑暗。计算数字要精准，却莫要计较得失。人生有得有失，一直在得，也一直在失，求得的未必是自己真正想要的，失去的也或许正是人生的累赘。

失败莫失落，莫失良好的心态。走在人间正道上，做好本分，该有的自然会有。走正道，要提防好逸恶劳，倒掉的油瓶不扶；捞偏门，需谨防大肆张扬，中彩票鬼迷心窍。

男人掉进女人海，女人失去男人地，都是不对的。男女成为夫妻，携手朝圣，才有可能修仁义道成真人，怀慈悲心成正果。

2. 人生如戏

人生如戏编导定，演员走的是角色路，只有演好了配角，才可能有主角的戏。

印度电视剧《人生如戏》讲述一对双胞胎女子的故事，一波三折，扣人心弦。

姐姐南琪塔与妹妹耐哈生长在受人尊敬、德高望重的莎玛家。南琪塔聪明好强，一心要当演员，耐哈温柔善良。莎玛为南琪塔物色罗杰佛做丈夫。耐哈接受追求明星梦的南琪塔的哀求，代姐姐出嫁，并令新郎罗杰佛对其一见倾心。

南琪塔飞往孟买之前留给耐哈的纸条，被姑姑看到，姑姑揭穿了顶包的诡计。夫妻两家长辈感觉蒙羞。耐哈甚至被赶出婆家，幸亏罗杰佛设法平息了风波。

表妹从小嫉妒南琪塔姐妹，利用耐哈的善良成了罗杰佛的助理，还闯进罗杰佛的生活，耐哈备感委屈，向姐姐南琪塔求助。南琪塔装扮成妹妹，揭穿了表妹的诡计。后来，耐哈死了，人们却以为死的是南琪塔。

耐哈是被罗杰佛同父异母的兄弟山姆杀害的。山姆却爱着南琪塔。南琪塔放弃演艺追求，安心做罗杰佛的妻子。山姆被庭审，却因为目击证人受威胁而当庭释放。山姆回到家，发现罗杰佛与南琪塔已举行婚礼，山姆指责哥哥夺爱，并发下毒誓……

印度电视剧的戏，显然已与佛教或印度教的传统相距很远，却与现代人的本能、与顺水推舟的情爱越来越近。如女人的泪水，变成了男人爱的海洋。男人不再是女人的情义大地时，女人就成了被本能掀动的狂风，完全不由自主。

人如果没有本能，后代繁衍就会成为问题。水太深，情爱苦海无边。水太干，女人冷漠无情。印度人以水、地、火、风为"四大"生命元素，组合成诸般色相。四大失调，人便生病，缺少了任何一样，人便死亡。

四大聚合成色，离散成空。泪水、感情、疲惫、苦难，都是色相，终究是空。人却还是会不停地去追。写好了巧遇和结局，戏剧才会扣人心弦。苦身不苦心，享乐能脱身，适可而止是智慧。

3. 男人与女人

人生须顺性，做男人，要承担社会责任，自强不息习才艺；做女人，要柔顺厚德载物，莫以从德为枷锁。有香港电视剧，讲述了一对男女的故事：江远生与孟思晨。

孟思晨是大陆偷渡客，偶遇泰国归侨江远生并互相爱上，虽然因生活所逼嫁给中年木匠贵叔为填房，又与江远生经常幽会，在马路边亲热，在树林里纵欲。贵叔赶工不回家，两人就偷情，即使躺在贵叔身边，却思恋着江远生。想给贵叔生孩子后嫁给江远生。

人在算，天在看。江远生买车，被骗去900元钱，气不过将骗子痛打一顿。江远生想通过洪拳和泰拳赚钱。为夺得总决赛的胜利而苦练拳击，如果获得胜利就可如愿。到美国做职业拳击手，然后

享受生活。总决赛日，江远生不顺从老板的旨意打假拳，老板指使教练骗他服下兴奋剂，使比赛成绩无效。

孟思晨在电视上看到江远生赢了比赛，急欲出去见他，匆忙中摔下楼导致流产。贵叔回到家，为孩子没了失魂落魄，绝望后摔坏了家里所有能摔的东西。电视机引起大火。远生带着失血过多的思晨去了医院。

电视剧最后的悬念是：等待孟思晨的命运，是被送回大陆，还是重新漂泊？

怎样解释孟思晨与江远生的命运？从孟思晨自愿跟四个以上的男人发生关系，或许其好景不长的命运就已经注定。查身份证时，遇江远生认她做老婆解围，并把她从自杀的危境中解救出来。她靠着贵叔，却红杏出墙，流产被弃是命还是运？

孟思晨从内地到香港，贪心没有尽头。做女人没有基本的妇道，能不惹祸吗？江远生不想打假拳，有夺冠的实力，却遭老板和教练暗算，是命运不公吗？

男人和女人有不被动物本能操控一生的性情，个人还要不要洁身自好？社会若是泥沙滚滚的黄河，或春水泛滥的长江，男女是否只能随波逐流地由着性情来主宰行为吗？当今家庭与国家，难道就只是男人和女人的巢穴吗？我们该为家与国尽怎样的职责？

4. 父椿母萱

父母，是父亲和母亲的总称。父母者，人之本也。《司马法》说："士庶之义，必奉于父母，而正于君长。"经验告诉我们：人类父母的存在意义比其他动物的丰富。

动物界，有雌雄的物种区别，交合成的新生命，世代野蛮，却也虎毒不食子。

对人类而言，父母不仅是子女来到人世的通道，更是超越兽类

野性的人伦火炬的传递者。文明社会，父母对待子女要有仁有义，不允许凶狠如老虎。人类的共性，尤其对于华人，天下之人中父母最亲，杀害父母之仇不共戴天。

不仅人类的血缘亲情有独特的温暖与和谐，养育更被法律规定为基本义务，以免有人声色犬马地肆无忌惮，做出禽兽不如、不顾子女死活的事来。

人类父母与子女的养育情爱不仅可以世代相传，还可以回报。这就是子女成年以后对父母的赡养义务。有人以商业眼光把这视为交易，却忽视了这其实是血浓于水的仁义。

无论人们生活多么艰难，或者自私到可以不顾法律的约束抛弃子女，终究会有愧疚的时候。这就是人类区别于禽兽的地方。天地造化人类时，已编好了父母跟儿女的恩怨相报的生命密码。天下味道最长的是盐巴，有盐万菜均出原味。

绝大多数情况下，父母能够为子女不计得失的献出时间和精力，甚至生命。这种可以从亲情升华为仁义的生命关系，是禽兽界没有的。老虎不管幼虎成家的事，人却要管，所以才有父母之命、媒妁之言的说法。

大狐狸对待小狐狸，出生没几天，就撵出去，让其自谋生路，让天赋的狡猾本能在无情无义的兽类环境里自然地产生出来。禽兽相传的只是本能。人却在大生命养育小生命的过程中，传授累积的经验常识、人际伦理和文化知识。这就叫教育。无论父母对子女有没有抚育的责任意识，都是最早的启蒙老师。

以植物比喻父母，父亲被称为"椿庭"，母亲被叫作"萱堂"。父爱刚如山，母爱柔如水。父母刚柔相济，可对子女启智益善。子女百善，从孝开始，万恶始于不孝。人类就在孝顺父母过程中开启佛性，体悟到对神与鬼的敬与畏。

5. 个人与心魔

个人想法，一旦演变成个人主义，如果不遵守伦常与法律，就会随私心走火入魔。

现代社会，个人主义可以有反抗权威的精神，却不能无法无天。有了享乐的条件，人想要超凡脱俗、圣洁如神，很难。但如果父女乱伦、夫妻仇杀、母女举报，内心邪恶失控，人就真的成了打着自由、人权的名义，行事如同妖魔鬼怪的心魔了。

私有制不可怕，可怕的是私欲膨胀、无所顾忌。西方人说，人一半是天使，一半是恶魔。这除了说人有善恶两面，还说明了如果被恶魔占据了人心，就会祸害世间。

心魔，不在社会上，而是在个人心里。并非是幻景，而是真切的仇恨心、贪念、妄念、执念、怨念，放不下，不能释怀。人常说，人最大的敌人就是自己。这个"自己"，说的就是心魔。

人如果不在社会中，没有对成功的追求和幸福的期望，个人心里也就不会有幻想，不会被心魔所控。兽群被动物本能操控，人却因为有心而可以不被操控。所以人要成长，心要健康，突破心魔，培育人的正气和正义感很重要。

美国小说《心魔》写一个美女杀手挟持侦探成功越狱，把侦探逼进了精神病院，其靓照却上了流行杂志的封面，许多地方开发了以她为主题的旅游景点。这个杀手曾答应侦探不再杀人，却说了不算，杀了人之后把死者的眼球和脾脏扔在厕所里。

这不是修行者心里的想象，而是美国法制社会里真实的事情。这些事情让人害怕，恐惧幻化成恐怖的情景，并越来越恐怖。所以文明社会要靠伦理和法制给个人增添力量，使人不被心魔所杀死。

但个人还是要经常面对自己的内心，所以人要坚强，要修炼，首先要超越自我，而后要找出让自己恐惧的观念，并设法摒弃掉。

一个人不够强大，就找两个以上的人，组成家庭、学校、公司等，通过共同学习，形成系统思维。当能走三步以上的棋时，就可以特立独行了。

6. 家庭与婚姻

人极少不结婚或不成家的。家庭是由婚姻、血缘或收养关系所组成的社会组织的基本单位。家庭最早出现在部落和氏族中，后来演变成由一夫一妻、一屋一庭院组成的小单位。说进化也好，说退化也罢，文明却真是以家庭为据点，散播出去的。

家庭是社会的起点，是摇篮，是学校，可以有很多说法。可是如果没有家庭，人类很快就会灭绝。因为，家庭提供给男人和女人婚姻的形式，使男女可以以夫妻身份稳定的结合，不至于像秋风里的落叶般四零八落，人才像船舶一样有了停泊的港湾。

家庭是儿童社会化与供养老人的地方。婚姻是夫妻结合，产生情爱的方式，当然许多怨恨也从这里滋生。但从普遍意义上来说，人类的亲密关系首先是从家庭与婚姻中发展出来的，社会制度也是首先从血缘和收养关系中产生出来的。

扩大家庭曾经是天下华人的梦想，"子孙满堂"是我们祖辈衡量成功与幸福的标准。所以，对于华人而言，结婚和成家是人生一辈子的大事，就好像修建庙宇。因此，离婚也是天大的事，如同拆庙。

欧洲人重视个人生活，有两三人的群体，就敢去追求个性。现代社会不再困在家大、业大、造化大的思维模式里了。单亲家庭也已出现了不少，由单身父亲或母亲养育孩子。这是社会的进步，也是人力有所增进的体现。

单身家庭，指人们到了结婚的年龄不结婚或离婚以后不再婚，一个人生活，所谓一个人吃饱，全家不饿。这已经脱离了老祖宗的

阴阳结合的太极生活模式，受到欧洲原子物理学思想的影响。

当今社会还有丁克家庭：夫妻有双倍收入，有生育能力，却不要孩子，把浪漫自由、享受人生看得比传宗接代更重要。

更有空巢家庭：只有老俩口生活的家庭。甚至还有试婚：男女双方更看重婚姻的寻欢作乐特性。婚姻与家庭已出现了很多新的变化。

但无论是在欧洲，还是在中国，丧偶、丧子或离婚之后选择再婚或重组家庭的人还是占多数。家庭与婚姻的情感需要和社会伦理的传承，还很重要，养老院、孤儿院还不能替换。婚姻和家庭，可改良，不可消灭。

7. 嫖娼卖淫

结婚成家，自有意义，但也涉及很多问题，于是就有了嫖娼卖淫的人和事：男子到妓院找妓女，或者女人为淫荡的需求或供养家人等需要，出卖身体。

嫖娼的主体是男人，卖淫的主体是女人，共性是金钱交易，性行为成了商品，男女自愿发生不正当的性行为。这种行为不正当，所以不能光明正大，而且会产生很多不良的社会后果。

卖淫、嫖娼，与通奸是有区别的。婚外性行为，自愿且没有金钱交易，是通奸；以金钱做交易，男的出钱嫖娼，女的收钱是卖淫。

嫖娼、卖淫不是好事，却也不是想消灭就可以取缔的形式随便消灭的事。这是文明必然存在的问题，就如同人类吃饭有可能会产生排泄或噎倒。

这主要是男人的问题。有男子嫖妓女，所以也就相应有女子卖淫。后来随着社会问题的复杂化，也产生出男子或女子专嫖男妓的社会现象。

嫖娼的方式多种，除了上妓院嫖宿，还有在旅馆或自己房间召妓女侑酒、弹唱、献舞，等等。曾经有过取缔妓院或禁娼的做法，但都没成功。嫖客可以变换出形形色色的地下场所和嫖娼方式。电影院、剧院、美容院、按摩院、蒸汽浴室、公园等，都可能演变成为寻欢作乐的地方，把正当行业也污染了。

所以，我们应当理智地看待嫖娼卖淫的社会现象。既然人类还杜绝不了这类现象的发生，就理应实行规范管理。古而有之的红灯区设置，就是一种方式，划出一个生活特区来，让婚姻生活不和谐的人有去处，让淫乱不至于成为社会洪水。

真正要防范的是如何不让独身女子、豪门弃妇、幼小儿童等卷入进来，如何不让政府官员用公款去嫖娼，如何不让贪污、受贿跟嫖娼搅和到一起，不让贪官污吏充当卖淫、嫖娼活动的"保护伞"，不让嫖娼与卖淫成为传播性病，破坏婚姻家庭关系，引起社会腐败，诱发刑事犯罪，以及严重扰乱社会治安等的主要渠道。

当然，说来容易，做来难。但想要解决这些问题，总比根本不去考虑要好。

8. 自然即神

人常说事在人为，又说不可赶鸭子上架。这就牵涉天道问题。战国大儒荀子论天，说："天行有常，不为尧存，不为桀亡。应之以治则吉，应之以乱则凶"。这里论的就是天道，即自然运动变化规律，讲要顺应的理。

天道，在西方，就是神道。孔子在《论语》中说："敬鬼神而远之"，这是说人事还得"尽人事而知天命"。谋事在人，成事在天。说的是同一个道理。

人谋事是人情事理，是人力可为的事。可是许多事情，人力是不可为的，例如天要下雨，地要地震，天高地厚。那就只有听天由

命了。天命、天意、天理，诸如此类，说的就是天道。

人行路有足迹，车路过有车辙，雨落地地要湿。这是人的意愿不可改变的事。这就是自然之理，也就是华人的神道：神秘而不见神，却抬头见天的道理。

古人以文言说的更精辟："积土成山，风雨兴焉。积水成渊，蛟龙生焉。积善成德，而神明自得，圣心备焉。"这里说的就是自然规则，自在本然之性。遵循规律办事，饭要一口一口地吃，路要一步一步地走。

曾经有人说：天上没有玉皇，地上没有龙王，我就是玉皇，我就是龙王，喝令三山五岳开道，我来了。这是口吐狂言，是反天道自然，结果是人为制造了许多荒山秃岭。

我们常说的天道，跟西方神道相通，所谓条条道路通罗马，却又没有那么玄。《圣经》说神六天创世，第七天安息。这个说法，信神的人相信，不信的当故事。但是信比不信好，相信的人行事有所羁绊，即使胆大，也不敢为非作歹。

我们较多地信孔子的说法，既敬神信天，知天命；却又不放弃人情事理，筷子掉地上，不是求它或等它跳到手上来，而是弯腰去拾。

天下没有免费的午餐，一分耕耘一分收获，不盼望不劳而获的事，知天命于经风雨、见世面之后。却又风雨之后，即便不见彩虹，也不怨天尤人，而是顺其自然。这就如同老子所说"天法道，道法自然"。天道自然，自然即神。

9. 人莫犯罪

人莫犯罪，说的是要守法，不要去行凶作恶，要遵守国法人道的理。

古代西方以神道禁欲来劝人守法，不合人情事理，因而不容易

做到。和尚、道士、神父，在庙宇、道观、修道院里才能做到的事，要一般人在人世间做到，实在是强人所难。这就像是赶鸭子上架，既违反自然天道，更逼人违法犯罪。

违法犯罪，就是做坏事。天道自然，人道规矩。做人做事，不能以身试法。宗教劝人行善做善民，教人做好事，学校教人守法做公民，要人莫做坏事。

可是人有私心情欲，为了自己不饿死，为了家人不被坏人害死，如同林冲为了老婆不被权贵的儿子凌辱，即使被陷害而忍气吞声，最后还是被逼杀了人。这是逼上梁山。

公正的法律是必须遵守的，比如不许偷盗和杀人。阻止特权者仗势欺人、以权谋私，不靠法律制度不行。人守法，也有特别的意义，是在营造阻止人犯罪和做错事的环境。但历史上施暴和撒谎违法的问题，至今还没解决。

健全法制是社会日益发展必须做的事情。但有人制定法律，同时也有人违法犯罪，这是文明国度的孪生兄弟。法律制度规定做坏事是犯罪，要受罚。

人莫犯罪，从根本上说，还是行人道。人道主义、理论学说太复杂，还是先贤的人道教诲明了易行。知仁行义，管束自己的心。这是治本。

孟子的具体的说法是：人有善心，有恻隐之心、羞恶之心、恭敬之心、是非之心，知善行事，就不会犯罪——见人摔倒了，知仁，就会上前去扶起来；见人掉河里了，知义，就会伸手拉他起来；开车在路上并行，知礼，就会慢一点，让有急事的车前行；听人搞宣传，知是，就会明辨好坏，不同流合污。

人知道依照斯文之道行事做人，不仅不会犯罪，更会懂得行善做好事。人道越来越好，社会也就会越来越文明。

10. 教书育人

教书育人，就是古人韩愈说的"传道，授业，解惑"，即为师之道。

做老师，在今天已被视为养家糊口的普通差事。但老师这一种职业，无论何时，都不普通。教书，不仅是教人获得知识，更要讲道理。

华人宗教传统不深，根深蒂固的是教人知书达理，即知情达理、与人为善。教人知天道或神道，在西方通常是教父做的事，我们的传统却是教师的职责。所以，我们看老师，光知识渊博、能解疑答难不够，还要求为人师表，做个好榜样。

教人知识，是解决具体问题的。好比不懂得使用电脑，就要去学关于电脑的知识，要会输入文字等基本技能。但光会教打字，或者教编程，不明白天道、人道，不能使接受知识和技术的人明道，对我们而言不能算是好老师。

所以，韩愈说："道之所存，师之所存也。"这是说，道在哪里，老师在哪里。的确，这样去衡量师道传统，评价很高。然而，这样的师道，已经失传很久了。

不明道的老师，别说教人做圣人，就是教人做良民，都不能够。质朴的人如果跟授业者学偷东西，那就成了小偷。这个小偷的授业者就将人领上邪路了，就不配被称之为老师。

我们祖先把老师当作一份崇高的职业，对当老师的人格外尊重，所以"有师者如父"的说法。师道对华人跟孝道一样重要。教书传授知识技能固然重要，但育人更为重要。教师职业崇高，不是因为教书授业，而是因为传道育人。

从传道育人上看，学生读书学习，至关重要的是闻道和明道。

教书，遇上聪明的学生，就可以培养出专家学者了，这不难。

难的是，培养有仁有义、知情达理、明智悟道的有德行的人，不会用知识和技艺去为非作歹、祸害社会。作为教师，为人师表就是为了育人，这更加重要。

11. 塑造品格

传道要为人师表，明道要塑造品格。人的品格要由他人来塑造比较难，须要人自觉为之。

品格，即人品和人格的统称。这里不谈论文艺作品的质量和风格，不谈物品的质量、规格与官品、爵位等，主要谈做人提高品位的问题。

酒有低档、中档、高档的品级，所以有品酒的职业，这里不谈；要谈，谈喝酒适量，莫要吆五喝六、寻衅闹事。这就涉及塑造品格的问题。

文章、作品，有质量、格调的品级，《红楼梦》雅致，不可与《金瓶梅》同论。一幅画也有同样的问题。这里也不谈论，谈的是作家、画家的人品问题。一个撰稿人，为了赚稿费，专门给中学生讲谈情说爱、乱伦、月黑风高杀人的故事；一个画家，为追求名利，专门画裸体画，还特别针对妇女……这样做，就是品格有问题所致。

无论酒、画、商品、文章，都是人生产或制作的。人的人品、人格高，就能做出高格调的东西，反之，东西就劣质。古人说"品格清于竹，诗家景最幽"，说的就是清雅、幽静的人品和人格。

林黛玉清雅、幽静，做演员肯定不合适。塑造一个林黛玉，肯定于演艺事业没有意义，却于女人世界的雅致清纯、诗情画意有特别的意义。存在就有价值。

大多数人是做不来林黛玉的，也不懂欣赏林黛玉，能做和能欣赏的倒是王熙凤的精明泼辣、平儿的善解人意、刘姥姥的世故幽

默。这些活法，更合乎世俗。

中国自古就有"三教九流"的说法，泛指传统宗教与各种学术流派。据传，从东汉就有印度佛教传入，与本土儒教、道教竞争。五百年后，北周皇帝召集三教论辩，最后判定"儒教在先，道教次之，佛教在后"。皇帝介入是人为因素。不过，这已经是在 500 年之后，三教秩序还算是自然形成的。

这既说明传统对人的地位和职业有等级划分，也说明古代很讲究人的品位，人很早就有了比较充分的自由，自然形成了多元化的人品与人格。

12. 出生与命运

古代希腊人相信人人都有一个精灵保护。精灵在人出生时已在旁侍候，并且看顾他的一生。罗马人传承了这种看法。

《西游记》说唐僧取经，孙悟空 500 年前就受罚在五指山候着。不仅如此，唐僧师徒及白龙马在明处，天上还有众神一路跟着，时不时地吆喝一声：大圣，您去搬救兵，我看着呢！

华人对生日比希腊罗马更讲究。尚书中说"惟天地万物父母，惟人万物之灵"。这里定义人为"万物之灵"，比希腊神话更早，更简明。

希腊罗马的先贤基本无生日可考。佛教关于释迦牟尼与基督教关于耶稣基督两位圣人的诞辰，都是信众的说法，是这门宗教传了几百年之后，才有的说法，没有史籍的记载和史家的考证。

中国孔子的生日却很早就见于史籍，属于史官考证后载入史册的。几乎就在孔子过世不久，《公羊春秋》《谷梁春秋》就记载了孔子的生日。但史家说法也不统一，这或许是标新立异的人所为，越往后，可能越有疑点。

华人生日精确的记载是用年月日时的天干地支命八字记载，孔子的生日就可见月日的明确记载：庚辰、庚子。是否有误，后人可考证。这种记生日的方法，据传命运信息就包含在里面。民间信仰由此认为命运早由天（或神）注定、可以用术数及占卜等方术来预测命运。

命指生命，注定一生的总趋势：生死、姻缘、富贵等；运指经历，用具体的年月日来预测显示。例如，一个富人，在幼年或者青壮年的某个时候，或者在财富刚起步时，可能会有暂时破财免灾的波折。

我们的八字说法，属于一种生日学，只是还不能用逻辑方法和数学思维整理出来。民间信仰只属意念，莫当学问。风水、术数、巫术等行业形成独特的职业风景，术业有精有粗，不可一概而论。但全信和全不信，都是极端的做法。

既然古代华人与希腊人都有共同的生日精（神）灵信仰，说明这是人类智慧的一部分，信命又何妨？不过人既然有运的演变，努力也自在情理中。贵在理智：既不搏命强求，也不懒惰混世。

13. 玩物丧志

有人很年轻的时候就有一手好厨艺，也不时地流露出办酒楼的志向。但几十年来一直玩古董，已经到了一进文物市场，不买物品就心痒痒的地步。而今五十出头了，仍不见酒楼。

《尚书》中说："玩人丧德，玩物丧志。"玩，与"耍"并用，"玩耍"通常指人的婴幼儿到童年的 12 岁以前，这是人在嬉戏中获取知识的途径，有趣则玩，无趣则弃。这是人由于兴趣、志向不确定与意志不坚定时，成长初期的自然状态。

自然玩耍，无所用心，所以幼儿贵在天真，即使顽皮，给大人、家庭和学校添许多麻烦，也属于天性，是成长中必经的磨炼。正所谓吃一堑，长一智；不经风雨，不见彩虹。幼儿的玩耍，通常

是五分钟热度，随兴趣而玩耍，是学习阶段。

过了玩耍的成人阶段，有了确定喜爱的事物，这就是把玩欣赏的"玩赏"了，也叫迷恋，跟恋爱的沉迷属同样深度的性质，只是恋爱迷恋的是人，玩赏迷恋的是物。成年人玩赏物品，比如古董、珠宝、字画、邮票等。玩赏的定向未必是志向。中年玩字画的人，有可能在青年时的立志是想做官，玩赏定向和事业志向不一定一致。

玩物丧志，就是指青年时代立下的志向，由于中年时代过于沉溺于某些事物，从而丧失了当初为志向奋斗的勇气和心劲，成为一个做事得过且过、不精益求精的人，也就是通常说的没有大的志向和志气的人。

对于和尚、道士、神父等僧侣而言，不求积极进取，倒是去除红尘执着、修行过程中去除心魔所需，不会陷入迷乱之中。但对于红尘中人，业精于勤，荒疏于嬉，若是眼高手低、志大才疏，长期不务正业，最后很可能会一事无成，没有事业。

春秋故事说卫懿公特别喜欢鹤，让鹤乘高级豪华的车子，整天与鹤为伴，养鹤每年耗费大量资财，常常不理卫国朝政、不问民情，最后遭侵略战败而死。这是我们要吸取的教训。

14. 异想天开

曾有商人经营公司时对人建议，用导弹或原子弹在喜马拉雅山轰一个缺口，可以解决北方缺水的老大难问题。这就可谓成语说的异想天开。

异想天开，如果对于心智不成熟的幼儿来说，可以说，就是胡思乱想、想入非非，是少儿学习初期思维的信马由缰，属于成长过程中的自然状态，不可过于训斥，甚至可以一笑了之，拍拍头以示鼓励，随之，由之。

对于从事发明的科学家，对理论思维有清晰的认识，若在思维尚无头绪的初期，能够发散思维，浮想联翩，将风马牛不相及的事情整合到一起，这又是一种能力，是把少儿时代的信马由缰化作成年人有意而为的一种思维技艺。

这可不是随便什么人都可以轻易做到的。任意妄为，画虎不成反类犬，就好比搞商业或实业的人不务实，却异想着把天弄开，到月亮里跟嫦娥跳舞，跟吴刚喝酒。这种离奇的思维若应用到诗歌中不算荒唐，诗情画意的创作需要超强的想象力，但莫要用于经商从政。

搞文艺创作的人，写小说、戏剧，异想天开对于编写故事是有帮助的，可以想象出出人意料的故事情节，让人读起来爱不释手，不忍中断，欲一口气读完。

在宗教的神话故事中，也有许多异想天开的故事，起初可能还不能算是天马行空，而是宗教创始人或真传使徒施展神通所表现的景象，却被误传为一般人做出的事情，流传下来可供信徒悟道、明道。但由于后人添油加醋，就越来越荒诞不经，让人觉得完全不可思议，终被今人嘲讽而轻蔑以弃之。

例如先秦古籍《山海经》，有人完全视为神话，有人则以为是上古部族，特别是东夷族人的史书，以图叙事，传承东夷及炎黄、华夏等远古族人的历史。其中涉及的许多异兽，当时很可能是真实存在的，只是现在绝种不见了，后人就认为其荒诞不经。

民间歇后语说："又要公羊，又要喝奶"。意思是说不合乎常识常理。但如果在超常思维中这样想问题，倒也可视为解决问题的一种创造性的思路。

15. 自私自利

自私，从来就是贬义，只是在古代被排斥，到了近现代却被广

泛地接受。无论哲学，还是宗教，或心理倾向，都这样，看书更能看到这种原则由负而正的转换。

自私，比较抽象，转用自恋，就比较形象。英俊的男人或美丽的女人，陶醉在镜子里的自己的模样，想象出各种各样的举动。这就是自恋。

自私变化出的自恋，在希腊神话里，典型的例子是那耳喀索斯，一名希腊的美男子，他拒绝了嗓子漂亮的女神厄科，却爱上自己在湖中的倒影，结果因为没有办法能令他变得更完满而日益消瘦，最后变成了水仙花。

以那耳喀索斯的故事，形象地说出了自私概念中的自满、自负、自我中心等。自恋的正面意义是羡慕，不走极端时，有利于心理健康。过于自恋，就形成病态的人格。过于羡慕别人，或自以为别人羡慕他，并逐渐变成只看重物质富足方面的快感，形成封闭、僵化的社会等级制度。

自私，常于自利并列，伴随很强的偏见，即利己主义。如将利己夸耀成牡丹或玫瑰，不管是从人际关系的伦理上，或者从个人主义的心理上，公说公的阳光理，婆说婆的月亮理，甚至有人以理性的超个人情感的理论思维，从客观的互惠互利的道德关系上，论证利己的合理性：我是红花要鲜艳，也少不了你的绿叶扶持。

自私自利的思想形成哲学，自圆其说，就成了唯我主义：没有两片一模一样的树叶，每颗水珠都有其独特性，每个人的自我经验，他人不可能有完全相同的感觉。

这就是个人主义的哲学，把个人视为分子世界的一颗原子，宇宙天空的一个星球。反对者则把社会似的气场或能量场当成淹没石头的沼泽，主张世界大同的无政府主义，以取缔可以吞掉个人原则和利益的政府力量，在政治上消灭掉国家边界。

自私，把人道绝对化，略去天道或神道，视损人利己行为为优先原则。但是在商场、战场中，自私者又被迫妥协形成了一种互惠

互利的原则，被称为"黄金规律"。

16. 私有财产

自私的黄金规律，体现在经济制度中，就形成私有财产，或称财产个人化：从法律上将财产的所有权归为个人。

通过法律，明确把财产确定在个人名义下，投资就有了流动资产（动产）与不动资产（不动产）区别。这种法定的私有财产制度下，人成了独立的个体家庭或家族的概念消失了。父权、母权、族权、君权、师权等全都没有了，只有个人。

于是私有财产成了最美丽的花。食物、汽车、衣物等人造财物，原本父母可以无私地传给儿女，现在法律鼓励父母自己享用。即便是看不见的卫星电视信号等，都可以由集团私有。只有阳光、水、空气等自然物质大众才有可能共享。

这就是最近这500年的自由主义思想花朵：我自由（即我可以选择的时候），我才是我，才区别于动物，活得像个人。这种自由主义，在文化上有积极的意义，使艺术、宗教、科学等有了自己的阵地，却把社群的商业关系绝对化了，消费高于一切，生活只是防卫和竞争。非商业交换的社会群体被损害和否定了。

当自我被当成中心，当成太阳之后，更大的银河系也就见不到了。在西方出现才百年的原子科学把千万年修养的学问当阵地攻克了，精英没了。这就使近代哲学与政治上的马基雅维里主义，不损人利己都不行。

这种自我被当成太阳的个人主义，以法律所有权仲裁一切，私产神圣不可侵犯，国家如同私人的鸟窝，政府就是搭建这种政治鸟窝的组织。凡合法都是好的，贪污、侵占、抢夺、诈骗、盗窃、走私，都是犯罪。但能在法律外，无罪就是智慧。

这样，人类也就不需要文学艺术了。一切价值的大小，都以收入、财产、产权等来衡量。黑格尔可能都没想到，法权逻辑传播着撒旦主义。

17. 自私与惩罚

撒旦主义的恶魔逻辑，是不是人类自私招来的惩罚？这个问题很值得探究。

惩罚，这个概念，中国早在春秋时代《左传》中就有了，说哀公六年"有罪受罚，又焉移之。"俄国作家陀思妥耶夫斯基以小说关注罪与罚时，已经是 19 世纪，比中国晚了 2300 年。

惩罚，词典上一般解释为：因为某种不当的行为所受的痛苦或损失。在哲学上，惩罚被视为是由权威作出的、对侵犯者的被控行为给被侵犯者造成的损失给予处罚。

心理学视惩罚为一种方法，为阻止个体继续侵害行为的，施予痛苦或剥夺利益，使其不再从事侵害活动。但这样看惩罚，道德便没有意义了。父母或老师处罚子女或学生，无论动机好与坏，其实只是为了自己管教子女或学生。

这样，人便不是什么宇宙精灵、万物之灵，仅仅是冤冤相报的社会动物。道德被视为"好人"的侵略行为或策略，忍气吞声只是为了引人同情、保护、打抱不平。这种逻辑把自私自利当作绝对标准，完全否定古代孔子、苏格拉底的思想。

这种用功利来制定刑法的思维，把人类古代先贤、宗教、国家几千年为公、为制裁罪人所定的刑律，完全视为罪恶，不是为了维护善良，只是以恶制恶的手段。因此，善也是恶，是隐蔽的恶。刑是国以牢狱给犯罪者规定的惩罚。人权就是个人的法定权利。

这种罪情与量刑裁处的罪刑法定主义思想，非常主观，断然把 19 世纪欧洲以刑法、法典确定下来的法律思想，当成评价全人类从古到今的行为是否恰当的标准。依照这种思维逻辑，当代人才能算

作是人；19 世纪之前，全人类都只是牲口。

罪刑法定主义如果被一个国家采纳，那么官员的想法就是法。长此以往，很可能会导致国家暴力伤害，甚至可能演变成要以核武器毁灭人类和地球的疯狂行为。

18. 交情与朋友

交情，顾名思义，指人与人在交往中产生的情感或友谊。异性之间互相爱慕的就是情人，用婚姻形式确定下来就是夫妻，形成生育关系就成为家人，结成亲戚就是亲人，朋友之交就是友人，等等。

普通的友人，理应劝善或提供一般性扶助。确立恋爱或夫妻关系的情人，交情较深，支援理应也比较深，若只是口头劝善或礼尚往来、些许财物支援，是说不过去的。

朋友，对华人来说，不只是西方法律关系下的那种泛泛之交，可以细分为同事、幕友、同学、学友等。果敢文说起来，不同的人理解不同。古人说的比较细微："同门曰朋，同志曰友，朋友聚居，讲习道义。"《诗经》说："无言不仇，无德不报。惠于朋友，庶民小子。"用言语和文字解释朋友，比较费事，具体情形下倒容易理解。

孔子说："有朋自远方来，不亦乐乎？"江湖故事说秦叔宝："为（朋）友两肋庄走岔道"。总之，我们的汉语不像欧美拼音文字那样浮光掠影，字形、字义、发音等都包含有信息和意思，能具体形象地反映出华人关系的复杂和细微。

由此可知，华人讲求与人为善、礼尚往来，是历史人文环境的必然。英法人文环境不过 1000 年，美国更不到 250 年，族人辈分、亲戚关系都很简单，打官司不打紧。华人打起官司来，人际关系复杂，恩怨情仇交织，上法庭如上刀山下火海，是最没面子的事，会

失去很多亲情与朋友的。

"朋友"的拼音，省略掉了我们的家人、朋党、友人、同志等多重关系，甚至省略掉了英语"friends"的意思。"朋"字中"两个月亮"蕴含着并肩走的双月双阴、物以类聚的关系，至于亲友、学友、战友等更深层次的情义，从字面上更加看不到。"我心如旧"的意思，高鼻子们很难理解。所幸拼音文字方案没推行，中国还是沿用传统的中文字体。

19. 同情值万金

果敢文有"家书抵万金"的说法，把"家书"一换，就成了"同情值万金"。

早些年如果批评某人没有同情心，这个人可能就要找个地缝钻进去躲着。而今这种批评没有力度了，被批评的人可能梗着脖子质问你："同情值几个钱?"

"仁"字能把人批评到找地缝，是尊孔文化的力量。在古代讲仁义的，并非只是儒家，道家也讲。司马迁在《五帝本纪》里讲"帝尧者，放勋。其仁如天，其知如神。"司马迁是史官，承传修道传统，说黄帝修德，说帝尧修仁。道德、仁义，这些在今天轻若肥皂泡的词语，在古代被赋予了天高地厚的位置。

所以孔子把"仁"作为儒家道德的核心，统帅孝、弟（悌）、忠、恕、礼、知、勇、恭、宽、信、敏、惠等思想，讲"克己复礼为仁""杀身以成仁"，的确意义非凡，不是今人站着说话、轻描淡写就能理解其深意的。

孔子说"仁者爱人"，今人觉得一般，是因为没有了尊孔的环境。细看"仁"这个汉字，示意"男人处于二人关系"之中，上横短、下横长，有主次，秩序井然。这就难怪有万夫不当之勇的关羽、张飞认刘备为异姓兄弟后，就对其无比尊敬。好比《水浒》中

梁山好汉认宋江为大哥之后，行事说话就有了一杆旗，有了主心骨。

果敢文的这个"爱"字，是由心来统帅的。今人讲"利益"好处没心没肺，所以制假酒、毒奶粉非常狠，因为根本没心了。所以，今人听"友人"这个词，跟听蒙古人说"安达"、日本人说"友达"或"某某君"，基本没有感觉。对传统称谓里的"石友、死友、挚友、素友、损友、诤友、益友"等，完全不如"盟友、网友、文友、密友、闺友、笔友"来得重视了，极少有不离不弃的恒友了。

尽管还承传下来些忘年交、忘形交、君子交、款交等词语，没几人能说清楚这些词语的真实含义，即使说得清楚，也很少人认真去交这样的朋友。为什么？因为大家都已经不知道同情心的价值了。

唐朝杜甫如果不具有从仁心中发出来的同情心，不可能写出"国破山河在，城春草木深，感时花溅泪，恨别鸟惊心。"的诗句。仁心仁术，伤残深重，实在惨不忍睹。

英国在18世纪才有人研究同情心。早在4000年前华夏帝舜就宽恕了父亲的无情与弟弟的无义。没有同情心绝对不可能宽恕。华人界，同情心是镇恶的泰山，万金买不来。

20．文明与国度

文明，泛指所有的人造财富，特指文艺审美、知识教育、经验科学等人类的思想文化。人类本性就在历史的演变过程中逐步、具体地体现出来：农民敬畏自然，市民遵守法律，工人以技术谋生，商人核算成本，族人和平共处……

同期发展的文明古国，唯独中国存活到今天，独具知书达理和为贵的气质。欧美以帝国的殖民主义为文明，最后被证明其侵略行

为并非文明，其实是真正的野蛮。英语说文明，主要指"开垦·拓展"。而果敢文中的"文明"意义则要丰富得多。

《易经》说："见龙在田、天下文明。"华夏摒弃野蛮，在匈奴耀武扬威蒙古草原时，以文明与文化的君子儒道光耀邦国，以"仁义礼智"心法管束言行，其结果是：汉唐文化千古。绩效是：南匈奴成了北国的屏障，北匈奴远走异国他乡。

在希腊人为女人跨海远征之际，中土君子吟诗道："有位佳人，在水一方"。待到西方君子文质彬彬之际，中土的礼仪则更令人向往："关关雎鸠，在河之洲"。经历三代而合成的文德光辉，更是"经天纬地，照临四方"。汉朝能够吸取秦朝苛政亡国的教训，君主以文治教化为天赋使命，因此才有400年的国运。

早在唐朝，海南岛就懂了"修明文教，使家国昌明"的道理。宋太祖懂得"马放南山、偃武修文"的道理，才有"杯酒释兵权"的睿智。明太祖不懂，所以才会杀戮功臣。满洲人、日本人不懂文昌之理，崇尚武力征服，因此才有"扬州屠城十日"和"南京大屠杀"。

在大地不见光亮的黑夜，以灯火来延续白日的欢庆，并非明智之举。能明察危难来临，内文明而外柔顺，家国、宗族才能避过灭顶之灾。周文王就曾经这样办到过。文明的魅力，不像武力刚猛让人害怕，却能将文明种子植入人们的精神。

新的、现代的事物，未必就是最好的。合于人道，不杀戮俘虏，更要合乎天道：以心神定魂，给文明人自由，教化野蛮人，使人内心重和谐，而不是一味镇压了事。

城市文明，不在霓虹灯。心法自律，比刑法约束人更为重要。管得住官，才安得了民。所有文明，都应在现代化的当代变异，否则急功近利，只会导致大乱不治。

若一个国度无主权，不能昌盛，人民将会很容易被煽动仇恨、制造阶级矛盾，更是国无宁日的根源。

21. 法规与纲纪

法律、法令、条例、规则、章程等法定文件，总称法规。欧美现代国度，以议会辩论后多数票通过的法律治国。这种法律被视为现代公民国的典范，世界仿效采用，以管治国家、城市和县镇。

一般而言，法规的作用在于命令或禁止一类事物，或用作颁布一项政策。欧美现代国家的做法是由议会通过法律，政府依据法律制定行政的法令、条例等。而后各类社团又在法律、法令、条例之下制定相关社会活动的规则、章程，等等。

各式各样的法规，使依法行政成为政府管理国家的依据，要更新秩序，先要变法。历史上的管仲改革、李悝变法、商鞅变法，就是先例。国家制度通常通过法规确立。但实施法治并非一定就能治理国家。曾经《汉谟拉比法典》举世无双，却没能让巴比伦王国长治久安。美国法典涉及的内容很广泛，提供给缅甸却未必适用。

和谐是立法的关键。任何法规，给予一个已无纲纪的国族，不会有人遵守。所以，建立与维护纲纪比立法和护法更重要。

纲纪，历代君王、贵族治理地方的根本。《镜花缘》里就有"经纬阴阳，纲纪万物"的话语，可能是从《诗经》"勉勉我王，纲纪四方"演化过来的。汉朝取代秦朝，更换的只是国姓，基本制度依然承袭秦朝，华夏族纲纪仍在，去除的只是苛政，所以很快就出现了文景治世与汉武盛世。

中华夏商周三代一直以姓氏贵族为纲纪，秦朝之后实行吏治，以高官品格为纲纪，官吏有德，家国有治；官吏缺德，天下大乱。儒家文化成为主道之后，家庭男主外、女主内，皇权治国，乡绅治村镇，家庭和社会早带有共和制的雏形。

在中国，君子的意思是君之子。君王若以"子"为师，孔孟就是帝王之师，儒家经典是王法的纲纪、法度、纲常。即使改朝换

代，只要纲纪不变，和平或治世也会很快来临。

22. 知彼与知己

中国长期是由"士农工商"四大职业阶层组合而成的社会。士在古代具有贵族精神，是专职的公臣或家仆，齐家治国，需要知彼与知己的才能。

士，在周朝，属于最末流的贵族，排在卿之后，通常都有一技之长，成为卿大夫的家臣、幕僚等。战国时代，士的才艺受到王侯将相等贵族（君）的重视，故而有孟尝君、平原君、春申君等养士成风。士有时也会充任侯国大夫的官职。

秦朝废除封国和世袭贵族之后，士、农、工、商都成了"庶人"，即俗语说的布衣、平民。又因为士普遍读书识字有治国才能，故被称之为"士大夫"，以示敬意。战国的士大夫，依诏命行事，因能深思以知彼，进而产生治国的智慧。

秦朝的士大夫为皇帝近臣。在中国象棋中，至今还能看到"士"官的这一特征。汉武帝之后的文官普遍都是儒士，逐渐形成在世界上独具一格的士文官政治：食君俸禄，替君办事，进而形成与儒家仁义道德相吻合的、忠君报国的"义士"品德：为知己者死。

士为知己者死，女为悦己者容。这其实包含了"知彼"的智慧与"知己"的高明。儒士为"知己"者死，是修习《周易》去"蛊"之"高明"道法：不事王侯，高尚其事。这种思想逐渐演变成了士为国尽忠的责任。条件是："邦有道则仕，无道则（隐）可卷而怀之"。

重义轻利，今人视为愚。若士大夫、君子儒知道人民需要仁官义吏时，就提供仁义，这就是智。智慧出自知彼。给了君臣可以共享的仁义环境，故而国泰民安，也就有了不求自得的职业收入，这就是高。

士文官以忠君为形式，以仁心之心追随仁君，报国是其目的。如果遭遇昏君，就会弃官而去。孔子出鲁国、周游列国就是典型例子。所以诸葛亮并非愚忠刘备，而是尽忠蜀国，为黎民百姓服务。东晋陶潜身处乱世，就挂冠而去，"采菊东篱下，悠然见南山"，躲过了兵乱匪乱之祸。

诸葛亮做官尽职，却不为高俸禄。这种精神，来自仁义道德，是"从道不从君"。刘备三顾茅庐，向诸葛亮表明的是"为民"的礼教道统。孔子更如庄子所说，见天子、诸侯不下跪，平起平坐地分庭抗礼。但这种士文官的贵族精神自宋朝后日渐失传了。

当今许多读书人做官急功近利，走权钱交易的钢丝，不仁不义，精神极度匮乏，活在被房屋、学位、轿车等物质所奴役的生活中，被折磨得精疲力竭，完全丧失了陶潜悠闲与健康的心境，也迷失了知己知彼的智慧。

23．人伦即福，知足常乐

据史书记载，从周朝起，我们的祖先便生活在礼教道统中，形成"父子有亲，君臣有义，夫妇有别，长幼有序，朋友有信"的五教关系。这种"人法地，地法天，天法道，道法自然"的人伦关系，在中华文明三千年中一枝独秀，功不可没。

五教礼法伦理，如同欧美国公民宪法伦理，都是历史形成的。而且显然中国人之间的各种伦理等级关系，跟欧美公民的职业等级关系，都是不可或缺的。

《管子·八观》说："背人伦而禽兽行，十年而灭。"《孟子·滕文公上》："人之有道也，饱食暖衣，逸居而无教，则近于禽兽。圣人（舜）有忧之，使契为司徒，教以人伦……"北魏鲜卑人侯景反复无常，把人与禽兽相提并论，为自己的反叛和凶残开脱罪责，最后其卖国求荣的做法惨遭失败，死后更是被挫骨扬灰。

鲜卑族入主中原后亡国，就跟其汉化时间短、喜欢背信弃义的反人伦行为有密切相关，验证了管子的思想，也间接证实：地中海地区的许多民族因反人伦而种族灭绝。君臣义、父子亲、夫妇别、兄弟序、朋友信，不可不遵。

幸福是什么？简单地说，幸福是一种愉快的心情，快乐，知足，并想持续拥有这些感觉的心态。

幸福在哪里？既然它是一种心情，自然就在心里。愉快，顾名思义，愉悦快活。看到活泼的小孩了，看到彩虹出来了，欢天喜地；作业得了一百分，满世界叫喊，要与人共享。

幸福如何获得？幸福就是一种人生价值观是在人生过程中获得的。

先贤墨子以为大众谋取兼爱互利的环境为幸福。战国杨朱以个人的食色本能而求幸福。西方哲人德谟克利特说：幸福住在我们的灵魂中，人要学会享乐上有节制和宁静淡泊的生活。若一毛不拔，则会无舍无得。节制如涓涓细流，细水长流才长久。

墨子和德谟克里特的观点都不错。人追求幸福的误区在于争斗，因而易遭报复。无义、无亲、无序、无别、无信，破坏人伦，自寻烦恼。遵守人伦即是福，应知足常乐。

24. 科技工业劫难

科技工业消耗能源如火烧大兴安岭，造成极大的环境污染，人为地酿成许多劫难。

科学在古代是哲学或伦理学的分支运用，思想感受多过技术革新。当今科学就像是许许多多把刀剑或各式各样的生活利器，要在能源有限的地球上开拓无限的知识空间，把天道改造成为自己的天堂，不再有荀子说的"应之以治"的睿智。

自从洋务运动把工业技术引入清朝，康有为把日文汉字"科

学"引入果敢文，先辈们逐渐开始赶科学技术竞争的时代潮流，造成士农工商流动开放的社会体系变异。

技术，无论是在古代希腊，还是中土华夏，都主要指手工业阶层的个人技能或技艺。具体地说来，是制陶器、车辆、宝剑、房屋等手艺、技巧，家庭世代相传的制作方法和配方。但到了17世纪，英国培根把科学知识跟实验技术结合，技术的含义发生了变化。

培根说：知识就是力量，人类要主宰世界。此后，科学技术泛指知识分子根据实验分析获取的自然科学理论，实际运用于工业生产中，获得的改变生活环境的发明，诸如蒸汽机、火车、轮船、飞机、大炮、核武器、人造卫星，等等。

从第二次世界大战结束后，人类用自动化机器和生产线进行生产，形成了机器生产体系。从19世纪80年代起，以微电子技术为中心的高科技工业获得了高速的发展。

近百年来，人类生活方式发生了翻天覆地的变化。曾经世代千年去不了英国伦敦，而今一张机票，10小时就去了。人飞来飞去，好像空中飞人。今人坐在电视机、电脑前，全世界的消息下一分钟立即就知道了。中美两国通迅比上村走到下村还快。

但头痛的事情也随之来临。如空难不时出现；恐怖主义劫持飞机撞美国大楼；据说污染曾经使淮河水面，几十里的水面燃起来；小孩喝牛奶，一不留神成了傻子。人世间的劫难，因为科技技术的发展，也来得比过去的干旱、战争更加迅速猛烈，猝不及防。

25. 轮回说与相对论

常言道，小心驶得万年船；是福不是祸，是祸躲不过。

佛教有六道轮回说，科学有相对论，放到一起讨论一下，看能聊出些啥来？

佛教看生命不只是地球上，是整个宇宙大系统的天道、人道、

阿修罗道、地狱道、饿鬼道、畜生道的循环往复。

轮回说看生命，认为即使是妖魔也有死亡，和人死后一样，都要走天、人、阿修罗、地狱、恶鬼、畜生六条道。也就是说，这辈子是人，下辈子可能就是牛马虎豹或花卉草木了。作恶多端的人，必有恶报，灵魂将被打入阿鼻地狱，受无尽的煎熬，永不超生。

轮回说以天、修、人、鬼、兽、地之六道说生命，听起来有些玄。相信轮回说，会让人活得有所顾忌，不能大鱼大肉、快意恩仇。不信的人就以科学来否定，说是愚昧和迷信。

理智地说，轮回说是一种大生命观，把时间与空间像楼梯似的分为一层又一层，死在这一层，又生在那一层。这种把时空分成若干层次，把善恶行为和生命形式选择都纳入其中，其实是更大的智慧，真正要理解，需要活着的人有超凡脱俗的思想觉悟。

科学至今未能证明生死是否轮回。实际上很多科学家对于轮回转世的说法，先是承认有自己无知的领域，而轮回转世正是无知的领域，有待自己去了解。科学就是先怀疑后证实。

现代物理学的相对论时空观倒是跟轮回说的生命观有一定的相容性。相对论提出了"同时的相对性"、"四维时空"、"弯曲时空"等新概念。这些新概念涉及的相对性原理，建立的有限无边的四维宇宙模型等，与轮回说中的一些概念有相似的地方。

轮回说，以佛法说生命，赋予人生更丰富的意义，给活在科学时代的人警惕，对自己的生活言行会更负责、更谨慎。

26. 政府问题

政府，古时叫官府，又叫公家、衙门等，是帝王授权、民众认可的政治大宅院——一套行政机构，执行法律，专职地管着一个区域，维持着秩序。

政府最初很简单、很原始，管农民的就是一座大一点的屋，管

牧民的就是一座毡包，执政者通过打斗或者信仰确立，发号施令，组织人手。这时候政府很小，管的人也不多，就是几个村落或部落，问题不多，都是些小问题。

渐渐地就分出了很多机关，现在叫部局、科室，诸如此类，有的立法，有的行政，有的司法，还有了专门的警察维护治安，有了专门的军队保护地方。这就有了很多机关之间扯皮的事，问题就由小变大，为了协调和领导各机关，就有了内阁。

政府组织变大、变庞杂，统治权力、政府官员的产生也多种多样，就有了多种形式的政府，被称为君主制、独裁制、共和制、民主制等。

政府若把管理的人当成压迫对象，势必就是独裁专制的政府。把管理的居民当成家人，被管居民把政府称为公家，这就是君主制，也有人笼统称为君主专制的。共和制一般是对独裁政府和君主政府不满之后产生的，由两组以上政纲不同的团体共同管理。共和政府通过民选产生，逐渐就出现了今日说的民主政府。

政府是税收的主体，服务意识强的，给人民好的福利，就成了好政府；服务意识弱的，总盯住人民口袋，跟人民争福利，贪官污吏很多，就成了坏政府。

27. 社会变迁

社会简单地说就是由若干个人或家庭组成的群体，有独特文化和风俗习惯，并长期居住在一块相对固定的地区像树林，像群山形成后基本不变。社会虽有小有大，却是不断重建的，正是在这不断重建的过程中，像林像山不断翻新。

社会变迁，就是重组元素，改变人与家庭的组合形式，形成新的文化和风俗习惯。一般都需要移居地点。无论迁移，或不迁移，人口、习惯、风俗、文字等变了，社会就重新组合了。

曾经鲜卑族越过长城，进入中原，逐渐汉化，成为汉族新人。近代有不少人漂洋过海，在印尼、新加坡、马来西亚组建出华人社区。最近的就是农村的人进城打工，由村民成为新市民，加入新单位。

古代希腊人有一种水、火、土、气四元素组合事物的学说，说爱和恨这两种情愫，爱是结合的力量，恨是分离的力量，爱将四元素结合成一个个新的个体，恨将四元素还原成水是水、火是火、土是土、气是气，爱和恨的平衡和斗争产生不同的植物、动物、人类等。

我们古代的五行元素组合的观念，认为社会的变迁也与五行有关。木、火、土、金、水五种元素，代表着"五德"，即五种德性，不同的朝代有不同的德性：禹土、夏木、商金、周火、秦水。古代皇朝就这样周而复始地交替变迁。

社会变迁，无论掌权者的斗争由谁获胜，或者是重排座次，都需要创造性地转换原来的社会结构，以形成新的文化和习俗。西方的转换注重创造力，不惜全部破坏，重头再来。中国的转换注重整合，像太极旋转，夫妻成家为二，生子为三，再添为四、五、六、七……到一定的时候，再分组新家，一、二、三、四，加入宗祠，共敬祖宗。

重建社会的转换，在西方很急速，最好一口吃成胖子；在东方，比较温和，不求人为，但求自然，比较按部就班。

28. 五行的神奇

相比印度"四大"（水、火、地、风）与希腊"四根"（水、火、土、气），中国古代"五行"思想具有特殊性与历史安排的优越性。

五行，金、水、木、火、土，是中国古代的元素组合万物的思想。广泛地用于中医和占卜。

我们讲的五行，不是希腊人那种思辨理论、由一元到多元辩证的哲学，主要是一种道术，用这五个物质元素的相生相克原理，解决华人祖先遇到的生存和发展的问题，所以就应用于医术和占卜术，还可以用于相面、撰文、讲演、写小说等等。凡术类涉及的领域，都可以用五行去分析，甚至是仁义礼智信五种品德。

用五行思想分析问题，据说跟分析者的道行有密切关系。西医看不起中医，认为中医五行不科学，没有西医的精确性，主要是不明了五行是道术，以"学"量"术"，犯了方向的错误。这跟在今天以技术来贬低理论一样不妥当。

大多数江湖术士，就是小道上的混混，糊弄一口饭，所以就是察言观色之类揣测，或者纯属经验之谈，准确性不高，牵强附会，很容易授人以柄。

五行术见于儒家六经，比如《尚书》，更早就涉及河图、洛书之数术。五行，可以跟东西南北中，跟春夏秋冬夹带四季土，跟子丑寅卯等十二时辰、甲乙丙丁等十天干，合成五行时空观，广泛应用。

八卦乾坤巽艮等与五行的配合应用，文王后天图像上可以见到。周易六爻也可以配五行。

29. 中国文明

天下华人难以不面对中国文明。中国之"中"，并非"天下中央"的解释那么简单，主要还是指文明发源地与儒家的中庸之道。

中国，除中土之名，还有中华、诸华、神州、华夏、中夏、诸夏、皇汉、汉国等代称。这个"中国"是什么？是中华人民共和国的简称吗？不是，是中华，是华夏，指的是我们祖先引以为荣、为华丽、兴旺、荣华的文化意味。

中国，最早指黄帝统一的中原之地，在夏朝、商朝、周朝，形成一脉相承两千年的礼教文化，简称中土、中国，再自然不过了。

春秋战国，各有齐、魏、赵等姓氏国名，却都自称中国。为什么？缘于骄傲、自豪、风度、认祖，尽在其中。

夏、商、周三朝代，共同见于古籍。在四夷眼中，三代都衣物华丽、光耀，是斯文的礼仪之邦，是天下的中心。商、周有考古实证，夏朝没有，古籍却只是并称华夏、中华，没有称呼华商、华周的。为什么？这不正说明夏朝其实比商周更文明，后人自愧不如吗？如果周朝人真是小人之心，哪会称呼华夏高度赞美？

中国古代崇尚礼教道统。这个道统，简单地说，就是君子统领小人之道。君子在中国古代，在周朝之前，是贵族的统称或雅称。秦汉以后，全民都是平民（布衣），君子就用以称呼其中有贵族精神的人，以区别没有贵族气质的小人。君子在中国古代治世、盛世，普遍为官，以礼仪与才艺教化小人，文化趋于温和。

礼教以培育君子的斯文礼仪、才艺为目的，虽非圣人，却也很有德行：有所为，有所不为；舍生取义；取财有道等。中国古代的君子贵族，与日本武士贵族、欧洲骑士贵族相比，内在涵养和学识有天壤（文武）之别。

小人，在中国古代，相对君子而言，特指不严格遵守道德和规则的人。今人说，我没文化，我很现实，莫跟我谈高尚，我是农民，我是个粗人……诸如此类，都是世风日下才会说的话。小人文化擅长搬弄是非、谋害诽谤、无耻下流成风。

中国文明很奇特。君子当道时，中国文景、贞观治世的现实就是柏拉图的理想国。小人当道时，无法无天，或有法不依，社会就会动荡不安。

30. 朝代问题

中国朝代，从夏朝到清朝，统一华夏的共12朝。

夏朝、商朝、周朝三朝代，简称三代，是最早有文字记录的封建朝代。三代，夏朝华美，最为后世称道，却至今是传说。周朝

800 年，春秋战国并计 500 年。三代交替时和前期，有短暂之乱，统一共长达千年以上，形成后来合的总趋势。

这个总趋势背后是华夏礼教道统：父子亲、君臣义、夫妇别、兄弟序、朋友信。礼教基于血缘亲情，比古希腊的英雄史诗文化文雅，比犹太人的圣经神话朴实。故而古希腊、犹太人统一难于上天。而中国却能于秦朝、汉朝再次统一。中国历朝承前启后，必然形成合久必分、分久必合的重组新生的自动机制。

分，是中国所说的乱世：有春秋称霸战国争雄 500 年，有秦汉交接之间楚汉战争 4 年、三国两晋南北朝约 400 年（其中西晋短暂的十几年统一忽略不计）、五代十国战乱 60 年、宋辽夏金元之间割据分治 300 年。

战乱绝非人民所期盼，所以我们有"宁做太平犬，不做乱世人"之言。但对于中国皇朝历史而言，乱世却促成游牧民族入主中原，促成北方汉族避乱南迁。匈奴、鲜卑等民族在中原建国，被人口多、文化高的汉族汉化而融合。中原王、谢等世族南迁江浙、两湖、两广。江南经济迅速发展。冥冥之中，中原战乱成了一只无形手，拨弄塞外人内迁接受汉化，逼中原人南迁传播中原文化。

隋朝和唐朝并称隋唐。唐朝治世时期，中国文化、经济都首屈一指，疆域广大也只有阿拉伯帝国可比。但阿拉伯帝国统一很短暂。隋朝为唐朝开道，犹如秦朝为汉朝开道一样。汉唐一脉相承的中国文化在宋朝登峰造极：文官制度成熟，政府以天下为公的仁义理念治世。

元明清三朝，稳定地给中国的是 1000 万以上平方公里的疆域，留下的汉唐君子文化与两宋文官政治残缺不全。元曲、小说文艺中遗失的思想和精神，奇迹性地出现在欧洲文艺复兴之后，分散在英、法、美多国的公民文化与公务员政治中。

中国在 1912 年建立民国以前，以帝王世袭制为主，国统由此稳定而有长治久安。

Selected Essays by Zhu Yuechun

English

On Adaptation

(Vol.1)

Preface

Mr. Zhu Yuechun prepared to publish a collection of some of his articles, and I was chosen to write a foreword.

Our friendship has been long and deep. Moral, just, kind-hearted, sincere and honest as he is, he also is in possession of erudition, modesty and amiability all of which make him a great friend as well as a mentor.

In the collection, Mr. Zhu has elaborated the main theme from the very beginning: "To those peace-loving people of the world". The first article is titled "On Adaptationism".

Harmony here refers not only to the harmony between individuals, but encompasses the boundless supreme harmony of the universe. Adaptation, following the law of heaven, is the survival guide for everything and the methods to attain supreme harmony.

According to Mr. Zhu, One should get along with each other and "show tolerance to history and future, to the current environment, and to oneself as well".

A nation should maintain internal harmony and unity. "Only an integrated and united nation brought about by ethnic reconciliation has the potential for flourish and prosper development."

Peaceful coexistence among nations should be adopted. Superpower's "hegemonism and unilateralism" shall be condemned.

Human and nature should seek interdependent and peaceful coexistence. Human should "employ the most sensible scientific way to develop and make use of the natural world".

Even the infinite universe has to move in a fixed orbit. "If the

Earth fails to fit in, it will also perish. "

To achieve supreme harmony, everything has to act in accordance with established principles. As an individual, one should " love oneself, one's family, career, nation and motherland". A nation should "respect the internal affairs of other states". As a human being, one should "cherish all components of Mother Nature".

In short, the universe must adapt to intrinsic patterns and rules, also called the law of heaven. Only when nothing goes against it and no ruthless acts are committed could all things coexist harmoniously and have room for growth. The adaptation theory and coexistence thinking are the very ideas that permeate Mr. Zhu's writings.

My understanding of Mr. Zhu's works is not thorough enough for a foreword. So may these few lines extend my humble perception.

Zhao Shanxiang
27 December 2011

On Adaptationism（Ⅰ）

The vast universe is infinite. The Earth that moves along a fixed orbit, It is a colourful material world where the objects with and without life coexist.

As a planet inhabited by living creatures, the Earth constitutes a part of the universe. If it fails to adapt to moving in the cosmos, it will undoubtedly wither away. If other planets render conditions suitable for life, then advanced and primitive species of flora and fauna that have already adapted to the growing environment there will certainly exist, all in varying life forms.

Judging from substances existing on the Earth, the Creator is indeed miraculous. For every substance He has made can be utilised and adapted by mankind.

All disciplines of science were formed in the process that humans lived with, enjoyed, and exploited the elements the Creator made. On this basis, mankind studied, invented, discovered and utilised those findings. Chemical phenomenon, physical phenomenon, biological phenomenon, mathematical phenomenon, written and spoken words were used to explain the principles of substances made by the Creator.

Each religious belief is conviction set up by people to reject the evil and publish the good and will stay as long as men survive. It also works to balance mankind's thinking, concept and mentality. For humans, earthly life is temporary. Religious faith is a field of study in which people learn to achieve a perfect peace of mind. People with a balanced mind will not vent their bad mind set on society or the natural world. Religious beliefs guide people to distinguish the good from the evil, the true and the false, the right and the wrong in the blink of the mind. Religious belief is a branch of learning that rejects the evil and publishes the good and a classical discipline that creates a peaceful and agreeable human society.

Among all beings in nature, human being holds the paramount status. Man can perform intricate thinking and possess high intelligence, improving along the evolution of human history. At all times, people live in two environments; the natural one comes first, followed by the social environment.

In a society created by mankind, people invent social systems adaptable to the survival and development of human being while overturning those harmful ones. People have to abide by and adapt to social laws and rules, so as to establish a social environment suitable for human beings to live in.

In the relationship between man and nature, the more natural resources man exploit, the worse the environmental pollution will become. Drastic changes have emerged between living colonies and non-living colonies, directly affecting the adaptability of the former. The huge transformation of non-living colonies has led to the extinction of individual living species. Mankind has to properly protect the natural environment suitable for human survival so that people can live and grow under an environment that they have been adapted to.

1. Foundation of Mankind

The birthplace would influence a man the most ever since he was born. Certainly, he would also be influenced by the national system, ethnical customs and creeds, local habits and practices as well as religious beliefs. However, hometown is the most significant.

In any nation or country, people's education starts from home, followed by that of schools, society and state. Only by this can one be properly educated and become qualified in the society.

Disparity in education is determined by family, national conditions, ethnic customs and creeds. Consequently, in the human society people vary quite a lot in the views of the life, of the world, of the social science and of the natural science.

However, as long as the people exist, there is the consensus on the foundation of mankind that the love for oneself, for one's family, for career, for the nation, and for the motherland.

Family is man's ultimate safe haven, the continuation of one's life and a component of the country. Family education as the groundwork of national education, family business as the pillar of state enterprise and family property as the source of national property, a nation cannot be founded without multitudinous families. As families compose a country, harmonious families will bring the peace to the country. It is the basic standard of a man living in the society that to guard his family and protect the country and to serve the country for the sake of his family.

From the gregarious primitive society to this day, a leader, or king, must be made once there are more than two persons. In this aspect, mankind is of no difference with any other animals. There is the King in human society, in the animal kingdom and in the insect world (Man would learn a lot from observing the bees). People are without king what the fishing net without netting twine. A king always adapts to solitude and loneliness. I believe in my good king. He will surely guide and civilize his people and will gain support from them.

 ## Quotes from Yuechun

Honesty and Integrity

A man of morality and integrity can exercise the self-discipline and self-respect in front of temptations of money, fame, power and beauty, which would not lure him. Not being

covetous and not toadying for personal gain, he therefore will not be mired in confusion and lose his personal integrity.

2. My Views on Man-made Disaster

Man-made disaster refers to the calamity caused by human beings.

Man-made disasters deprive people of their lives, dying an unnatural death. Was as the biggest catastrophe, it also includes all sorts of sudden injury and fatal accident like the mine disaster, marine casualty, traffic accident, natural calamity, terrorist attack, homicide, execution, suicide, robbery, affray, fighting with weapons, and murder.

Each leads his own life, and death is the only and the most equal destination for them. People die in different ways, yet they can be categorized into two, the natural death and the unnatural one.

That people die in childhood is called the premature death, in middle age the untimely death, and at old age (over 60) the natural death. The old people have gone through the course of life-being born, growing old, getting sick, and dying. So the passing of the aged people is a natural.

Man-made disasters would happen somewhere in the world at all times. During the World War II, Hitler carried out the cruelest genocide in concentration camps, in which over 12 million Jews and Gypsies were massacred. When Japan invaded China, merely in the Nanking Massacre, Japanese soldiers killed more than 300 thousand people. Those being massacred in the above two events, men and women, old and young, were all bare-handed. Even babies were thrown into the air and stabbed with bayonet. How atrocious! How inhuman! These people died unnaturally. They were totally different from those who engaged in warfare and were killed by guns on the battlefield. As long as the mankind continues to exist, one should never forget about these tragic

events.

In human history, it was the countless unnatural death that made the generals with honours and glories on the battlefield, the emperor ascended the throne by war to overthrow the previous king, and the billionaire mine owner, coal mine owner in particular.

However, since ancient times, someone dying an unnatural death are remembered and venerated by others forever. They sacrifice their lives for the country and people and always live in people's heart. Soldiers, fire fighters, Peacekeeping Force, marine accident rescuers, public security officers and epidemic disease physicians, all of them would come forward n every critical moment and dedicate their lives for the national safety, for the security of the general public and those suffered from natural or man-made disasters. Died an unnatural death, they are the heroes cherished and commemorated all the time.

 **Quotes from Yuechun**

Man's basic virtues

It is the basis for being a decent man and the source of happiness to perform the filial piety, have fraternal love, be responsible for jobs, be honest and upright, be courteous and law-abiding, act appropriately, be incorruptible, have the sense of shame and correct faults.

3. Family Rules, Clan Regulations and Laws

Human beings' own quality also remains a principal problem of the society.

Since mankind the creation of mankind, the mate of men and women, the miracle has thus begun. The numbers of people growing

from one to two and then to three, people have been reproducing themselves without ends. In the process of evolution, mankind has constantly attached importance to their quality and quantity.

So far, billions of people with different complexion, languages, races, culture, religious beliefs, customs and creeds, coexist on earth. People have their right to live; who are all equal. Man is just a sojourner on earth; his whole life resembles a growing cycle of plants.

People are different in wealth, status, occupation and nationality. On the whole, disparities will always exist. People with no difference would have no aspiration to forge ahead and be better. Men are born to seek, to compare with, to argue and to fight over all sorts of things amid differences constantly. Due to the variation in desires, material wealth, social status and ideology, people will always take actions. Thus legal standard has to be set up to decide whether the actions are right or wrong.

The earliest legal standards originated from family rules and clan regulations, which had generated and gradually developed since primitive life.

In the evolution process, men realised that the standard ethics code must be complied with in order to improve hereditary traits. So sex morality is put in the first place. People want to raise children with beneficial genetic traits, with the hope that the next generation will outshine the previous one. Thus the prohibition of consanguineous marriage and incest was stipulated in the sex morality as the basic rule to regulate the marriage. Today's advanced laws, legislations, clan regulations and family rules came into being step by step, playing the part to guide the family and clan behaviour, to guard the national safety and to defend human rights. In Chinese history, there is a book on comprehensive family teachings and rules, *The Family Instructions of Zhu Xi*.

In human society, every country, nation, religion and sect would

unexceptionally formulate laws, statutes and regulations to satisfy their own needs. It belongs to their domestic affairs, which should be respected. Any country should not interfere and impose its political views on other countries or fabricate an excuse for coercion, invasion and wars.

Quotes from Yuechun

Integrity and modesty

Having a happy old age and the thriving descendant, one must have been a man of integrity and modesty in his early years. Understanding the principle that "take a step back, and the world will open up", he is blessed with fortune, prosperity and longevity, as well as a happy and peaceful life.

4. Great Power and Cold War

In human society, everybody hopes to perfect himself, his family, and his country. All citizens share a common responsibility for the fate of their country. They are all duty-bound to devote themselves to their country and family, despite their precious life.

Since the history of human warfare has been recorded, it was as easy for a great power to attack a weak nation as an adult hit a child. Conversely, if the child wanted to strike back, he had no alternative but to play tricks.

Since the Cold War between superpowers (Cold War era refers to the period from 1945 to 1991, when the communist bloc led by the Soviet Union and the capitalist bloc headed by the United States began the armament race, competing in various fields including arms, space, hi-tech, intermediate and long range missiles. Both contested against each other and carried out infiltration in opponent's sphere of influence), countries and regions such as Afghanistan, DPRK (Democratic People's Republic of Korea), Vietnam, Cambodia and the Middle East had become the testing grounds for hegemonism. Cold War officially ended after the dissolution of the Soviet Union into 15 republics in 1991. Since then, hegemonic powers, to vie for resources, once again began to proclaim their dominance of the world, to contend for territory, and to dispatch troops for garrison duty.

In those years, small or weak countries, facing with hegemonic powers, had no choice but protect the country with people's life. They devote lives for their country to accomplish the ultimate sacrifice. Suicide bomber was thus born – that is what called the terrorism.

Everyone in this world should press his chest with both hands, pat it thrice and ask the Heaven, the Earth and the conscience, how could such practice, judged by human rights and moral standard, be worthy of himself? Be fair to his family, elders and children? To live up to the king, the fellow townsmen and the general public? Kings, high-ranking officials and decision-makers should also apply the same actions and ask themselves. When mapping out the strategy to you have to defeat the enemies, please put yourself in the other party's shoes and ask, can you bear the consequences resulting from your decisions? If everybody thinks in this way, there will be the hope for peace among human beings.

Between 1922 and 1939, the events confirmed with regard to the terrorist activities, terrorist organisations, terrorist leaders or terrorists happened. At that time, only over 80 000 Jews inhabited in Palestine. World War II brought about an influx of more than 0.45 million Jews to Palestine, and the number surged to over one million in the following two years. However, Arabs and Great Britain could not accept the reality all at once, and made troubles deliberately to the Jews. The already-unfortunate Jewish refugees became desperate, and organised

terrorist attacks from time to time. Terrorism-related words and actions thus emerged in diverse forms. Between 1945 and 1947, large-scale terrorist war was ignited in the Middle East. In 1947, the United Nations voted to divide Palestine into two. The new state of Israel was born, which fulfilled the Bible prophecy that a Jewish nation must be created in Jerusalem.

The Middle East problem has been labelled as "terrorism" for over 60 years, and the situation is getting worse. That region is utilized for the superpowers to promote and experiment hegemonism. Their behaviour has deprived Middle East countries and the surrounding states of peaceful days. It is both detestable and lamentable. If revenge breeds revenge, will there ever be an end to it?

 Quotes from Yuechun

Good friendship is beneficial

Confucius said, "Helpful friends should be upright, sincere and erudite". It is conducive to one's character and mind to meet more people in daily life and strike up friendships with upright, honest and learned persons. When in trouble, the good friends will become a benefactor and lend a hand in necessity.

5. War and Man-made Disaster

Warfare is a kind of man-made disaster. Since the beginning of mankind history, all kinds of wars, large and small, break out all the time. Unexceptionally, wars with any property are ignited by those in power, in which arms merchants reap unfair gains while civilians suffer.

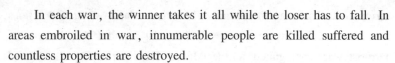

In each war, the winner takes it all while the loser has to fall. In areas embroiled in war, innumerable people are killed suffered and countless properties are destroyed.

For thousands of years, war has been launched for obtaining territory, resources, treasure, or sometimes just for a beauty (in late Ming Dynasty, Wu Sangui revolted against the dynasty for Chen Yuanyuan). Consequently, vicious fighting dragged on.

There are two kinds of war in terms of property. One is aggressive war in which other countries or regions are invaded, the other is civil war resulting from power struggle within the country or region, or citizens fighting against despotic rule.

With the progress of history, pretexts used by invaders in aggressive wars have become increasingly insidious and sly. Nowadays, superpowers easily resort to military force as a means to resolve conflicts, thereby exposing the domineering essence of hegemonism and unilateralism. Resources of subservient small states will be manipulated and monopolised by them. Slight disobedience will incur coordinated attack by land, sea and air, which is a pretext of superpower. And the invaded state will be razed to the ground in a few days. This type of warfare threatens human beings with extinction.

In ancient times, each war would last for several years. From 636 to 642 A. D. , Muslims occupied Pakistan, Syria, Persia and Egypt. In 1243, the Mongols invaded the Seljuks, who had already occupied Afghanistan and six other countries before the Mongol invasion. In 1592, Japan invaded the Korean Peninsula, which directly threatened China, at a time the Ming Dynasty still flourished. From 1824 to 1886, in which British invaded India, Burma was also invaded on many occasions. In 1886, Britain made Burma a province of India. In 1937, Japan invaded China. In 1942, Japan occupied Burma and six Southeast Asian countries.

Flames of war have never come to a cease in human history. In

modern times, World War I resulted in a loss about 50 billion, and casualties at almost 40 million. The human and financial loss incurred in World War II was several times higher than those in World War I. A slight error made by the authorities resulted in innumerable deaths and incurable injuries. How many people's lives and properties that a war had deprived!?

Quotes from Yuechun

Read good books, say good words, perform good deeds, and be a good man

It is hope that people could adopt a modest and sincere attitude to the world. One should vigorously carry out charitable acts amd disseminate benevolent thoughts in everyday life. Thus, the society will be imbued with peacefulness and serenity.

6. No Interfering the Internal Affairs

Every state, region or nation has its own political system, laws and legislations, clan regulations, social contracts, family rules and ordinances which comprise part of its domestic affairs, clan affairs, and family affairs, namely internal affairs. Every state, religion or family has its own hard nut to crack. Under the prerequisites of independence and self-determination, they should choose solutions adaptable to them. It is utterly unjustifiable that any country tries to impose its own conventions onto others.

However, in every country or region, the inadaptability of policies or system concerning people's livelihood will undoubtedly breed rebellion, or even trigger internal wars, or civil wars. Any foreign

political or economic interference in country or region undergoing civil war is unjust.

Some countries, especially hegemonic states have to poke their nose into others' business, enjoy looting a burning house while that nation is in a civil war for personal gain. They tend to nurture their own agents in both political and economic spheres, which is more cost-effective than attacking the region. In cold war era, rumbling cannon sound is nonetheless around. Arms dealers cash in, while resources of the weak nations are seized by strong powers and hegemonic states as usual. If small countries maintain stability, hegemonic states have nothing to gain; once military conflict erupts in the former, the latter will be profited in many ways. Amid every country's civil war, there are hegemonic states taking advantage of the occasion to reap unfair gains and righteous countries lending a helping hand.

War is a kind of man-made disaster, an inevitable product of human society. Where there is a war, there will be loss of lives and properties. Human consciousness is the fundamental source of social systems. All strategies of social system are standards for upholding social order. If serious mistakes occur, it will turn into gunpowder for war. Once ignition fuse is applied to it, war will break out.

Quotes from Yuechun

A sense of honour and justice in the noble spirit of upright men; Discipline and rules of conduct in his loyal heart

A gentleman conducts himself with morality and integrity. Guan Yu was such a man. He had praised as the model of justice and influence people for hundreds of years.

Importance should be attached to disciplines and ethics for

everything in the world. Guan Yu had accomplished all the eight virtues. His loyalty shined like the sun and moon.

7. Greed is the Root of Corruption

Greed is the root of corruption for mankind.

If the dot in Chinese character "贪" (meaning greed) is changed to a falling left stroke, it will become a character with an entire different meaning, "贫", which means poverty or end.

Man was born with selfish desire ever since the existence of human beings. Selfish desire constitutes the watershed of morals, regulations and laws. One is entitled to the normal and legitimate incomes, while illegal gains pertain to greed. No greedy person has good end. The greedier one is, the worse his fate will be. To satisfy the greed, one would unscrupulously exploit others. Indulge in drinking and one will be drunk. Greed for money makes one perish. Lust for sex messes up one's life and even deprives him of it. One would lose his aspirations by seeking pleasures and have the health harmed by gluttony... As the old saying goes: men would die for money while birds would die for food.

In the world, the more venal officials there are, the more corrupt the officialdom will be. Take the trade of government official positions for example. For the people who was longing for a position, he had to spend considerable money to get a lucrative post. Then he would take one third of the term of office to recover the cost of buying the post. In the remaining time, He had to continue to take bribes so as to make financial preparation for a second term or higher position.

For those selling official positions, they managed to get money from the lower ranking official and used it as the bribe to get an even higher post. They amassed large quantities of fortune, antiques and famous paintings. Their residences were commensurate with the imperial palace; their vehicles were better than the emperor's. They had abundant beauties and female servant girls. They used public money for their own expenses. Some built villas privately and were wealthier than the imperial court. n the Qing Dynasty, a notoriously corrupt official named Heshen emerged. He owned the total property that amounted to the imperial revenue of the Qing government for 13 years.

It is known to all that Ancient Greece and Egypt became powerful and prosperous based on the scientific and economic achievements. But in later years, they declined due to the large number of corrupt officials. Yi Le, an extremely corrupt official, also brought about the fall of the powerful Bagan Kingdom of Burma. Likewise, bunches of corrupt officials in the late Ming Dynasty compelled the most industrious and thrifty Emperor Chongzhen to commit suicide at Jing Shan.

In each dynasty, accomplishments were achieved by the loyal and upright officials, and ruined by treacherous and corrupt ones. Yet the former were easily framed, such as Yu Chenglong in the Qing Dynasty of China, and the later, on the contrary, were protected, Qing Heshan as an example. Though born in the same country and region, people live with differentnationalities, cultures, religions, beliefs, social systems, customs and creeds. However, people hold a unanimous attitude towards their government and officials on whether they are loyal or treacherous, upright or corrupt. Therefore, the historyof every country and region is co-written by a variety of opposing characters in human society – wise and despotic rulers, loyal and treacherous courtiers, upright and corrupt officials, law-abiding citizen and scoundrel, good and bad guys, as well as man and woman. Those characters appeared and disappeared in the historical stage, with the valuable and adaptable recorded by the later generations as the human history for people's reference.

8. Population Issues

Population distribution and density of a country or region is a

significant issue that influences the national economy and people's livelihood.

Population size and quality are key factors to determine the annual national income and the national economic development. Population issues encompass the following aspects which are crucial to the comprehensive development of the nation: the sex ratio, national health, care and education for young children, enrolment rate for adolescents, employment rate for adults, pension ratio for old-age, cultural education of the whole society, health care, infectious disease control, nationwide fitness programs, physical quality of the public, and social welfare, etc. People constantly work for the basic necessities of life, producing what we need and consuming what we have to use. Both production and consumption cause pollution. All these are closely related to the population density. People seek the effective and harmonious methods that accommodate to Heaven, Earth and men between the population and society as well as between the population and nature. And put them into practice.

Human beings are living on the earth which is a relatively limited space in their life time. Thus to control the population growth has become a practical problem for the countries and regions spreading over the surface of the Earth. The higher the population density, the greater the pressure and the more tension the society and nature would face. As a result, it would be more difficult to tackle the relationship between the production and consumption (social management and natural resource usage) and the pollution they generate. Population is a significant factor influencing the social stability.

Cold war lasting for several decades, the world did not see another world war, just some minor regional warfare, which gave many countries the opportunities to continue to live and develop. In a relative stable situation, agriculture, forestry, animal husbandry, fishery, light and heavy industries, that all trades on which mankind relied to live, co-ordinately developed so as to offer the basic necessities of people's life. If one could live in peace, he would surely be devoted to work. Increase in productivity was followed by rapid population growth. Only when basic needs for living have been met, can people spare the effort to care for life quality. On the contrary, hunger and cold breed wicked intentions. That is how human beings have developed.

When new China was founded, it had a population of just over 0.4 billion. At that time, the government offered incentives to families to have more children. In 1965, the population surprisingly surpassed 0.7 billion. The authorities were alarmed and immediately adopted effective family planning programme. Only through tough measures could the population be controlled to stand at 1.3 billion currently. In India, another populous country, feasible methods regarding family planning are yet to be sound at present. Its population is expected to exceed that of China by mid-21st century.

Nowadays, only Russia has seen negative population growth. Viewing from the perspective of rational population growth, Russia should not encourage population growth. Rather, it may be a blessing for Russia to let nature take its course.

Human population is increasingly growing on Earth. To survive, humans would exploit the society and Nature at any cost. The resources are consumed up by large

The greater part would use up the lesser. There is a not very nice saying: human is more vicious and ferocious than the viper and the fiercest beast, because the latter two have been swollen by men. Once they completely disappear from Earth, human being will die out too.

9. Elementary Analysis of Moral Standards

Humanity, known as the moral conduct or disposition, is the way of getting on in the world.

Dispositions can either be good or bad. The former includes being

true, sincere and honest; the latter, being false, wicked and hypocritical. Good or bad, all are constantly reflected in one's words, deeds, manners and behaviours. One always behaves out of his disposition.

Dignity matters in regard with the ways of getting along with others, as well as people's words, deeds, manners and behaviours. And characters comprise individual character, national character, family character, ethnic character, party character and faction character. To sum up, distinction should be made between the internal contradiction, friend and foe, as well as principle and non-principle. Such kind of classification is internationally recognised, boasting general and universal significance. Whether they are good or bad, all depend on the group to which the people belong.

But for all human material products and commercial contacts, which consist of all the commodity, public welfare undertakings, scientific research findings, news reports, historical documents, works and advertising medias, as well as the whole world, entire country, all regions, ethnic groups, factions, families and individuals, there must be certain difference in disposition, to be true or false, sincere or wicked, honest or hypocritical. As long as humans exist, one has to comply with public morality. Otherwise dreadful man-made disasters would be brought about.

Fake drugs, adulterated wine, quack medicine and unqualified food have killed countless people. Fake technology, adulterated products and false commodities have deprived people of their money and life. Pseudo scientific research projects, false advertisement and information have misled people and swindled them of their life and money. It is not only related to certain individual, certain family, certain region or certain country. This is concern of, all man kinds the a matter of prime importance. Humans should join efforts to advocate public morality, earnestness, sincerity and honesty.

If such public morality is not advocated, everyone in the world will be hurt by each other. People would be the victim of their own.

To alive is already a blessing in life. And life is for living.

With the material living standard be satisfied can people lead a healthy and safe life. Only with health and safety can one reach longevity, and can he make contribution to himself, to the family, and to the nation.

Therefore, the discovery, research and creation of all living necessities must be truly conducive to the improvement of human life and health. Human should make choice between "Genuine and fake", "beneficial and harmful".

10. On Religious Belief

Religious belief has been a lifelong conviction in people's mind ever since human came into being.

People are wondering where man comes from and where he goes; why the heavenly bodies operate cyclical; why there are millions of species on Earth from generation to generation; why the climate changes capriciously or regularly... bewildered by these mysteries, mankind therefore decided that the Creator will bless the human world from Heaven, so that man could live peacefully throughout his life. Man is living for the happiness, peace and good fortune for himself, his next life and his posterity. So in the process of human history, man had created the divine concept of prophecy, and believed that god is ubiquitous and omnipotent.

Man has set religious belief as the spiritual pillar upon which harmonious life can be established. It is a stable spiritual refuge. From the beliefs they rely on, people may also revise and purify the blemishes in their daily life. So mankind has found Buddhism, Christianity, Catholicism, Islam, Taoism and Confucianism, etc. Religious belief will always keep man company in their life journey as long as there is

human being.

Since scientific theories are known and proven, they are real facts. In this vast universe, the number of unknowns far exceeds that of known, but the unknown is a material phenomenon set up by the Creator. It is what the religions believe-the phenomenology.

Doctrines of the major religions fully show the existence of phenomenology.

In Buddhism, Christianity, Catholicism and Islam, it is believed that God exists in heaven, where human come from. When men are born on earth, they are going to experience the pleasure and pain in their life, feel various emotions and desires. After going through the stages of birth, ageing, falling ill and death, the eligible human will go back to heaven, while the ineligible human will enter the next transmigration again and again until they are up to the standards.

Confucianism was established over two thousand years ago in the Central Plains of the East, which embraces the doctrine that man is an integral part of nature and they interact with each other. Three principles and five virtues in human world are instructions from heaven, which guide men to achieve long-term peace and stability. One should maintain orderliness, or "heavenly commandment" will be violated and "divine punishment" will be inflicted on you. It instructs people to follow the will of heaven to make their family and country thriving and prosperous.

Taoism emphasizes "this life". Followers try to obtain immortality by self-cultivation. The doctrine aims to enlighten the public based on the principle of "interaction between human and heaven". Man should "respond appropriately to the situation and help others" so as to "return to one's true self", fully enjoy worldly emotions and feelings. After going through the penance, human will become the immortal, living a leisure and carefree life.

Religious belief is the conviction of rulers and common people.

Scriptures, which suit the ethnic groups of the country and region, let people make the choice upon adaptability and gradually practice what they have chosen. That is religious belief.

11. On Doing Things

As a human, the most important things in this world are to get married and build a career. Day after day, one has to take care of all kinds of issues—large or small—of family and career. They are working busily throughout their life and only at the end of tunnel can we find out whether we did it valuable or not. There is no need to analyse the process of one's life in a certain period or at a specific issue. It is the outcome that matters. If a man committed all sorts of crime during the prime of his life, and in his later years serving as the wellbeing of his country, nation and family by achieving insurmountable contributions, he could be described as a bad flower producing good fruits. A wrongdoer may become a man of virtue once he does good things. Conversely, if he already made significant contributions during the prime of his life, but did harm to his country, nation and family in his later years, then he is a good flower producing bad fruits. He has become a sinner or a person condemned by history. So there is no need to comment on the process of things we do, the result says it all.

To judge good or bad, one should take into consideration the laws, legislations, religious belief, clan regulations, family rules and morality of that country or region in which the incident occurred. If things are involved with different countries and regulated by international law, one also has to take international law into account to avoid making mistakes in that field.

If someone makes a mistake or breaks the law in deliberately, for example a failure in operating a machine, he doesn't fully consider the result. This is not induced by human thinking. A wrong behaviour results in mistake. For this kind of error, people should take

circumstances into account when commenting and deal with it differently.

Men live on earth and among people. Anyone who intentionally carries out abominable deeds, outrageous acts or mean things will come to a bad end. God's mill grinds slow but sure. Those violating the law will be punished. This is what "evil will be recompensed with evil" is about.

People in this world should live for his family, for his country, for just and honourable causes. Throughout his life, man must follow the dictates of conscience to act. Doing things with good intentions and in compliance with rules and regulations, the outcome must be favourable. Behaviour like this is consistent with the philosophy of calmness and philanthropy. This will be beneficial to the country, to people, to his family and himself.

Quotes from Yuechun

One who shows filial piety is the smartest

One who shows filial piety is the most smart. It is because filial to our parents will be emulated by our children, and they will show the same respect for us when grown up. Deities will bless our family with peace and smoothness. Therefore, one who shows filial piety is the smartest.

12. On Principle

Inside a country or region, between the ruling party and party out of power, ethnic groups, and armed forces of national unions, political disagreement, military conflicts or embroiling into a marathon civil war happen quite often.

However, since ancient times, whether there are relevant constitutional clauses and public praise or not, in everyone's heart, those who split the country, harm national interests and dignity, commit treason, defect to the enemy, or betray national interests have lost citizens' common heart, and become the black sheep of the state. This standard should top the list of principles for citizens of a country or region.

Based on this principle, factional conflict within the country, between ethnic groups and armed forces are internal warfare.

For the past two hundred years, countries involving in civil war have been rising all the time. Those include Civil war between Upper and Lower Canada from 1837 to 1840, American Civil War between the North and South from 1864 to 1865, Chinese Civil War from 1947 to 1949, Vietnamese Civil War between the North and South from 1964 to 1975, Cambodian Civil War from 1963 to 1975, Nigerian Civil War from 1967 to 1970, as well as civil strife in African nations such as Rwanda and Zaire. For over 50 years, ethnic armed conflict in Myanmar has never ceased. In short, the world has never seen a day without civil war and internal strife.

There is no doubt that where there is civil war, there is infiltration and intervention of a third country or party involved. One kind of infiltration is positive, which aims to help end other country's civil war and reach a peaceful unification as soon as possible. Another is to get profit from other's misfortune by supporting separatists to plan sinister plots.

For any country mired in civil war or internal strife, all parties, sects, factions and ethnic groups should put national unification and ethnic unity as the ultimate goal. All sides should take part in discussion to seek reconciliation, compromise for a new path despite political discrepancies and agree to differ. They should regard national interest and well being of the larger group as more vital, prioritise the right and

wrong on issues of major importance, be proud of general unity, feel ashamed for secession, and be mortified by internal strife. If every citizen manages to do likewise, there will be hope for ethnic unity in the country.

Quotes from Yuechun

Be selfless and kind, and make friends with neighbours

A man will get the magical affinities if he could voluntarily care for and help friends and relatives near you with a kind heart. As the saying goes, "A good neighbour is more precious than a luxury house." Mutual help and protection, especially among good neighbours, are substantial blessings.

13. *Living Up to One's Word*

If a person can always be responsible for consequences resulting from one's words and deeds throughout his life, then he is a man of integrity for his whole life.

As Chinese sayings go, "What's said cannot be unsaid", "Gentleman is a man of his words". Both of them describe a person living up to his promises. Fulfilling what one has promised, and then his word is believable.

To make words and deeds generate satisfying effects, one must treat them responsibly. When we make mistakes in our own words or deeds and cannot fulfil our promise, or even, violate national law, clan regulation, religious doctrine, or worst trigger trouble and disaster, we face the results of what we say and what we did squarely, and bear the necessary legal responsibility. In that case, this is still a form of integrity.

Language is an audible way for human to express his thinkings and sentiments. (While the deaf-mutes use sign languages). One must keep to his word and what you said has to be carried out, and you have to shoulder the responsibility regardless of the result. This is also a demonstration of integrity.

As regard to putting human language into written words, for example: making a contract, agreement, promise, signed document and bill, you should answer for the contents of this kind of oral or written promises. If you manage to do so, this is another representation of integrity.

Man's behaviour, including directing others to act, as well as planning and organising team play, responsibilities of all consequences generated from this behaviour should be respectively borne by the primary plotter, participants and enforcers. Only this is a display of human integrity.

It takes two to dialogue, whereas talking to oneself does not have to be responsible for the other party. Benefits and harms of suicides, self-abandonment, self-enlightenment, self-awareness, self-realisation and self-study are totally borne by oneself. You are accountable for your own words and deeds. As man suffers from one's own actions, responsibility lies on you.

Integrity is manifested in three different levels:

(1) Elementary level: personal behaviour, referring to words and deeds between individuals, or between an individual and an organisation or a state.

(2) Intermediate level: group behaviour, referring to words and deeds between families, between religions, or between groups.

(3) Advanced level: national behaviour, referring to words and deeds between countries, or between regions.

All parties must always be trustworthy, resolute and responsible pertaining to these three levels of words and deeds. This is the kind of

integrity suitable for building a harmonious society.

14. Class Society

Ever since there is a class society, there has been the classification of people into levels. Class or stratum comes from marketplace. At the market, men will supervise other people, take care of things, and manage money. In that case, the economic foundation is established, and management hierarchy is set up, all the way to the central government, imperial court, king, and president...The marketplace has developed into today's modern market economy.

As an oriental saying goes, "Marketplace emerges before an imperial court but later than a barter kiosk". Originally, a barter kiosk was chosen as the venue for contact between individuals and families. As trading thrived, kiosk transformed into a market. All cities and towns in the world were easily accessible by land or water transport. Marketplace grew in the same pattern.

Marketplace was an economic distribution centre. Someone had to be selected to manage the property, and charge management fee, taxing thus began. The manager allocated sites for stalling, processing and storage to merchants. Running the marketplace evolved into business management. Religious or tribal leaders supervised the marketplace manager. As the society developed, a hierarchy of upper-level human management comprising government departments of town, county, state, province and centralised state power was established.

From the perspective of world history, the earliest relevant example was the unification of China in 230 B. C. by Qin Shi Huang, the first emperor of a unified China. Primarily enforced at marketplaces, the standardisation of weights and measures facilitated easy trading for market economy. After the Roman Empire's conquest of Greece and other regions, weights and measures at marketplaces were also standardised around 146 B. C. From 1044, the Bagan monarchy of

Myanmar had been attaching importance to market economy for over 230 years. In 1776, the Americans overturned

British colonial ruling. In the wake of the country's independence, its market economy developed rapidly, and had taken a dominant position in the world to date. Audacity grows with one's purse.

Quality living is supported by material wealth, the amount of which reflects grow or decline of a market economy. Without economic or material abundance, governance success will not come to a country or family no matter how it is run. Yelling slogans is no national welfare and people's livelihood. From the general public to the central government and from the central government to the general public of a country or region, all should seek workable methods compatible with national conditions and popular sentiment to invigorate the economy. Relying on science to boost productivity so as to strengthen the economy becomes the tops of the agenda of nations worldwide.

Days of harmony and unity have to be supported by economy.

15. *Egotistical Ethnic Democracy*

Ethnic issues often top the agenda of multi-ethnic state's central government, concerning the general direction, stability and unity of the country.

Multi-ethnic countries fall into two different categories. One is a country comprising many states (a single nation accounts for the bulk of the population) and run by a union government, such as Myanmar, the United States, Iraq and the former Soviet Union. The other is the historical multi-ethnic state where different ethnic groups have been interdependent for several thousand years, such as China and India.

Substantive difference between these types of state lies in the contradictions between national democracy and ethnic democracy, and between ethnic democracy and hereditary tribal chieftaincy.

Crux of the issue is whether the internal democracy within the local

ethnic group and democratic line of the federal government and all factions can look at the big picture, work for the benefits of all, and find the right way adaptable to the survival and growth of the federal government and local ethnic states. This is ethnic democracy.

The obstacle to ethnic democracy is hereditary tribal chieftaincy of local ethnic states. Any hereditary chief ascending the throne is reluctant to make his exit. However, it is not that making one's exit is good while not exiting is bad. Heritance and abdication, democracy and dictatorship, all must be primarily decided by citizens of ethnic states. Internal affairs of local ethnic groups are decided by the majority within the ethnic group. This is essentially ethnic democracy.

If every ethnic state is able to attain local ethnic democracy, then turn around and take the federal government into consideration. A unified country and authentic ethnic unity are the first and foremost conditions of building the road to prosperity for an ethnic democratic state. Under an environment of national stability, every citizen can then give expression to their rights and obligations pertaining to democracy. The federal government has to deal properly with ethnic democracy of local ethnic states, and approve guidelines that bring peace and stability to the country and the people constitutionally. In addition, adjustment has to be made concerning ethnic policies and strategies of different period. Ethnic democracy keeps pace with the times; one should never be careless about it.

Quotes from Yuechun

Kind persons are blessed.

A man should show respect for life. He should spare creatures' life, not kill ants or other insects, and not kill fish by poison or electricity. He should have gratitude for what have

been bestowed by Heaven and Earth. If one can earnestly act in this way, God will bless him with more fortune, more happiness, and longer life.

16. Learn to Conduct Oneself well

To get on in the world, it is essential for people to learn how to conduct themselves well.

Conducting oneself is like the carpenter shaping neat wood planks. First, one has to precisely cut out right angles at the edge of the material with a set of square rulers, and then make square openings or holes with which various shapes and patterns can be carved at will. After perfectly joined with various frames or equipment, the entirety of an elegant utensil takes shape.

To behave oneself, one must start with learning the rules, principles and common sense of conduct, and be a person of uprightness. With painstaking attention, whatever you do will naturally come out fine.

Confucianism in the East embraces some good doctrines in regard to learning how to conduct oneself well. "Three Principles and Five Virtues" and "Law of Heaven, Law of Humanity, Law of Things" are codes for man to observe throughout his life, when socializing with people.

Throughout one's life, there is a thread of humanity hanging between the heavens and the earth. High and low, left and right, front and back go together in the world. Man lives in the time and space, always being inside. In other words, we are living in the circumstances always surrounded by others, taking the middle course and being tolerant towards those around. And only in this way can we learn to tolerate ourselves and survive as men.

Confucianism provides people with spiritual enlightenment, making them realize "what law of heaven is, what law of humanity is, what

law of things is⋯" It appeals to people to devote themselves to the right thing, be upright before making others upright, and discipline themselves before disciplining others. Being reasonable, which is the guiding principle of conducting oneself   defines the way we behave.

Unscrupulously trying to satisfy their selfish desires, people will definitely violate the "Law of Heaven, Law of Humanity, Law of Things". The loss of principles and virtues means chaos, which will lead to a complete destruction of humanity and outrageous acts.

The resolution of global turbulence, national unrest and family discord depends on the decision-makers behavior, which is supposed to conform to "Law of Heaven, Law of Humanity, Law of Things". The decision-makers here include those who can make decision on international and domestic affairs, on affairs between organizations and families, and on affairs within organizations or families as well.

Men's consciousness is guided by the code of morals forever and turns to direct our decisions and actions. If the code of morals is wrong, then consciousness, decisions and actions are all erroneous, and that error induces misdoings.

 ## Quotes from Yuechun

Good nature makes good fortune

A man's fate can be changed, just like land. If he is lazy, fertile soil will turn barren and crops will grow poorly. If he works industriously, barren rock will turn fertile and yield bountiful harvest. Therefore, as long as one repents sincerely, continue to rectify the inner mistakes and be kind-hearted and impartial, he will certainly be blessed by deities with peace and safety.

17. National Democracy

National unity and democratic governance are the mainstream in today's society, which is also the top the agenda of multinational state's central government.

National democracy should first be adaptable to its own national conditions. More specifically, when compared with countries of immigrants on the new continent, democracy is presented differently in countries with ancient civilisations. Good for cross referencing, but detrimental if copied entirely. The reason is that culture, creeds, religion, living habits, local customs and practices as well as ideologies are key factors to differentiate ethnic groups.

Culture and customs are manifested in languages. With respect to customs, much importance is attached to marriages, ceremonies, and rites. Major life events such as wedding and funeral encompass different rituals. These have laid the foundation of an ethnic group.

There are two varieties of religious beliefs. One is the local religion, and the other is foreign religion imported in later times.

Take ancient China as an example. Taoism and Confucianism are its local religions. Prior to the Tang Dynasty, people were sent to the Western Regions for Buddhist Scripture. In early Tang Dynasty, Hsuan Tsang, a Buddhist monk, was on a mission to the Western Regions (now India) to obtain Buddhist scriptures.

India, the origin of Buddhism, had been a British colony for nearly a century. Burma was once incorporated with British culture. From then to 1947, British colonists forcibly introduced Christianity into India and Burma. In Kachin State (Jingpo people) of Burma, even English spelling has been converted into Kachin word by adding Jingpo phonetic transcription. The entire ethnic group embraced Christianity. Even at present, part of Indians and Myanmar people still believe in Christianity.

In the social environment of human beings and religions living and growing, the fittest will survive and thrive, while those unable to adapt to the society died out. For example, in 15th century, with the large flow of European immigrating, the native American Indian tribes living in the United States, Mexico and Canada of North America as well as the Mississippian culture of temple mound before the 15th century withered away.

National groups have diversified customs and practices, which include local features and those of the neighbouring national groups, a result of interpenetration. Contact between different peoples is normal in a human society. In history, intermarriage and trading is inevitable. "When in Rome, do as the Romans do" is common sense. Few national groups are completely closed itself off from the outside world in every corner of the world. To gradually adapt to the rapidly developing society, even a hermit nation has to learn ballroom dancing.

National unity and democratic governance are the most complicated issues devoid of standards. Absolute concentration was once the source of productivity, creativity and cohesion in human community, driving the growth of society. However, absolute freedom has disunited people, making them inferior to a swarm of ants. Cohesion, concentration and unity of ants and bees facilitate clear-cut division of labour and give expression to individual freedom. Herds of elephants, prides of lions and flocks of birds also adapt themselves to nature for survival in this manner. Those committed to brutality would sometimes be portrayed as "inferior to a beast". In human society, owing to the disparity in social systems and lifestyle as well as the dissimilarity in democracy and concentration of authority, national democracy significantly varies from one country or national group to another. With respect to countries made up of immigrants, such as the U. S. , Canada and Australia, to deal with aboriginal inhabitants, they have cultivated the practice of deciding by voting and adopting policies that are adaptable to the survival of non-native national groups, namely themselves. Today, "democracy", which we take pride in, is not adaptable to a lot of regions in Europe and Asia. There are two special cases worth mentioning. Under British colonial rule, Burma was annexed as a province of India. Democracy never existed there. Since 1947 when it gained independence, two extremes have emerged. One was the military government holding highly concentrated power, and the other is the factions indulging in a high degree of freedom. Democracy had turned the federal government into a chaotic government. The other example is Hong Kong, China. Being servants under British colonial rule, none of the party even mentioned anything about democracy. When the territory returned to Chinese sovereignty in 1997, being master of their own, citizens began to cry for democracy all the time. Few Myanmar people and Hong Kong citizens would rather be a slave than a master.

First of all, it should be certain that national unity and democratic governance are internal affairs. It means that each country and region have the freedom and rights to define its people's rights and interests which is adaptable to their country and region. To make it simple, a man may not agree with the meal from another family; and he will suffer if forced to eat it. A man should live in a way adaptable to himself. So, in each ethnic group within a country or region, the system of democracy and centralization shall be formulated by themselves so as to enjoy a better development.

18. Second Talk on Natural Disaster

Mankind always encounters natural disasters. People will be on tenterhooks upon receiving disaster forecast, and more terrified at the news that epidemic disease is found. A catastrophe may result large casualties and huge economic losses. It is the way Nature punished mankind.

Similar to man-made disaster, natural disasters, big or small, happen every day. Between 165 and 167 A. D. , a plague swept through the Roman Empire. From 1347 to 1351, the Black Death, the most severe epidemic in human history, ravaged Europe and the Middle East, killing a quarter of the population in the five years. In 1353 and 1354, plague pandemic erupted in China. In 1976, he Tangshan Earthquake claimed hundreds of thousands of lives. In 2005, the Indian Ocean tsunami swept away hundreds of thousands of people from coastal countries.

Natural disasters such as earthquake, tsunami, hurricane, tornado, mountain torrent, debris flow and volcanic eruption would take away thousands of lives and hundreds of billions of property in the twinkling of an eye. Nature inflicts sudden severe punishment on mankind and in just a few minutes, man would suffer both losses in life and property, which is really shocking and frightening.

Plague or epidemic disease is even more horrified. It can last for long and affect a large area. The dead is difficult to dispose and bury, and the sick is hard to be treat. The spread of disease would be speeded up if the carriers escape. Dreadful and lamentable, people are frightened on hearing of the epidemics.

The infectious disease can be controlled and cured through the immediate and simultaneous prevention and treatment once the epidemic is found.

For the sudden natural disasters, such as the earthquake, tsunami, tornado, ice storm, thunderstorm, lightning and volcanic eruption, etc. , precautions are being taken and forecasting techniques are being improved gradually with the hope to reduce the unnecessary losses.

However, there is a special phenomenon between mankind and Nature. The dividing line between the man-made and the natural can be described as "Man can devise a thousand-year plan, but can never forecast a sudden natural disaster". It is also the natural law formulated by the Creator, and mankind has no choice but to obey. The blessed would always survive confronting the natural disaster.

Facing the natural disaster, Effective actions should be taken in the prevention and relief. People should place the natural environmental protection in the first place, as the more serious the humans destroy Nature, the more punishment they will get.

 Quotes from Yuechun

Cumulate merit and virtue, and be kind towards everything

One should perform good deeds and cumulate the merit and virtue, be compassionate and cherish all living things on earth. If he industriously cultivate the field of happiness at heart and cumulate the merits and virtues, he would get help from God and other people, and be blessed in everything.

19. Saving the Earth

Living on earth, humans make use of resources provided by Nature to satisfy their daily needs. Resources, after direct utilisation or being processed into end products, will inevitably turn into refuse, industrial waste and domestic waste. The amount is directly proportional to man's demand. Waste, degradable or not, recyclable or not, will all contaminate the natural world, polluting the soil, water and air to a various degrees. Conversely, a polluted environment hazards human beings.

Humans use various things to improve their living condition in the scope of food, clothing, housing and transportation so as to enhance quality of life. Certain raw materials are directly harmful to human

body, while some become noxious during processing and manufacturing. Waste released is definitely a pollutant; what differs is the degree of pollution.

The more resources men utilise, the more pollution there will be. The more people eat, the more human waste there are. The more vehicles run in the streets, the more tailpipe will be emitted. The more factories, especially chemical plants and pharmaceutical factories, the more wastewater, toxic smoke and poisonous gas will be discharged. In other words, more people, who make use of more resources, will produce more waste and bring about more pollution to the natural environment.

The man-made pollutions threaten mankinds and endanger every living animal and plant. According to research, scientists have initially confirmed that dozens of living species die out from the world everyday. Mankind would probably become extinct if only few animals and plants left in this world.

Human beings are powerful in the world. The law of the jungle applies to Nature where the big, the fierce, the smart and the wise eat the small, the meek, the dumb and the foolish. Humans eat edible things in Nature. For example, millions of whales have been caught annually in Japan. In various countries, nearly all the edible animals from sky, on land and under water are offered as food or hunted for money. Elephant, rhinoceros, crocodile, lion, tiger, snake and bird are all included. Man is the most ferocious advanced animal in the world.

However, it is human beings who have created material wealth of a society and also destroyed the natural world. Man has to figure out by himself whether it is a blessing or a disaster. Immediate actions are demanded to take to protecting mankind's only homeland, the Earth. On As to the utilisation and protection of natural environment, man should seek self-enlightenment in self-amusement, self-awakening in self-lost. God will save he Saves himself.

Quotes from Yuechun

Practice benevolence and righteousness, and perform self-cultivation

A man should practice the benevolence and righteousness. In this case, he would be blessed by Guan Yu with the ubiquitous integrity. He also should cultivate himself and strive for excellence, so that Guan Yu's reputation, glistening like stars, will shine the earthly world forever.

20. Understanding of Nature

Subsequent to the invention of written words, recording of events gradually appeared. The appearance of events recording is the beginning mark of mankind's history. The history of human beings knows about the nature, summing up the phenomenon of natural material changes in the nature, scientifically classified dozens of material elements (dozens of elements), physical phenomenon, chemical phenomenon, biological and physiological phenomenon for explanation and analyse that there is are infinite variety of fantastic phenomena in the natural world.

Chinese people in ancient times already made use of the Five Elements consist of Metal, Wood, Water, Fire and Earth to explain and analyse the yin and yang changes of all substances. Based on the concept of mutual generation plus mutual conquest and infinite transformation of the Five Elements, it clearly explains and analyses the universe, planets, phenomena and all substances on the earth. Similar to natural substances, human sentiments and passions, heaven, earth, man, deity, spirit have also been explicitly presented.

During life and production, mankind observe and analyse nature discovering the changes of natural substances and creating living

materials. While improving the life quality, men wreak havoc on the natural environment. Mankind needs to make choices after weighing the pros and cons.

Please embrace what is adaptable to human utilisation with little environmental pollution generation. And reject what is adaptable to human utilisation with enormous environmental pollution generation.

21. Man and Nature

Nature is the origin as well as the ultimate destination of men. Destiny means that people follow the course of nature. In the long process of history, men's life, no matter how long, is as short as the falling star flashing in the sky. Where there is life there is death, which is the natural law for Creator to renew the lives. All the species including animals, plants and micro-organisms cannot escape their ultimate fate.

Lifespan for humans varies, with the average of less than a hundred years. They could be as short as a while, yet the oldest person ever recorded in history had lived for several hundred years. Man is totally powerless in front of death. The Creator has been partial to mankind. Everything in the natural world seems to be made for men, which illustrates the greatness of human wisdom. However, will mankind adopt the most sensible, scientific approach to develop and utilise substances in the natural world, and cherish them all? This is the issue that humans should explore and discuss.

The basis necessities for humans to live in this world include clothing, food, housing and transportation. Materials come from two sources, one of which is Nature. This kind of materials is non-renewable, which means that they will finally be used up, such as oil, coal and all mineral resources. They were created by the Creator. Nowadays according to the researches, both with and without evidence, scientists infer that they were gradually formed during millions of years.

The question is, how could human beings, a life of less than a hundred years, give an accurate description about the things billions of years ago? It is mere speculation.

Mankind is asking for more and more materials from Nature. These non-renewable resources will gone forever once consumed. With the imminent exhaustion, an era of human survival being threatened looms large.

Mankind knows how to regenerate substances. With animals being domesticated, fishes that used to live in the sea, the river and the lake being farmed in ponds, wild grain being planted as food crops, man has these carried out in annual cycle and material increased, which constitute the non-exhaustive sources for human existence. It is the way adapted for human beings to acquire materials and survive.

Nature boasts much renewable energy. Not being utilized by man, they are gone for nothing. Such renewable sources as solar energy, wind energy and hydroenergy are clean and pollution-free, and should be adapted and utilised in no time. The exploitation of the almost-exhausted natural resources should be slowed down for the sustainable development of the future generations.

Quotes from Yuechun

Do favours and practise virtue at all times

One will be blessed if he could do favours to others timely, constantly perform charitable acts, and persevere and strive to enhance moral integrity.

22. Flora, Fauna and the Environment

The Creator made all substances in the universe, which constantly

vary along the time and space. Living species will naturally die out if they fail to keep up with the changes.

The mangrove at seaside lives by the seawater and the coastal mud. To adapt the living environment with frequent ebb and flow, hurricane and great waves, it develops the viviparous propagation to make sure its continuation. The mangrove doesn't produce seeds, but the propagules which are the "mangrove baby" with root, stem and leaves well developed. They detach from the parent tree to sea mud and then settle down. Therefore, it represents a most adaptable plant among organisms. Men have made the ocean pollution aggravated and them angrove is endangered.

The reason is that, according to scientific study, thousands species of plant have disappeared from Earth. The amount is shockingly large.

Confronted with the constant climate changes, animal species, individuals and groups, are evolving continuously, marine animals in particular. They tend to evolve gradually from aquatic to amphibian. It is probable that one day the large terrestrial animals are predominated by their counterparts from sea.

Man's continuous abuse of the material resources on Earth leads to the destruction and pollution. As a result, the good climatic environment deteriorates and the aquatic and terrestrial species become extinct from time to time. Humans have destroyed the ecological balance of the natural world, and it will seek vengeance on mankind-it is the law of nature and no one can break it. People should take measure to protect the environment in no time, which is the only solution.

Statistics reveals that scores of fauna species and over 50 flora species disappear from Earth on a daily basis. Well aware of the environmental problem, humans should take immediate actions to save every creature on Earth, videlicet to save themselves.

Quotes from Yuechun

To cultivate the righteousness

A man of integrity boasts his righteousness. Thus he can dissolve the selfish desire and prejudice. If one could conduct such proper behaviours as to be loyal to the nation and filial to parents, he must be influenced by the righteousness. In this case, he could be fair and impartial to everyone, getting rid of harmful acts. Meanwhile, he could complete apprehend the feeling of resentment, hatred and bitterness. All in all, he would gain a sudden enlightenment and has an open and carefree mood.

23. My Views on History

The time and space in which mankind exists on earth represents the evolution of human society. The time and space with all of the substances in the natural world stands for the evolution of natural substances.

The subjects on evolution of society and nature, which was recorded in the nongovernmental literature, falls into two types of knowledge-social knowledge and natural knowledge, namely, the past is history. It is wrong to comment on history by modern standards. History is both the social and natural environment in which generations come and go. The thought of Human has to adapt to the social conditions and natural conditions at that time, namely, the history then, for each generation of mankind is unexceptionally striving for survival and development. Human are writing their own history at every moment which composes the history of their family, nation and country. The whole history is the records of society and nature through the time and

space.

Acting as salutary warnings and lessons, history is passed down to future generations for reference, which helps them carry forward the achievement and avoid repeating past mistakes. By comparison and reference, they can create an even better future ahead of them.

There are two types of heritages left over by history-material and non-material, both of which are significant. Carrying forward our history is mankind's mission, while failing to do that is incalculable losses. Building on the past and forging ahead is the eternal aim of mankind.

The history is the records of individual, family, nation, region or country through time and space, which differ significantly from each other. The history in conformity with the law of heaven, humanity and things, is regarded as an honor, While history violating the law is supposed to be taken as disgrace and warning.

Against the law of heaven, humanity and things, countries wage war brutally on another for land and financial reasons, plunging people into misery and suffering.

The most abominable and hateful thing for mankind is war, while the most pathetic and pitiful thing is also the war. War is caused by human. Regardless of the scale and whether it happens between countries, nations, groups or families, wars are the blackest fragments of human history.

Whether the war breaks out between countries or within a certain one, it inevitably causes heavy casualties, economic losses and refugees. After the war, new political power emerges, which is also called the change of dynasties. All industries are beginning to revive and there comes a new era of history.

24. Out of Reason, Dictated by Disposition

Man living in this world means an individual life taking a trip in

social space. Human comes from nature where he must return. No one can be spared.

Humans are animals with intricate thinking, endowed with the wisdom to create and utilize the substances. What will run throughout a man's life are the sentiments and passions, or his disposition and habits.

Dispositiondetermines a man's fate. In family and society, man first expounds his ideology on himself, and then interacts with others' ideas via etiquette, wisdom, credibility and courage. Ideas are conveyed with one's disposition as the basis and knowledge as the manifestation of wisdom. One might either be modest, prudent and sensible, or bullying, insolent and unreasonable, which are all out of his disposition. In a word, one's destiny is decided by his disposition.

Habits determine a man's health. Clothing, food, housing, transportation, work and rest are the basic necessities as long as one is alive. People have developed the habit to start labour with sunrise and stop work at sunset ever since the ancient times.

Human life has its natural course to abide by. In this case, man shall not overly pursue such pleasures as to hangover in nightlife or sleep till late in the day all the time. The regular work and rest are the key factors for physical health. One's health is decided by his dressing, taste preference, living environment, behavioural habits, capriciousness of sentiments and passions, and so on.

Man lives in time and space, and is greatly influenced by his disposition and habits. That's why life comes out of reason but is dictated by disposition.

25. Sizing up the Situation

Humans are good at sizing up the situation.

What a man cannot chooses when he was born are his country, region, ethnic group or family. It is a magical fate, natural and predestined.

Once born, man is destined to take his life journey. Time, fate or luck, it is all the destiny that will determine one's life span, whether the life is smooth or tortuous.

Through the life, one shall never act rashly no matter how learned he is and how often he succeeds or fails. Rather, he should rather size up the situation earnestly.

Situation refers to the social trend. In each country or region, the new government will bring in the new policies just as the seasonal vegetable goes with seasonal diet. In different times, the policy, decree and regulation are determined by the one who is in power and ever change. It is the strategy.

A man should assess his current situation to adapt to the policies and decrees enforced. Like weather, policies and decrees will change in no time. Alteration may also be made even they are relatively stable. For the individual, family and small unit of a small group, any unexpected change may bring about a destructive blow on them.

A man must live in certain time and certain space. During one's lifetime, natural climate and social ethos are ever changing, which fulfils the old saying, "in nature there are unexpected storms and in life unpredictable vicissitudes." Over thousands of years, when facing natural and social transformation as well as the capriciousness between people, one would usually comment with a proverb that, "times have changed". The old saying clearly states that it is essential to seize the time and chance, which is vital for people to judge the situation. Those good at sizing up the situation enjoy high successful rate and safety rate. Otherwise obstacles will be meet everywhere, and not even a single step can be moved.

Quotes from Yuechun

Resign yourself to fate, be optimistic
in poverty and devote to work

Everybody has his own opportunity. One should be modest, grateful and cherish everything he already had in favourable circumstances; abide by the law and perform his duty, act along nature, and strive to enrich himself in adversity; be optimistic, spare no effort to work hard and wait for an opportune moment in poverty and financial straits.

26. Nationalism

Based on the reason of environment, society, nature, history and human evolution, the ethnic groups vary from each other all over the world wherever human beings in habit. These groups manifest the distinctive ethnic rules despite their difference in size. The ethnic attributes are usually distinguished from language, custom and tradition.

Countries and regions are basically composed of multiple ethnic groups, the original inhabitants and the foreign-migrated people. The original inhabitants are called the aborigines. People both immigrate from a foreign place or emigrate elsewhere. Owing to the variations in history, time and space, tremendous differences exist in the ideology and religious belief of each ethnic group. This kind of ideology is called the nationalism.

There are two types of nationalism, in a narrow sense and in a broad sense. In the multi-national countries and regions, the acts of state, externally, strengthen the national defence within its administrative boundaries; and internally, endow all the nationalities within the same administrative boundaries the rights to discuss and

formulate the national policies and plan the people's livelihood. All nationalities are equal and all the citizens enjoy equal human rights. This equality is prescribed in and realised according to the constitution, law and regulations. All the actions that violate the common interest of all ethnic groups for the interest of one's own nationality belong to the narrow nationalism. All the actions that combine the interest of one's own nationality with the common interest of all ethnic groups and take the interests of the whole into account belong to the broad nationalism. Certain nationalities blindly raise the banner of narrow nationalism to seek independence and secession, threatening the unified administration of the state. Some countries stipulate the ethnic autonomy policies in their constitution, which is kind of tolerance towards the ethnic policy. Even though, some of the nationalities fail to appreciate this, instead they seek independence and secession in the name of anarchism and narrow nationalism. This is not tolerated in any country or region.

Only through ethnic reconciliation can all the nationalities united as one, can a country be likely to prosper and attain global renown.

 ## Quotes from Yuechun

The key to goodness is sincerity

Sincerity, rather than quantity and magnitude, is most valuable when performing goodness. The kindness and goodness will come to perfection if one devotes his sincerity selflessly from the bottom of the heart without the longing for fame, profit or repay.

27. *Control the Temperament and Choose the Habits*

As man of flesh and blood, everybody has both hardness and softness in his sentiments and passions. It is a kind of adaptability for one to express his emotions normally. A man would cause big trouble if he gets mad at something that should be tolerated, would do harm to his country as well as himself if he doubts the major issues that should not be questioned. That is to say, one should be restrained when it is time he endure the disgrace in order to carry out an important mission. At the same time, he should act quickly and seize the opportunity to uphold justice and bring his talent into full play. Let go what should be let go. Yet what should never be abandoned include the national territory, national dignity, family prestige, human rights and law of nature. Not even the slightest degree of righteousness and dignity of human rights and law of nature can be given up.

Therefore, to obtain something else one must learn to give up, and to reach out with force one must first restrain himself. As the decisive display of temperament, the better it is put to use, the better one's fate will be.

Living habits lay the basis for health. The right thing one should do is to have some fun on joyous occasion, to proportionately vent the anger when facing infuriating things, to appropriately smooth away what should be anxious about; to discreetly settle what should be thought of, to swiftly deal with sorrowful events and get himself out from the shadow of fear, to convalesce after shock. Suitable tonic should be taken to nourish one's weak body. For those with interior cold, warm and hot taste food should be eaten. For those robust, attention should be paid to the balance of *yin* and *yang* as well as the gentle breathing. When heat attacks the viscera, one should consume detox drinks to relieve heatiness. In case of dryness and vexation, one should consume

food that can lubricate the bowel. For those with internal heat, the source should be traced to address the problem. All these ailments are induced by improper living habits and can only be completely cured through adjusting such habits. Each person prefers different flavours- sweet, sour, bitter, spicy and salty. Food preference is related to one's daily life, living environment, climate and physical quality. Daily routine has decisive influence on health, and daily routine is interconnected with one's diet that needs to be adjusted. As a result, imbalance would lead to diseases.

Quotes from Yuechun

Perfect morality has to be cumulated. One should constantly do good deeds, and avoid making mistakes. Once mistake is made, one should correct it immediately. One will not be able to take the money with him when he dies, except for his morality. For the peace of this life and next life, one should carry out charitable acts perfectly, big or small. of the scale. No excuse should be found for the mistakes. Persevering in this, one will go to heaven with morality after death.

On Adaptationism（Ⅱ）

A New Year Wish.

In the process of human society, sincerity and friendliness are most desired between countries, families and persons when in times of peace. Cooperation is established in terms of communication, material exchange, economic trade as well as the natural environment conservation and rational exploitation. In one word, it is the ideal for the Peace Party of Myanmar that people can live together in peace and harmony so as to accomplish a peaceful human and social environment.

One will be blessed with boundless happiness, prosperity and longevity if he could work for the world peace.

1. Behaving with integrity and working with confidence

This is a motto for everyone himself. Life is bitterly short, one hundred years merely represents slightly more than 36 thousand days. One grows stronger in childhood and weakens in old years. Not so many days are left without counting the beginning and the end of life. As a saying goes: "Life is limited and a hundred years may fly in a flash."

People come together and form different ethnic groups, nations, ranks and classes. With various levels of integrity and confidence, they lead totally different lives. The prime time of one's life for associating lies in one's youth. Therefore one has to, every day, put his own trajectory under control to live and work. Everyone should own outstanding past, grasp the ongoing moment, and hope for a brighter

future. Life comes in a full circle while "yesterday, today and tomorrow" work alternately. A one-hundred-year cycle just operates for 12 thousand days, which is rather transient.

During one's lifetime, one should behave with integrity, which is a virtue of people, and the basis on which one socializes and gets on with his pursuit. Quality is about grading. It is all about observing and evaluating whether one behaves or speaks with integrity when it comes to everyday life, like living, socializing and operating. This conclusion is drawn from time and space by men.

It is wildly seen by all how much one performs integrity. For a person of high integrity, his deeds accord with words and he can be fully trusted, so things can be done without obstructions. For one with low integrity, he cannot even set their mind in ease as for people on his own side. For someone with no integrity, everyone is afraid of him. Only those without associating or unfamiliar with such kind of people will be taken in.

Integrity is the foundation of a character, the guarantee of a success life career, and the ultimate way for people. If one does not believe in himself, he will accomplish nothing because one has to understand oneself before understanding others. Know yourself, know your enemy, and you will be invincible in every battle.

A person knows his own physical strength and intelligence the best. Act according to one's real capability will generate a good chance of success. Give full expression of one's wisdom, carry things through, and victory is within one's grasp.

Integrity is the most significant asset in one's life. Only with confidence can one's capabilities be brought into full play. A man of integrity can go anywhere anytime unobstructed.

To realize your dream and aspiration, you should assess your capabilities and then act accordingly. Work with confidence and be realistic. Only when one's confidence and realistic actions are conducted by overcoming difficulties and trekking through hard paths can his goals be achieved. Referring to social realities and details of situation developments as well as knowing yourself before knowing others, you will always win. In the case where there is a thing, even you do not believe that you can plan, act and accomplish it, you may as well leave it alone. A man with no confidence has too much fears; a man with enough confidence, on the contrary, dares to think and take actions.

Failing to keep faith in one's limited life will result in having no friend and none of his wishes will come true. Acting with no confidence is a waste of time.

2. *Common sense is more important than cultural knowledge*

To live well is the top priority of human life. As days pass by, people having or not having a good living enjoy the same amount of time, while the space they possess is vastly diversified. We started learning cultural and scientific knowledge from our adolescence with the purpose that we can lead a quality life in lifetime. Cultural knowledge is essential, no matter it is traditional Chinese cultural knowledge or that of the whole world. Through learning and utilizing knowledge, not only one's quality of living can be elevated, traditional culture of different groups can also take shape and grow into global culture. Cultural knowledge enriches human life, defines accomplishment and taste, and gives rise to human civilization.

Nevertheless, common sense is more important. Cultural knowledge is similar to oceans, while common sense resembles rivers, hundreds of which converge into an ocean. The cultural knowledge ocean of China and the world comprises countless rivers and streams of common sense.

In bread baking process, amylose in flour has become aged, thus

creating the elasticity and soft texture of bread. Study the cause and effect relationship of starch aging and bread elasticity, the staling phenomenon in which soft bread gradually turns hard and the grasp the time, rate and temperature of staling generate baking knowledge.

Drink more tomato soup, boiled water or diluted saline in summer. Yogurt can relieve hangover's anxiety. Honey and leek taken together will cause food poisoning and fish cannot be stored for too long. These sorts of everyday knowledge come in great variety. Many scientists and writers learned and discovered, studied and summarized findings and drew conclusions from their daily life.

For an individual with good common sense, the fact that he has not received any proper schooling will not hinder him from becoming an educated person. Someone who could not write his own name grew into maestro all the same, for example Huineng, the Sixth Patriarch of Zen, was the greatest master of Buddhist philosophy.

If rice is not thoroughly cooked, use chopsticks to poke holes in the rice to the bottom of the pot and pour in a little yellow wine and stew again. For perfect scrambled eggs: crack eggs into a bowl, add a little lukewarm water and whisk thoroughly. Put oil into frying pan and then pour in the eggs and stir. Put in a few drops of wine when stirring to produce softer scrambled eggs. Those who eat them will be highly impressed. One who masters a skill or a unique craftsmanship is proficient in a particular field. He can lead a well-off and plentiful life.

One can live without cultural knowledge, but not without common sense. One must live in normality.

3. Facing the Capricious Life with the Ordinary Mentality

In most people's life, one has to go through three stages that being born, growing up and dying. This from-life-to-death process varies for different individual. Some enjoy longevity, while some have a short

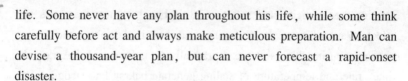

life. Some never have any plan throughout his life, while some think carefully before act and always make meticulous preparation. Man can devise a thousand-year plan, but can never forecast a rapid-onset disaster.

In order to trace the past, anticipate the future and understand the present, one has to upgrade and accumulate the experience, common sense, and cultural knowledge, upon which his talents and skills develop. Mistake will be made in words and deeds if one is not good at computation. Mathematics, a major subject at school, aims to cultivate people's arithmetic ability.

Any mathematic question can be precisely calculated. Life, similar to a computer or a star, has the default programmes or fixed orbit to follow. Life, with the established rules, can be calculated precisely and its value can be measured to several decimal places.

However, we can by no means foretell the length of human life. Life is the reproductive and transformative process of the cell and the organism, which include metabolism, growing, genetic variation, and the process of adaptation by selection. This process is pre-decided by the Creator and "programmer", while people, the created, are not told. Therefore, in the Gospel of Matthew, it reads, "Seeing ye shall see, and shall not perceive". Owing to the incomprehension, natural and man-made disasters are encountered, thus endowing life selection with significance. With the designated name, the clans are created; with the common practice, the social conventions are established, and with the social agreement, the laws and regulations are made in the country.

Each has his experience and destiny. Man proposes, God disposes. The meaning of life is to find oneself. The ancient people compared the course of life to the changing process of icing or burning-Ice melts into water and things are burned into ashes. Life is capricious, hence meaningful.

According to Buddhism, all worldly things are transient. *Diamond Sutra* says, "The mind or thought of the past, present, and future cannot be held fast; the past is gone, the future not arrived, the present does not stay." Transiency means the cycle of life and death, and from where the meaning of life emerges. It is transiency and capriciousness that offer hope to those subjecting to different forms of miseries. Hence, life may be planned but is dictated by fate. In this case, one shall neither make importunate demand nor be lazy.

A good mentality is essential for a man to be assiduous and get along well with life, which includes tolerance, a sense of balance, self-respect and self-confidence. Mentality is the deciding factor for fate. One with the bad mentality will become impatient when encountering difficulty, thus making things worse. Good mentality may not guarantee success, but it can help people well embrace the present life, enjoy the process, and elevate the happiness index.

The good mentality, in essence, refers to the ordinary mentality. Ordinary means behaving properly and having a balanced mind. Not be disrupted by confusion and keep things in order. Bluntly, one should adopt the middle course, neither following the trend blindly nor departing from established practices. An abnormal mind will cause the failure, so an ordinary mentality must be maintained.

4. Virtuousness breeds Easiness

Ancient Greek had famous saying goes "Virtue is knowledge". And ancient Chinese further enumerated those virtues as continuously striving for self-improvement, practicing the social commitment, being vigilant and introspective, working cautiously with order, cultivating and performing virtue and morality, posing good influence to others, being dutiful but not beyond one's authority, discussing and learning form others, etc. Anyone who is able to reach one of these virtues can be regarded as a gentleman, who can achieve significant accomplishments.

In Sima Qian's records, Huang Di cultivated virtues and boost morale. Collaborating with Yan Di, he defeated Chi You and suppressed the rebellions. In China, importance is attached to virtue and morality which are honored by the gentlemen. As Heaven keeps vigor through movement, a gentleman should unremittingly practice self-improvement. As the Earth's capacity is to hold, a gentleman should constantly cultivate virtue to shoulder the world. If one holds the virtue of commitment, he is endowed with the adaptability, a virtue of the utmost importance.

Commitment and tolerance are what man has learnt from the nature. Anyone, poor or rich, superior or inferior, can step on the earth. This noble quality is regarded as being magnanimous, a neutral attitude neither positive nor negative. Trodden by a multitude of people, the earth manifests its indomitable quality and becomes the support for the mass. If man is a piece of iron, earth must be the magnet. No one can jump up to the air without falling down eventually.

Man practices virtue and right deeds what the compass keeps the ship from getting lost at sea. Man, therefore, has the ability to foresee the future. A thin layer of frost signifies the forthcoming of icy season, in which one should dress warmly and store food for winter.

Immense earth produces strong magnetic field; virtuousness breeds easiness without restraint; do nothing irrational and everything can be done. If man can be upright, selfless, fair, broad-minded, dispassionate just like the earth, he would be hurt by nothing at all. He who longs for nothing would be asked for help by everyone.

The beauty of a man lies inside and defined by fortitude. Inner beauty and gentleness can keep pretty ladies and gifted scholars from ill fate. Even in peacetime when there is no opportunity to have military exploits, one would achieve success with the proper conduct.

A magnanimous man has the insight not only to see but also to comprehend. A committed person is well educated and knowledgeable.

He will not show off his learning and will not make a remark until the opportune moment. To the contrast, those morally defective are inevitably narrow-minded and belligerent. They would end up similar to the heavenly dragon battling at countryside, blood spilling, leaving only parts of the body.

As Huang Di ascended the throne of all tribes with the virtue and inspiration, a man of virtue and morality would be outstanding and admired by all. As the spirit of endeavoring for excellence, the unremittingly striving for self-improvement and commitment should be always upheld. Trouble emanates from a careless talk. Virtuousness breeds easiness. When waiting for the opportunity, if one can be self-disciplined and practice morality, he will sure to reach his goals one by one.

5. On Degradation and Self-sublimation

During one's lifetime, everyone has to face the choice between life depravity and personality sublimation. This is the condition for people to enjoy freedom. Depravity may refer to variation in or degeneration of human nature reflected in situations such as abandoning oneself to vice, committing suicide or homicide, which occurred in low-spiritedness caused by adversities including illness-induced physical suffering, alcohol or drug abuse.

For example, some young people developed melancholia because of loving frustration in their growth period. They were then reduced to shower peepers, or committing adultery, visiting prostitute, using drugs, wounding others or suicide. Ultimately, not treasuring their own life, they drowned themselves in a river, committed homicide or other crimes. Unlike humans, animals do not boast rationality or freedom. They are manipulated by their innate survival instinct. They live for ecological balance, neither depravity nor sublimation is involved.

Ego refers to the independence and consciousness of your own

identity, or the initiative, as well as each individual's character, interest and viewpoint. Plainly put, life is primarily controlled by one's established concepts. If a certain person agrees with the remark "my father said I am hot-headed", he then engages in fighting, kills someone, gets suspended death sentence and thus having no chance to work as a criminal police officer who can make contribution. If another person approves of the remark "my teacher said I am stupid", he then collects rubbish for the next several decades, his culinary talent is thus neglected.

Self-realization of an average person is not necessarily his true self, but an evaluation of him by his teachers, parents and classmates, namely mass experience. Ego is generated after an individual managed to transcend social consciousness of the masses. Either he is paranoid and depraved or he boasts a sublimated personality.

Examples of sublimation include: drying wet clothes in the sun, thinning of tungsten filament in an incandescent bulb, candle burning into ashes, camphor balls getting smaller, and melting of ice in rising temperature. It is the gradual transition of substances such as water, iron, wax and camphor from one phase into another. In the field of philosophy, it refers to motion pattern being upgraded from mechanical motion to physical motion and chemical motion.

When one's conforming personal experience or social consciousness turns into something unusual or different from that of their teacher, superior or father, ego thus comes into being. If the realization of ego targeting oneself and society tends towards evil and sin, degradation and depravity ensue. If it tends towards goodness and rightness, sublimation and transcendence follow. Degradation of an individual is similar to landslide, in which mud flows down along the terrain, carrying more and more sundries on its route. Ego at this point resembles a face being smeared with sand and covered with leaves, can no longer be seen. Sublimation is like trekking uphill with a heavy burden, the higher, the

more outstanding. In a clear and lovely atmosphere, tranquility yields transcendence and supreme good is magical.

6. On Good Deeds and Evil Doings

Good deeds are the opposite of evil doings. Doing good deeds means to perform charitable work and accumulate virtue incessantly. It is a kind of action and practice. To practise virtue, one must have his statements and actions beneficial to others.

Practising virtue was first seen in the *Book of Changes*. In the *Kun* trigram, it is said, "the family that practises virtue is sure to have abundant happiness". Practising virtue and accumulating goodness are of the same meaning here, which means that one should perform the five constant virtues (benevolence, righteousness, propriety, wisdom and fidelity), do no harm and lend a hand to others. Virtue is equivalent to such gaining as good family, school and offspring.

Practising virtue is a presentation of humane quality, a personal practice of moral teachings, a cultural tradition of self-discipline which manifested in personal words and deeds. In this society, activities for public benefit are the virtue practised by the citizens for their country.

Buddhism teaches people to practice virtue through almsgiving, morality, patience, vigour, meditation and wisdom. These six approaches help eliminate the six spiritual taints (greed, harm, anger, slackness, confusion and ignorance) for the re-emergence of one's innate temperament.

If greed is the taint of moral conduct, extreme greediness will make a person never contented. The way to get rid of this acquisitive impulse is through almsgiving. Morality, patience, vigour, meditation and wisdom help eliminate the impulse of causing harm, anger, slackness, confusion and ignorance respectively. Instead of giving a few dollars to the beggars, enhancing one's character is the key for him to authentically practise virtue.

Performing evils doings, to put it simply, refers to doing all kinds of wrongful acts. One who does evil is full of intensely wicked ideas and negative thoughts. He is vulnerable and vengeful. The man who will revenge a slight insult with outrageous act must be self-abased and envious. He has to destroy the cultured person in order to free himself from envy and hatred.

Besides vindictiveness, some people perform evil doings out of profit for which he would go all length to swindle, to steal, to hit and to kill. Some corrupt officials have so much strong avarice that he would violate the morality and abuse their power and money to keep a concubine.

The Evildoers regard the wrong as the right and never forgive. They stress their improper thoughts in the extreme and falsely mistake the absurdity as the truth, claiming that those are applicable everywhere. Consequently, evildoers rightfully carry out the bad things, even calling on others to commit crimes together.

7. On Undesirable Results

Evildoers will eventually turn extremely vicious and run into a dead end, because they go against all rules and disregard the natural and social laws. However, the natural laws coexist with the social laws and will not be changed by human will.

Nature and society are both ever-changing. Every new sovereign brings his own courtiers, and seasonal vegetable goes with seasonal menu. One hopes that all his wishes can be fulfilled, but the result is always disappointing.

Human fortunes are as unpredictable as the weather. Man often acts beyond his capability. Everything is closely bound up with the time, place and human relationship, thus nobody can get whatever he wishes for. If so, the law of nature, human society and things will no longer exist and the rules and regulations for mankind will disappear. If

man can do whatever he wants, nature and society will fall into chaos.

It is wise for a man to calm down for meditation to adjust his mood when everything goes against him.

It is advisable for a man to take the effective and feasible measure to save himself with sense and coolness when encountering natural or man-made disaster.

It is the high time for a man to face the problems with courage and senses when violating the laws and regulations. Any avoidance and escape will make him repeat his mistake, even do something wrong desperately. The reversible error would eventually become an irreversible one.

One will face to face with so many unsatisfactory situations in his life. Yet, man must act within the limit of social reality and natural laws. As the old saying goes, "Man proposes, God disposes."

8. To Follow the Natural Laws and Social Trends

The word "Nature" in primary school textbook refers to the natural world which is the empirical research target of today's physic. In other words, it is the material world, or the whole universe, encompassing the tiny neutrino to the colossal galaxy. It also includes the life in the general sense. If someone is described as dressing up in an unnatural way, it means that his original features or temperament has been concealed. Nature, for most of the time, refers to the "natural environment" (climate and geology, etc.) or the wilderness without human intervention (wild animals, rocks, forests, beaches, underground mineral and energy resources, etc.) It is a word used to differentiate the above from the artificialities such as garden and commodity.

Law must be mentioned when associating with nature. Nature has its own law from which the social law is derived. Law is the superordinate of rule, regulation and principle. Just like the undressedup face and the undiscovered or un-mined mineral deposits, it is the innate attribute of the natural object and will not chance with man's will. Law cannot be created, changed or eliminated. Although water can be pumped uphill to build a reservoir so as to irrigate highland area, it will always flow downhill without external force.

In Chinese language, nature and law can be expressed in one word "Dao". "Dao" is equivalent to deity, law, truth, spiritual master, and the universe. "Dao" was originally found as the very first word of the first sentence of the first chapter in *Tao Te Ching*, a Taoist classic. It refers to the so-called "ultimate truth" which can be talked about but what talked about cannot be regarded as the truth. Man cannot specify the essence of Dao. As man talking about a table, what described is merely the aspect they have already known about.

Dao possesses divinity, giving rise to myriad things. It is also a ubiquitous principle which must be adhered to by man, earth and heaven. "Dao", for ordinary people, only means road or reason, without the implication of practising Taoism to get rid of sentiments and passions. The ancient people often interconnected Dao with goodness, as if it was the railway track on which the train of human virtue moved.

Since the law of nature lasts forever, man must always adapt to it, rather than change it, even with slightest notion. It is the social trends (or popular culture, especially modern culture) that can be followed, leaded and changed by mankind. The typical feature of modern culture is the increasing coarseness. With the development of industrial technology, popular culture was created in the interaction between public taste and media industries. However, it will be fashionable only at a specific time and place.

The modern industry and commerce have accelerated the emergence of new trends. In ancient times, something would remain fashionable for hundreds or even thousands years; nowadays, only a few or ten-odd years. Popular culture is generally rather shallow, since

profundity cannot coexist with popularity. Man should adapt to social trends, but never depart from the classics and rebel against orthodoxy.

9. Courtliness, Responsibility and Evilness are all born in mind

Courtliness and responsibility among the man's four principles do not refer to etiquette in the association with people. Manner and appearance can be prettified, whereas courtliness and responsibility cannot be disguised. Mencius once said that courtliness is the feeling of modesty and complaisance; responsibility is the feeling of shame and dislike. Human devoid of courtliness and responsibility is not a real man, an evildoer, worse than a beast. Without courtliness and responsibility, a man without would do harm to the society and an official would bring about misery to the people and the country. In one word, the ignorance of courtliness and responsibility would make men and women behave shamefully, inhumanely and without benevolence.

There is an anecdote about Su Shi playing pranks on Fo Yin, the Zen Master. Su said that Fo Yin looked like a pile of cow dung, while Fo Yin claimed that Su resembled Buddha. Why did the two have so different opinions? Because they had different hearts. Su was aggressive, so he compared Fo Yin to cow dung, while Fo Yin was modest, so he compared Su to Buddha. The metaphor might not be appropriate, but kindness was involved in Fo Yin's words and he requited evil with good.

According to Confucianism, humanity leads courtliness, responsibility and wisdom to jointly manifest man's benevolence. Courtliness springs from heart, and it makes one behave properly. Only with courtliness at heart can one put courtliness into practice. A well-dressed man may also behave rudely and resort to violence in times of disputes.

In December 2012, a campus shooting occurred at Sandy Hook Elementary School, Connecticut, U. S. A. , in which 20 children were killed. The tragedy once again triggered the debate over gun control. 250 millions firearms are privately owned in the US. If mass incidents took place there, what would happen? How many gunfights will there be when civilian ownership of firearms becomes the self-defence right and Christ worship turns into a custom and courtesy.

Su Shi had already deviated from the principle of the gentleman and the learnt to differentiate between right and wrong when humiliating Fo Yin with the cow dung comparison. He had been irrational and abused others. Had Su been provoked, scolded or even slapped by Fo Yin, he might have committed wrongful acts. In modern society, many criminal cases are triggered by verbal dispute. Evil arises from heart, pushing people to be rude and commit crimes.

Troubles come out of careless talk and officious actions. What is evil is not the feudal society, but the deliberate unconventionality. It is easy to dodge an open attack but difficult to escape from a malicious and clandestine one. With the criminal intent, wine bottle, rice bowl or fist can be used to kill. Even the most robust security system cannot curb man's sinful nature of doing evil. Compassion shrinks as the legal framework grows sounder. Man would become a chessman if the compassion is systemised. Man's sinful acts are prompted by the sinful nature of lacking in moral sense. Both the sinful nature and act are villainous.

Those devoid of benevolence and belief are most dangerous. The sense of courtliness and responsibility comprising modesty, complaisance, and shamefulness is man's inherent virtue. Without it, manner and appearance are just the speciosity, being the package of all kinds of evil. It is difficult to be enlightened and become a Buddha, maintaining benevolence as its key. Through courtliness and responsibility, the dissension can thus be diminished and ultimately resolved. The mind is bodhi: enlightenment, giving up and carefree.

10. Heaven Secrets Shall Not Be Divulged Casually

Heaven Secrets, literally, are the confidential information known only to heaven. It is related to natural divine law in Taoism and Buddhist doctrine and is the alternative expression of the Confucian law of nature, justice of nature and the will of heaven. All military strategies, like Zhuge Liang's clever schemes, belong to the Heaven Secret. Doctrines of gods, Buddhism, Taoism and Confucianism unexceptionally comprise mysteries of heaven.

Heaven Secrets can be described as the confidential and ultimate essence of knowledge. Be it the philosopher's contemplation or celestial being's meditation, Classical quotations or essays that have been handed down to the later generations convey meanings with figure of speech so as to conceal wisdom between lines. This allows people to perceive, to memorize, and then with the enhancement of common sense and sublimation of moral conduct, to realise and to appreciate its significance. To comprehend Heaven Secret, association is a must. One has to treat the world with reason, not to be confused by personal feeling.

Heaven Secrets contain the essence of wisdom. Wisdom allows one to profoundly understand man, events, things, society, universe, present, past and future, and enable him to ponder on, analyse and pursue the truth of gods, Buddhism, Taoism and Confucianism. With wisdom, man would achieve a natural success. People rarely discover the Heaven Secret. They would get lost in the ocean of knowledge and miss the real wisdom.

The impurity in knowledge would be out-of-date in a little while, but yet attractive due to the remarkable look. The experts and scholars that addicted in this would be trapped in offices and laboratories, with the brains imprisoned. As a matter of fact, only virtue can release them. Since essence is the best and the most important, it is said that "the essence should be assimilate and the dregs rejected". However, few can actually accomplish it.

The essence of wisdom in Heaven Secret is the splendour and glory of doctrines embraced by deities, Buddhism, Taoism and Confucianism. It resembles the vitality of the five viscera and the essence of the sun and moon. Therefore, to learn the Heaven Secret, one must get rid of the inner perversity and evilness in care the brain is invaded and injured by them. Socrates once said virtue is knowledge. Confucians maintain that humanity, righteousness and courtliness lead the wisdom. The significance is that one should absorb the essence for self-improvement by virtue of his noble character.

People of noble character stand out of such political disputes as feudalism and democracy. Leading a hermitic life, they practice the benevolence silently. In places where pleasure seekers can only see the beautiful scenery, they can discover the intelligence of the world as well as the essence of the sun and moon with their all-seeing eyes.

Heaven Secrets are enlightened, abstruse and definite and shall not be divulged casually. An egg can never be hatched if poking a tiny hole into the shell. Similarly, to reveal the Heaven Secret, opportunity must be waited and divine providence be followed.

11. On vanity and pragmatism

Human society is full of menace, which hinges on whether it is true or false. All the false, including untrue statements, false incidents, fake objects, pretended affections and phony righteousness, continually breeds maliciousness. Serious falsity gives rise to grave sins, prolonged falsity has enduring influence and the larger the extent of falsity is, the larger range will be harmed — one is directly proportional to the other. Insincerity makes couples and friends turn into enemies, and eventually go their separate ways, or in worse cases, it makes people inflict hurt on families or neighbors and leads to disaster.

Vanity makes efforts go in vain, while pragmatism brings actual effects. Vanity is an excessive and twisted self-respect, a kind of defect of personality pursuing superficiality, and an emotion trying to obtain honor and attract wide attention. Abnormal behaviors include blind comparison, craving for grandeur, giving undue importance to others' comments, insatiable passion for self-expression, and intense jealousy.

Vanity, commonly known as face, has a most vivid explanation that one slaps his face until it's swollen in an effort to look imposing. To show off their power and influence, ancient court functionaries rode in sedan chair with eight carriers and sounded the gongs to clear the way, which is driven by vanity. Out of mere vanity, man may commit crimes – cheating and even stealing. Pretending to be rich, they may treat others to feast, although they will fall into financial straits for the following several months. In addition, they may get into trouble because of borrowing celebrity's title to impress people and get involved in law cases.

Man relies on integrity to get on in the world and on self-confidence to work. Self-reliance is most reliable. Craving for Vanity, one decorated with appearance, knowledge and property would merely show his arrogance, eventually losing all friends and being isolated. Craving for commendation and praise, one would employ dishonest approaches to protect his self-esteem. When falsity is exposed ultimately, everything goes wrong and all yearnings end up in nothing.

Man seeks superficial honor or false glory out of dependency and insufficient self-confidence. One wants to rely on others for success in work, hopes to take shortcuts to get favorable results, and longs to reap without sowing. All of this usually stems from inappropriate upbringing by parents in one's childhood, which results in children's inferiority on account of weak capabilities.

Yet, the key for one to get somewhere is adopting a pragmatic approach. Being pragmatic is to be realistic. Due to the practical efforts of collecting folk prescriptions from various places and having them verified, Li Shizhen managed to complete the book Compendium of Materia Medica.

No matter it is an agricultural, nomadic or merchant culture, if a nation can survive for five centuries in the age of civilization, its traditional culture must have nurtured pragmatism. Confucius said to his disciples, "Don't pretend to know what you don't know", which is just the doctrine of pragmatism.

The spirits of Confucian teachings is that eminent person does not pursue a glamorous facade and honourable man strives for pragmatism. Do not go after false reputation and what replenishes one's heart is a mind of pragmatism. Keep in mind that pay attention to reality, be a doer, reject falsity, and refuse to fantasise. One can make it, if he makes friends in a down-to-earth way. A skyscraper is built from the ground, and success is the result of accumulation. Pragmatism has become the bedrock of Chinese traditional virtues and of the civilisation extending five thousand years.

12. On Rights, Consciousness and Life

Human beings die in pursuit of wealth while birds die in pursuit of food. The proverb states disastrous consequences for things overdone. Although wealth can improve living standards, men are not supposed to be greedy for money, which is incorrect and abnormal. The correct and normal attitude is that no matter how high your status is, you should maintain a mentality of the commons when associating with people; no matter how wealthy you are, live in accordance with the virtues practised by the poor; and do not waste food, natural resources or useful belongings. Despite high status and enormous wealth, a virtuous man would still preserve the mentality of the commons and lead a hardworking, thrifty, plain and honest life.

If someone compares human to a computer, what he means is that

human being has default programmes, that is, the individual characters determined by genes. Evolution of the species remains forever a subjective idea and philosophical inference. Thinking can evolve, but not species. Dogs do not eat cow dung and monkeys cannot turn into men.

During the overthrow of tyrant Zhou of Shang Dynasty, King Wu, the supreme commander of the punitive expedition, vowed when meeting with vassals to form an alliance, "Only the heavens and earth are the parents of all living things and only man is the paragon of all creatures". These words were said not out of human's outrageous arrogance, but based on the fact that man is able to manage and subdue all things on earth. Meanwhile, King Wu explained the reason for this military rebellion by this statement, which is not an act of treason, but an operation responding to the will of heaven and people, complying with the divine providence, and reviving the good administration.

Revolution is not revolt, which does not mean to kill. The significance of revolution lies in putting an end to despotic rule and defending life. Human life is of utmost concern and should never be taken away casually. Therefore, one of the works in Yuan-dynasty Drama reads as follows, "Human life is beyond value, so culprit or accomplice makes no difference." What it implies is that one who kills an innocent person has to pay the forfeit of his life or to be severely punished.

In history, whether a religion is a legitimate faith or an evil cult is judged by its doctrines and whether a school of thought is upright or crooked is judged by its views. Any religion or school of thought that teaches followers to be decent, to eradicate evil and do good, to care for others, and defend human life is legitimate or upright, while the opposite that teaches followers to be immoral, to invert right and wrong, to kill or rob, and to treat human life as worthless is evil or crooked.

Evil cult and crooked views preach violence, instigate hatred and terrorism, and deceive or force others to be wicked, which is renegade and against the law of nature as well as common sense. Legitimate religion and upright views teach followers to respect deities, show filial piety to parents, help others and coexist peacefully, guiding people to abide by the law of nature, to behave in a down-to-earth way in accordance with common sense, and to face difficulties with courage. If one's doom is sealed, he is supposed to accept it rationally. One who survives a calamity would be blessed subsequently.

Rationality is the guardian angel of life. Philosophers regard human beings as political and rational animals, guiding people to believe in god and go back to heaven. Sages regard human beings as the paragon of the whole Creation, teaching people to get on in the world with spirituality, help others, choose the right path and follow it, and accept all good advice.

With the story of hesitating to pelt a rat for fear of smashing the dishes beside it, Jia Yi persuaded the emperor not to torture court ministers, so as to preserve the regal dignity. Nowadays, the same story can still be used to advise people not to crave for money so as to avoid troubles and cherish precious life. Seeking nothing but profit, those selling fake wine for money may take away the lives of innocent people.

13. On Development

Development means evolution and upgrade. Development of the country, family or nation, big or small, without exception, would fall into the following categories, 1. too politicised and short-lived; 2. civilised management for long-term peace and stability.

Political entities in ancient Babylon, Egypt, India and Aegean area changed constantly, and their partial shadows only can be found in mythology and archaeology. The "civil politics" we mention today

was defined by Sun Yat-sen as "management of everybody's affairs", which have developed into the three principles of Nationalism, Democracy and People's Livelihood. His principles had been put into practice in mainland for only two decades, while Chinese ancient political ruling method of "world for all" had endured for five millennium ever since the legendary emperors Yan and Huang to the Qing Dynasty.

According to ancient books such as the *Book of History*, Chinese monarchy believed that if the ruling method was correct, the country would be run well; if graces reached down to all communities, people would live in peace and work happily. Leading the principal ministers, monarchs ruled the country with the political and ethical ideology that "people are more important than the sovereign". Before the Western Zhou Dynasty, emperors and vassals had to cultivate themselves so as to undertake the heavenly mandate to carry out the good governance. If the emperor enforced the evil policies, he would be overthrown in the revolution by the vassals who upheld the benevolent rule.

This is what called ruling by virtue in today's society. It was not just in word, but in the actual implementation in every aspect of daily life. Cultivation of mind tops the agenda for ruling a country. From the higher level to the grassroots, self-discipline was advocated and controlled by the public opinion. This kind of education-oriented flexible management had provided freedom and civilisation with plenty of leeway. Innovate at the right time will push forward the development of the society.

A civil governance will last long with the strong military power as its backing. For example, it is said that the Shang Dynasty had lasted for 510 year, going through 31 cultivated emperors in 17 generations. In western civilization, military power had played a leading role in its urbanisation and citizenization. Military force was used to conquer the foreign states and transform them with the urban civil life style directly.

The original civilization must be destroyed in the first place and then it would be rebuilt as slavery or serf system. In this process, different ruling modes including aristocracy, republic, democracy, and oligarchy were put to test. If all of them failed, the autocratic monarchy would come into effect. However, this kind of civilisation, characterized as military colonial conquest followed by the rule of law, would last no more than 500 years.

Throughout the five millennia of traditional Chinese civilization, military have all along been the backup force. It has taken such a development path as ruling by virtues for the overall peace and civilization. That is, scholars show their power with their works full of righteousness and literary grace. The rules rule by virtues, culture and education. Military force is prepared but seldom or never used. The people practice the filial piety and self-disciplinary so as to live in peace and work happily.

14. Man's Three Qualities to Demonstrate

First of all, one should demonstrate his cultural attainment.

Are you well educated? When asked such a question, does an intellectual examine himself rationally or be ashamed into anger? Are you to be patriotic? As to the violent behaviour in the demonstration on the dispute over the sovereignty of the Diaoyu Islands, it is believed that few can probe into its source with parents at home, can trace back to such incidents as burning house and beating diplomats during the march of May Fourth Movement. With many things being known, it is claimed that it is the evolution to satirize when sympathy should be shown and cheer when condemnation is needed, and claim that this represents evolution.

If the mind evolution is not the advancement of rationality but the fall into the mental slavery, happiness must be faraway and unattainable. In 1950, national literacy rate was only 9%. Yet, at least

95 percent of the people would be willing to help others, like directing the way with a smiling face and showing the way voluntarily. Nowadays, the literacy rate has risen to over 90%, but only less than 1% will stay calm if his foot is stepped on. It is not rarely seen that people with high academic qualifications walk vulgarly, squat everywhere and swear others. Some of them are even the professors of famous universities, bragging about being descendants of notable families.

In the second place, one should demonstrate his enterprising spirit.

Today's utilitarian culture and education have deviated from the traditional values. The doctrines of striving continuously for self-improvement and cultivating virtues to practice the social commitment are no longer prevailing. Pursuing high GDP as the top priority, people are misled by the following: only Official position and money can endow a man a meaningful life. People would seize every opportunity and spear no efforts to achieve career success and become famous. In this way, the persons of virtues, erudition, low profile and refinement are seldom seen.

Mencius said, "He who know what to give up will make great achievement." And Mencius practised what he had preached, and was revered as the second sage after Confucius by Confucian scholars of the later generations. The book *Mencius* has been passed down through the ages, but still fresh and brilliant as ever. This is in itself a great achievement. If Mencius had compromised his principles to work as prime minister or senior official for a vassal, the famous quote that "people are more important than the sovereign" and *Mencius*, the classic, would not have come into being. Mencius' teachings have subtle but increasing influence, and his enterprising spirit is in urgent need to revive at present.

Thirdly, one should demonstrate his willpower.

Bruce Lee had a strong and awesome figure. He managed to bring the techniques of free combat into full play. He developed his strength at the cost of health and lived only for 32 years. According to Mencius, what can overthrow the tyranny is not the physical strength, but the unshaken, uncorrupted and unyielding willpower.

15. On Being Strong and Weak

There was one popular article on Internet written by a 15-year-old junior school student in 2006, announcing that there is no distinction between what is right and what is wrong, but what is strong and what is weak. Judging from the chaotic phenomena inside and outside junior high school, he concluded with limited vision, hearing and report that one should be worldly wise and make oneself safe, meanwhile make remitting efforts to make oneself strong quietly. Try to be stronger than everything else!

The severance that he had seen was as follows: the 50cm-long fruit knife was taken into the dormitory; buglers robbed and blackmailed students; teachers just had no courage to restrain the cut-in-line phenomenon; the one who was crueller would be the winner in the school fights. Actually numerous that kind of phenomena had existed. And his words just mixed with so much surmise. When he said that teachers had no courage to do that, he was just biased with no analysis of the effect to people's inner hearts of this kind of society.

The severance that he had heard was also as follows: there would be a big distinction whether you have power or not; dressing too dazzling would die early; famous heroes can not outrun the big brother of sinister gang. And all these were just gossip from parrot people and the wrongly informed information. We can use these public words to condemn the evil spirit, but we are not supposed to find excuse for cowards. Sima Guang and Wang Shouren knew about the ancient common saying before 10 years old. These sayings were examining self thrice a day, the world belongs to all, the benevolent loves others, not

decline to shoulder a responsibility, die to achieve virtue, do what by humanity and duty, and using peaceful means before resorting to force, know black from white. But this student did not know that, just like the coal was used up under the city of Taiyuan.

And students just blindly accepted these warnings as follows: The outstanding usually bear the brunt of attack; drawing out a sword to help but find it was flat. And when you were in trouble, your friends were just onlookers. They just cast you aside when you have served your purpose. Then students did not learn any useful knowledge and gained nothing at school. What was the real weakness was that you did not doubt prejudice or have self-identity.

Triad members and policemen shield each other which causes that there is no (legal) equality in this world, but officials shielding one another. Taking bribes is inevitable. It is forever true that winners take all. Words like this, "in this world", seems that learning physics and chemistry is only for examination purposes. Originally, a boy who is 15 years old could be a hero. Now, he is so week and easy to float westward following "the balloon of power". In his two-thousand-word article, there is no single word about benevolence, righteousness or propriety. Absolutely, he is not a wise man.

"Even if you wanted to become a hero, you must be a hero unknown to the public; if you want to report the bad things, you are supposed to do it secretly. And what you should learn are not only to protect yourself, but also take care of your families' safety", the person in power said weakly. Could we achieve these two dreams of being a merchant and a thief at the same time?

16. On Being Poor and Rich

Poor and rich are not equivalent to weak and strong. Poor is not necessarily weak, while rich is not necessarily strong, both in terms of body or mind.

What fearful is not being poor with little money and distress life, but the self-humiliation caused by poverty. With this inferior complex, one would be jealous of the rich and their children and be resentful at the unfairness in his fate. Certain people are born with good destiny in which success can be easily attained without hardworking, while the poor are born in a slum or a destitute peasant's family in which they have to money to access to higher education and engage in farming all the life … The impoverishment drives them to revolt. They have no choice but take desperate action and often commit crimes.

There are reports about the poor people being treated unfairly. For instance, the Urban Management officers beat a poor old woman who kept a stall on the roadside to death. Two persons killed in a car accident, damages paid to the poor peasant girl was less than half of the amount paid to the other, a city dweller. People of the same conditions are treated unequally. The notion that "poverty gives rise to a desire for change" has been distorted. The poor were incited to rise in revolt, but their descendants still suffer from poverty, which means the process is totally meaningless. What fears the most of being poor is the loss of will and moral integrity. Frustrated by poverty, one would be subjected to either death or starvation.

There will not be any social class barrier between the rich and poor as long as the mobility of residence registration and occupation is ensured. One, who is now poor, does not lose righteousness and morality. It is the foundation of affluence. He will get rich when there is the opportunity. Old yet strong, poor yet firm, he who sticks to the path of virtue will eventually change his poor condition. What important is that the poor man should not yield to the poverty, but to work even harder and become outstanding.

Different form the poor natural environment which is objective and unchangeable, a man is able to change his destitute situation as long as he keeps the moral integrity and has the willpower. Ouyang Xiu,

scholar in the Song Dynasty, poverty-stricken, once could not afford the pen, paper or books. However, he had a noble character and the willing to learn. He wrote on sand with a reed and, read the transcript of the borrowed books. At the age of 23, he finally passed the imperial examination and became successful.

Undoubtedly, poverty is not an ultimate state, rather it is just the current situation or what had been left behind by the previous generations, so being poor is not coming to a dead end. Assiduous practice makes perfection; misery nurtures brilliance. Heaven rewards the diligent; those destitute but talented just have to wait for an opportune moment. It is advisable for the poor to make use of each favourable condition to attain to affluence.

Some say that human relationship is money and a billionaire can let his son go unpunished by paying money. These are one-sided words of indignation. Poverty is temporary, so is wealth. One's being rich wouldn't fleet very soon if he was lack of the virtue and morality. The rich, departing from the right path, would seek power and indulge in luxury and extravagance. Their good times would not last long. Poverty will end if the poor endeavour with willpower. Wealth will last for long if the rich act with moral integrity. He who can conduct himself with courtliness and responsibility will enjoy the most glorious life.

17. On Courtliness, Responsibility, Wisdom, Fidelity and Courage

Human ideology is primarily manifested in courtliness. Of the four virtues depicted by Mencius, namely "benevolence, responsibility, courtliness, and wisdom", benevolence and wisdom are innate qualities, which can be faked. Responsibility devoid of courtliness is unnatural. Only courtliness is universal, which can be seen between monarch and subjects, parents and children, teachers and students, the older and the younger, neighbours, as well as at workplace …

Courtliness between people brings along order which serves the base of a harmonious society. Courtliness is the cornerstone and source of rules and regulations, the cradle of human emotions. Without courtliness, benevolence, responsibility and wisdom will no longer exist.

Responsibility is a human action in which personal loyalty and obligation must be carried out. According to human affection, strong measures would be taken only after courteous and humane ones fail. Affection comes up naturally after the conventional courtliness. The faked filial piety could be recognised through the discourteousness. Responsibility precedes behaviour. The quality of responsibility is determined by the nature of sentiment behind etiquette determines. The fine sentiment comes out of mentality and the grand responsibility out of action. A responsible behaviour is the embodiment of nobility. Heroes and martyrs represent the zenith of responsibility carried out.

Wisdom is knowledge like sunlight. Although man's IQ is inborn, it has to be accumulated gradually over the years-development to be exact. Man constantly draws lessons from practice. In the evolution of human mind, man, in the ever-changing world, builds up the common sense, develops the culture knowledge and accepts the faith within the social and natural environment. In this process, intelligence is sublimated into wisdom. The wisdom is either brilliant or significant, creating miracles on earth and recorded in history forever.

Fidelity is the pillar on which mankind depends to behave and cope with things. It encompasses integrity which refers to the way one treats people and handles things, as well as the self-confidence which refers to how one conducts oneself. To succeed, one has to uphold both integrity and self-confidence all the time. A man of integrity can make lots of friends. If he could show kindness to others, numerous good karmas would come, thereby making him infinitely resourceful. Working with self-confidence, having the courage to face difficulties, sticking to the right way despite the destined calamity, and getting rid of the evilness

in character, one would turn failure into the opportunity of success and enjoy the happiness.

Courage is the fulfilment of man's courtliness, responsibility, wisdom and fidelity. One must be with the courage to examine the people and matters he faces, to detest the evil and to loves the kind to the end. A brave have the courage to love what he adores and to hatred what he resents. Only the brave man could become a real hero. A man of noble character who knows precisely whom or what to love or hate must have the courage to choose and follow what is right.

Courtliness, responsibility, wisdom, fidelity and courage make the mental resources for those who are truly benevolent, righteous, wise, devoted and brave.

18. Envy Harms Both Others and Oneself

Envy is composed of suspicion and jealousy, which is very abnormal, harming both others and oneself.

Life is capricious, but one's mind must be normal, which serves as a social norm. Human is a creature of seven sentiments and six passions. The former seven kinds of emotions include joy, anger, anxiety, thought, fear, and fright, while the latter refers to six physical conditions comprising dampness, pathogenic cold, sthenic symptoms, heat, dryness, and fire. Six passions, which give rise to the seven sentiments, are the biological perceptions of human body. An appropriate degree of them is required, while excessiveness will lead to illness.

Desire is shared by both men and animals, which is actually a state of feeling and the cause of it. Owing to rationality, human enjoys selfhood and freedom, and have the chance to choose a living style besides natural instincts. Because of spirituality, man can be awoken to the right way from the code of morals encompassing the law of nature, humanity, and things. If one is able to comply with the law and modify

his behavior, he can attain the truth while observing the world.

If one could be reasonable and genial when associating with others, he is able to look upon others' growth, improvement and success with a balanced mind, and sincerely extend his congratulations. If that party happens to be his relatives or friends, it is a sheer joy for celebrating and sharing. If one's mentality is abnormal or unbalanced, envy will emerge. Man should never be envious. It is impossible for those who are jealous to open up one's own career and make great achievements.

An envious mind would, for no reason at all, be suspicious of others doing something bad to him. When witnessing other's success, he would nurse a grievance and suffer from mental imbalance. One has to query himself, clarify the doubts in his thought through contemplation, and guide his own behaviour with clear cognition. A doubt without cause or reason is unfounded. It is totally wrong to make wild guesses casually, and always have negative thoughts over other's words and deeds. The whole envious movement of a person almost begins with groundless suspicion and jealousy behind a dignified facade.

A domineering or indecisive person is most envious. One who lacks the senses of propriety, righteousness, integrity and honour has an unbalanced mind, and is easy to be jealous and suspicious of person at any age, whether male or female. A jealous mind would inevitably take pleasure in others' misfortune, while in the eyes of those being envied, he is sick with jealousy. When misery comes to those lucky people, he will get even more pleasure, which is a representation of an abnormal mind.

Suspicion at heart will undoubtedly nurture jealousy. Once jealousy grows out of hand, it will unavoidably bring evil consequences that should not emerge, or even results in massive bloodshed. Throughout history, cases that began with envy and developed into war, poisoning or murdering plot had been innumerable in every dynasty, era or year, which made the way to survive and living gradually changed.

19. Ways of Living

The way of life refers to one's way to get on in the world and socialize with others, while the way of living means one's lifestyle, including food, clothing, housing and transportation.

Nowadays, the way to get on in the world is regarded as an interpersonal communication skill for getting along with people and associating with others, a kind of technique that can be taught. Yet it is not that superficial. The way one gets on in the world and associates with people is the foundation upon which man conducts himself. It is the approach to adapting to the natural environment and integrating into society. Demonstrating human virtues including benevolence, righteousness, propriety, wisdom, fidelity, loyalty, courage and honour defines the morality for man to get on in the world, which distinguishes humans from animals.

In early days of human civilization, the way of getting on in the world was mainly manifested by capable and honorable man. Honorable men valued righteousness and would not to be shaken by poverty or submit to force, based on which moral conducts formed, such as sticking to reciprocity, being refined, keeping promises, and being willing to die a martyr, and only those who could accomplish all of the above were considered real men. As time went on, people were becoming more and more worldly-wise, and the way of getting on in the world gradually degenerated into political and social association, which emphasized skills. For instance, Su Shi of the Song Dynasty was demoted due to his incompetence at toadying, while He Shen of the Qing Dynasty got promoted because he was good at pleasing Emperor Qianlong.

The way of living is concerning the basic necessities of one's life, no matter whether he is an honourable man or a villain, noble or ordinary, of high or low moral. Yet there will be some differences under different natural environment, such as diversities in geographical and climatic conditions. Dissimilarities can be found in terms of clothing, food, residence and transportation in ethnic groups of temperate zone and tropical area.

In modern society, the way of living has turned into an art for the public to achieve success and happiness, relating to interests and feelings. Following the demise of hereditary aristocracy and moral conduct no longer being popularly advocated, people have been decreasingly worried about death, especially at the early age. Their main concern is life and living, which turns out to be the social trend and a consequence of popular culture. Discussion topics about life and living prevail, which include sincerity, love, gender, time, anger, fear, patience, compliance, forgiveness and happiness.

The hero's way of living is not widespread. However, everyone has to think about issues of clothing, food, housing and transportation, which serve as human's basic necessities. Our particular attention to clothing, food, housing and transportation has led to social development. Cloth coupon, food stamp, cottage, dirt road and the like man-made have been of the past.

Following the living way of the sage and honorable men for generations, Chinese have been moving forward, which has turned out to be our root. Our existence has developed into the continuation and expansion of ancestors. Greening and enhancing the wilderness, storing water at reservoir, developing multiple industries such as agriculture, forestry, animal husbandry and fishery have become our missions of existence and living, for which mankind is not confined by economic factors and manages to live a life of high quality.

Regarding the way of getting on in the world as an art or philosophy is a Westernised concept. Instead, it is a skill of the East, especially in China. An existence-oriented issue within the social context, living also involves policies and laws of a country; social

contract of ethnic group, race and clan and the way of a family to run one's home. Those adept at associating with others and living a carefree life, remain serene and contented, in prosperity or adversity.

20. Be an Upright Man, Not a Corrupt Official

The Chinese character implies not acting severely. It may also be understood as: no matter you are a private citizen or a government official, neither overdo something nor be greedy. In a material age of soaring desire for power and wealth, one was blinded by lust for money, to fill his stomach and be warm a junior official feasted at a cost equivalent to two years' normal living expenses of a six-person family, the price of a designer coat equaled the three years clothing expenditures of a six-person family, the money paid for a pair of shoes or a wristwatch could be used by a citizen for 70 years on clothing, food, housing and transportation. Consequently, some became corrupt officials and their life was so depraved that their body was overburdened with nutrients and resulted in death from gluttony and covetousness.

Status brings people the money, one having money craves for position, one of some standing high wants to climb higher. Man's instinct of scrambling for power and profit has been fueling power struggles between countries, blocs and individuals for generations and years without any moment of relaxation. Certain country, claiming throne, seeks regional hegemony. This has induced blocs, companies and tribes to consolidate their sphere of existence, enlarge their sphere of influence as well as achieve position and power so as to reap economic benefits. Likewise, individuals, families and ethnic groups strive for power, status and interests in the same way.

Society is constantly making progress. Rapid economic growth has intensified the gap between the rich and the poor. Man's desire is affected by this disparity, and they want to reduce the inequality with their own hands. Male and female, old and young, doing and saying

wicked things with bad intentions, one will be heading down the wrong path. You reach the precipice, one more step and you will drop into a bottomless abyss, shattering into pieces.

On the fast track to economic development, poverty stifles ambition while wealth fades moral character; desire has turned into a bottomless pit. Much richer, more villainous; much poorer, less motivated. Looking only for fast return, one would rather lose long-term great interest for instant small benefit, quenching his thirst now but would die of it in the future. Man without aspiration is like a sailing ship without direction. Sinking into the mudslide of society, he grows less humane and will soon be more villainous. Society is supported by moral which is moral outline comprised by the principles of propriety, righteousness, wisdom, fidelity and courage. Villainous human beings are no different from beasts.

Living in society, man must be upright in being a man or doing something. Once to do one thing, you should have a thought in your mind first and the thought should be good which means upright. The law of humanity is similar to that of things. In regard to the law of things, carpentry is a simple trade in which as wooden items are manufactured and processed, to make joints strong, tight-fitting and good-looking, every strip, plank or mortise hole must be measured precisely with a pair of compasses and framing square for accuracy. Be upright first, then it will not slant. The way to conduct oneself is more complicated, but it is identical to the principle of carpentry. First and foremost, be upright and straighten one's mind and behavior; moderate one's greed and resolve mistakes. Rectify oneself before rectifying others. It is being a righteous person and right career that is a real career.

21. Good Citizens Should Learn to Be a Bridge Between Past and Future

Unavoidably, every citizen has no choice over a number things including country, ethnic group, region, family background, parents and life expectancy. Yet he can choose what kind of person he would be: a law-abiding individual or one who violates disciplines.

Good citizen should primarily learn to conduct oneself and the first step is to put yourself at the central axis and learn to identify all those around.

Those at the level above are your parents, grandparents, great grandparents, maternal grandparents, maternal great grandparents, elder brother, uncle, older cousin and chief, and your elders include parents, grandparents, great grandparents, maternal grandparents, maternal great grandparents. The essential points in dealing with elder members are filial piety and respect, which is an unshirkable duty of human being. Towards our leader, chief and teacher, we should be obedient and loyal, carrying out responsibilities in good faith. Towards our superiors, we should do our filial duty, practice loyalty, not to rebel against them, and fulfil our life obligations in accordance with the law of nature, law of humanity and law of things.

Those at the level below are your children, younger sister and brother, student, staff and servant. You are their elder. You should raise and teach children, younger brother and sister with love and patience. Teach your subordinates as if they were your children, younger brother and sister.

Those on your left are your colleague, classmate and spouse; those on your right are your neighbor, fellow villager, clansman, one of common ancestor, fellow countryman and one of common origin. Groups on your left and right should live in harmony and help one another. A neighbor that is near is better than a brother far off. During

our lifetime of tens of thousands of days, we have to get along with those on our left and right with mutual respect and care.

Things before are what you have experienced, they are yesterday of your own, history are events, days and antecedents which you have gone through. What man should not forget is not one's class but antecedent. The remembrance of the past is the teacher of the future. Once born, man went through days by three days: the sum of passed days is increasing day by day, while that of future days is decreasing on a daily basis. To seize today is most important. Current hardworking forms a bridge between the earlier and later stages. Today is passed on from yesterday and opens tomorrow. Life goes round and round forever revolving around yesterday, today and tomorrow. Just like this, man lives his whole life.

Getting along in an interpretation of three days human has to constantly adhere to the six-word rule of "above, below, left, right, before and later" to live and spend the days. To get on in the world, one should thoroughly comprehend and make good use of this rule. One who is adept at conducting oneself must be good at handling matters, just that different interests give rise to different matters. Each has his own ideal, but career achievement is a day-after-day sediment accumulated with one's personal effort.

22. Be Down-to-Earth Before Achieving the Dream

Stepping into society, one has many dreams. If they are goals planned in a scientific attitude consistent with the law of nature, humanity and things and together with unceasing effort towards them, then one's dream will come true.

Some have too many wishes and some, too few. The former are insatiate. Their selfish desire bloats into a marsh, lushly verdant lawn, so tempting that one might want to lie down on it. But the consequence is sinking into the marsh and life stifles. Or desire inflates into a

balloon, getting bigger and bigger, floating higher and higher, and finally blows itself up because of strong atmospheric pressure. Those belong to the latter category but unable to practice Taoism will blame everyone and everything and they themselves would feel indignant all the time. Meanwhile, those having high aspirations but little ability are fastidious but incompetent, unwilling to be down-to-earth and work at junior position first. Without past experience and personal connections, they are incapable of handling major matters, thus making themselves unusable.

Certain people live for their faith, devoutly believe that God will arrange everything for them, so they just wait, instead of fulfilling their obligations. God plans everything and for peace of mind, they hold themselves aloof from the world, but one has to stand on solid ground and work and learn one or several trades that can be relied on. Most people in the world, especially the toiling millions, should first be resigned to destiny, handle present things in a satisfactory way and clear all arrears in this lifetime. Only by doing so can one achieve a perfect peace of mind, can get the assets and achievements brought along by destiny.

Those who behave and work in a practical way while having a clear conscience are looked after by gods and deities of all faiths. Inviting immortals manifests the heart of deity worship, while one working with feet on the ground is being responsible and diligent. Simply treat the wealth; peacefully face towards poverty. This is the normal thought from the general public. Rule of the common people is that endure for a while and things will be calm and tranquil; take a step back and you will see a new horizon. In countries and regions of multi ethnic groups, rulers should embrace freedom of belief, and provide law-abiding people with ample freedom that make them free to choose which god to believe in. Praying for peace, one stands up to fight only when things turn unbearable.

Criminal law is mostly employed to punish people with extreme thinking. As for the masses having an ordinary mentality, what they need are guidance and consolation. Life is capricious, but one's mind must be normal. Normal-minded individuals can use the insight acquired through meditation to rectify mistakes, enhance wisdom in self-sublimation and size up the situation with magnanimous mind; a contented mind is a perpetual feast; enlightenment and learn the true way to life.

23. National Tradition is the Root of People's Thoughts

In Chinese language, the word "country" is the common term of motherland and home. Home is the general term of family and hometown. Family is a stable place where one rests and settles down in one's current place of residence or birthplace. The origin place of our forefathers is the hometown. Motherland refers to the country in which the hometown is situated. Throughout one's life, man constantly bears his hometown in mind. A poem by Li Bai in Tang Dynasty reads that look at the bright moon, lower the head thinking my hometown.

Born into this rich and colorful world, man would always keep thinking about his motherland wherever he travels to. And it often lingers in his heart and his mind.

A song expressing emotions and feelings have been circulating among overseas Chinese. The lyrics are roughly as follow: "The sky is clear, the wind is cool, sound of my native accent floats near. On my mind, how are those at hometown? In faraway places, lonely and miserable. I am willing to return, live life as before, reliving the joy of getting together with relatives and friends." This illustrates the attachment of Chinese living on foreign soil to their motherland and hometown.

In the book *Roots*, written by black American writer Alex Haley,

he sets the root of life in Africa where is the traditional land of his ancestors. Judging from this, we may see that turning against traditional culture is to excavate the ancestral grave, to cut one's own path to life is similar to that to dug up the roots of a large tree.

Where does root come from? It originates from the depths of one's life memory in which indelible emotions such as fear over natural and man-made disasters as well as joy over childhood anecdotes are stored.

No matter which country or religious belief one belongs to, all those civilians passing away on foreign soil or soldiers killed in action overseas wish their soul could return to their native place. The British aristocrat Bertrand Russell and the Chinese commoner Su Shi both achieved a perfect peace of mind throughout their life.

Man moves forward by generations. There were definitely ancestors before us, but whether the descendants to be continued exist is the question that whether the root would be continued. Conservatism can help carry on one's ancestral line but not radicalism. Among different people, different countries and different individual concepts, there are myriad diversities. Each understands one's own situation; each treasures one's own values. It is a problem of good or evil that should not be advised by others.

24. Greed Leads to Poverty

Greed tops all sins. In Kokang language, the form of character meaning greed is similar to that denoting poverty. In Buddhism, greed, known as desire, together with hatred and ignorance are called the three poisons. Desire here refers to a man's appetency for material and fame, which makes people intoxicated by the illusion arising from the favourable circumstances at the moment. He who has the insatiable avariciousness and disregards the consequences would do harm to both others and himself.

Greed is placed the first among the three poisons. Wallowing in drinking is the earliest manifestation of drug addiction. Purportedly, alcohol boasts a history of almost ten thousand years. It is a relaxing drink that can arouse sexual desire, confuse one's mind, generate pleasure feelings and enhance entertainment. According to historical records, there were quite a few nations perished due to the emperors' greed for alcohol, examples including Xi He, Jie of Xia, Zhou of Shang, Yang Guang, and so on. It is not good to indulge in extravagant orgies.

Lust, as ancient as the greed for alcohol, stems from human's year-round instinctive sex drive. Trapped by sexual desire, one would be out of his sense and commit crimes. Jie of Xia, Zhou of Shang, and You of Zhou, all of them were subjected to the moral decay due to the sexual misconduct, thus bringing calamity to the country and the people.

Greed for money is a sin emerged in the enlightened time after the extreme disparity between the rich and the poor happened. To commit murder out of greed should be regarded as an Unforgivable offence evil brought about along with the civilization.

Gluttony refers to the physiological symptom of excessive longing for food, which usually results in obesity. When I was an educated youth (sent to work in farms during the Cultural Revolution), my appetite for food was enormous so as to sustain the physical activity. I later learned that women, in annoyance, would eat indulgently rather than have no appetite. Obesity leads to the clumsy movement and increasing disease.

It is the most difficult to control the excessive desire for alcohol, women, food and money. As a result, there are insatiable people never satisfied with what have been already gained. They are greedy for greed's sake and without considering whether the coveted object is truly required. What they do is to reap profits at the expense of others, or even do harm to others without benefiting themselves. Greed for alcohol

would bungle the important job and tarnish the reputation. Lust for women would cause the collapse of the nation and Paris the Trojan prince and King You of Zhou were examples. Gluttony is harmful to one's health which is also a critical danger.

Greed, a phenomena all over the world, is threatening the whole mankind. Alcoholic triggers disaster; lust leads to tragedy; avarice perishes life; and gluttony jeopardizes health. Endless greed makes one eat his own bitter fruit, ending up with penniless and unspeakably misery. Greed for material possessions induces fetishism in the commercial society, enslaving tens of millions of people. The incontrollable greed, human's inner devil, degrades one to a pleasure seeker without ambition. Once falling into the crooked business, one would bring the everlasting grief with a tiny false step

Among the seven deadly sins of the Catholic Church, lust, gluttony and greed (belong to the category of avarice), taking up three of the seven, are all induced by rapacious desire. According to China's Confucianism, waste of food and unrestrained accumulation of wealth are regarded as evil, while lechery tops all the evils. In Chinese Taoism, Confucianism and Buddhism, the significance of curbing the avarice had been aware of even earlier. From the public opinion to the actual action, the anti-greed campaign has been forging ahead step by step with rationality.

25. Hero, Mediocrity and Idler

Everyone in the world would lead a different life and behave in a different way. Yet, to sum up, they fall into several types-a small number of heroes, a majority of mediocrities (ordinary guys and women), and a minority of idlers.

Heroes cherish the country and family, having family success and national prosperity in their mind. They would attach more importance to people's interests than those of their own or his party. They could lead an ordinary life, but at the critical moment, they would give up what they has got and show the true quality of hero. Regardless of their personal safety, they would contribute their strength or even sacrifice their lives for the nation or people. This makes a true hero.

Mediocrities are ordinary people. Among them, the selfish are regarded as petty persons by the Confucians. Petty persons treat their lives as a business. Their self-interests are always put in the first place. They would calculate their own interests all the time and regard it as the ability to take advantage of the society or other people. For them, the only standard of success is to obtain self-interests. They even gain advantage at the expense of their parents, brothers, wife, children, relatives and friends. To pursue self-interests, they would commit all kinds of evil, harm other's interests, discard virtue, fidelity, righteousness and propriety completely. They run out of mind in scheme, but end up hurting themselves.

Idlers are extremists among petty persons. They, having grandiose aims but puny abilities, will accomplish nothing. Believing in Hedonism, they always want unearned things and reap profits at the expense of others. Those who steal, rob, cheat, fight and take drugs come predominantly from this kind of persons.

Idlers are jealousy of the society. They are good at comparing their strong points with others' shortcomings. They are cynics and even hostile to ethics and morality. Having neither the fundamental conscience of being resigned to the fate nor the courage to compete, they only want things to be given without the willing to pay back any debt. What they do is to consume and enjoy, but create nothing for the world. Their anti-tradition thinking remains the strongest. Among each ethnic group, there are not a few idlers who constitute the root of social instability.

Hero, mediocrity and idler are three categories of people in human society. There are only a handful of heroes, a lot of mediocrities, and

not many idlers. Common people are mostly law-abiding and rule-following. They resign to the fate which serves as their self-consolation and let nature take its course. It is a sensible choice to be a good citizen who has been providing for himself, high-ranking government officials, the rich and the famous. However, in certain times, the good citizens have also supported various corrupt officials, fatuous rulers, treacherous ministers, and even villainous traitors.

26. Organization and Ethics

There are two main characteristics of human: one is organization, which refers to the combination form of groups; the other is ethics, serving as the initial principles of the combination.

The loosest organization is a hasty collection of people, without discipline and cohesion. The original compact forms of organizations were clans and tribes, which were linked together by blood. Subsequently, there emerged villages, religions, cities, armies, prisons, courts and countries comprising people with different family names and blood relations. At present, more and more groups have been set up on the basis of money, regulations and contracts, such as factories, companies and political parties. Society expands owing to organizations, which we call development.

Society became increasingly complicated and lager on account of the emergence of organizations. The fundamental track was: from blood relative communities to cities comprising people with different family names and from tribes (ethnic groups) to chieftain states (nations). The initial combination rule was ethics, namely, the generation status in the blood relative community, based on which there appeared family ethics, including the relationship of mother-child, brothers and sisters, as well as worship of nature and gods.

Primitive tribes were highly close-knit and outsider-rejecting, so as to maintain the stability of the organization, and because of that, war ensued. According to the historical records, four or five thousand years ago, fighting breaking out in the Central Plains of China were emperors pursuing federal monarchy, who cultivated virtues, strengthened military powers, selected the good for public posts, and gave the crown to the capable one. And then there emerged tribal kingdoms ruled by feudal aristocracy, just like poker combination, high-or-low rank aristocrats forging the vassal states and protective relationships. In the Mediterranean region (River Nile and Mesopotamia), the situation was based on the racial or city-state slavery relationship, whose essence were conquest and destruction. Raging war continually broke out, and tribes with loose ethics were short-lived.

That was how the Oriental culture formed, which complying with the Chinese tradition of believing in god of nature as well as embracing the heavenly and royal laws and mandate. In this form of organization, wisdom was under the command of benevolence, righteousness and propriety. "Harmony is precious", there was always a flowing relationship between aristocrats and common people in terms of liabilities, integrity and talent. After the military struggle for hegemony in the Period of Spring and Autumn and Warring States which extended about 500 years, the hereditary blood relationship of commoner and aristocrat was broken. For two thousand years from the Qin to Qing Dynasty, China saw a cycle of benevolent administration and tyranny, of peace and chaos in a monarchy founded on the belief of heaven, earth, monarch, parents and teacher.

From Europe, North Africa to West Asia, Central Asia, South Asia and western China, the religious tradition of monotheism (belief in Jehovah, Jesus or Allah) supports the hierarchy and Shinto teachings that emphasise military force, the countries adopting the form of national organisation resembling Japan. Therefore, in the circle of Confucian culture, Japan accomplished the departure from Asia to Europe and developed smoothly into a commercially-managed society,

while China was confronted with a great number of setbacks.

27. *Seeking Truth from Facts*

After organizations, ethics and believes developed into traditional culture, factional confrontation gradually emerged between cliques stressing Confucian orthodoxy and those embracing pragmatism, based on which there came the law of humanity that truth is sought from facts. When trying to make a difference, man should find out what he should do and should not do. Seeking truth is the cornerstone of the law of humanity.

Based on the principle of seeking truth from facts, the *Book of Han* tells the story of Liu De, namely, Prince Xian, the son of Emperor Jin, collecting ancient books. After the First Emperor of Qin gave orders to burn existing ancient codes and records, books of the Zhou Dynasty, written in classical Chinese, were rarely seen, and the transcripts of those books going along with the writing way of Qin Dynasty were mingled with later generations' thoughts. Liu De attached much importance to the authenticity of the text and left behind the tradition of textual research, namely, seeking truth from facts.

The tradition of collecting books followed the principle of seeking truth from facts, from which Confucian's learning on classical works derived and developed into a study of identifying the original meaning of classical texts. After Wen Tianxiang dying a martyr to the cause of dignity, Confucian scholars used a Buddhist approach to talk idly about the law of nature. Intellectuals in the Qing Dynasty put forward the principle of seeking truth from facts again in tectology, advocating the tradition of learning on classical works, that is, respecting the original meaning of the old texts and learning in accordance with it. Yuelu Academy adopted "Seeking truth from facts" as its motto.

The law of nature refers to the rules governing seasons shift, climate change, mountains, rivers, oceans, tides and natural motion in the workings of the universe and celestial bodies. The coming and going of wind, thunder, rain and snow are determined by the law of nature, which is cosmic principle perceivable by mankind and the reason to revere nature.

The law of things is the physical, chemical and biological nature inherent in all substances of the universe, the genetic phenomenon of species, and the variation principles that can be generated by intrinsic elements. The rationality of this kind of substance transformation is collectively called law of things.

The respect for the laws of nature and things brings human ethics into being. Men exist, live and move forward. How could they live a life with honorable character? Throughout one's lifetime, how to live a respectable and moral life? How could one follow the path of virtue while pursuing material comfort in everyday life? The human history of thousands of years has stipulated the rules of co-existence, which include family rules, clan regulations and national laws. If one consciously observes ethics as well as the law of nature and things, he will lead a free, easy and unrestrained life. His family will be peaceful and happy and society will be well-governed and ordered.

Based on the three laws, every country formulates its own laws so that people will have orders and reasons to follow in everyday life, so that family rules, clan regulations and national laws will have principles and standards to comply with. Society will thus be well-governed, the country will be prosperous and citizens will live in safety. Adhering to the law of nature, law of things and ethics, as well as the compliance with family rules, clan regulations and national laws, is the fundamental factors to establish a peaceful world.

28. Enough is as Good as a Feast.

That enough is enough means one should advance no further when he is pleased with himself. One's words and actions are just right

without going beyond the limit, which is the guideline of his life and social activities. Take human body as an example, hands would drop down naturally without exceeding the knee.

The ethics, derived from the law of nature and universe, are not the social conventions, religious beliefs or legislation. For instance, the ethical relationships between parents and siblings are portrayed in the Eight Trigrams as heaven, earth, thunder, wind, water, fire, mountain and lake. To be brief, ethics are the relationships between humans and those between man and nature as well as the rules for dealing with these relationships.

The Chinese embrace "heaven, earth, monarch, parents and teacher" as the five worships, stipulate "loyalty, filial piety, fraternal love, forbearance and fidelity" as the five principles, and regard them as the reasons behind the five human relationships between ruler and subject, father and son, elder and younger brother, husband and wife as well as between friends. This is similar to the norms of conduct naturally derived from professional identity between manager and staff in modern society. Today's professional ethics emphasize the reciprocity of benefits. In ancient times, the interpersonal ethics focused on mutual kindness, thus gave rise to family happiness and principles of human relations, i. e. the reasonable ethics.

Man should behave in a rational way and take the logic or the human emotions into account. The ability of logical reasoning determines one's IQ. It may only take one second for a man with a high IQ to solve a problem that has puzzled the slow man for one minute, one hour, one day or even one year. However, the thoughts of a cleaver man should never go too far. If one's ideas go beyond the limit, he would go against the law of nature and the law of things, as well as go against the laws of humanity such as ethics, laws and logic. In this case, he would become radical and disregard the social norms and law of nature. Cleverness means not to overstep the limit or not go against the social norms and law of nature. Or else cleverness may overreach itself.

Most people have the average or lower IQ, and some of them are even described as foolish and dumb. The slow need to start early. Those with the average or lower IQ should think thrice before act. They would reflect that to what extent his behavioural direction deviates from the law of society and nature. It would take an hour for a slow man to ponder a clever man's instant thinking. Yet it is worthwhile because at least the fooleries which may result in the loss of face and dignity can be avoided.

All sorts of people cohabitate in this world. A quiet thinking is needed before action. Man's intelligence and abilities are witnessed in the special behaviours. To pursue knowledge and accumulate experience are man's essential life skills.

29. Intelligence Evolution and Moral Degeneration

The time and space experienced by mankind is the evolvement taking place in the increasingly complicated combination of social classes. This is similar to the situation in which the time and space gone through by all substances in the natural world is the evolution of the complex permutation and combination of natural phenomenon.

A civilised society evolves in the intricate permutation of the constituent elements, including social entities (family, guild, government and so on), objectives (established by regulations, spontaneity eliminated), systems (internal key elements, structure set up by evolution rules and so forth) and activities (interpersonal communication both internally and externally, economy, politics, culture and so forth).

At first, it was the kings and nobles who formed societies, built cities and established countries, adopting both religious beliefs and secular laws. War was primarily waged to suppress internal rebellion

and defend the homeland. Confucian orthodoxy can last over a millennium in a country, while the republic existed no more than 500 years and the glory of democratic administration came to an end within only one century.

Modern society has fundamentally and originally transformed the tradition of aristocracy laws, adopting the constitution established by the legislative body to direct the judicial act of lawyers and judges. Organisations, comprising the government, army, political parties, schools, hospitals, enterprises, labour unions, charities and religious institutions, have to observe laws either formulated by the legislature or promulgated under imperial decree. Morals and ethics are less important now than in ancient times.

As in mathematic calculation, law has divided or equalised the freedoms and privileges enjoyed by aristocrats in the hereditary hierarchy. Skills of craftsmen and merchants, which were initially imposed by religion or Confucian ethics, have now become patents that can be popularized. Industrial workers and merchants strata made a fortune by means of hard work and diligence. Meanwhile, countries have undergone industrial, financial and technological innovation. Yet when civilisation advanced to the stage where welfare system came into being, French tended to be riding a hobby which sapped their will to make progress, living the life just like the descendants of the Eight Banners in Qing Dynasty of China. Derided as "the laziest people in the world" by Chinese tourists, Greeks were so lazy that their government went bankrupt in 2010.

Chinese gradually turned assiduous in the 1980s, but failed to inherit the Confucian ethics prevalent before 1949. Advancing step by step, reforms made use of concessary measures such as preferential land premiums in special zone and development zone as well as tax exemption to attract investment. At the expense of the environment as well as farmers' and labourers' welfare, economy has indeed grown,

while unscrupulous businessmen's concept of seeking nothing but profit has also been popularized.

Intelligence evolution trades with moral degeneration. Spanning thousands of years, historical civilisation is achieved with the hardship and toil of good people as well as the management knowledge of aristocrats and high ranking officials. When the rich and powerful adopt the epicurean motto, the rebellion against exploitation will break out, which makes the system even more complex and the natural vitality will be damaged.

30. Natural Vitality is the Source of the Social Development

Depending on social relations, rationality and intelligence, mankind has established total supremacy over all species on earth. In the course of the development of human society, natural vitality plays a decisive role in influencing the ebb and flow of the tide, constituting the foundation of the social system.

Vitality is concerning people's well-being and national policy. The masses constitute the base of the nation and laid the economic foundation, serving as the cornerstone of the superstructure of society like government, legislature and judiciary. The public vote in general election under the republican system represents the will of people, which comes from the traditional vitality of one heart and one mind. Without Protestant for white Americans, there would be no charity foundation. Likewise, the Republic of China opposed Confucian ethics, consequently, there were less heroes like Song Jiang, Wu Song and Yang Zaixing, but more adulterous couples like Ximen Qing and Pan Jinlian.

If good citizens are unable to make a good living, their families and nation will crumble and the economy will decline. The common people's will which is cultivated by good guidance and good living

represents the social system suitable for them. This type of social system is the soil for people's well-being. Americans believe in God and Jesus, while Chinese stand in awe of heaven, earth and parents. The two different will of common people are respectively the two countries' vitality concerning the welfare of the nation.

The natural world relies on energy. Planet Earth counts on suitable space, sunshine and water of the universe to offer source for survival. Flora and fauna on the ground and mineral resources underground are interdependent, using the other for one's own end, counteracting each other. In a balanced, natural environment of mutual reinforcement and restraint, air, soil and water are normal in respect to the law of cosmic motion.

Loss of balance will damage the natural fountainhead. Without the balance of water and air, natural disasters will ensue, including deteriorating conditions of river water and seawater, earthquake, flood, abnormal climate and epidemic of disease. Mankind, flora, fauna and all life on earth will suffer a lot. Mankind deserves the consequences after wreaking havoc on the environment. Protecting environment is to protect the source of survival and development of human society.

Currently, Shennongjia in China is the only place on earth where vitality abounds. With undamaged vegetation cover and four distinct seasons, Shengnongjia is ideally suited for the living and growth of organisms and fauna. Vertical climate created by north-south and east-west current movements reflects kaleidoscopic changes. Ocean currents of Siberia and South China Sea collide here, and give rise to strange rains. The vitality of Qinghai-Tibet Plateau joins the dry wind of Loess Plateau circulating between the Yellow River and Yangtze River year-round, and the two flows back from the North China Plain. Shennongjia promises divers life, with abundant precipitation, capricious clouds, ice-coated mountains in winter and rich mineral resources, which make it adaptable to the growth and reproduction of all

elements underground as well as fauna, flora and all other living things on the ground. The name *Shennongjia* comes from the name of the legendary emperor Yan, namely Shennong, who built a ladder to gather medicinal herbs and tasted hundreds of them, and *jia* means ladder. The vitality of Shennongjia upholds the Mausoleum of the Huang Emperor. National vitality implies the secret of Chinese culture.

On Adaptationism（III）

1. Temperament and Righteousness

"人"（a Chinese character meaning "human"）means, in its written form, walking in the middle direction while the way is divided into left and right—being graceful and sympathetic, and knowing when he should give up even in wild eagerness.

A man with moral character keeps improving himself on personality and never deprave himself in the aureole of glories. The biggest failure of one's life is to move to a dead end in a single direction, without knowing there will be an alternative in the front only if he could a step backward. A man of great talents will surely be given important assignments; making perfection more perfect gives a person more shinning points. Those who are always stubborn can be nothing but a failure.

As human being, one should be straight and finish doing everything well from the beginning to the end. People live in feelings. Feelings with faith are pure; without faith, feelings can be out of one's control-turning into endless desires and in turn controlling people, which would do great harm to a man himself. Children do things according to their interests and are propelled by the feelings of delight. Growing into an adult, one should comply with certain principles—being free from all desires and worries when stepping into the society; while in society, seeing everything clearly and correctly and insisting his principles.

It is just well to have enough money to use. The real hero is the one who is not haunted by the thirst for luxurious cars, elite housings, women or social status. Being rich, one should not worry too much about the security of money; in poverty, one should not eat too much in a hard-won meal. Only by not changing his mind in poverty, not becoming lascivious in good times and not yielding to force can a person see how wonderful life could be. The splendidness of life stems from self-cultivation. Sharp blades can cut the Gordian knot, and the sword of wisdom can cut evil thoughts.

Setbacks always plays jokes on people who challenge itself. Listen to the arrangement of setbacks no matter you are young or old, male or female —do not evade sufferings, since after sufferings comes happiness; and do not be addictive to entertainment too much to lose your minds. Live your life seriously because your life is on live everyday.

Life is a process. Some live in a rich and colorful world and have different life experiences everyday, while others live monotonously as if there is only black and white exist in their life. People who have principles and take opportunities seriously would get success even though he does not in tend to pursue it. Those who have not principles and are proud of temporary achievements are doomed to lose in their whole life. Keep morality in your mind even you are in a barren land, and finally you will find your vibrant fairy land.

In this world with varieties, nobody is absolutely right, because all the human emotions can be sins. God's evil is not as horrible as that of men. Rainbow comes after wind and rain, but person doing evil voluntarily will be in the hell forever. One can make calculation accurately, but he should never be serious on personal gains and loss. This is because life is full of gains and loss. Things you have acquired may not be what exactly you want, and things you have lost may just be the burden of your life.

Do not lose your heart and keep balance in your mind when you fail. Walking to the right direction you can get what you need only if you perform your own duty well. If one walks on the right way but

prefers leisure to work, he will achieve nothing; If one enters into a forbidden field, he will end up nothing.

Men dropped into the sea of women, while women lost the island of men. Men and women becoming couples should pilgrim hand in hand. They can be true humans if they take the way of righteousness, and be buddhas once they take the way of mercy.

2. Life is Like a Play

Life is like a play made by scenarist, in which players act their the roles. Only by playing the supporting role well can they have access to the lead role playing.

The Indian TV series *Dishayen* (its literal meaning: life is like a play) narrates about twin sisters Nikita and Neha. The serial is full of complications and cliff-hanging.

The elder sister Nikita and the younger sister Neha grew up in Shama's family who is respectable and venerable. Nikita is clever, competitive and eager to be a actress, while Neha is gentle and kind. Shama selects Rajive as Nikita's husband. Neha accepts the persuasion of Nikita who was chasing her Star dream to marry Rajive and make him lose his heart to her at the first sight.

The paper left to Neha by Nikita before her flight to Bombay was seen by their aunt. The parents realise the truth and feel ashamed of this. Neha was even driven away from her husband's family, but fortunately, Rajiv poured oil on the waters.

The consin of Nikita and Neha has been jalous of then since they were children. She took advantage of Neha's kindness to become the assistance of Rajive and gets involved in Rajive and Neha's marriage. Neha felt wronged and asked help from Nikita. Nikita dressed up as Neha to expose the trick of their cousin.

Neha was killed by Sam, stepbrother of Rajive. But Sam loved Nikita. Since Neha was dead, people took her as Nikita.

Nikita gave up her pursuit for performing arts and contentedly to be the wife of Rajive.

Sam was in court trial but was finally set free for that eyewitness was threatened.

When Sam went back home, Rajive and Nikita had held the wedding ceremony. Sam blamed his brother Rajive for taking away his lover and swore the serious oath. . .

From this play we can see that Indian TV series are obviously far away from the tradition of Buddhism and Hinduism but become much closer to the modern people's instincts. In these stories, love develops naturally.

Women's tears stream into men's sea of love.

But men are no longer everything to women the relation-ships.

Women are helpless in the swirl of love.

If there is no instinct in people, producing offspring would be a problem.

Women are water to men in love affairs. If there is too much water, the sea of love will become an endless abyss filled with miseries. If there is little water, the sea of love will go dry as a woman be come ruthless.

Indians take water, earth, fire and wind as the four prime biological elements which can be combined to form the different creature.

Once the four elements are out of balance, men will be sick; people will die if there is a lack of any one of them.

United four into expression, fall apart they become nothing.

Tears, feelings, fatigue, sufferings are all expressions and they will become nothing at the end. However, people chase after them constantly.

Playwrights always intend to write the end and coincidence well so that the story will be cliff-hanging.

Endure sufferings physically but not mentally, thus the body can enjoy the happiness. In a word, moderation is wisdom.

3. Men and Women

Men and women should play the social roles of their own. Being a man, one should take his social responsibilities and strive to become stronger and always equip himself with new knowledge and skills; while as a woman, one should be of compliance, self-discipline and social commitment but never be trapped by morality.

There is a Hong Kong serial play which narrates about a couple: Jiang Yuansheng and Meng Sichen.

Arrived illegally in Hong Kong from mainland China, Meng Sichen meets and falls in love with Jiang Yuansheng, however, she has to marry to the carpenter Uncle Gui, a middle aged widower. But she can't help but date Jiang Yuansheng frequently with a tempting heart.

Meng Sichen wants to marry Jiang Yuansheng after having a child with Uncle Gui. She lives with Uncle Gui but longing for her lover, Jiang Yuansheng, around the corner of every second.

When Uncle Gui is too busy at work to get back home, Jiary and merg have secret liaisons.

Something unexpected happens.

Jiang Yuansheng is cheated out for 900 dollars when purchasing a car and beats up the cheater badly. Then Jiang Yuansheng decides to make a living by boxing. He thinks he could enjoy a good life after having his success in his boxing career.

He practices hard and aims for the victory in the boxing championship. If he could win the match, he would have the chance to go to America to be a professional boxer.

In the finals, Jiang Yuansheng doesn't play the game according to the boss's requirement and is forced to take the exhilarant by his coach. In this case, the results become invalid.

When seeing Jiang Yuansheng win the game on TV, Meng Sichen is so eagered to meet him that she falls down from the stairs and suffers a miscarriage.

As Uncle Gui goes back home, on seeing this he crashes all the things at home in desperation. The broken TV causes a big fire. Yuansheng takes Sichen to hospital. The suspense of the play is what is waiting ahead for Meng Sichen, being sent back to the mainland or beginning a new life?

How can we explain the fate of Meng Sichen and Jiang Yuansheng?

Since Meng Sichen begins to fall in love with more than four men, she has been on the way to a miserable fate.

As being checked the Identity Card, Jiang Yuansheng's taking her as his wife to help her out of the siege, and later rescues her from the dangerous situation of self-suicide. She depends on Uncle Gui but have affairs with other men.

From all these, we can conclude that Meng Sichen comes to HongKong from the mainland with the endless greed.

Being a woman lacking virtues, how can she avoid those troubles?

Jiang Yuansheng doesn't want to cheat in the boxing game. He has the chance to win the champion but was set up by the boss and the coach. should he blame for his fate?

Men and women all have the temperament which can't be controlled by the animal instincts for a lifetime, should a man preserve his moral integrity?

What men and women only can do is go with the stream following their own temperament?

For the present family and country, are they only the nest of men and women?

What responsibilities should we shoulder for our country?

4. Father and Mother

Parent is the general name for father or mother.

It is father and mother that are the root of human beings.

The Methods of the Sima says that men's justice is followed by father and mother but corrected by brothers.

We can learn from experience that the significance of parents for human being is much greater than that of animals.

Animals are divided as female and male. They mate with each other to regenerate, barbarous for generations . However, dog doesn't eat dog.

For human beings, the parents are not only the ones who brought their children to the world, but also the ones who pass the porch for ethics which beyond the beasts.

In a civilized society, the parents should treat children with kindness and justice rather than the curelty as tigers.

A common value is accepted as that, especially for Chinese people, the parents are the most intimate people in the world and there will be irreconcilable hatred for the death of parents.

Kinship brings human beings special warmth and harmony. Raising the children up is regulated by law as obligation to avoid one from abandoning his children without mercy and living with sensual pleasures at his will.

The love between parents and children can be passed down and paid back. It is the children's responsibility to reward their parents when they grow up. Some people take it as a deal, but as we all say "blood is thicker than water".

Regard less of the hardship in life or the selfishness, one will feel guilty one day if he abandoned his child.

It is the very instinct that tells people from the animals.

When human being were created, the life program of gratitude or

resentment feeling between parents and children were set well.

Salt has the strongest taste in all flavors, with which all the dishes will retain their original taste.

In most cases, parents can devote all their time and energy to their children, in spite of any cost. The relationship which can rise from love to kindheartedness and justice does not exist during the animals. A tiger never cares about the family life of his offsprings. However, human being do care about this, so their marriages are arranged by parents.

Several days after a little fox was born, elder fox would force him to get out from their den to live on his own, which makes his instincts naturally come into being in a savage animal circumstance.

What the animals pass down to their offsprings is only instincts.

However, during the growth of the little ones, the elder one hand down the accumulated experience, common senses, interpersonal ethic and cultural knowledge to them.

This is what we call education.

Whether they have a sense of responsibility or not, parents are the earliest teachers to their children.

Comparing parents to the plants, the father is called Tsubaki and the mother is called tawny daylily. The love from a father is strong and steady like a mountain and that from a mother is soft and tender like water. Father and mother complement with each other well would inspire their children's intelligence. All charity stem from family life and sins come from unfilial deeds.

By being dutiful children to their parents, people could generate their Buddhist nature, realizing the respect and fears for gods and ghosts.

5. Individuals and the Devil Inside

Once an individual is regarded as the center of all, he would follow his own selfishness and be possessed by the devil if he disobeys

the laws.

In the modern society, individualism can help fight against the authorities, but it should not be out of control by laws. Once people are addicted to enjoyment, it is difficult for them to be extraordinary and refined.

But in the cases of incest between father and daughter, the vendetta of husband and wife and the accusation of a mother by her daughter, the inner devil is out of control. Under such circumstances, people will do things like evil spirits under the name of freedom and human rights.

The most terrible thing is not private ownership but the expanded and unscrupulous selfish desires. The western people say that people are half-angel and half-devil creatures.

It means not only that people have two faces of good and bad, but also that devil occupies people's hearts controlling them to do harm to the world.

The devil inside does not come from the society but in the people's heart. It is not the illusion but emotions of hatred, greed, delusion, obsessiveness and resentment. It can never be released easily. It is often said that the greatest enemy is yourself. The "yourself" here means the devil inside.

If people are not in the society having no pursuit for success and happiness, there would not be the devil in people's heart and they would not be controlled by the devil inside. Herd are controlled by the animal instincts, but people can't be controlled by their instincts. Therefore, it is important to defeat the devil inside and cultivate righteousness and justice if one wants to grow up.

The American novel named *Evil* tells the story that a female killer succeed to break out of prison by holding the detective as her hostage. She forced him into the madhouse and her picture is posted on the cover of popular magazine. Many scenic spots were even named after her.

This killer promised the detective that she would not kill people any more but she failed to keep her promise. After the killing, she leaves the eye balls and spleen of her victims in the toilet.

It is not the illusion in the Nazarite's heart but real things happened in the American legal society. These things are frightening. Fears are reflected as the horrible scenes in the novel and become more and more dreadful.

That is why we say civilized society gives the strength to individuals by ethics and legality, protecting people from being killed by the evil inside.

But one has to face his heart, so he should be tough and need the practice. Firstly, one should go beyond himself. Then he should find out the conception that makes himself scared and try to abandon it.

If one is not strong enough, he should find another one to form a family, school or company to study together and systematize their thought. One is independent by making three decisions on his own.

6. Family and Marriage

There are some people who don't get married. Family is the basic unit of the society and it is formed by marriage, blood and adoption relationship. Family emerged from tribes and clans and then was divided by husband-wife relationship. No matter it is evolution or the degradation, family is the footstone of human civilization. Family is the starting point, cradle and school of society. Human beings will extinct if there is no family. Family makes men and women stably combine with each other in the name of wife and husband.

Family is the place to raise children and take care of the old people. Marriage is the method of love coming into being by the combination of wife and husband. Many resentment also breed from here. However, generally speaking, the intimate relationships of human beings develop firstly from family and marriage, and the social system also emerges from blood and adoption relationship.

Enlarging their family is the dream of Chinese people. Sons and grandsons are the success and happiness of the family. Therefore, to the Chinese people, marriage is a great matter in their life like building a temple, and divorce is the great thing like pulling down a temple.

The European people focus on the individual life. They show their personality even in a group of two or three persons. In the modern society, the thinking mode is not confined to that only one who has the good background of family will have great success. There are many single parent families in which the mother or father has to raise the child on his or her own. It is not only the progress of the society but also the demonstration of labors.

There exists the single-person family in which people do not get married when they reach certain ages or after their divorce. A person lives all by himself. It goes with the sayings that the families will not be hungry once he gets himself full. It has been divorced from the ancestors' Taiji theory of Yin and Yang Combination in living mode.

In the modern society there are DINK (Double Income No Kids) families, in which both wife and husband have incomes and the ability to have children but they pay more attention to the romance, freedom and enjoyment of life than carry the family on.

There are empty nest families in which there are only old couples living together without their children. And there is trial marriage in which people focus on the merrymaking features of the marriage. Marriage and family have changed much.

More and more people lost their company, son or get married again after divorce to reconstruct family home and abroad.

Marriage and family are still important for people to pass on social ethics and bear their emotions. Nurseries and orphanages can never be replaced. Marriage and family can be improved but not perished.

7. Prostitution and Whoring

There is significance and problems caused by marriage. There comes prostitution and whoring. Men go to the brothel to have fun with prostitutes or women sell their bodies for lewd demand to raise their families.

The subject of whoring is a man and that of prostitution is a woman. The cores of both activities are pecuniary exchange. Sex becomes the commercial products. Men and women have improper kind of sexual behavior as they wish. It is improper so it has to be sneaky and will cause many bad social consequence.

Prostitution and whoring is different from fornication. Fornication is under free willing and has no money exchange. Under money exchange, men offer money for whoring and women take the money for prostitution.

It is not good affair of prostitution and whoring but will not be easily eradicated by prohibition. They are natural products of civilization and it is like that men would produce the excretion after having meals. It is mainly men's problem. There are men as merrymakers in the first place and there are women as prostitutes consequently.

With the social problems being more complicated, there occur the social phenomena that men or women would have fun with male prostitutes.

There are many ways of prostitution, besides the whoring in brothels. There are other means such as calling prostitutes to serve the wine, singing, dancing and so on. There are some regulations banning the brothel or prostitution, but they did not succeed. The people who go whoring can change various places and methods. The places such as cinemas, theaters, beauty salons, massage parlors, saunas and parks and so on could be changed into places of pleasure.

Therefore, we should treat the social phenomena of prostitution and whoring in a sensible way. Now that it cannot be resisted by human nature, the regulated management should be carried out. From the old time the red light districts are to divide a special living region to allow the people whose family is disharmonious to relieve themselves. This would help easing some social problems.

What we should do is to prevent the involving of the single girl, abandoned woman and young children, to prevent the prostitution by government officials with government expense, to prevent the mixture of corruption and bribe-taking getting involved, to avoid prostitution and whoring to be the umbrella of the malfeasants, to prevent the prostitution and whoring to be the main channel to spread disease,. It can destroy marriage and family relationship, causing social corruption, induce crimes and badly disrupt social order.

Certainly, said is easier than done. Taking the solution of these problems into consideration is better than leaving them alone.

8. The Nature is the God

People often say that human efforts can achieve anything, but on the other hand they also say that do not force a donkey to dance. It is concerned with the law of nature.

In the Warring States period, the learned man Hsun Tzu talked about the nature that it has its law and won't exist or perish for men, even lords like Yao or Jie. It will be good if regulations are applied and be ill if disorderliness occurs. What here is talked about is the law of nature, which people should follow.

The nature, in the western countries, is the God. In *The Analects*, Confucius says that you should respect the ghosts and gods and keep yourself from them at a distance. It also says that things should be done and the god will help.

The saying "man proposes, God disposes" has the same meaning.

What men propose are the things that are available to them. But many things are beyond the control of men, such as storms or earthquakes. They should be submitted to the will of Heaven.

Words like destiny, fate and heavenly principles refer to the natural law.

Footprints will be left when men walk by. Tracks will be left when cars run over. The floor will get wet when it rains. These are the things that cannot be changed by men's will.

It is the natural principle and the principle from God for Chinese people that God is so mysterious that it cannot be seen by mortals. .

A brief saying in the old time says that earth to piles up to make a mountain and then wind and rain will rise up from it. Collecting water can make a deep pool and then dragons will appear in it. Good deeds can create virtues and insights will come itself. Here it means the natural law holds the features of nature. We should do things complying with the rules, eat things bit by bit and walk one step after another.

Some said that there is no Jade Emperor in the heaven and no Dragon King in the sea. I was the Jade Emperor and the Dragon King who can order high mountains to clear the way.

It is against the natural law. As consequence, many barren hills were created.

The Law of Nature that we often talk about is the same with that of western countries, it is not that mysterious but likes the saying that all roads lead to Roma. Bible says God created the world in the first six days and took a rest the following day. For this saying, people who believe it would take it seriously, but people who do not believe it would take it as a story.

However believing is better than not-believing. People who believe it do things with hesitation and they would not commit primes even they are audacious enough.

We most believe the sayings of Confucius that those who worship

the gods and believe the fate would accept their destiny. However, they do not give up humanity. When chopsticks drop on the ground they bend to pick them up rather than pray or wait for them to jump back onto their hands.

There's no free lunch. The more ploughing and weeding, the better the crop. One should not hope for something to be reaped without sowing. But knowing the fate is after sufferings. And they do not complain and just let it be. It is same with Lao Tse's saying that the god controls laws and laws control the nature. The nature is the god.

9. Do Not Commit Crimes

Not committing crimes means one should abide by the law and do not factitiously break the law or their laws of humanitarian.

In the ancient western countries, people suppress their sensual passion by the laws of God, persuading people to abide the law. This is irrational and unavailable. It is inconsiderate for normal people can hardly complete the things performed by the monks and priests in the temple. It is like forcing a donkey to dance, which violates the natural laws and pushes people to commit illegal crimes.

Delinquency is doing the illegal things. The god governs the nature and the people control the laws. Do not defy the law as being a man or doing something. Religions persuade people to do good things and be good men. Schools educate people to comply with the laws for being good citizens and not to do illegal things.

But there is selfishness in people's heart. Everyone has to make a living and protect his families from being killed by others. As in the story of Lin Chong in the novel *Water Margin*, he is forced to kill the people who wants to insult his wife. He is forced to join rebels. One should obey the laws, such as no theft and murder. To prevent the people who have the privilege from abusing power for their own ends, it is necessary to build up the law system. It is of special significance for

people to obey the laws. It creates the circumstances to prevent people from committing crimes. In history, problems of violence and violation of laws have never been solved.

Improving the legal systems is necessary for the development of the society. Someone makes the laws and someone else will break the laws. It is not a rare phenomenon in a civilized county. Under the laws, it regulates that people committing crimes will be punished.

Fundamentally speaking, not to commit crimes is to follow the laws of humanity. Humanitarian and its theories are too complicated. It is the creeds from our ancestors that are more comprehensible. They tell us to understand the kindness, do what is right and control our own minds. These are the basic steps to take.

The saying by Mencius is that men are kind-hearted as they were born. They had senses of compassion, shame, respect and the conception of right and wrong. One will not commit the crimes once knowing what is good. On seeing someone fall on the ground, one would help him up. Seeing someone fall into the river, one would pull him up. As driving on the road, one would give way to others who has emergency. When listening to the broadcasting, one would tell the good from the bad and avoid going along with others in their evil deeds.

People know that men should never commit crimes and do good deeds.

A society will become more civilized, as its people behave better.

10. Imparting Knowledge and Educating People

Imparting knowledge and educating people is the saying by HanYu. Preaching, fundamental nursing and answering questions are duties of a teacher.

Being a teacher has been treated as nothing more than the means of earning a living. But teachers, in any way, are not ordinary jobs. Education is not only teaching people how to obtain the knowledge but

also how to learn.

The religious tradition of Chinese people is not as profound as education. People are educated to be sensible and have good manners.

Teaching people to know natural law or the wills from God is usually conducted by the Godfather in the West. Yet our tradition hands this responsibility to teachers. Therefore, for the teachers, having a wide range of knowledge to solve the problems is not enough. They should be good examples to their students.

Teaching knowledge is to solve concrete problems. You have to learn the knowledge of computer and basic skills like inputting, if you know nothing about using the computer.

But if the teachers can only teach you how to type or programme without showing you the significance of the computers in natural laws, they are not good teachers.

Therefore, Han Yu said that it is the natural laws that make the teachers exist. That is to say that where there are the laws, there will be the teachers. Indeed, teachers are thought highly of in this way. However, we could hardly find such kind of teachers nowadays.

The teachers who understand little of the laws could not teach others to be good people. For to an ordinary man, if his teacher show him the way of stealing, he might become a thief.

A thief was led to the bad way by his teacher in a sense. His teacher is not qualified then.

Our ancestors looked on teacher as a privileged career and highly respect their teachers, so there is a saying that a teacher is like the father to his students. Respect to one's teacher and that to one's parents are both important for Chinese people. Imparting knowledge and skills is important, but educating people is more important. Teachers are honorable not for imparting knowledge but for educating people.

In terms of educating people, it is most important of knowing and understanding the laws for students.

If a teacher encounters bright students, he can mould them into professional scholars. It is not that difficult. However, it is difficult to cultivate the people to have kindness, wisdom and enlightenment for laws. If they are sensible and virtuous enough, they would not use their knowledge and skills to do harm to the society.

As a teacher, one should be the good example to educate his students, which is more important than any other matter in the world.

11. Moulding Characters

If a teacher can be served as an example, he can impart his knowledge to his students more effectively. One is hard to be moulded, but can be inspired.

The morality of a person is reflected by his characters. Here we are not talking about one's taste on art and life style, nor his social status. We'll be discussing how to improve one's tastes in life.

The wine has the grades of low, medium and high, so there are the issues concerned by the professions. As regard to the manner of drinking, one should never shout loudly and cause troubles once gets drunk. It is a matter of virtues and manners.

Article and works have the grades of quality. Works like *A Dream in Red Mansions* is delicate and cannot be degraded to the works likes *The Golden Lotus*. It is also the same as regards to paintings.

What we are discussing is the moral quality of a writer or painter.

If a writer writes stories on love affairs and murder for middle school students only for money, a painter paints the nude figures only for fame, it is their moral corruption that drives them to do all these deeds.

Wine, paintings, commercials and articles are artificial.

If one has high moral quality, he can produce products with high quality in good style. The ancient people said that if one has characters as elegant as bamboo, he could rhyme the most beautiful poem. It is a

vivid example of good characters.

Lin Daiyu is elegant and beautiful enough, but being an actress is not suitable for her. To study the characters of a Lin Daiyu is definitely meaningless for one's career as actress, but it has special significance for women on how to live in an elegant and poetic way.

For most people, Lin Daiyu is not their role model that they appreciate. They prefer women smart as Wang Xifeng, considerate as Ping Er and humorous as Granny Liu.

The latters are more secular.

From the ancient times, our country has the saying that the three religions and the nine schools of thought, which generally refer to the traditional religions and various academic schools. It is said that Indian Buddhism had been introduced from the Eastern Han Dynasty competing with Confucianism and Taoism. Five hundred years later, the emperor of the Northern Zhou Dynasty called up the discussion of three religions and finally decided that Confucianism came first, followed by Taoism and the Buddhism. The intervene of the emperor is a human factor. But the order of the three religions is a natural product in the five hundred years.

It demonstrates that we had the tradition of grading people on their status and professions. It can also reflect that people had freedom in ancient times to form their characters.

12. Birth and Destiny

The ancient Greek believed that there is a spirit for every man to protect him. The spirit has been on the man's side when he was born and would look after him for a lifetime. The Romans inherit the belied and pass it on.

Pilgrimage to the West says that Xuanzang goes on a pilgrimage for Buddhist scriptures. Sun Wukong (the Monkey King) had been punished to wait for Xuanzang under the Five Finger Mountain for five

hundred year.

More than that, Xuanzang and his apprentices are watched by gods on the heaven following them along.

Our country is more particular about the birthday than the Greece and the Romans do.

In *Book of History*, it says that only the heaven and the earth are the parents for everything in the world; only human beings are superior to all the other things on earth. Here human beings are defined as master to all the other things. It is earlier and more specific than that in the Greek mythology.

Ancient Greek statues are noted to the wise scholars in the past. There is no evidence for the birthdays of the ancient wise men in Greece and Rome. The birthday of the two Saints, Sakyamuni of Buddhism and Jesus Christ of Christianity, are from the sayings of their believers and the arguments after these religions were passed down for hundreds of years. Even though the two religions become prosperous, there is no historical records and researches by the historians on the dates of birth of the two saints.

The birthday of Confucius is seen in the early historical records, and it was written into the history by historiographers after their research and confirmation. Shortly after the death of Confucius, the books *Gong Yang Zhuan* and *GuLiang Zhuan* had recorded his birthday. The different records by historians may be caused by the novelty of humanity.

The accurate record for the birthday of Chinese people is by the Chinese horoscope of year, month, day and hour the birthday of Confucius is exactly recorded as GengChen and GengZi. Its accuracy needs to be researched and confirmed. This way to record birthday is said to have concluded the information of one's destiny. Based on this, the folk think that one is destined by the heaven (or the god) and can be predicted by the methods like astrology and divination.

The destiny is related to life and the general trend of one's life, like death and birth, marriage, wealth and so on. All these can be shown by concrete year, month and day. A rich man might have twists and turns when he was a child. Misfortune might occur at any time.

Our believes about horoscope stem from a theory of birthday, but no one has ever sorted them out in a logical way and mathematical thinking. Folk religions only come from belief rather than knowledge.

Geomancy, divination and witchcraft are self-taught professions with skills. To believe or disbelieve completely are extreme views.

Now that there is common belief on birthday spirits for both ancient Chinese and Greek, it can be regarded as a part of human wisdom. Then, why don't we believe in destiny? Since there is development of luck, it is understandable for one to make efforts. But we should remember the instruction that one should not risk his life to pursue and should not be lazy to hang out all day.

13. A Playboy without Ambition

A man is good at cooking when he is young and has the ambition to run a restaurant. But he is fond of collecting antiques for more than ten years. He can not fight against the temptation to buy antiques when stepping into the antique market. Now the man's more than fifty years old and the restaurant is on the way forever.

Book of History says that excessive attention to trivialities saps the will. "Playing" usually means amusement to children before 12 years old. It is a way for people to get knowledge through amusement. This is because children at this age don't have strong wills. It is their natural state.

Playing freely without intention is important for children who are innocent. Even though they are naughty and cause troubles to adults, family and school, it is their instinct and progress of their growth.

It is said that a fall into the pit, a gain in your wit. The infants

have fun on their interests. It is a way of learning.

The adults have less interest in playing. They have certain things that they fancy and adore. It is called "fascination". Its degree of addiction is similar to that of love. The difference between them is the aim of the former is the things but the latter people. The adults are fond of antiques, jewelry, paintings and stamps, etc. Interests are different from ambitions. Middle-aged people are fascinated by paintings. young people may want to be the government officials. That is the difference between interests and ambitions.

Being a playboy without ambition means that one lost the courage and strength to strive for his aim for he might be addicted to something in his middle age. Finally he becomes a man who muddle along the things without improving himself. These are the people without great ambition and courage.

For monks and priests, no aggressiveness may be the requirement to get rid of the evil in heart during their practice. This would keep away from fantasy. But for the people in the secular society, practice makes perfect and vice versa. They must have grandiose aims but puny abilities, have high aspirations but little ability. They should never hang out without purpose for a long time and accomplish nothing in the end.

The Book *Chun Qiu* tells a story that Wei Yi Gong likes cranes very much. He lets them sit in his luxurious carts and companies them all the time. It costs a lot money every year to raise them. Eventually, he neglects the state affairs and does not care about the living of his people. Finally he was killed by the invading army. It is the lesson that we should learn.

14. The Fantasies

There is a merchant who runs a company tells others that blasting a gap with missiles or bombs in the Himalayas can solve the problem of water shortage in the North. This is what we call a fantasy.

For the child whose mind is not mature, the fantasy is like a bee in the head or dreams. It is random thoughts during the learning period of child which the nature status in his growth. It should not be scolded but taken as a joke or give them proper guidance instead.

For scientists engaged in inventions, a clear description of the theoretical thinking can produce the divergent thinking and imagination when there is no early clue in the thought. They can connect irrelevant things together and inspire children to make good use of their imagination.

It can not be easily done by anyone. It is not pragmatic for a business man to live in his illusion.

Outlandish thoughts are not absurd in poetry. If one has the poetic imagination and live with it, he should not do business or enter politics.

It is helpful for the writers and artists who write novel and make up the stories from their fantasies. They can make up surprising plots to attract people. In the myths of religions, there are plenty of fantastic stories. At first they may not be suggestive, but shown by religious founders or apostles using their "powers". Actually, these ceremonies are as simple as those that most people can do, so they are handed down by the believers. But by adding the trimmings by the descendants, they become increasingly bizarre and totally incredible. Eventually, they are abandoned by modern people.

For example, the book *Guide Ways of Mountains and Seas* is fully seen as myth by some people, and others think it is the historical book for ancient tribes especially Dongyi clan. It narrates things with pictures, passing down the history about the ancient people. It also mentions animals which actually existed at that time but extinct now "imaginary".

As the saying goes you can't have your cake and eat it. It means that do not accord with common sense. If you are thinking freely, it may be taken as the creative thought for solving problems.

15. Selfishness

Selfishness is always negative. It was rejected in the ancient times but is accepted in modern times. No matter in philosophy, religion, or psychology, we can see a paradigm shift of this term from negative to positive.

Selfishness is abstract. But if it is defined as narcissism, it may become more concrete. Handsome men or beautiful women tend to be enchanted by their own reflections. It is narcissism.

In Greek myths, Narcissus, the Greek god transferred selfishness from narcissism. He refuses the love from the goddess Echo who has a beautiful voice, but falls in love with his own reflection in the water. Finally he becomes a daffodils by the pond.

In this story, Narcissus is very self-centered and selfish.

A positive definition to narcissism is self-satisfaction. If things do not go to extremes, it is okay for one to stay in such kind of mental status. If one is too narcissistic, pathological personality will be formed: if one is too envious of others or admire others too much, a closed and rigid social hierarchy will be formed.

Selfishness, often going with self-interest, forms very strong bias, namely egoism. It boasts self-serving as peonies or roses. From the mentality of individualism, people talk about their own reason.

Some people even demonstrate the rationality of selfishness from the objective moral relationship of mutual benefit.

Selfishness may form a whole set of philosophy, which is called solipsism: no two pieces of leaves are; each water drop has its uniqueness. For everyone's own experience, others can't fully understand that.

This is the philosophy of individualism, taking individual as an atom in the molecular world or one planet of the universe. It is opposed to advocate world anarchism or eliminate the national borders

politically.

Selfishness absolutizes the humanity and neglects the laws of Heaven or God. Self-interests become the priority. But in business or battlefield, selfish people is forced to compromise. Mutual benefit is called Golden Rules in these fields.

16. Private Property

The Selfish Golden Rules are implemented as economic system forming the private property and the private ownership. The individual becomes an atom as the basic unit of molecule.

According to the laws, properties are individualized. Investments are divided into current assets and real estate. Under the legal system of private property, an individual is the basic unit. The concepts of family and clan disappear. Patriarchy, matriarchy, clan authority and sovereignty all disappear, leaving only the individuals.

Then private property becomes the most beautiful flower. The artificial property like food, car and clothes which could originally be passed down from parents to their children selflessly, are encouraged to keep to the parents themselves. Even the invisible satellite TV signal is occupied by the financial groups. Only the natural resources like fish, water and air can be shared by people.

They are the fruit of liberalism in the past five hundred years. I have choices to be different from animals and living things. Likeralism is positive in most cultures. It gives chances to art, religion and science to develop without restriction. But on the other hand it commercializes the relationship in the communities. Consumption is given top priority. Life is just in competition. Non-commercial exchange communities have been compromised and rejected.

If one takes himself as the center of the world, just like the sun, the other parts of the galaxy could not be seen at all. It took one hundred years for the western atom science to conquer the knowledge accumulated for millions of years. Without the elites, the apathy was deduced from the equality. It is the machiavellianism in modern philosophy and politics in which people had to to reap profits at the expense of others.

This individualism taking oneself as the sun, arbitrates all the things by the ownership in law, and worships the inviolable private property. The country is just like the bird's nest for the personal use and the government is the organization to build this political nest. They are all good if abiding by the law. Corruption, embezzlement, robbery, fraud, theft, and smuggling are all crimes. But out of law, it is the wisdom to be not guilty.

In this case, there is no need for people to have literature and art. All the value, large or small, can be measured by the income, property, and ownership, etc. All virtue turn into the abominable fat. Hegel's probably did not have the idea that the logic of law spread with Satanism.

17. Selfishness and Punishment

Could the devil logic of Satanism be the punishment to the selfishness of human beings? It is worthy of research.

The conception of punishment occurred in the *Commentary of Zuo* during the spring and autumn period. It said that, in the sixth year of Duke Ai, "the guilty should be punished and should be transferred." The Russian writer Dostoyevsky's novels focus on the crime and the punishment. It was in the 19th century and 2 300 years later than that of China.

The dictionary generally explains the word punishment as the pain or loss resulting from the improper behavior. In philosophy, it is considered as the penalty made by the authority and used to redeem the losses of the offended caused by the offender.

In Psychology, punishment is regarded as a method. In order to

keep the individual from continuing the violations, the offenders are imposed with suffering or deprived of their interests, so as to stop them engaging in violations. Looking at the punishment in this way, moral becomes meaningless. When parents or teachers punishing their children or students, they just teach their children or students the lesson to their own convenience no matter the motive is good or bad.

From this aspect, human beings are either the universal spirit or the lords of all creation, or the social animals revenging wrong with wrong. Moral is regarded as the aggression or strategy of the "good guys", They bear insult just to gain sympathy, protection and the justice. Such logic takes selfishness as the absolute standard and entirely deny the thoughts of Confucius and Socrates in ancient times.

This is the thought that enact the criminal law with utility. It completely regards the laws formulated by the by the ancient philosophers, religions, and countries for the public and the sinners in thousands of years as the evil. Such laws are merely used to revenge wrong with wrong rather than to maintain the goodness. In this case, Goodness is evilness, a hidden evil. Criminal law is the punishment for the criminals in the form of prisons. Human right is the legal right of the individual.

It is extremely objective in the doctrine of a legally prescribed punishment for a specified crime, which indiscriminatingly sets the legal thought based on the criminal law and legal code in the 19th century Europe as the standard to evaluate whether proper or not the behaviors of all human beings from the ancient to the present. According to this logic, the people born after the discovery of the atom were real man, and before the 19th century, all mankinds were animals.

If the criminal law interpretation is adopted by the country, the authority of officials would be the law before the criminal law is enacted. As long as such tests are permitted, the national violence would come to resurgence. Even the humankind and the Earth could be

totally destroyed by the nuclear weapons.

18. Fellowship and Friends

Fellowship refers to the emotion or friendship produced through the interaction between people. Love is the fellowship between the opposite sexes. Couple is the fellowship bonded by the marriage. There are also the fellowships of family members, relatives, friends and so on.

The ordinary friends would provide some good advice and lend the general help. For the lovers and couples who have intimate relationship and deep affection, the support should be much greater. It is unreasonable for them only to give the verbal advice, perform the courtesy demands reciprocity, or provide the financial support.

Friends, for Chinese, do not refer to the nodding acquaintances under the western legal nexus. They can be subdivided into colleagues, assistants, classmates, schoolmates, and so on. In Kokang, different people have different understandings about it. The ancient people explicated it as, "People who are studying after the same teacher are classmates, who have the same ambition are friends. Classmates and friends gather to talk about study and moral". *The Book of Songs* says, "one should always respond to other's words. If he pay back other's favors. If he only be kind to his close friends, he must be petty man. " It is difficult to describe friends with only the sayings and words. Friend should be talked in certain circumstances and it will be much easier.

Confucius once said, "Is it not delightful to have friends coming from the distance?" The story goes that Qin Shubao once risked his own life to help his friend. In one word, our Chinese words cannot be simply and easily understood like the European and American words. The information and meanings of Chinese character are conveyed by its glyph, meaning and sound, which reflect the complication and subtlety of Chinese people's relationship. It cannot be made clear without friendship.

It can be seen that Chinese people attach importance to the kindness and reciprocity, which is a necessity in the historical cultural environment. On the contrary, the humanistic environment of England and France is for only 1000 years, while that of American is for no more than 250 years. In this case, the family trees and the relationships between relatives in England, France and America are simple, and it is quite easy to deal with the litigation. It would be much more complicated if Chinese people are engaged in a lawsuit. Due to the complex relationship and interwoven love and hatred, they would fill ashamed and even lose the family bond and friends, which is very humiliating.

"Pengyou", the Pinyin of "朋友"（meaning friend）, omits the multi-relationships between families, cliques, buddies, comrades, and even the meaning of "friends" in English. In Chinese character "朋", there are two moons（Chinese character "月"）side-by-side. It implicates that the people of the some group will be friends. Besides, it contains the in-depth affections between relatives, friends, schoolmates and comrade-in-arms. Foreigners can hardly understand the meaning of "我心如舊"（Literally, it means that my heart is like the old one.）Fortunately, the alphabetic writing system is not put into operation and there are still the traditions in our country.

19. Precious Sympathy

In Kokang language, there is a saying that "a letter from home is precious". If the word "letter" was replaced by sympathy, the saying becomes "sympathy is precious".

In the early years, if criticized for no compassion, one may hide his face with shame. However, at present the power of criticism disappears. The criticized one may straighten his neck and asks you, "how much is compassion?"

Criticizing a man with "benevolence" can makes one fill ashamed,

which is the power of Confucian culture. In ancient times, not only Confucianism but also Taoism respected righteousness. Sima Qian, in the *Five Emperors Biography*, said "The Emperor Yao released Xun. His kindness and wisdom are comparable to the God". Sima Qian is a historiographer, whose task was to pass down excellent tradition. According to him, the Yellow Emperor cultivated morality and the Emperor Yao cultivate kindness. Moral and kindness, as light as soap bubble now, were entitled the significant position in ancient times.

Therefore, Confucius takes kindness as the core of Confucian ethics, leading the thoughts such as filial piety, respect, loyalty, forgiveness, propriety, knowledge, brave, purge, generousness, honest, wise, kindness and so on. He said that humanity means to restrain oneself and observe the rites and die to achieve virtue. It is really of great significance and would not be easily understood by the people in modern society.

Confucius said, "the benevolent loves others". Nowadays, people think it is common because we don't live in the environment of respecting Confucius. Looking carefully at the word kindness (Chinese character "仁"), you will find it means "the man is in the middle of two persons' relationship". The above horizontal line is shorter than the below one, which means the order. It is no wonder that Guan Yu and Zhang Fei, who were brave enough to match ten thousand warriors, respected Liu Bei so much after they swearing the brotherhood with Liu. In *Water Margin*, after the Robin Hoods made Sung Chiang their head, the guidance for their action and speaking was set and and Sung Chiang became their mainstay.

The word "love", from Kokang's perspective, is guided by heart. When modern people think about interests and benefits, they will become heartless. So they produce fake wines and poisonous milk powders mercilessly. As a result, when people hear of the word "friend", they have the same feelings like hearing of "anda" from

Mongolian, "yota" or "Kun so-and-so" from Japanese. People pay much less attention to traditional titles such as the "profound friends, life-long friend, soul friends, sincere friends, bad friends, candid friends and good friends" compared with the "ally, net friends, literary friends, close friends, bosom friends and pen friends", let alone the forever friends who will never forsake each other.

Although there are some words inherited from the old days, like "the good friends despite great difference in age, the spiritual friendship between a noble and a commoner and gentleman friends, and the most intimate friend", few people can explain them clearly. Even though they can make it clear, few people really make such friends. Why? It is because they have no idea of the value of sympathy.

If Tu Fu of the Tang Dynasty had no compassion from his kind heart, he would not write out the poem, "On war-torn land streams flow and mountains stand; In vernal town grass and weeds are o'ergrown. Grieved o'er the years, flowers make us shed tears; Hating to part, hearing birds breaks our heat." With benevolent mind and heart, deep impairment, it is horrible to see.

It wasn't until 18th century that someone started doing research of sympathy. Four thousand years ago, Chinese emperor Shun forgave the heartlessness and relentless of his father and his brother. There would be no forgiveness without sympathy. Among the Chinese people, compassion is the Mount Tai to suppress the evil, which is too precious to buy.

20. Civilization and Country

Civilization generally means that all the man-created wealth, especially referring to the thought and culture of human beings, such as literary aesthetics, education and empirical science and so on. Human nature is gradually and specifically manifested in the process of the history evolution-Farmers fear the nature; citizens abide by the laws;

workers make a living by the technics; merchants do the cost accounting; and the clansmen live in peace...

Within the ancient civilizations, only our country survives to today. We believe that education and harmony is most precious. The imperial colonialism in Europe and United States proved that that their aggressive behaviors are not civilized which is the real savage. Civilization in English mainly refers to "reclaiming wasteland and expanding". The significance of "civilization" in Kokang is far more rich.

The Book of Changes says that "the dragon is seen in the field, and the world is in civilization". When the Hsiung-Nu bullied Mongolia grassland, HuaXia abandoned the savage. The Confucianism use civilization and culture to make nations famous, and use the four cardinal virtues, humanity, justice, propriety and wisdom, to control the words and actions. Therefore the culture of the Han and Tang dynasty spread through the ages. The results were that southern Hun becomes the barrier of the northern country and northern Hun goes abroad. .

When the Greek started the military expedition overseas for the sake of women, the Chinese poet chanted, "The girl I love is so far from me". As the gentleman is elegant, Chinese etiquette was desirable, the poem read, "Guan! Guan! Cry the fish hawks on sandbars in the river." The glory of accumulated by the three generations brought about China the prosperity and the worldwide renown. The Han dynasty could draw lessons from the tyranny Qin dynasty and tried carry out the culture and education government so that it lasted for 400 years.

As early as in the Tang dynasty, the idea that culture and education make the country strong and rich had appeared in Hanna Island. Knowing principle to desist from armament and promote culture and education in peacetime, Emperor Taizu of the Song dynasty had the

wisdom to relieve the generals of their commands at a Feast. Without understanding this, Emperor Taizu of the Ming dynasty killed the man of merits. The Manchurian and the Japanese people don't understand the principle that education prospers the country. They upheld the military conquest so that there existed the 10-day YangZhou massacre and the Nanjing massacre.

It is not wise to prolong the daytime festivity in the night with the light of the lamps. A country of a clan would be able to pull through the great calamity if they can sense the coming crisis and get cultivated internally and externally. King Wen of Zhou was a successful example. The strength of knowledge is not as fierce as the military power, yet it can plan the seeds of civilization in people's heart.

The new and modern are not necessarily the best. Out of humanism, soldiers don't kill prisoners. The Cod's will means more — to calm down with spirit and soul, to endow the civilized people with freedom, to civilize the savages, and to focus on people's inner harmony rather than resorting to repression.

A civilized city cannot be reflected by the neon lights. The self-discipline is more important than the restriction of the law. Only with the well supervision of the officials can the people live in peace. All the civilizations are changed in the contemporary modernization. The society would fall into chaos if all the people were anxious to achieve quick success and get instant benefits.

A country with no sovereignty cannot be prosperous. It is the root of instability and unpeace for a country to stir up the hatred and fabricate the classes.

21. General Rules and Regulations & Social Order and Law

Laws, decrees, regulations, rules, regulations and other legal documents are called the general rules and regulations. In modern

European and American countries, governing the country by the laws, which are passed through the majority vote in the parliamentary debates. It is regarded as a model of the modern citizen, which is followed by many other countries around the world.

In general, the role of laws is to command or prohibit something, or to promulgate a policy. Modern states in Europe and the United States pass a law by parliament, and the governments formulate the administrative laws and regulations according to this law. Then under the laws, decrees, regulations and articles of association, all kinds of social activities are associated with the rules.

Rules and regulations vary from one region to another. Administration of laws and regulations forms the basis for governmental management. If people want to reform their society, the first thing is to re-establish the order. In history, the Reform by Shang Yang and the revolution led by Li Kui are unprecedented. State institutions are usually established in accordance to laws and regulations. But the laws are not necessarily to govern the country sometimes. The code of Hammurabi was unparalleled, but it failed to bring peace and stability to the kingdom of Babylon. The code of United States is widely used, but it may not be applicable in Burma.

Harmony is the key of the legislation. To any laws and regulations, if given to a nation that has no justifications, no one will abide by it. Therefore, the establishment and maintenance is more important than legislating and upholding the laws.

Social order and laws are the root of Chinese society, since the generations after the Xia dynasty. In the book *The Marriage of Flowers in the Mirror*, "Social order and law rules everything", which might come from the *Book of Songs* saying "laws rule over the whole country". When Qin Dynasty was overthrown by Han Emporer, the legal system remained the same from that in Qin Dynasty. The right legitimacy intention and the ancient tradition still works. What they

removed was only tyranny. So there came the prosperity in Wen Jing and Han Wu's reign.

From Xia, Shang and Zhou Dynasties, the Chinese have used surname nobility as justifications; after the Qin Dynasty, there came the bureaucracy management, which took official character for justifications. If the officials have good virtues, then the state can be prosperous; if the officials are lack of virtue, the country would be a total mess. After the the times when Confucian culture becomes dominant, husband is the one who earn money to support the family, while wife is the one who is responsible for housework. Nobleman rules the country by imperial power, while squire rules village. Family and society has already been a republic.

In China, gentleman means a teacher of king. Confucius is the teacher of the lord, so his philosophies be come the justifications of laws. Even the regime has changed, the social order and laws remained the same throughout the dynasties in Chinese history. Peace will come.

22. Know Yourself as Well as the Enemy

China has long been seen as a society composed of four major professional classes namely, scholar, farmer, artisan and merchant. In ancient times, scholars who lived leisurely with noble spirit was a full-time ministers or household servants. It is necessary to know yourself as well as the enemy if you want to regulate the family and rule the state.

In the Zhou Dynasty, scholars were among the lowest rank of the hierarchy, after the Qing (senior officials). Usually they had certain skills, and worked as senior officials' home ministers and chief staffs. In the Warring States period, scholars' talents caught the attention of the lords. So it was popular for those famous lords as Meng Chang, Ping Yuan and Chun Shen to hire a lot of scholars. And scholars often acted as officials.

After the abolishment of the hereditary system in the Qin Dynasty,

scholars, farmers, artisans and merchants had become "the common people", which is called populaces and civilians. Because they could read, write and have statecraft, they are known as "scholar-officials" with respect. In the W ring States period, scholar-officials acted in accordance with the order from the emperor. So they lived leisurely so that they could focus on the strategies to deal with their enemy.

The scholar-officials in Qin Dynasty were close to emperors. In Chinese chess we can also see the character "士" as the officer. After emperor Wu in Han Dynasty, civil officials were generally Confucian scholars and gradually formed the unique civilian politics of the times: They work for whoever pays. Then there formed the virtue of righteous which is associated with the Confucian morality of the loyalty: They die for those who appreciate them.

Gentlemen die for those who appreciate them and ladies try to look good for those who love them. It contains the wisdom for knowing the enemy and themselves. Confucian scholars died for those who appreciate them, which is the philosophy in *Zhou Yi* : work for the emperor even in their tough times. It forms the responsibility and loyalty to their country with the condition that "working for the country when the national policy is correct; when the national policy is not correct, people should withdraw themselves from society and live in solitude. "

The idea of valuing loyalty over money is taken as a foolish act. In fact scholar-officials and gentlemen of Confucianism know that people need benevolent and righteous officers. This philosophy which comes from knowing others brings benevolent environment that can be shared by emperor and ministers. The country is prosperous and people are at peace, which brings income to oneself. It is a brilliant for one to know himself.

Scholar-officials' loyalty to emperor is reflected by their righteousness. Patriotism is essential. If they serve a bad emperor, they

should quit the job. Confucius, traveling to the state Lu was taken as an example. Zhuge Liang didn't have blind loyalty to Liu Bei, but dedicated to the state Shu and serve its inhabitants. In the Eastern Jin Dynasty, Tao Qian quitted his job. As his poem goes, "While picking asters neath the Eastern fence; my gaze upon the Southern mountain rests." So he could survive from the turmoil and chaos of war.

Zhuge Liang worked as an official with responsibility but not for salary. This spirit comes from morality that "follows the righteous instead of the emperor." Liu Bei visited Zhuge Liang three times to show the moral codes of orthodoxy of "for the people". Zhuang Zi said that Confucius didn't kneel down to the emperor and governors but stand up with them equally. However, after Song Dynasty, scholar-officials' spirit gradually lost.

Today's scholars work for fame and wealth like walking on a wire of money and power. One day after these sinful acts, the spirit is soaked in extreme poverty. People become slaves to houses, degrees, and cars. They didn't have the wisdom of knowing the enemy or themselves and They care little about Tao Qian's state of mind and finally become sick with anxiety.

23. A Contented Mind is a Feast.

According to historical records, our ancestors had already followed Confucian orthodoxy of ethical code since Zhou Dynasty, thus forming five kinds of relationship as "affection between fathers and sons; affiliation between monarchs and courtiers; distinction between husbands and wives; order between seniors and juniors; trust among friends". This kind of human relationships like "human follows land; land follows sky; sky follows Taoism; Taoism follows the nature" make Chinese civilization outshine other civilization for 3000 years and contribute a lot to the world.

The Chinese traditional laws and regulations are similar to civil constitution or ethics in Europe and America, both of which are products of history. Obviously, ethics and hierarchy are important and indispensible in all countries.

According to the book *Guan Zhong · Eight View*, "If one is against human relations and does things like an animal, he would be defeated in ten years." And in the book *Mencia · Teng Wengong*, it said: "If one is free from all burden from life, he was something like an animal. That's why the sage shun was worried about that, then he dispatched Qi as prime minister to educate the common people with the knowledge of human relations..." Hou Jing, a Sabir in the Northern Wei Dynasty, is a volatile man. In order to discipline for his rebellion and ferity, Hou equated men with animals. Then he came across tragic failure at last. People drank his ashes along with wine to express their hatred to him.

After entering the central areas, Xianbei suffered national subjugation and genocide. This historical fact is closely related to Xianbei's short-time Chinesization and their behaviors against human relations such as be unfilial and perfidious. Their results tested and verified Guan Zhong's thought. As you see, "affection between fathers and sons, affiliation between monarchs and courtiers, distinction between husbands and wives, order between seniors and juniors, trust among friends" —these are the laws we should follow.

What is happiness? To make it plain, happiness is a kind of cheerful mood, pleasure or contentment. It is the perfect condition that we want to sustain.

Where does happiness lie? It lives in our heart. Pleasure, just as its name implies, is joyful and cheerful. Look at those children. They will be rapturous when seeing the rainbow come out; they will go around to yell and share with others when their homework got full marks.

How to get happiness? We should learn how to get pleasure and

how to protect it. We can know that happiness depends most on noe's values of life. That is to say, happiness could be pursued in our life.

Mozi regarded universal love and mutual benefit for the people as happiness. Yang Zhu in the Warring States Period held that people always lived for their personal instincts such as food and sex. The western philosopher Democritus said that happiness lives in our soul. It's necessary for a person to learn how to control when indulging in comforts and how to live a peaceful life. One won't get anything without giving up. Abstinence is just like building a reservoir. It makes water flow slowly, so that it can flow for a long time.

It is right to follow Mo Zi and Democritus. When people pursue happiness, they always fight with others or hurt their rivals. People have no faith, no affection, no order, no distinction, no trust, and destroy human relations, which will cause troubles. Therefore, a contented mind is a blessing.

24. Science and Technology Industrial Would Bring Disasters

Science and Technology can do harm to the environment. Pollution is one of the disasters caused by human.

Science is a branch of philosophy or ethics in ancient times. Today's science is like a sword to the earth, which wants to tear open the earth to acquire the limited energy. It is not as wise as what Xun Zi said: if you use the correct management measures, things can work out night.

Since the westernization movement, industrial technologies were introduced to China to in the Qing Dynasty. Kang Youwei introduced Japanese characters "science" into Chinese. Chinese began to catch the trend of the times. Science and technology competition and open policies on politics brought great changes to the society.

No matter it was in ancient Greece or China, technologies mainly refer to personal skills. Specifically speaking, they are skills to manufacture crafts like ceramics, vehicles swords or to build houses. These skills are handed down from the older generations of the family. But in the 160 os, Britain's Francis Bacon combined scientific knowledge with experimental technology, which has changed the nature of technology.

Bacon said: knowledge is power; human will dominate the world. Since then, science and technology refer to the theories acquired by the intellectuals through experimental analysis. The application of these theories in industrial production has changed the living environment New inventions emerged, such as steam engines, trains, ships, aircraft, cannons, nuclear weapons, satellites and so on.

By the end of the Second World War, people had known how to use automatic machine in production lines, which had changed the system of the machines. Since the 1980s, the high-tech industry enjoyed a rapid progress.

Over the past century, human's mode of living has greatly changed. A trip to London had taken several generations' efforts, but now with a ticket, people from the other hemisphere can be there in ten hours by air. People sit in front of the TV set and computer and the next minute they know the news around the world. The communication between the United States and China is faster than that word came from village to village.

However, what makes people worried is that plane crashes happen from time to time. Terror attack made the plan crash to the buildings. children drank milk and was poisoned. Because of the science and technologies, the disasters happen more often than before. They come even more fiercely than droughts and wars.

Buddhists believe that people will pay debt in their present life for what they have done in their previous life. If they did something evil, the revenge will come to this life. The film *2012* rendered frightening

disaster of doomsday. However, the year 2012 has passed and nothing happened. Can science and technology industry help people avoid disaster?

25. The Theory of Samsara and Relativity

As the saying goes, "Caution is the parent of safety." One often meets his destiny on the road he takes to avoid it. Since the blessing and evil are different and good days will not last forever. When the evil comes, can we avoid it by keeping caution? Should we just live for today for the reason that we couldn't avoid disasters?

Buddhism has the theory of the six great divisions in the wheel of karma, while science has the theory of relativity. If we put them together to discuss their influence on men, what kind of conclusion shall we get?

Buddhists not only believes there is life on earth, but also believes that there exists a big system of the universe with heaven, humanitarian, Asura, hell, the hungry ghost realm, and the animal realm.

Samsara stresses in the circle of life: even the demons must die, and after death, they have to experience those six great divisions in the wheel of karma. That is to say in the present life you can be a man, and in the next life you might be an animal or a plant. It is not easy to get a human body, which may take over a hundred years. If you do good things, you can keep the human body or go to the heaven after your death. However, if you do the evil things, your soul will be burnt in the hell and you will suffer endless pain; you will never be a man from then.

Samsara thinks any living thing needs to go though the six great divisions of heaven, Asura, people, ghosts, beast, and hell. It sounds fascinating. Believing in Samsara will make men live with fears. You cannot eat too much fish or meat and live a luxurious life. Those who

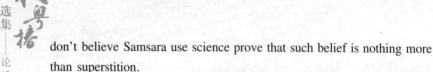

don't believe Samsara use science prove that such belief is nothing more than superstition.

Rationally speaking, Samsara is a kind of Taoism, which divides the time and space into different layers and people never know where they will die or be born. How do people with out wisdom figure if out? Superstition means anti-science. Seriously speaking, this kind of time and space division includes the good and evil behavior and life forms actually has more wisdom. If you really want to understand it, you need to live freely from vulgarity.

Science cannot prove whether life moves in cycle or not. In biology, the life after death is beyond the discussion of science. However, many scientists believe Samsara. At first, they acknowledged that they have their blind spot, and Samsara is one. Samsara is what one needs to learn about by himself. On the contrary, science is a subject that requires one to believe some facts before he can proove them.

Modern physics theory of relativity on time and space has something in common with Samsara. The theory of relativity raises the new concepts of "relativity at the same time", "four dimensions of space-time", and "curved space-time" etc. These new concepts reflect principles of relativity, and the establishment of limited boundless four-dimensional universe model. Using these principles to define Samsara will help to make the concepts clear and easy to understand.

Samsara uses Buddhist doctrine to talk about life and gives richer meaning to life, as well as ultimate care to those who live in the era of science. Those people will be more responsible and more careful about their words and behavior in their life, and keep distance from corruption and evil spirits.

26. The problems of government

The government, which is called official government or public

government, etc. , is authorized by the emperor and approved by the people political—a set of administrative agency, law enforcement; full-time monitor a region-to maintain the order.

The government initially is very simple, very original. They control farmers in a bigger house; herdsmen in a package of carpets. Through fighting or establishing mutual belief, the rulers make orders and organize groups of people. At that time the government is very small, controlling a few people, several villages or tribes. However, they have to work and deal with some frivolous problems.

Gradually it is divided into a lot of branches, now they are called bureaus, departments and so on. They are in charge of legislation, administration, justice, and specialized police to maintain public order, the troops to protect the local. Then there are a lot of disputes between the institutions. The problem has changed from small to big. In order to coordinate and supervise each part, there comes cabinet.

Government organization gets bigger, more complicated. The controlling power and government officials have also varied. There is a wide variety of government, known as the monarchy, a republic and a democracy and autocracy.

The government uses management as an object of oppression, which will inevitably become the authoritarian government. However, if the government takes residents under management as a family and residents call them government official, this is the monarchy, and some generally call absolute monarchy. A republic generally comes after dissatisfaction authoritarian government and monarchy, which is managed by two or more persons. The republic government is selected by people, and gradually appeared in the democratic government today.

The government is the subject of tax. With a strong sense of service for the people's benefits, it will become a good government; with a weak sense of service and always focus on taking people's money and welfare, there will be a lot of corrupt officials and became a bad government. Government theory includes monarchy, democracy, autocracy, and republic. People don't need to care about it. The most important thing is to distinguish good from bad.

27. Rebuild the Society

To make it simple, society is a group composed of several individual or family, which has a unique culture and customs, occupies a certain areas of land like the trees and mountains. After the formation, the woods and hills hardly change. However, although society can be big and small, it is constantly reconstructed. In the process of constant reconstruction, it feels like a mountain or forests growing unceasingly.

Reconstruction of society means the restructuring of elements, which changes the combination of form of people and family and forms a new culture and customs. Typically it requires changing locations. If there is no migration, people will have to be isolated, experiencing the procedure like MLM brainwashing. Whether migrating or not, as long as population, habits, customs, language change, the society will be reconstructive again.

Once the Xianbei ethnic group crossed the Great Wall, came into the central plains and gradually became the Han nationality. In modern times many people travel across the ocean, and form the Chinese community in Indonesia, Singapore, and Malaysia. It happens every day that rural people come to cities to find jobs and the villagers join the new unit as new citizens.

The ancient Greeks had a doctrine that four elements including fire, earth, water, air compose everything; love and hate are the two kinds of feelings respectively stands for the energy of combination and separation. Love makes four elements combine into a ball and hate turns four elements back into their original object. The balance and struggle of love and hate produce different plants, animals, people, etc. This is

the first class struggle restructuring of social philosophy.

The ancient society was the combination of five elements restructured by five virtues. It is said to be the history of social reconstruction. Wood, fire, earth, metal and water are the five elements representing five virtues. Different character stands for respectively dynasties: Yu, Xia, Shang, Zhou, Qin. Ancient dynasties come in cycle like that.

Society reconstruction requires creative transformation of the original social structure to form a new culture and customs regardless of the struggle, win or lose or the rank. Western reconstruction pay attention to the creativity and do not hesitate to destroy everything and start from scratch. We pay attention to the integration of the conversion, like Tai Ji. Two people get married and have children and grandchildren. At a certain time, they are divided into a new family and join the ancestral hall worship ancestor together.

Transformation of reconstruction in the western society is very rapid, like an oak felled at one stroke. In the east, it is mild and not artificial; natural and on track. The country is now following the west which cannot exploit the advantages to the full.

28. The Magic of Five Elements

Compared to India's "Four Theories" (water, fire, earth, wind) and "Four Roots" of Greece (fire, earth, water, and gas), the ancient "Five Elements" has the advantages of particularity and the historical arrangement, if you think it through you can understand.

The theory of five elements including gold, wood, water, fire, earth, is combination of everything the ancient Chinese, which is widely used in Chinese medicine and divination. The five elements theory covers the weakening or theoretical philosophy and it's said that the thought is more appropriate.

The theory of five elements we talked about is mainly a kind of magical power, different from speculative theory of Greek. It is a kind of philosophy changing from monism to pluralism, based on principles of mutual promotion and restraint between the five elements to solve problems of survival and development of Chinese ancestors. So it can be used for medical skill and divination and also used for face reading, writing, speaking, writing a novel, etc. Every kind of areas can use five elements to analyze, even for the five characters of righteousness and propriety wisdom.

Using the theory of five elements to analyze problems has close relationship with the analyst's way. Western medicines look down on Chinese medicine because they think neither traditional Chinese medicine theory of five elements scientific or as precocious as the western medicine, which mainly for the reason that they don't fully understand that the theory of five elements is a Taoist magic art. Using the perspective of academic to see magic art is wrong direction. It's as inappropriate to use technology to be little theory.

Most of charlatans like gangsters on the street only want to keep alive. So speculation of sense motive or a rule of thumb with the low accuracy and far-fetched reason is easy to be charged.

Five elements theory has been seen in Confucian philosophical, such as the *History*, which involves the River Maps and Luo Book. Five elements theory can be combined with all the directions, seasons, nature, time, and heavenly stems, form view of time of five elements theory and used widely.

The Eight Diagrams, heaven and earth and the elements such as Burgundy match five elements theory can be seen on King Wen's image. The book of changes can also be equipped with the five elements.

29. Chinese Civilization

The Chinese cannot live without Chinese civilization. As the

character "中" in the word China, it isn't such an simple explanation as "the central of the world". It mainly refers to the civilization and the birthplace of Confucian doctrine

China, in addition to the name of middle earth, there are names as well as Zhong Hua, Zhu Hua, Shen Zhou, Hua Xia, Zhong Xia, Zhu Xia, Huang Han, Han etc. So what is China? Is it the abbreviation of Republic of China or People's Republic of China? No, it refers to gorgeous, thriving and glorious cultural meaning of which our ancestors are proud.

China, which firstly refers to the central plains the Yellow Emperor unified, formed the two thousand years of Confucianism culture which comes down in one continuous line with the Xia, Shang, and Zhou dynasties. It naturally referred to middle earth or China. In the Spring and Autumn and Warring State period, there are names as Qi, Wei, Zhao and other surnames country names, but all claiming to be China. Why? There are pride, honor, grace, recognize ancestors involved.

Xia, Shang and Zhou dynasties are commonly found in ancient books. In the eyes of other ethics, these three generations had luxuriant clothes as polite countries and centers of the world. Shang and Zhou dynasty had archaeological evidence, but Xia dynasty didn't. There is a saying of Hua Xua or China in the Chinese ancient books. There is no such call as Hua Shang and Hua Zhou. Why? This is the clear evident that Xia dynasty was more civilized than Shang and Zhou. If the people of Zhou dynasty are mean, how could they speak highly of China?

The ancient China advocated Confucianism orthodoxy. To make it simple, it was the time gentlemen controlled the villains. Before the Zhou dynasty, a gentleman in ancient China was a general or elegant name of noble man. After Qin and Han dynasties, all the people were civilians (ordinary people), gentleman was used to call one with the noble spirit, to distinguish them from those villains with no aristocratic spirit. In ancient China Gentleman would be an official at the

prosperous time to educate villains with etiquette and talent cultivation. Then the culture tended to be more modest.

Moral codes take fostering gentle manners and talent of a gentleman as purpose. Though there is no saint, a virtue still alive: Do what ought to do, don't do what should not do; give up one's life for righteousness; A man of honor makes money by a lawful way etc. Compared with the Japanese warrior aristocrat and European knight nobles, ancient Chinese gentleman have huge difference in inner quality and scholarship.

Compared to the gentleman villains especially refers to people who do not strictly abide by the moral and rules in ancient China. People said, "I have no knowledge and. I am very realistic. So don't talk to me about ideal. I am a farmer or I'm a clown..." That is the word said when the moral degeneration of the world is getting worse day by day. Villain's culture makes gossip, trap, libel, shameless and mean become popular.

Chinese culture is very unique. When the gentleman is in power, Plato's republic is the reality in China of Wen Jing and Zhen Guan emperors. When the villains are in power, there will be lawless, or failure to abide by the laws.

30. Issues on Dynasty

Chinese dynasties covered a period from Xia to Qing dynasty including twelve different united countries. However, this seems as if they make an unworthy continuation of a great work.

Xia, Shang, and Zhou dynasty, referred as "the three generations", had the earliest feudal dynasties of written records. In the three generations, Xia dynasty was the mot gorgeous one with the most compliments by the later generations. But till today it is still a legend. The Zhou dynasty lasted for eight hundred years and the Spring and Autumn and Warring States period lasted for five hundred years. In the alternate and early period of the three generations, there was a short

time of disorder. Then the time of unity lasted for one thousand years in total and formed the general trend of unity.

What behind the general trend is the Chinese moral codes and tradition: There should be affection between fathers and sons, affiliation between monarchs and courtiers, distinction between husbands and wives, order between seniors and juniors, and trust amongst friends. Moral codes based on blood kinship are politer than the ancient Greek hero epic cultural refinement and simpler than the Jewish Bible mythology. So it's overwhelmingly difficult to unit the ancient Greek and Jews. But China can be united in Qin dynasty and Han dynasty again. Chinese dynasties which serve as a link between past and future must form a new restructuring automatic mechanism of unity and separation.

Separation means the trouble times in China. There have five hundred years of hegemony in the Spring and Autumn period and the Warring States period; Chu and Han' war lasted for four years between Qin and Han dynasties handover; The Three Kingdoms, Jin dynasties and the Southern and Northern dynasties lasted about four hundred years (neglecting more than ten years of short time in west Jin), five dynasties and ten states had conflict for sixty years; Song, Liao, Xia, Jin and Yuan had partition in three hundred years.

War is not what the people expect. So we have a saying that "We would rather live ordinarily in peaceful society than being famous in trouble times." But for history of Chinese dynasty, trouble times allowed nomadic people invading in the central plains, which made the Han nationality migrate to southern to run away from social upheaval. The Xiongnu and Xianbei nationality establish their countries in the central plains, and merged with the culture of the Han nationality of large population and rich culture. The king of the central plains and noblemen migrated south to Jiangsu, Zhejiang, Hubei, Hunan, Guangdong and Guangxi provinces, which leaded to the rapid economic development of Yangtze River area. The wars in the central plain became an invisible hand forcing the people outside the Great Wall move in to learn culture, and forcing the central plains people migrating south to spread the culture.

Sui dynasty and Tang dynasty are called Sui-tang. In the times of peace and prosperity of Tang dynasty, China's culture and economy were second to none; territory was almost as large as Arab empire. But the Arab empire unification was short. Sui dynasty was to Tang dynasty what Qin dynasty was to Han dynasty. Chinese culture of Han and Hang dynasties reaches its top in Song dynasty: mature civil service system; the righteousness concept for government which hasn't seen the descendants in the world so far.

Yuan, Ming and Qing dynasties left a territory of more than ten million square kilometers as well as incomplete political of civil official of Song dynasties and culture of Han and Tang dynasty. The thought and spirit lost in Yuan opera (a type of verse popular in the Yuan Dynasty) and novel surprisingly appeared in the European Renaissance and scattered citizen culture and politics of public servants in Britain, France, and America etc.

Before China was established the republic of China in 1912, it gives priority to hereditary Kings, so that there are stable and lasting stability.

Selected Essays by Zhu Yuechun

朱粤椿选集

——论适应主义 下

On Adaptationism（Vol. 2）

朱粤椿 著 李南哲 译

·广州·

广东省出版集团

新世纪出版社

目录

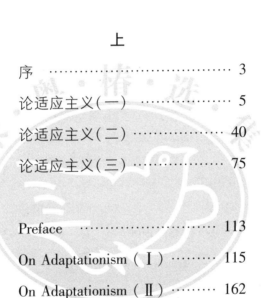

朱·粤·椿·选·集

——论适应主义下

论适应主义（四）

1. 人生如树

人生如树，有一个自然的生长过程，在一日复一日中量变，在月积岁累中质变。人由精卵细胞结合成形，在母腹中孕育，由微型而显形。人十月怀胎，如同树种在土壤里培育根系。人破胎而生，如同树苗破土而出，身柔如树，干枝难分。

人蹒跚学步到学前，犹如小树在风中摇曳、在雨中颤抖，经风雨见世面就有了生活。人上学形成思想，分科学习，犹如树开始分枝，年级晋升如树枝伸长。人从小学到初中，从初中到高中，从大学到硕士、博士、博士后……思想在点点滴滴中累积，在人文环境中潜移默化，由感性而理性，由直观而客观分析。

人生如树，由小到大的过程即生长的过程。自然生长，树大根深，根深叶茂，身体增长和思想演进都是这样的理。树叶长宽增长多、厚度增长少；人体高宽增长大，厚度增长小；东想西想容易，沉思审视却难。经验数量可以因经历丰富和勤奋而增加，但思维抽象分析、概括综合，只能按部就班，如同枝叶慢慢生长。

树叶吸收阳光、二氧化碳，树根吸收土壤中的水分和矿物质，都通过其表面。树无论根系、叶系，要有足够大的面积与体积，才有足够的营养供应。人也是这样，无论小学、中学、大学，都要有阶梯式的年级，要有班级中一定数量的同学，相互促进与制衡，还

要有一定数量的学友，以了因结缘。

不仅完备的思维能力需要层级不同的训练，需要与同学、学友的相互扶助，竞争促进。人的品格形成，更需要朋友，所谓一个好汉三个帮，好花需要绿叶衬。朋友形成的环境，对人品的好坏有重要影响，所谓近朱者赤，近墨者黑。

物以类聚，人以群分。树有种类，人有品类。好人莫与坏人为伍。老鼠过街人人喊打，正气也须扬威。除恶趁早，莫让老鼠屎弄坏一锅汤。药医不死病，佛度有缘人。强辩者愚，深思者智。

2. 遗传基因

生命前后代相似，是因为遗传基因的传递。遗传是前代通过基因传给后代的特征，正所谓人模人样。人模人样，是人的 DNA 得到复制。人样狗习，结合佛教思想推理，是说狗的 DNA，在人身轮回中，遗传效应得到发挥。

生物遗传学研究需要有对生物实验的谨慎观察与分析。人类文化留有不少遗传方面的知识，足够我们理解为什么要重血缘亲情，讲孝悌伦理。

司马迁在《史记》中为扁鹊立传，说："庆有古先道遗传黄帝、扁鹊之脉书，五色诊病，知人生死。"这是说扁鹊的医术，是医药先辈留传下来的，是医道师传的，并非靠自己聪明琢磨出来的。许多聪明人执迷不悟，窗户纸不点破，外面的阳光就透射不进来。人没有名师指点，就须留意高人暗示。遵守礼教，是很重要的。

许多遗留下来的传闻被史家记载后，千百年来后人读史借鉴、体悟、推广后约定俗成，形成文化。秦朝的隶书被汉朝认可与承传，成为汉朝隶书。历代书法，就这样代代遗传前代，才有了书法的留存和演进。琴棋书画等诸多技艺的遗传，都是文化的流传。

物种、人种，不能隔断 DNA 的遗传基因的传递。绝种，就是遗传基因没有了种族传人。古代希腊文化被日耳曼人的军事侵略和基督教阻隔，希腊就不再有苏格拉底、柏拉图、亚里士多德的思想传人了。国家要防止这样的悲剧发生。

华人承传祖国文化。我们绝不妄自菲薄，西学引进了，也还不回去了，只是莫要废弃老庄、孔孟遗传给我们的文化矿藏。做先哲思想基因的传递人，推陈出新。

3. 三岁定向

常言说："三岁看大，七岁看老。"金庸笔下的韦小宝，在妓院长到十几岁，好色、骂人、骗人、赌钱作弊，早在三岁就定向了。

三岁看老的科学依据是：婴儿出生时脑重量只有 370 克，快一岁时，接近成人脑重的 60%；两岁时，约占成人脑重的 75%；三岁时，已跟成人脑重相差无几，以后脑重的 25% 要到几十岁。

英国伦敦精神病研究所与伦敦国王学院，1980 年将 1000 名三岁幼儿分为五种类型：自信型、适应型、沉默型、自律型和多动型。到 2003 年，这些孩子二十六岁时，研究者走访了他们及其朋友和亲戚。调查结果显示，这些成年人的性格，其三岁时的言行就准确预示了。

调查者卡斯比教授在 2005 年发表报告中说道：一个人对三岁之前经历的事情会像海绵一样吸收。这意味着一个人在三岁之前，生活在什么样的环境下，就会形成相应的性格。可以说，金庸笔下的黄蓉、韦小宝，性格都在三岁就奠定了。

1920 年在印度发现的七岁的狼孩卡玛拉，跟狼一样用四肢行走，白天睡觉，晚上活动，怕火怕光怕水，只吃肉食（放在地上用牙齿撕开吃），不会讲话，吃饱了就睡，像狼似地长嚎。卡玛拉死时十六岁，智力只相当于四岁的孩子。

美国科学家用"正电子发射计算体层摄影"技术，扫描幼儿大脑，研究表明，三岁以后大脑的复杂性和丰富性已经基本定型，并且停止了新的资讯交流，这时大脑的结构就已经牢固成形，如同电脑一样，硬盘已经格式化完毕，就等待编程了。这就是说，黄蓉成侠客、韦小宝做官的兴趣方向，在三岁就定了。

美国男人丁大卫、台湾女人张平宜，能来中国贫困地区支教，都是在三岁时就形成了助人为乐的快感机制。

而许多农村孩子从小就被父母唠叨，长大要进城，所以一心就想逃离乡村。很多人好辱骂孔孟，是三岁就有了对传统文化的仇恨。

4. 读书启智

读书上学，基本上是文明社会为孩子定制的学习过程，一般有小学、初中、高中、大学。当代国家义务教育，有的从小学到初中，有的到高中。

"小么小二郎，背着书包上学堂，不怕太阳晒，不怕风雨狂，只怕先生骂我懒，没有学问，无颜见爹娘……不是为做官，也不是为面子光。只为做人要争气，不受人欺负不做牛和羊。"读书从小确立的是如此目的，长大就会学孔孟，兴中华。

当今读书，从小学到中学，都以西学为主，汉文识字、数学抽象、英语与国际接轨，而后以科学、电脑、美术、音乐强化华人对西学的兴趣和对技能的志向。中学细分科学为物理现象分析、化学物质变化、生物种类进化等。物理、化学是西学特长，中国要与国际融为一体，自然要学习。事实上，华人能够学得更好。

读书学习，一般而言，都须从师听讲，态度很关键。文子，周朝先贤老子的弟子，曾经将听讲学习分为上、中、下三个层次，说："上学以神听，中学以心听，下学以耳听。"倡导听讲要聚精会神，做不到也要用心聆听，不要当耳边风。

近代洋务运动倡导"中学为体，西学为用"，开启近代工业发展之路。以中庸之道启蒙、以仁德教化明礼，应始终是华人文化教育的主道。

这正是今人要负起来的责任。不要为了私心，让老庄斗孔孟；让愿意把猴子当祖先的人自学进化论；让以斗为乐者自修斗争哲学。地理、历史、政治教育，立足于传统。老师要以人的灵性培育为本，以人的自强与厚德为先。

5. 果行育德

果行育德，语出《周易》，是讲启蒙的道理：师者，传道最重要，培育人的德行。

这是教人做君子、善民的第一步。人总是自求善与福的，何谓善，何谓福？就是美德品行。这听起来是陈词，却不是滥调。父母留给孩子万贯家财，孩子无品无德，吃喝嫖赌，家财很快就会被败掉，弄不好，还惹来杀身之祸。

唯天地万物父母，唯人万物之灵。这两句话，就蕴含了果行育德的道理。人是天地的造化，宇宙的精灵。于是，做君子，仿效天地精神，就要自强不息、厚德载物。能做到吗？无德，千难万难；有德，万难可以排除。

做老师，首要的是传道。那么做学生，首要的是什么？那就是行德。学生受教之初，通常都会觉得"道"不着边际，大道理没啥用处，不如具体知识、技术实在，比如书法，学生想学习各种技法，可是大书法家给学生强调的就是德。

道，从老师口中说出来，学生自然会觉得是空的。但如果学生去履行，将"道"化作一个个细微的德行，那就是具体的，也很有用，很实在。德行伴人，受益终生。

早上起来，见到父母，说声："爸妈，早上好!"电梯门口，遇到邻居，说声："阿姨，您先请!"见到同学提重物，主动上前帮忙……日本有个教授，每次去学校，一路行，一路拾垃圾，到学校门口，扔进垃圾箱。这样的老师，到哪都会得到注目礼，到哪里都是朋友。我们知道，做正事难，可做人到这份上，就不难了。

果行育德，意在德，重在行。社会人都自觉行德，刑法就会没用了，当然这只是理想。但据史书上记载，在中国古代文景、贞观治世，确实有过路不拾遗、牢里无人的好景象。

讲行德，有人会觉得保守、老土。瞧英国保守党，老土吗？很绅士的。人，初生是混沌的，所以求知启蒙，如果首先学了偷盗，就毁了大半生。所以古希腊圣哲苏格拉底说："美德即知识。"

6. 十五志学

一个人，三岁定向是通过家教，读书启智在小学里，成为自觉行德的人，再在人生教育旅程中前行，就进入十五而志学的阶段了。

中国古代教育，过去总给人一个印象，那就是聪明活泼的孩子老被打手掌，被父母罚站或打屁股。这如果不是无知的宣扬，就是刻意糟蹋私塾老师。

私塾从孔子时期开始。孔子教学生，有教无类并因材施教。哪有训斥和体罚？孔子幼儿时期也嬉戏、玩耍，何罪之有？幼儿、小学时期，活泼是天性，天真可爱，不必强求他一坐一个小时，做作业到晚上，学而不厌就学，厌了就去玩，体罚干吗？

孔子自述"吾十五而有志于学"，还说"我非生而知之者，好古敏以求之者也"。联系起来，我们就知道了，对于学而知之的人，专心学习在十五岁左右。

十五岁已是少年了，一般人这时候都心志坚明，所以这时学习者"志于学"没什么困难，是可以做到的。十五岁在儒家经学时期，是入大学学经术之年，学格物致知、修身齐家、治国平天下之经术，也非志于学不可。这既必行，也可行。

而今学习，经学内容很少，所学皆术，基本失道，学校基本上是西方式的。西方学生多数小时候就要受洗礼、进教堂，这是西方"果行育德"的方式之一。没有这样读小学启智的过程，如果一个人在幼儿园就被强迫写字，在小学晚上十一点还要做作业，这样到十五岁，对这种被强加的、让自己劳累而无趣的学习，是很厌烦的，躲避还来不及，怎么会"志于学"呢？这时候孩子很向往独立，反抗学习成了起点。

一个人如果能够活到七十岁以上，十五而志于学做到了，之后，才可能三十而立、四十不惑、五十知天命、六十耳顺、七十随心所欲不逾矩。

所以，十五志学很重要的。否则，三十以后，接二连三来的是失意和重重难关。

7. 成家立业

一般而言，人成家立业在三十岁。所以孔子有"三十而立"的说法。当然，就知书达礼、学以致用而言，三十而立指学有所成。"有所成"当然已经能自立于世了。

古今中外，只有少数人有避世隐居，以修道求仙或修佛求涅槃的心愿。大多数人都是红尘中的性情中人，他们是要活在家人中，需要事业为生甚至扬名。所以成家立业，是大多数人的诉求之一，是人生的一个阶段，达成了，就有成就感。

古时候成家立业，一般在三十岁，通过科举成了进士的有了县官一级的品级，这自然能够挺胸做人，父母也觉得荣耀。作为读书人，父母与自己都以此为期盼。对于寒门学子，读书的意义也在于

此：书中自有黄金屋，书中自有颜如玉。

一般志不在学的人，也不是人生就了无期盼。安心务农，或者学门手艺，或者外出经商，或者就地摆个水果摊之类的，这类人也希望能在三十岁成家生儿育女。

三十岁的时候，农民有了十几亩田、一座小院，工匠出师带艺有了职业收入，商人已经历过盘货、验货、囤货、出货等风波而于商场有立足之地，都可以为女人夫，为儿女父了。

必须承认，而今时代跟古代有很大的变化，科举制也早被废除了，农民也不困在土地上了，工匠与商人这些过去的低贱行业现在已然是城市文明的主道。社会职业结构已从"士农工商"，重新排位，成了"工商士农"了。"老板"称呼，喊得有人心颤、有人心痒。大学毕业即失业的很多，很难期盼黄金屋、颜如玉。

社会结构变化引发名流变化，旧时王谢堂前燕，飞入寻常百姓家。但在三十岁成家立业这个指望，还是很有激励意义的，如果忽略这个阶段，中老年问题会有很多。

总之，成家立业能给所有人一个人生目标，有成年人的意识和责任心，不至于只是穿衣吃饭干活睡觉，活得糊里糊涂。

8. 四十不惑

有种消极的说法是：人到中年万事休。说它消极，是相比四十不惑的说法。

电视剧《人到四十》，讲述一个职业为精神病医生的丈夫，与职业为重症监护室主任的妻子的生活波折和情感战争。在事业有成的四十岁，两人都不满意自己的生活，妻子期望丈夫调动工作，以减轻自己操持家务的压力；丈夫被查出癌症死亡将近，向妻子坦承自己喜欢上了别人，妻子默认了第三者的存在。

这对夫妻活得够累的，也彼此够折腾的。这固然有生活在上有

老、下有小的四十岁的沉重，更主要还因为人到四十还迷惑，还没真正活明白。

人到四十，如日中天，依照自然规律，不仅学业进入了不疑惑的明智阶段，而且进入了处变不惊，遇事知道什么该做，什么不该做，能够理智地予以取舍的阶段。

孔子说他四十而不惑，既是经验之谈，更是智者的明察和洞见。

黑格尔说中国智者是一种散文式的理智，这是以近代哲学家的成见衡量古代儒家先贤的睿智。如果孔子就是个哲学家，他确实应该把这个"四十"与"不惑"给予定义，而后分析哪些情况下会不惑，哪些情况下未必。但孔子不是这样的人。

18 世纪的黑格尔是大学教授，是搞理论研究的。春秋的孔子是诸侯的老师，与诸侯分庭抗礼，收了三千私塾弟子，以传道、授业、解惑的方式教他们如何治国安邦，如何做君王老师。黑格尔没这么牛，在诸侯面前只是个顾问。

其实孔子的这句格言，联系"十五而志于学、三十而立"来理解，就真正是学术了。一个人十五岁的时候能够静坐三小时，诵读《诗经》《周易》《春秋》有乐趣，有自强不息、厚德载物的功夫，三十岁时就能为人师表，坐怀不乱，四十不惑就水到渠成、自然而然了。

再看这位精神病医生，十五岁忙中考，胸无经典，脑无学术；三十岁以西医谋职，以医疗技术安身立命，虽成家立业了，却还是个马步不稳的花拳绣腿者。四十岁一边被告知"所剩时日不多了"，一边听玉女说"我爱你"，他能不晕倒吗？

9. 五十知命

有位老师五十岁了，突然迷上炒股，白天忙着观察股市行情，

晚上钻研证券术。最后教学任务被耽搁，股市遭遇熊市，钱被套牢，人活得像热锅上的蚂蚁。这是五十不知命所致。

生命，生而有命，五十知命，知足常乐，活得安稳。五十岁的老师，快退休的年龄，如果这时候他想搞教育学研究，著书立说，把自己的经验理论化，改良现有的教育学理论，这倒是知命。现在做准备，退休依然有事业，活得就很充实。

孔子五十而知天命，是另外一种形式。孔子是在礼崩乐坏的时代背景下，成为私塾老师，以教人知仁讲礼而门徒络绎不绝。五十岁的时候，他知道教人知礼是他一生的使命，最重要的是教儒士做官，教君王克制私欲教化民众。于是他进入官场，业绩不断，从县令升到司法部长。

孔子治国若烹饪，五十三岁时，使鲁国大治。但鲁国君臣迷恋歌舞，不理朝政。孔子知道鲁国不是久留之地，也知道诸侯都是这样，但知其不可而为之，他必须把上天让他知道的关于仁与礼的道理教给这些诸侯，于是他周游列国。

诸侯们既爱他，需要听他的高见，又接受不了他不叩头而平起平坐"高尚其事"的帝王之师的姿态，也就是说，消费不起他。而孔子又必须这样，给天下文人，尤其是以入仕为职业的儒士做个榜样，所以他就一直做他国客卿，被作为顾问而不用。

"知天命"，是懂天意的意思，也是说知道自己一生的使命是什么。这倒不是说，五十知天命是人老了，要不求上进、不思进取了。而是说静则静，动则动。

孔子人在鲁国，心在诸国，懂的都是诸侯该懂却不懂的事，所以去各国把他所知道的学术，告诉无知的诸侯，就是天命，是他必须做的事。

如果鲁国给孔子机会把鲁国变成强国，诸侯都来访问，他就不用远游了。鲁国没给他这个机会，这就是天意要他远行，离开故土。采纳与否是国君的事，告知他们是孔子的事。

而今这位五十岁的老师突然转向炒股，纯属心血来潮，大环境浮躁，他也躁动。

10. 人是万物之灵

在地球的众生中，唯人有机灵劲：理智，有灵感，能灵机一动、急中生智。

这确实是人与动植物相区别的地方。植物靠根深，而增加其生长的高度，却因此被大地牢牢陷住，一步也不能移动。动物能飞跑，能游泳，却一生被本能所困，身边有根棍子，却一辈子不知道借来敲打或支撑。

理性的抽象分析和归纳概括，能让人改变本能习性，跳出经验陷阱，进而得以借助器具，做成光凭身体力所不及的事，所以跳起来抓不着的果子，可以拿棍子打下，可以制作梯子从坑道里爬上地面。这就是人所拥有的动植物没有的理智。

人尤为奇特的在于，还能不用感官就能超距离地知道远方的事，知道他人的事，他人心里所想的事，等等，很奇妙。科学上叫远隔知觉，文艺上叫灵感思维，修行者叫神灵的感应……汉朝史官班固称之为"通灵"能力。

人的灵感玄妙的一面，未必都能理解，但感觉敏锐这一面却是普遍能认知的。有人不用温度计，凭感觉就能精确知道气温；不用秤，手一掂，就知道几斤几两。

有时候，百思不解的事，因为见到、听到、嗅到、触摸到什么，就能得到启发，突然间得到解答。

修行有成，听"鸡肋"口令，知道军队要撤退。修大道有成者，还真的如老子所说："不出户，知天下；不窥牖，见天道……不行而知，不见而名，不为而成。"

成语"灵机一动""急中生智"，就蕴含有人的灵性思维。没

有神妙难以言说的灵性，人何来灵机、急智、机智？灵性使感性升华，归正理性，驯化野性。

孔子说他六十耳顺，却有人八九十岁还不能。逆耳之忠言，许多人拒绝，不能明察话中的微言大义。表面上看，是人老顽固难变，其实是灵性缺失。人因为有灵性，才有"听君一席话，胜读十年书"的洞察和醍醐灌顶之醒悟，才能够格外物致良知，从常识中洞见天理，才可能不习逻辑，思维也有条理。

11. 疲劳与休息

无论思维、说话和做事，都有劳苦困乏的时候，需要休息。这是自然规律。

军事进攻，除了选择敌方戒备松弛的时候，再就是选择其疲劳、抵抗无力的时候。一国政府，使人民疲劳，就会促成各式各样的骚乱，上慢下暴，这个国家就开始瓦解。鲜卑、蒙古历史上穷兵黩武，就是在官民疲惫之际灭亡的。

家和万事兴，是以和谐协调的关系，使人免于紧张和疲乏。士农工商序列的国家和社会，控制工商业竞争进程，比较有节奏，疲劳在后。游牧部族军事侵略，最容易疲劳和瓦解。战争结束，马放南山，和平来临；整肃兴风，官民颤栗。

河流下游，泥沙增多，水势减缓，是河水的疲惫态。大山绵延，由巍峨到山峦，草木稀疏，山石风蚀，是山的疲惫态。中老年皮肤干燥，缺乏弹性，也属疲劳。

疲劳是自然和社会会普遍出现的状态。个人呼吸急促，打哈欠，伸懒腰，都是疲劳表象。疲劳乏力，疾病容易发生。病人又容易疲劳。疲劳了，要及时休息。

马放南山是军队休息，熄灯睡觉是个人休息。休息是生物具有的缓解疲劳、恢复精力的生理机制。感觉累了，减少活动，做体

操，听音乐，睡一会儿，疲劳感觉就会消除或减轻，精力就能得以恢复。好政府、好官员，就要懂得与民休息。

苛政、暴政就是政府利用权力加强人民的劳动量，并剥夺财富，使人民重复劳动，以至于不得不反抗，最后天下大乱不治，群雄纷争，战火纷飞，文明财富耗尽。轻徭薄赋甚至免税，就是中国道家传出来的让民众休养生息的执政方式。

中国历史上尧舜、平章、文景、贞观治世，都是掌权者与民休息，不与民争利。欧洲历史上，国家政府很晚才懂得这个道理，大部分国家政府是第二次世界大战之后才明白。

儒家仁政礼教的王道政治，说白了，就是君让民休息，官不争民利。当今民主宪政，其实就是由人民来实行仁政。

12. 家庭与事业

家庭不仅与婚姻关系联系紧密，而且与事业也息息相关。

家和万事兴，国睦百业旺。这个道理，中国在四千年前的尧舜传说中就有了。尧不传帝位给儿子，而传给舜，原因之一就是舜很有齐家的美德。舜的父亲、继母、弟弟多次合伙陷害舜，用火烧、坑埋等方式，舜都巧妙地一一化解，而且息事宁人。

就从舜时代，传出父子亲、君臣义、夫妇别、长幼序、朋友信的人际伦理。亲、义、别、序、信的“五教”伦理，贯穿中国所有和平时代。这个家庭伦理在，国乱，天下不乱，换句话说，天下小乱即止。

一般而言，人一生要经历两个家庭阶段，与父母在一起的出身家庭，在这里习得最基本生活经验与五教伦理；因结婚、生子而建立的生育家庭，在这里把在出身家庭所得的、能传的东西传给儿女。这就是祖国几千年文化和文明的传统。

现代公民国，是经历富人革命、穷人运动创建出来的，首先在欧美，再到全世界和中国，然而"为民谋福利"的"公天下"政治理念，却是从中国传到世界的。当今世界，家庭是最基本的社会设置之一，是人类最重要的一种制度，具有儿童社会化、供养老人、经济合作、两性欢悦等多功能的人类亲密关系的共同体。

家和万事兴，国睦百业旺。这两句话的意义，将比中国造纸术、印刷术、火药、指南针带给世界的意义更为重大。现在已经显现出来，时间将最终证明。

中国"成家立业"这句话，也真切指示人类每个个体获取成功与幸福之路。几乎无人不想拥有自己的事业，即创业，为此人们被各式各样的外来宣传蛊惑。然而，上苍却在安排人出生的时候，只安排了半个你，另外半个需要你通过婚姻去寻觅。

家庭，说白了，就是男人与女人的第一个事业。成家即立业了。知足息争，长久欢乐。古今中外，无论男女，双双自由欢悦点燃红蜡烛的时候，事业就开始了：关爱对方，生儿育女，白头偕老。这才是主业，其他财富、声誉只是副业。

所谓先立业后成家是会引人误入歧路的。《易经》说事业，做自己喜欢的事并帮助他人；更以恒卦说出家庭恒久与事业成功的黄金法则——男如雷主外、女如风主内。

13. 工作与公司

女主内就有了家务和宅院，甚至家庭纺织业。男主外便有了工作和产业。

工作就是社会上的劳动生产，在长时间内，做着重复的一系列动作，以产生价值。中国在汉朝史书上就有"苦役、工作"等词语，以后"工作"这个词常用于指劳役做事、工匠制作、官史及机构办事，通常指男人从事的家外的社会事务和劳作。

用词不考究的诗人、词人、文人，更把带孩子、搞运动、执行

任务也说成工作，这样泛指以后，职业也称为工作。宋朝甚至将在货行居住的匠人称为工作。

现代社会的公司，其实就是"士农工商"国家的工商业在欧美公民国演变出来的劳作组织，以营利为目的，多人投资折成股份，以董事会形式集体管理。

"公司"一词最早出自《列词传》："公者，数人之财；司者，运转之意。"庄子也以"公司"说"合小而为大"的"为公之道"。《礼记》说中国历史是退化：先是"天下为公"的"大同"社会，后是"天下为家"的"小康"社会，再后是礼崩乐坏的霸雄社会。士大夫的职责就是遵循圣人教诲，礼法治国，使天下为一。

这就是说，中国古代"士农工商"就是公司社会，以"士"阶层"齐家治国"的方式，领导"农工商"阶层，主旨是国泰民安，不是发展成由西方来的聚财公司。再明白地说，在中国古代，家是父立母治的小公司，国是君立臣治的大公司。

中国这种家国公司是在亲、义、别、序、信的"五教"伦理上创建的，人际关系亲情第一，血浓于水；远疏近亲，仁义统领，以礼为主道，以法为辅助。这才有改朝换代，万变不离祖国的中华儿女礼教道统的荣耀。

全世界部族消亡了千千万万，中华民族却悠悠千古，也因此尾大不掉。我们现在需要明辨家与国、与公的分别，莫再让家的私情破坏公的章法，切实负起责任。

宪政公司是最为广泛高效的经济组织形式，以图谋利益为宗旨，集合私人资源，分散风险，跨越血缘、地缘，好似动车急速前行，迅速耗散人类的能源。公司型的全球经济政治网路，正神秘地输入一种觊觎人类灵性的技术文化。中华天下为公的仁义理念，正有排毒护灵的积极意义。

14. 国泰民安

宋朝儒生吴自牧活在元朝，被蒙古人强行列入"臭老九"，比妓女地位还低下，深感元朝统治的黑暗，缅怀南宋临安的太平盛世，写《梦粱录·山川神》，记述："每岁海潮太溢，冲激州城，春秋醮祭，诏命学士院，撰青词以祈国泰民安。"这一民俗，记下南宋政府的人民性——求神灵护国安民。

看祖国古代民间艺术，看不到人民对政府的敌对性，没有"万恶的旧社会"的诅咒。中原的麒麟舞，多在节日、喜庆中出现，以示国泰民安的庆贺。

在香港，依赖渔业和农业为生的村民常以太平清醮的盛大仪式，酬谢神恩，祈求国泰民安，即使是在殖民统治的时候，依然相信太平盛世是神灵给的。

华人只要不被迫，总是"和为贵"的。这种期盼，在台湾更是普遍，每到佳节时，当地信道教的人、各地信徒纷纷到关渡玉女宫、大雅区永兴宫、东港东隆宫、指南宫进香贡献，并祈求风调雨顺，国泰民安。

台湾龙舟比赛中，二龙村渔民龙舟竞渡的船尾插着两面旗，一面是"风调雨顺"，一面是"国泰民安"。这种求民安的国泰旗在大陆贵州苗族龙舟节上也有。由此可见，台湾和大陆的同文同礼同俗。大陆要更多恢复传统礼俗才能赢得台湾人民的心。老人星在台湾人心中、眼中就是一颗象征国泰民安的吉星。

在泰国本头妈祖庙，前山门招牌上有"国泰民安"四个字。韩国的首尔社稷坛用以祭祀社神、稷神，重要的心愿就是：祈求国泰民安、风调雨顺。犹太人在古代信仰上帝，国王治国祈求赐给他的智慧，主要就是让民强国富、国泰民安。

清代皇帝的祭天仪式是国家祭典，是一种国态，每年都有国泰

民安的祈求。这是满族跟汉族文化一体化的表现。

据说身上有胡人血统的唐太宗更是积极认同汉族道家政治中"休养生息"的理念，由此开创国泰民安的贞观之治。这种清明政治延续到开元盛世，一片国泰民安的景象。

国泰民安是祖国礼教道统的重要内容，官民共盼天下太平、歌舞升平、河清海晏。人民由此认同政府为公家。统治者主国策"恩威"并施。

15. 竞争与合作

现代社会利益至上，竞争成了人能够成名成家的首要法则。当群体组织关系僵化、伦理关系偏私的时候，竞争很有必要。但人际之间，合作更重要。

果敢语文，一音一字，一字一意。古人说："并逐曰竞，对辩曰争。"在近代，华人用竞争说优胜劣汰之时，主要是指行动。现代商场竞争激烈，企业视竞争为生存斗争，人类关系被恶化为生物关系。

生物学中所谓竞争关系，是自然界的生态制约平衡，实质是斗争。牛吃草、羊兔也吃草；豺狼虎豹吃肉，人类也吃肉。生物因此产生了争食物的关系。当食物越来越紧张的时候，争食物激化生存矛盾，就出现了生物之间的生存斗争。

从理论上论述竞争，是从中国废科举后，德国法学界开始的，法学家罗伯把"竞争"概念明确定义为职场活动，仅仅是工商业界同类商品的供应之间的行为。这样定义竞争很严谨，跟体育比赛、升学考试、总统竞选、议员辩论等区别开来。

的确，人类历史上的纷争不能笼统用竞争来模糊，宗教信仰组织的"圣战"，政治党派发动的革命或暴乱，都不宜用竞争来表述，以免混淆。商业竞争是现代宪政国家和社会中企业组织的合法活动，是契约式的游戏。历史上的圣战、战乱等，通常是国家、党派之间的非理性的强霸争斗，是非契约式的。

把竞争与争强、争霸、斗争等更激烈、非理性、难调和的纷争从形式上相区别，我们就能理性地发现，竞争可以与合作相容，成为商业组织的互动方式。

争强、争霸、斗争等是竞争的升级，不会有真的合作，往往是你死我活的战争。这种必死其一的斗争，特定时候能带来新制度，但主要会造成人性沦丧。

合作或协作，才是人类社会文明化的主要互动形式，把商业竞争引向为共同目标而共同工作的共和社会。这样的话，商场经济关系逐渐就会演进为超利益集团的同盟，像中国古代家庭，却是世界范围超种族的，就会走向大同社会。

其实人类早就有共同创作、从事的活动，有依法制作、合奏音乐等合作的事情。果敢文里"人心齐，泰山移""水涨船高，柴多火旺""夫妻同心，其利断金"等格言，都讲到合作的道理。读书人有意识地合作，可以共用知识，有更多的发现。

16. 同志斗士，同人大有

近现代世界斗争中产生同志斗士。中国古代和谐诉求中出现同人大有。

同志是个西化名词，首先出现于法国大革命中，后来在搞革命斗争的时期，成为斗士之间的称呼，主要表示互称"同志"的人政治立场相同。

在中国近代，"同志"最先是光绪皇帝用以称呼康有为、梁启超等人的；后来同盟会以及中国国民党也以此称呼共同参与革命的志士。中国国民党现在也还用这个称呼，马英九曾在竞选中要党员称呼他为"马同志"。

中国现在"同志"这种称呼逐渐少用了，政治意味很淡了，甚至被用以对同性恋者的称呼。

"同志"称呼其实不是小事，包含对君子敬天传统的挑战。光绪称同志之前，读书人志同道合，称"同人"。这不同于"同志"，这种称呼很温情，没有斗争的政治气味。同人，出于《周易》，以"天火"比喻君子协同。

中国君子之中不提倡党同伐异的斗争，主张和而不同。但君子也有独自做不了的事，需要同心同德地会同他人一起做，这不是组织约束的，而是志同道合的，"道不同，不相为谋"地去会同。

同志要结党，靠斗争信仰和组织纪律联结。君子同人却是同心亲和共事，合则同道，分道扬镳。这样谋求的不是新人斗争与改造新社会、新国家，而是"火天"大有的景象：火在天上，普照万物，万民归顺，顺天依时，大有所成。

同志斗士，一阵风，极端化者战天斗地，挑战伦理。同人大有，会聚君子，学天效火，共同敬天，光明磊落做朋友。和谐社会需要的是同人。

17. 鞠躬尽瘁

鞠躬尽瘁，是汉语成语，指勤恳尽心地做公仆，不惜操劳到生命最后一刻。这句话是三国时代蜀国诸葛亮所说，语出《后出师表》："臣鞠躬尽瘁，死而后已。"

这并非诸葛亮自我标榜，而是西晋史官陈寿整理蜀国历史，记下来载入《三国》志史册的。有人不相信有这么公心的丞相，总有这样或那样地质疑。这或许是质疑者自己不能尽职，而推己及人；或许是标新立异，要引人注意；或许不太会思考。

陈寿立场在魏国，要这样捧人也该捧司马懿才对。但作为史官，稍有操守的，都不会这么做。因为这就是蜀国诸葛亮的历史。

刘备三顾茅庐请出诸葛亮，诸葛亮做蜀（汉）丞相后，为报刘备知遇之恩和履行伐魏的承诺，他亲自率兵出师北伐，第一次没有完成而撤兵，准备发动第二次北伐时，遭到一些官员的反对，诸葛亮就此上表，其中"鞠躬尽瘁"之言表现的忠贞气节令人感动，也因此流传下来。

榜样总有人效仿。以后忠臣在向君王表示忠心的时候，都时常引用这句话。

后人用"鞠躬尽瘁"来说人说事的更多，说的人与事都不同，但在表彰努力尽职上是共同。我们知道，做事随便、工作应付的人很多，努力的人不多。

凡努力的人，必费力费心，这需要很强的意志力。人只要图安逸，就会玩忽职守，做事马马虎虎或虎头蛇尾。"努力"这种品质很难得，各行各业都需要。

努力一旦成为人做事工作的习惯，要这人偷懒或玩乐都很难了。这时候，谁要委托这样的人去办事，叮嘱都免了，他考虑的问题多过委托人，做事做好，不仅是给委托人有交代，更是让自己安心。努力可以使人进入做人做事的佳境。

努力也可能使人"进"到"井"里，瞧瞧敢文简体的"进"字。人专心致志地做事，会很有钻研精神，这正是努力的可贵之处，但也要防止成为井底之蛙。切忌。

18. 海阔天空

海阔天空，跟天南海北、高谈阔论、漫无边际、夸夸其谈相近似，但词性却是褒义的。这个词并不是说某某浮夸或不踏实，而多用来指广阔天地、博大胸襟、性格豪迈、话题宏大等。

看大海，游鱼从海边往中心游，越游越远，最后不知道是不是去了龙宫。望天空，老鹰高飞远去，越飞越高，最后不知道是不是

去了天庭。

一生走过很多地方。见水是井水或溪流，见天在山顶上，仿佛登上去伸手就可触摸。这是穷乡僻壤，让人清心寡欲，没什么可追求的，要么就进洞闭关学庄子去。见水是西江入海口是海水，见天在头顶高高的，山一个个都是小山峦，衬得天格外高。这时候，就真有化成游鱼、苍鹰，去体会海阔天空的心境了。

说话海阔天空地侃侃而谈，主要是令人见多识广，再加上从容不迫。

真正要从"海阔天空"这句成语里悟出一些什么来，还是要超越乡党之间的学问谈论，从人生适应自然和社会这方面来思考和领悟。

有些人一生没走过多少地方，却不怯生，在任何地方都像在自己家里，自由自在的样子。你可以说他是山野村夫，他却土得像大山，容得下整个森林。

这其实就是一种气概！我的身体我做主，它属于我，我胸怀世界，它就是世界。这就不是口若悬河在那里表现口才，而是展示自己的世界观、宇宙观。

海阔天空更是一种心境，从来不活在谈论中，而活在适应自然和社会的生活中。在水一方时，就是水，是溪流汇成江河并奔腾成海的水；在山那边时，就是山，是峻拔、对峙、绵延的多种姿态，最后高耸入云去了天外。

《周易》说乾卦：天行健，君子以自强不息，从潜龙勿用，到见龙在田、飞龙在天……过程中是对一个个已有的偏见的放弃、阶段的超越。人不在自囚中，就可以看见海阔天空了。

19. 随心所欲不逾矩

孔子在《论语》中说他七十岁时的学成情况：随心所欲不逾

矩。这是一种自由自在却不逾越人际伦理的自主境界。这无论言行都很难做到，要几十年的训练。

从十五岁到七十岁，五十五年，大半生啊。从时间上说是够了，比如挥手，五十五年天天挥舞，左右上下，圆形、曲线、波浪……到手与心合一的境地，是什么甩手动作都可以做出来，却不会有所碰触。为什么？因为心不想碰触。

这是一个以自由自主为目标的人生旅途。人，在热情与冷漠、厌烦与兴奋、正与邪、真与假、善与恶的正负两面性中，做辨识与选择，开始时总是不想什么来什么，比如想热情却冷漠，总也高兴不起来。可渐渐地，能够达成心愿了。即使君子自强不息也能了，但终究还是不能完全如愿，有时候也做小人懒惰一下。

这就需要调适，逐渐减少这种疲劳的松弛状态，这个过程真正漫长。聪明的人从不会选择到会，可能就是瞅几眼后，试几下就可以了，要做到熟练随心，也就是半天或一天的事。但后来"不逾矩"的达成过程就漫长了，滞留期很长，有时还会退步。

很多人就在滞留或后退阶段放弃了。如果宿命不在这上面，那倒是退一步海阔天空，新的机遇到面前。如果虽然宿命在这，但经不起时运不济或不到的磨炼，心灰意冷而退，过不了自己的心魔关，那就前功尽弃。后来的也不是机缘。

做人就这样难，人生如戏，真正的角在哪儿，你不知道，看似知道最后不是。人生如树，你可能就陶醉在根系很多或幼树青皮的阶段美里，自满而失去圆满。

孔子说的主要是君子修养——"仁义礼智信"的进程。德行有七十随心所欲不逾矩的境界，其他人生领域的品格修养也有同样的道理，比如做官同流不合污。

孔子很睿智，从志于学开始，在正道上而立、不惑、知天命、耳顺之后，他就将人世间与自然界连通了，做到天人合一，从天看无为而无不为，从人看自由而不逾矩。

20. 弱者与强者

经济学研究角度看弱者是社会资源占有的份额相对较少的个人或组织。伦理学研究角度看弱者是指嫉妒、显示、争斗等恶性强的人与组织。这两学应相结合。

古代诸葛亮、陶潜等从经济学角度看属于中产者，却让当时世族司马氏、王谢氏自愧不如。他们不仅有真才实学，更有对世道不公的正确看法，没对世风日下推波助澜。官场洪水泛滥成灾，陶潜审时度势及时上岸。诸葛亮入仕在三顾茅庐之后，保持住了智者对于勇者必须的指导权，这才能够依法治蜀使世族无存。

所谓弱者需要保护，定义不准确。当世需要政府保护穷人与专利被侵夺者。他们不是被保护的弱者，而是人权必须被尊重的人群，竞争必须有公道。

智者和勇者，如果在公平竞争的法律起跑线上比试，很多人可能是杰出的律师、教授、企业家、商人……却被权贵结合的组织打压成了穷人、牢犯等。这些人并非真正社会、法律、经济意义上的弱者，而是被弱者以组织侵权的强者。

人权被侵害者中有很多真正的强者（智者、勇者），他们被权力伤残，而后被冠以社会弱者、法律弱者、经济弱者、家庭弱者的称呼，再以所谓人道主义名义扶助他们，给贪官污吏逃避制裁并获得荣耀的机会，这很歹毒。

当世许多地方筷子似的弱者，以权钱交易方式合成木棒、木槌，借助意识形态，以一些莫须有或刻意捏造的罪名，把强者削成钢丝后横扯绷紧，不停地敲打，摧残宁折不弯者至死，让受不住摧残的示弱者自我作践，给摧残者送鲜花、锦旗……

呼吁法律保护妻女笼统地称呼为家庭弱者，首先是认可权钱交易的组织权力，这不对。我们理应做的是重组社会。

总之，当世需要以孟子说的恻隐心与羞恶心重新立法，还社会朗朗乾坤。

21. 虐待让人狂

心理学上有个名词"虐待狂"，特指性虐待。据说，性虐待狂男性多于女性。

研究性虐待现象，是心理学领域的事，可以由专家或想成为专家的人去做。我们应该超越这种以虐待方式寻欢作乐的心理学领域研究，而从更为广大的社会领域，寻找出生时健康的人，在婴幼儿或童年时期被人为变得衰弱与萎缩的原因。

古龙笔下的小鱼儿，就是童年被逼入恶人谷，最后被训练成为施虐者。理性地说，小鱼儿会比从看当代小说、影视节目学成的虐待狂更疯狂。古龙超现实地把小鱼儿写成了一个神仙似的英雄剑客。古龙这样写，跟其环境和认知状况有关。

虐待是邪恶的。受虐者痛不欲生而又死不成的时候，就会被逼成疯狂的人。理智地看古龙描写的人物，小鱼儿能受虐从恶人谷出来，必定认可了施虐的正当性，并转为施虐高手，出谷就是施虐作乐，恶瘤似的散布虐待病毒。

当世，有个名人不满母亲包办婚姻，却又不愿公然反抗以背上不孝骂名而失去留学游玩等机会，于是把不满藏在心里，以多种方式折磨妻子，以辱骂方式报复所有权威，以文章施虐而显示自己的力量与征服，从中获得快感。这是自卑惹的祸。

奥地利心理学家阿德勒曾指出，出于对过度自卑感的补偿，人们通过追求优越感来补偿自己的自卑感。男女老少人群中都有人因为自卑而伤害他人。

历代以"均贫富，等贵贱"之类旗号造反的农民，大肆虐杀富人达官，就是因为自卑而滋生嫉妒、显示、争斗等不良心理，在乱

世中变成虐待狂，一旦握有生杀予夺的权力，最爱用打骂、恐吓等方式虐待人，以寻求满足与快感。

虐待狂更乐意用下流的调戏动作，羞辱让他自惭形秽的人，看他们跪地求饶，不一定非要对方死，或者肉体痛苦。虐待让人疯让人狂。所以重建君子国家很重要。

22. 负罪伏法，愧疚悔罪

过了文言关，读《周易》《尚书》《论语》，能更多更深地领悟君子治国之理。

《论语》记载孔子教道卫灵公："己所不欲，勿施于人。"朱熹加注："推己及物。"说白了，这就是将心比心，自己不愿意挨打，就不要去打人。

有个春秋时期的故事，说齐国有年冬天，连下大雪三昼夜。齐景公披着皮袍，在厅堂赏雪，期盼多下几天，更饱眼福，对身边的晏子说："不冷，是春暖时节了。"晏子是个君子，直言不讳地说："古之贤君吃饱了，会想还有人饿着；穿暖了会想还有人冻着；安逸了会想还有人累着。君王，您呢？"景公被晏子问着了。

今日少有晏子，更多齐景公，身在好光景中，想不到要扶助逆境中的人。许多达官以权谋私而获罪，还只怪运气不好。

西周时代"刑不上大夫"，几乎没有以身试刑的贵族，都以犯罪为耻辱。礼崩乐坏到唐朝，因负罪而销声匿迹的人，不为世俗所容，如同今日美国对待诈骗者。宋朝王安石变法，以酷刑逼富人与官吏将从民众口袋捞的钱送进国库，许多富商逃之夭夭。元朝更以酷刑折磨廉官洁吏，逼汉人造反。

春秋之后以身试刑的贵族越来越多，还是有很多恪守礼制的贵族拒绝做乱臣贼子，年老者惭愧"力不能制，负罪先公"。

礼教道统以"义"德培育人的抱愧、抱歉意识。所以东汉关羽宁可被俘，也不丢弃义兄家眷逃命；赵云虎胆狮艺，宁可命丧乱军之中，也不卖身曹营以求荣。直到明朝不少官吏还有"受人点滴之恩，当以涌泉相报"的恩义情怀。

传统礼法政治以伦理齐家，以王法治国。皇权使宋江之类终能负罪伏法，即使为活命被逼上梁山，心头也不轻松，期望有招安机会获得正道出身。礼教道统使即使匪气如李逵者，错了也能自感愧疚，真诚悔过悔罪，不惜损名誉。

23. 成名的意义

红尘中人成家立业之后，很多人想成名。心理学的需求层次理论研究发现，人由低而高先后有生存、安全、爱、尊重、自我实现五个楼层。成名排第四。

大多数人只是跟着感觉走，但上天确实给几乎每个人预定了这样的需求楼层：面包、房子、婚恋、名人、天使。这些是比喻，跟理论能一一对应。

面包、房子是第一、二层楼，不容选择，活着就要。这是生物普遍需要的，植物要水、光、大地等，禽兽要食物、窝等。没有这些，就得死。人高于动物之处在于，会用工具制造食物、房屋，可以不吃嗟来之食，可以建楼房、搞装修……

婚恋是第三层楼，在面包、房子需求得到后出现，是环境影响后有的，也是人在参与营造人际环境，这就有了夫妻、父母的生命旅程，叫成家立业。古人普遍重家庭，婚恋是家族事业，个人意愿次要（如果首要，就做隐士了）。现代人个人乐趣首要，更看重夫妻小家庭的小日子，家族没落，这就是公民社会。

成名是人生旅程的第四楼层。人在成家立业之后，若想不平凡，引人注目，光宗耀祖，这就有了事业奋斗：庄园、战斗、钻营、改造社会（甚至自然）……王侯将相的疆场功名、达官贵人的

衣锦还乡，动力都是名。

今人的名片，都要弄个头衔，哪怕是个虚名。这就是虚荣心或好面子的表现。成名不容易，过程中不仅可能被批斗，还可能被竞争对手、嫉恨的人诽谤、伤害。成名让人忐忑，总担心说错话、做错事，又怕被忘记，又要炒作自己……

有些人说，我不想成名，只想做郁金香……这基本是奋斗之后失败的人的自我安慰。红尘中人，三十左右成家立业，不想成名的人很少，自己的内心、家人都要自己有一定或相当的名气。有名不仅有誉，还有利，只要还留恋红尘，说不想成名是自欺欺人。不想成名，奋斗干吗？不想吃猪肉，却爱看猪跑，是一种病。

想成名，没有错，只是看成名的范围有多大，知名度有多高，好爸爸、好丈夫也是名。无论什么名，大小不重要，大小有命。奋斗不成就去死或者颓废一生，是偏执搏命，自讨苦吃、自寻烦恼。成名好坏是最重要的，恶名传千里，一失足成千古恨。

显然成名是有意义的，是对一个人做人做事、工作职业的肯定、褒奖、社会的信赖。成家立业后，自然成的名有好爸妈、好夫妻、好科长、好老师……这才真正属于自己。刻意挣来的，最后才发现，失去的更多。成名常伴随着不幸。

24. 人为何不幸

关于人不幸，众说纷纭。圣贤的说法比较恒定。老子说，不幸源于相争；佛陀说，不幸源于把幻象当真；孔子说，不幸源于不仁；耶稣说，不幸源于不义。

今人谈论不幸，总是源于当时的感觉：苦、累、痛、郁闷……或者前后矛盾：爽与不爽，感性与理性……跟圣贤相比，这些说法太随意，像天上云彩，飘浮不定。

2006年9月，网易网站以《如果有来生，你愿不愿意再做中国

人?》为题，搞了一次调查。有 10 234 人参与调查，其中，64% 的调查答卷说"不愿再做中国人"。其中，37.5% 的人说"缺乏人的尊严"；17.6% 的人说"买不起房子"。

思维混乱，是人不幸最表象的原因，无论哪个国家的人。美国黑人，几百年后还回非洲寻根，谴责殖民主义，并没因为现在住洋房开轿车，就说"我恨黑非洲，殖民万岁"，仍然堂堂正正地说："我的根在非洲，我爱非洲。"这就是思维明晰。

人的不幸，透过表象，明察本质，综合圣贤的说法，源于忘恩。相争，不仅有人与人之间的忘恩，更有人对自然的忘恩。把幻象当真，以至于把异乡当故乡，必然辜负老家人。负恩必然不仁，继而不义。忘恩负义，这句成语更明了。

历史上许多部族，融于文化更博大的民族之中，比如赫梯人、亚述人，是由于被征服后失掉祖庙，迫于无奈融入其他民族。

作为个人，如果天天骂老爸坏、老妈脏、哥哥姐姐是流氓，自己不幸生错了家庭。这样的人的不幸源于什么?

个人不幸，理应探寻历史原因，以史为鉴，那么就读史、读古籍，重听圣贤的教诲，温故而知新。

25. 幸福人生

幸福是什么? 托尔斯泰说过，幸福的家庭都是相似的，却没接着说相似的幸福是什么。但在《家庭的幸福》中说了："生活中唯一可靠的幸福就是为别人而生活。"后来在《战争与和平》中借玛丽亚公爵小姐的心理活动，说："我的天职是以另一种幸福为幸福，以仁爱和自我牺牲的幸福为幸福。"

当然，正如托尔斯泰说"不幸的家庭各有各的不幸"一样，各人也有各自的幸福观或家庭幸福观，尤其是名人。名人为成名所累，答案总要各有不同。

这样，也许我们回到托尔斯泰对家庭幸福与个人幸福的观点上去，比较明智。其实真正经得起时间追忆的观点往往是圣贤或先哲的观点。所以回到托尔斯泰，因为我们可以从他说的，透视到老子的"清净无为"、佛陀的"色相是空"、孔子的"仁者爱人"、耶稣的"爱你的敌人"……名人的观点之所以吸引人，是因为把先贤的珍珠制成了面膜。

当渴望幸福人生的人将诉求关注在财富或物质上，比如金钱、名车、美人、兰花等，为此父母抱怨、家庭分解，甚至一生是病，最后会觉得失望：这不是我要的。这说明，这个人并不了解什么是幸福，不知道幸福人生是什么？

很多人大半生都如同瞎子摸象，在玩弄自己的感觉。托尔斯泰就有过这样的感悟："过去的感情就像过去的时间本身，已经不可追忆了；要追它回来不但不可能，抑且痛苦而不愉快。"从托尔斯泰婚姻最后还是不幸的可以看出，那曾经"觉着那么幸福的时光"昙花一现，小说中构想出的列文的农家爱妻并不属于他。

人的所谓上半生、下半生，只是时间上的划定，人活的只是当时，是现在。可如果就此把生活变成感觉，变成证券交易，最后必定满手是废纸。每个当时、现在，都连着过去，接着未来，如果硬要割断过去而自绝传统，自堵去路背水一战，这样做任何事，都变成了赌博，赌的是感觉，博的是命，必为心魔所控。

幸福人生，首要的就是要从自我中心、瞎子感觉、赌徒搏命的生活中走出来。有自我不盲从，却懂得为他人考虑；有感觉，却心明眼亮，不把象鼻子当蛇去为此争斗；做事要思前想后，却也莫谨小慎微，怕掉悬崖就不迈步，循道而行就是。

这样看来，幸福人生就是明智地思考和生活，遵循先贤的教诲，做好人生当下的小事大事，并时刻听从灵性的召唤。

26. 通过黑暗

人，追求幸福，如果听不到或者听到却不从灵性召唤，就将坠入心的黑暗之中。

人之初，没有感觉，没有兴致的事，是不会去做的，被迫也不能持久。人是趋乐避苦的。良药苦口利于病，避苦拒绝吃药，该治能治的病就会被延误，害了身体。忠言逆耳利于行，避苦拒绝听从，自找该避能避的危险，掉进陷阱。

沉迷于甜的口感，结果满口虫牙，痛得直叫唤。沉溺于乌的快感，结果吸毒上瘾，不能自拔：人生的天空塌陷，啥事也不能干；心乌黑的，只认毒品是光亮。

人在追求幸福的路上，从感觉起步，一旦不能升级需求，陷在面包、房屋、婚恋中，就走不出来了；或者升级到名人，就晕在炒作更大名声的虚荣中。

这样，大多数人在三十岁左右，就基本在踏步走，在生存线上踏步，在安全线上踏步，在爱情线上踏步。如果思想没有从感觉到理性的升华，有人就"我的命苦，吃饱就不错了"；有人则"我的房屋太小了，何时能有三室两厅？"有人在有妻有儿时，又左顾右盼，认为昨天的选择是错误的，需要重新选择。

成功人士则在尊重线上踏步。这些人正奔四十，或已过四十了，衣食无忧，名声在外，这时候很需要不被感觉和成见所迷惑，需求升级到天使的自我实现上层。

古人范蠡功成名就时就及时身退，据传在家道的桃花园地、商道的神仙洞天里自在。家业、商业成了范蠡的时空隧道，一日千年地悠悠。

范蠡的同僚文种，不知道另有活法，不懂退一步海阔天空的道理，结果被越王勾践赐剑自杀。文种这是为成名所累，进入名利所

致的海底世界，这里是无光的黑暗。在春秋战国杀戮的时代，正义之路被暴虐之恶人包围。勾践的心是个黑洞，就成了文种的黑暗之谷。

美国比尔·盖茨是现代范蠡，2008年6月，他与妻子捐出580亿的全部身家，不留遗产，"希望把它回馈社会"；从此退出企业经营，全身心投入慈善事业，"希望为世界作出积极贡献"。这一年盖茨五十二岁，知天命而行，成"天使"了。

27. 恐惧情结

恐惧，即害怕，指生物面对危险所产生的惊慌，或者面对自己厌恶的事物时出现的应急状态：心跳加速、血压升高、瞳孔放大、尖叫、盗汗、颤抖等，严重时心脏骤停、休克。有人极度怕狼，被狼包围，还没等狼扑到身上，就吓死了。

一些恐惧是面对现实产生的，比如人站在悬崖边，怕掉下去，自然会产生肌肉紧张、人往后退等生理现象。另外一些恐惧出于人的想象，例如考试成绩不好，担心回家被父母责怪，在外面晃荡很晚，最后砸橱窗玻璃。恐惧会引发焦虑与敌视。

心理学上看恐惧，主要原因在内心，出于个人的认知。当某事或某物被人确定为有危险或恶心时，这个人生理上就会出现惊慌失措、很不正常的状态。

初生牛犊不怕虎，长处犄角反怕狼。这句俗语，就是说恐惧纯属心理现象。实验显示，所有婴幼儿最初在不知道什么是黑暗、高处（高楼、飞机）、水中央（船上）、火等事物时，没有恐惧；看见狼来了，有的还会笑；不怕触摸蛆虫。

后来人因为被狼咬过，或者看见狼咬人留下的伤口，从高处掉下摔得很痛，看见人淹死等，这些经历让他很不舒服，不想再体验，心理上就有了害怕，生理上就相应出现紧张、变异的状况。于

是就有所防范或隔离，也就避免了危险。

由此可知，恐惧是人和动物的一种感觉，有自保的作用。被吓死是自保机制失控。一般而言，恐惧是本能行为，由此而产生的防御或逃跑等行为让人得以避免危险。当突然感觉地面晃动，或者发现蒙面人，立即逃跑，可能就躲过了地震和被劫持的灾祸。

心理学研究证明，甚至植物也有恐惧。这有心理学家以测谎仪做的实验报告为证。

恐惧，以及引发的焦虑与敌视，是人人皆有的正常心理。天不怕地不怕的人倒是不正常，俗语将这类人称为恶魔。

但当恐惧成为一种强烈的情绪纠结，也就成恐惧症了，成为个人成长的心病，俗语说没长大。很多成年人被三岁时的恐惧经历及心理纠缠，相关的仇恨与敌视的心魔挥之不去，恐惧社交、某些场合、人或事，人生中失去许多机会和乐趣。

28. 超越恐惧

恐惧的生理机制，人先天具有；恐惧的心理现象，人普遍有之。这就是说怕是难免的。人可以一怕、二怕，不可三怕。人不可以让怕成为心病，需要超越。

超越恐惧是心理健康的需要。谁说"我就是不怕""我天生大胆"，这是打肿脸充胖子，是强作镇定，是自卑所生的优越显示，却也是超越恐惧的初级方法。

1920 年，美国心理学家华生以"小亚伯特实验"证实：恐惧感是可以通过后天培养出来的。原本不怕动物、不恐高、不惧花、不怕云等的大胆幼儿，通过重复相关的可怕现象给他看，让小胆儿陪看展示恐惧，大胆儿逐渐出现恐惧。

恐惧来自对事物的认识方式：可怕的事密集地给予重复，让恐惧感传染。土匪强盗树立威信的方式就是"小亚伯特实验"的方式，让被绑架者或者所控制的村民看杀人、剥皮等，让人质互相打骂，进入敌视状态时，他来使敌视停止，甚至给予保护。这就叫斯德哥尔摩综合症，人质爱上绑匪。

这也就是说，可怕的事不让人见到太多，如果给看也要间隔较长的时间，让不怕的人（成年父母、专家学者、勇敢者等）陪看，并给予解释分析，恐惧感也可以改变。由此可见家教的重要性：父母以仁义与智慧保护和教育儿女。

家教中确有一些应该纠正的错误方法。最严重的是父母互相指责。父母作为家长是一个整体，犹如人体的左与右、上与下、前与后，是互补的，而不是你错我对。

父亲严不起来，那就母亲来，但不能借此去诋毁对方，争夺儿女的爱。父母的敌对，会让家庭成为战场，加重孩子的恐惧感，不愿回家，成人后恐惧成家。

严父慈母搭配，父亲威严如天，让儿女有所敬畏，就不会恣意妄为，会遵纪守法；母亲宽恕如地，让儿女跌倒休息后爬起，给儿女犯错成长的时空。华人父母，从小读三字经、千字文获得的仁义与智慧，对于帮助婴幼儿超越恐惧很重要。

社会无论如何进步，价值观无论如何改变，都无法改变人类对瘟疫、火灾、洪灾的恐惧。这就是说自然的力量大过人，从根本上说灾变是人冒犯自然规律自找的。所有改造自然都是徒劳，是在制造荒原、淤河、干旱等，是噩梦、怪病之源。人真正能做的还是循道修德，知仁行义，礼让息争，明辨是非，择善而从……

29. 君子道术

春秋战国时代，在五百年的乱世中，华人祖先，士贵族君子纷纷出山给君主献计献策。这可不是中华民国时期基于当世所理解的毛找皮附，而是做帝王之师。

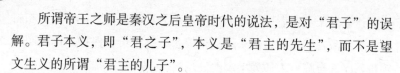

所谓帝王之师是秦汉之后皇帝时代的说法，是对"君子"的误解。君子本义，即"君之子"，本义是"君主的先生"，而不是望文生义的所谓"君主的儿子"。

老子、孔子之"子"，就是后世"先生""老师"的尊称，老子即老先生，孔子即孔先生。另外，孙子、墨子、庄子、韩非子，都是以"子先生"给的尊称。

韩非子著《权术》，献给秦始皇，后世皇帝只要学习，那就是韩非子的学生。历代帝王凡修习儒术的，莫不是孔孟之道的传人，差别只在于，有的称职，有的不称职。韩非子的《权术》，属于法家道术，教皇帝"驾驭群臣"，很长时间不外传。

《权术》外传官场之后，被称为驭下之道、迎上之道、为官之道等。权术险恶，所以后世有人认为韩非子下场不好可能与此有关。韩非子这类君子道术，跟先前孙膑兵法、张仪或苏秦的辩术，都是历史的特定安排，以促使魏国衰微，秦国强大，跟相应的人之恩怨相关。

之后民间官宦家族类似《权术》的经验总结，就属于受控的邪术，所以不见光，都是口口相传，极少著书。中国古人，尤其是君子，读书前先要打坐、调息，道家传人还特别讲究时辰：子时、午时，卯时、酉时等对时修炼。欧美没有这些。

欧美的权术，以马基亚维利的"实力原则""不择手段"双重角色"等为代表。马基亚维利读书、著书，最后也是为指点国君的，却没有中国打坐的讲究。

马基亚维利的政治权术，主要还是个人经验之谈，跟耶稣神道没有关系。韩非子、李斯师出荀子礼教儒门，当秦始皇的老师是履行君子职能，但以权术、霸术引导君王为统一霸业走速成捷径，改变君臣之间的主客坐而论道、分庭抗礼的关系，这在华夏叫离经叛道，是欺师灭祖、不教人学好之罪。所以李斯下场很惨。

正统华人不可以不循道修行，无论在何时何地。德行修为，教

人学好，从家里到家外，是个人真正的立身之道：神，如来，天道，自然……

30. 修身养神，通情达理

循道修行，立身之道：神，如来，天道，自然……何谓神？上古评判君王，把民众无能不争善恶时代的天子冠名神宗，这并非说他是神人，而是说道行很高。

华人有的父母很有能耐，不用打骂，婴幼儿就一切顺从，如同基督徒顺从神道。不能安定民心，人民必定相争，即使和平时期也不能太平，怨天子无能。

神、如来，其实都是不同的部族民众的说法，精神实质都是顺应天道自然的灵性生命，能行神迹：手到病除、移山倒海、创世造人，等等。

人世间循道修行，无论君主、君子、道士、佛教徒、基督徒，未必真的就能飞到天上，或者哈口气铁杵成了绣花针。但有修为的儒、道、佛、基督之信徒，都很通情达理：说话讲道理，做事持善意。他们的存在，很像世人与天人的联络人。

通情达理，指设身处地地体会、感受对方。这种能够体验别人内心世界的能力，佛教说是他心通，心理学说是读心术，无论什么说法，施用这种方法与人沟通，必须是非常友善的人，温文尔雅，言行如和风细雨，让人不戒备地敞开胸怀。

这种能力，现代咨询师只凭心理学知识和咨询技巧训练并不能达到。咨询，从求助者的言谈举止，探测对方内心的情感、思维，跟木匠、医师同在经验层面。这当然有一定的效果，阅历和经验越丰富，效果越显著。但还达不到举一反三。

知识和经验丰富的同时，人会非常世故和成熟，很会揣摸人心，却因为拿咨询当医术，自然也就成了病魔的敌人，受到很强的

抵抗：互相玩"猫鼠游戏"。

神通不是用知识去征服人，而是用善念去感动人。这种善念好似婴儿开心的笑，没有功利、指引、评判、说教等，就是通情达理的疏导；没有旁征博引也就没有很多战场，就是心神合一的举一反三：一个事例类比千万。

华人传统的通情达理就是真正的与人为善。这让受助者能感受到，一句"还有吗"，就能让他推心置腹地说出他的秘密。

论适应主义（五）

1. 百无一用是无长

所谓百无一用，即毫无用处，或者说一无可取。清朝黄景仁《杂感》说："十有九人堪白眼，百无一用是书生。"这句话流传至今，但说的并不在理。

书生是有学问与知识的人，位居中九流之五，在琴棋、僧、道、尼之上，往上走可以参加科举中举人，进入仕途可以做文官治国。说"百无一用是书生"是酸话。

百无一用也不是无知。无知是一种婴儿状态，所谓初生牛犊不怕虎。却也因为这种无知的幼儿态，人可以通过老师，获得知识、明白事理。

也就是说，无知可以学。孔子说庶民：听使唤的人，给他们自由；胆大妄为的人，教育他们知晓厉害、危险，让他们不要乱来。教育即教无知者有知。

另有百无一用是深情的说法。深情让人执迷不悟，对于修道、向佛的人，深情是要逐渐去除的。但对于红尘中人，情是摆脱不了的，也是正常的人类社会必不可少的。人深情就不会出忘恩负义或薄情寡义的人。社会需要爱国爱家至深的人。

真正的百无一用是无长，即没有一技之长。没有一技之长，便成无用之人。"人"字一撇一捺，左右两脚直立，左右两手交替或配合使用，即可自立于天地间。人生有长可取，才不会寄人篱下招白眼一生。

人有一技之长，即可吃香喝辣。换句话说：一招鲜，吃遍天。一技之长乃人的社会价值的体现。对于多数人而言，术业有专攻，学识不在博而在于精。在古代社会，贵族文人博览群书、通晓古今，还需有诗画琴棋射御等技艺；在现今社会，上大学就在于学一技之长得以谋生与养家糊口。

人要发挥自己，首先要能够认识自己。知己才不会犯傻。熟知法律，就去做律师，莫去做农民；懂得财务，就去做会计，莫去做推销员；擅长美容，不去做美容师，却要去做画家，就是犯傻。是诸葛亮，就要等刘备上门。是赵括、马谡，去当军事教师，都可以成明星，而不至于丧命。

2. 有悟人生无大错

悟，指理解、明白或觉醒之义；前面加一个字，可构成感悟、领悟、参悟、醒悟、觉悟、彻悟、大悟等等。瞎子摸象说鼻子是蛇，读书只知其一都是悟性差。

文天祥在抗元失败途中遇异人，得大光明法，之后写诗说："谁知真患难，忽悟大光明。日出云俱静，风消水自平。功名几灭性，忠孝大劳生。天下惟豪杰，神仙立地成。"文天祥诗中"悟大光明"是修"大光明法"有所参悟、觉悟之意。

文天祥之悟，非常人所悟，是不是得仙尸解而去，不得而知。修道、修儒、修佛，各有其不同的领悟与解说，毋须说这对那错。思想认识，兼听则明。

有悟，人生无大错。悟心了性，理解和分析事物的能力非同寻常；悟宗，明了佛理，心境升华；悟悦，因了悟而喜悦；悟理，领悟道之理。悟道参玄，或许就有了文天祥"悟大光明法"之玄妙的

觉悟。悟物，了悟物理；悟明，了悟真言；悟佛，了悟佛理；悟禅，参悟禅理。所以文天祥能够义尽仁至。

人类之初多苦修。据传印度的婆罗门教走的就是遁入深山的苦修路。后来的印度教实修者持守苦修，却另有对立于苦修的享受主义。佛教行的是中道。

只要是正教，无论修道、修佛、修儒或信基督，说到底就是要悟圣人的教诲。一般人对世间本质及生命的真相无知而沉溺于享乐与堕落之中。有悟就能解脱。

唐朝王维有诗说："碍有固为主，趣空宁舍宾？洗心讵悬解，悟道正迷津。因爱果生病，以贪始觉贫。声色非彼妄，浮幻即吾真。"王维，字摩诘，有诗佛之称。由此可知，王维之诗是居士修佛的参悟。修道或修佛，重在感悟。

道禅是天天功课，把握道理修行，明心见性，终有悟道、开悟而大成的一天。

3. 细节培养品性

人处世做事，天天过日子的生活细节，从小可以看到大。如随地吐痰，随便丢垃圾，开口粗言……这些无关紧要的小事、小节，累积起来就成了人的品性。

一个人偶然吐一次痰在地上，那不是问题。身边没有痰盂，身上没有纸，附近没厕所，迫不得已吐在地上。但是随便吐痰在水泥地上，形成破坏环境卫生的习性，成年后当白领就很难。可以说，白领光靠读书读不出来，还得从做小事上培养细心与耐性等。

看小说、戏剧、电影、电视，人物的性格、事件的发展都是从细节上一环环演变过来的。孩子一生下来就把父母杀了，绝不可能。例如《上海滩》的许文强成为黑帮老大，是从闹学潮、打架、舞刀弄枪，一步一步走过来的，先伤人后杀人。

东汉班超说过："为人有大志，不修细节。"但他的成长历程就有反映细节的戏。班超出生史官世家，因为心不在文史，虽然做了管奏章与文书的官，也因为小过失而免职。

班超当文书时心仪西汉出使西域的张骞，曾投笔感慨，被嘲笑时发出壮士之言，找人看相受激励，居家不畏劳苦，能言善辩，博览群书并能审时度势，北伐匈奴做小官打仗获胜，终于获得出使西域建功的机会。

刘备去世前给刘禅留下遗诏，说"勿以恶小而为之，勿以善小而不为"，告诫儿子要"唯贤唯德"，不要光凭权柄立威，要进德修业，让人心服。

这是合乎事物演变规律的。好事从小事做起，积小成大就成了好事业。慈善家的事业，也是因为从小有这心，不断行小善，后来财富多了才有心有力援助社会。罗马不是一天建成的。黑帮老大也不是一天做成的，是累积小恶的结果。

所以做人要从点点滴滴的小事上起步。好事，搭把手推车也要做；坏事，即使是偷根针也不宜做。都按人生要细细品味的道理做人，世上就太平了。

4. 管住嘴避病免祸

管束对人来说是必要的，随心所欲、恣意妄为必然害人害己。什么东西都吃，就可能患病或中毒。

西晋傅玄写《口铭》："病从口入，祸从口出。"傅玄在官场历任县令、太守、典农校尉、司隶校尉。人缘复杂，官场险恶，傅玄晚年被免官。但终因管住了嘴，善终于家中。

病从口入。早在《论语》中就有不吃生果的记载。《本草纲目》中明确说："饮食不节，杀人顷刻。"管住了口，就能预防饮食中毒，延年益寿。所以古人说："晚饭少吃口，活到九十九。"病

从口入在现代社会已成医学常识，父母、阿姨都要告诫幼儿。

祸从口出。同义词有言多必失、多言买货、直言贾货等。这是说，人说话不谨慎容易招致出人意料的灾祸发生。这在华人圈子里促成说话成了艺术。儒家讲君子以直报怨，即直言不讳，不能包庇纵容坏人坏事；也讲慎言，不要乱说话。

乱说话容易招惹事端。不小心说话犯了谁的忌讳，招来打骂甚至杀身之祸。这样的事例在历史上、现实中屡见不鲜。说话随便更是商场大忌，随便承诺几年包修，一切损失包赔，助长了顾客的贪念，也放纵他们不负应该负的责任。

信息交流与能量补充如果都从口这个通道进入，口舌就要出问题。同时其他的信息、能量入口，比如书信表意、眉目传情、举手示意等也就闲置了。

当然万事都要适度，不能过头。啥事都不用手，就等于把手废了。该说的话说，不该说的话不说。人说话心中有个尺度，如同河堤设有闸门，也就有了安全防护。人为了自己的形象工程（面子），包揽承担不起的责任，势必失信于人，使自己多年信誉毁于一旦。

病从口入，患自口出。是非皆因多开口，百病九十源于嘴。嘴不可不管。

5. 万万不可小瞧格

格，最明了的说法，是格子。小孩子写字最怕格子，觉得受约束，很不自在。

格，万万不可小瞧，后面加一个字，有格范、格尺、格令、格法、格条、格样、格调等，前面加一个字，有人格、品格、官格、国格等。

人格，通俗地说，就是人品的格式，如同人有了一个无形的格子，其人品风貌好似拍摄电影定格，形成了独自的品性风格气度。

人因此而有了内向与外向、好人与坏人、收敛与张扬、节俭与奢侈、大度与小气的区别。孔子说人十五而志学，三十而立，四十不惑，五十知天命，六十耳顺，可以理解为人格发展的阶段性。

品格，是人格在道德方面的体现，也就是所谓人品。人生来并无好坏之别，却因为善恶心性并存，后天环境的影响与各自的倾向性选择，才会出现好人和坏人。

官格，顾名思义，官的样式或品格。父母官，以管家的模式治国，把管辖者当成自家的儿女看待，情理交融地去管理，这是儒家君子官的样式，好官即清官，坏官即贪官。公民官，以法官的模式治国，把管辖者当成政治、法律上平等的人看待，一切依从法律，这是欧美地方官的样式，好官依法行政，坏官贪赃枉法。

国格，与官格、人格有区别，指一国有别于他国的特别样式，即有别于他国的民族、人群、风俗、语言、文字形成的独特的国样。有失国格，便国无国样。

心中有格，做人有典范，行事有标准，政府有确定的法令及条文等。心中自有法度，人也就活出了自己的模样：吃有吃相，喝有喝相，坐有坐相，站有站相。

格，如同"囗"，里面是"或"，是繁体的"國"字；是"玉"，是简体的"国"字；是"人"，成"囚"字；是"古"，成"固"字。政府厚今薄古，人如同坐过山车似的头晕，国命不长；厚古薄今，国如同长江、黄河，源远流长，江山牢固。

6. 无知者无罪，明知故犯者重罪

这里说的无知，特指缺乏知识和重要常识、不明事理的婴幼儿状态，不泛指失去知觉的昏迷状况。成年人说自己无知，是谦虚，是说自己还有未知的事物。依照儒学理论，无知是小人状态，致良知做正人，信歪理成恶人。

人，生而无知，却又先天具有学习的能力，具有天命所赋有的才智。无知是婴幼儿的正常状态，也是成年人求知学习的心态。年幼无知率真而童言无忌，不是罪过，而是生命本身存在之必要阶段。如果人全知全能，将无法在地球上待一刻。

人因为无知，所以才有钦佩与忠诚的情操，所以才有宗教信仰的精神需求，也因此越是大科学家或真正具有科学求知精神的人，越是坦承自己一无所知，不执着于自己的成见与偏见，以不断接近真理。牛顿是这样，爱因斯坦也是这样。

人不怕无知，最怕把无知当成有知，把歪理当成真理，把邪说当成科学的少年轻狂状态。轻狂则胡说八道、虚荣傲慢、恣意妄为，为埋下犯罪的种子。

轻狂的无知者不学无术，心灵宛如寸草不生的荒地与缺乏油料的灯，这比无知与贫困更可怕。无知可以通过学习而改变，轻狂才敢为非作歹、作恶多端，像一只没有翅膀的海燕在暴风雨里瞎折腾、瞎叫唤。无知是瞎子，轻狂是疯子。

英国有句格言说："知识是光，无知是黑暗。"意大利留有"无知是智慧的黑夜"的名句。由此可知，人如果不学习，不汲取知识之光，心灵就可能会被黑暗笼罩，就可能会被歪理邪说蛊惑，成为以犯罪为乐趣的恐怖分子或危险分子。

人因为无知而怕上帝的惩罚，怕恶鬼的纠缠，进而不去作恶，这是好事。人生最大的不幸是被无所顾忌、行事没有底线的心魔操控，唯利是图、以权为天、以斗为乐，以歪理邪说操控军队，胁迫民众，违反道德规范，大张旗鼓地违法犯罪。

苏格拉底说：我知道我一无所知，毕生引导轻狂青年回归"美德即知识"的正道，爱国更敬神。幼儿无知无罪，成人犯罪伏法，明知故犯罪加一等。

7. 因缘、良缘与恶缘

中国人很讲"缘"。信佛者讲因缘，信儒者讲情缘，信道者讲机缘。

哲学上解释"因"为直接原因和间接原因，"缘"为直接和间接的结果。因缘，又称缘分，是佛教对因果的一种说法，没有哲学因果那么广泛，主要是指人与人前世今生之间轮回转世中的无形的联结。

佛教徒常以宿世的"因缘"来解释人们今生的关系：前世之因，种下今生的聚会之缘。直白地说，前生你挨了我一耳光，所以这一世来打回给我。佛教故事说，前世的鹿王善待了国王，这世就成了释迦牟尼与徒弟的关系。

儒道不说因缘，但情景、机缘与因缘有相同的意思。有首歌唱有这样几句歌词："爱总是短暂，情总是简单，为什么曲终人会散？如果还有来世，今生诺言算不算？一生难得缘分，为何轻易留下遗憾？

良缘，指美好的因缘，即行善而使人今生或来世得好报。唐诗说："新知遭薄俗，旧好隔良缘。"良缘有获得好职业，进入好学校，结为好夫妻，遇上好婆婆，等等。

恶缘，指恶劣的因缘，即行恶而使人今生或来世得恶报。佛教徒有"六恶缘伴，阻坏净心"与"烦恼内催，恶缘外牵"等说法。依照佛教的说法，人不能获得好职业，读书不上进，妻离子散等，都是自己的恶缘带来的。

电视剧《前世今生》：20 世纪 30 年代上海滩黑帮人员，花心的苏云飞爱上富家女子秦婉莹，为她报杀父之仇而谋杀黑帮老大潘四爷，同时与潘四爷的小妾段小玉纠缠。苏云飞杀死潘四爷后，也死于非命。20 世纪 90 年代苏云飞在北京，再遇转世为餐馆服务员的沈小慧，不再有爱恋，却通过沈小慧认识了段小玉转世的湘兰，爱上了湘兰，最后娶了湘兰。这一世苏云飞被潘四爷转世的陈老板害得很惨。苏、秦、段、潘等因为因缘两世相遇，苏、秦、段了结良缘，苏、潘了结恶缘。

因缘、良缘、恶缘，玄而难信，却包含劝人行善的思想。相信倒是有利于和谐的。

8. 人生绝境十四

人生绝境可用两个成语描绘：十面埋伏与四面楚歌。这是人生最怕。

早在西晋时代，史官陈寿就在《三国志》中记下："高祖诛项，十面埋伏。"这里说的是楚汉战争的结局：气吞山河、不可一世、百战百胜的项羽，最后被他不瞧在眼里的刘邦与不用的韩信一战而胜，一败涂地而不想再战，不想活了。

元曲唱戏、三国演义，讲述军事故事，都以十面埋伏说战争中的重重包围。项羽由于被十面埋伏而陷入军事绝境。夜间项羽周围四面楚歌，使他误以为汉军已经攻占楚军阵地，以为天要灭他而斗志消失了，与虞姬饮酒悲歌告别。项羽率军突围到乌江，只剩下二十八名士兵。项羽拒绝乘船渡江东，带兵再战，自杀于江边。

历史上的项羽只有一个。但有类似项羽艰难处境的人却不在少数。假设某个公司的董事长，在商场上叱咤风云远近闻名，但终因花无百日红，商场如战场，最终企业破产，自己找事做，却又到处碰壁，此时公安立案调查他，他还可能因为行贿锒铛入狱。同时女儿吸毒惹上的毒贩也要找自己要钱，老婆也跟人跑了，情人翻脸要青春损失费，不得也要找他算账。他想死，却只弄瘫了自己。

人是万物之灵，不牺牲灵性，不会有绝境。也就是说，做人不离经叛道，水有高山，树有土壤，困难只是一两面，终有柳暗花明

的时候。

人厄难中十面埋伏重重包围的逆境，四面楚歌的孤立无援的窘况，大多是自己激进和非理性造成的。

人最为不幸的是由两脚直立变成四脚着地的动物，由安居乐业变成无休止的丛林战争。相信人的祖先是猴子，人生的适应主义就变成了战争主义。每个人最后都是项羽。将人定义为政治的动物，就将人推上了你死我活的都市丛林路。

人最怕做项羽，风光一世，输在最后，输得无颜再活下去。

9. 说说夫妻的笑

夫妻相伴既是人生幸事，也是很多烦恼事的源头，所以有时欢笑，有时愁。

夫妻欢笑多半是在年轻的时候。年轻是性情不太稳定的时候，因为相恋结婚，生活中如果没有双方家人的干扰，工作过得去，没有孩子的拖累，异性相吸，趣味相投，自然会产生两情相悦，想不笑都难。通常年轻夫妇笑声多，且响亮。

夫妻欢笑更多是在婚庆的时候。当然也有例外，例如因为某事被迫在婚礼庆典的时候紧锁愁眉，但这种情况很少。婚姻通常是大喜的日子，两情相悦到以婚姻互托终身，过程中的艰辛这时候像酿酒一样发出浓烈的醇香。无论夫妻是否年轻，尤其是那些因为各种原因年轻的时候没有结成夫妻而大龄时举行婚礼庆典的，更是喜笑颜开。

夫妻都希望欢笑永远。趋乐避苦人之常情，夫妻相处更是如此。所以无量寿经说："言色相和，无相违戾"。这是说夫妻之间应和言悦色相处，以免乖戾之气影响感情，引起夫妻的争吵、打闹，甚至离婚。先前的笑成了自嘲：那时候太傻。

夫妻成家随之带来了许多责任。诸如谁赚钱养家，谁做家务，

等等。古代男主外，女主内，家庭是个共和制公司，责任明晰，所以婚姻比较恒久。故而中国早就有琴瑟之好的比喻和相敬如宾、举案齐眉的故事流传。而今婚姻家庭大变革，夫妇共同工作、共同操持家务，职责不再泾渭分明，争执冲突在所难免。

有争执与冲突，未必是坏事。这就如同河水傍山而流，时而也惊涛拍岸。夫妻之间山高水长，小溪潺潺，撞击石子，前行迂回，波涛之后徐徐流淌，道窄湍急，道宽平缓。恩爱一辈子的良缘夫妻少，吵闹一辈子却不离不弃的锅铲夫妻多。

炒菜必需锅铲，夫妻反目只在这个阶段，不砸锅摔铲成仇，依然能携手到老。

夫妻应笑着白头到老。《诗经》说"执子之手，与子偕老。"这时候笑，最美好。

10. 结婚成家不是枷锁

部族成员的夫妻关系一确定，就有了婚姻与家庭。一般说来，一夫一妻、一屋一庭院的家庭形式多半在欧美，一夫多妻、多厢房、多庭院的家庭形式主要在亚非。从现象上看，家庭具有繁衍有世系的后代、防范性病、优生儿女、耕织分工等多功能。

家庭是社会的细胞，不是牢狱。故而婚姻不能变成枷锁，成为男人与女人正常生活的桎梏。男人与女人没有夫妻的婚姻形式与名分，完全不要家庭也不行，使部族酋邦形同妓院，乱伦、同性恋等淫秽之事层出不穷，所以被灭。游牧部族农耕化的过程同时是家庭形成与稳定的过程，夫妻名分与责任明确。

据说"丈夫"名称有两个起因：丈夫怕老婆不贞，跟在后面一丈远的地方；老婆希望被保护，要找一丈高的巨人做老公以应对酋邦的抢亲野俗。是否有如此说法，由史学家去考证，但可以确定的是，婚姻与家庭至少具有优生与安稳的双重功能。

基本可以肯定，婚姻最初并无多少情爱成分，主要是部族群体稳定的需要，阻止抢妻内战，也是女人个体的需要。"婚姻"的"女"字偏旁隐含了这一点。

这个过程看似自然，但猩猩、猴子再自然一亿年恐怕也不会有人类的婚姻和穿衣相处的家庭。逻辑地说有天意神旨，历史传说验证了"人是万物之灵"一说。

看中国式的圣经周易，可知"男主外，女主内"是夫妻关系恒定的原则，荣誉与责任、忠贞等伦理都由此而生。但无法调和的夫妻反目、离婚的个案也有。

看历史记载，人类荒淫现象在距今两千五百年的时候就日趋严重。欧洲、西亚、北非没有阻止住，文明邦国成千上万地自灭或被灭。中国孔孟之道确立，礼仪之邦延续到公元1911年的清朝末年。过程中女人不得随便，但允许再婚。

北宋范仲淹的母亲再婚是为养儿，并非为激情搅拌情感泥塘。男须忠女须贞。

11. 大众给面子，自己笑自己

面子是东方人际关系中的一种跟名分相联系的荣耀，很难有个明确的、能够得到大家确认的具体定义，大致上指家庭、党派、朝国（党国）中的成员依照传统习俗所需要获得的尊重，是重视而不是轻视、嘲弄、笑话。

华人圈中常有"给人面子"的说法，果敢文中相应有"给面子""给脸面""给脸"等词语。这里的"面子""脸面""脸"特指思想意识精神上需要的荣誉、显耀、尊重等。这就是学者所谓的社会性。

人有社会性的需要，就会有面子、脸面的需要，如男人讲官职高低，女人要跟娼妓区分，职务要有等级，诸如此类差别的要求，

都是面子范畴。东方人关注社会性，故而面子观念重，男人纳妾、女人偷情等等都与面子相关。绝对不要脸的人很少。西方人只是面子观念没有东方人强。

由此可知，面子是大众给的，给个人心理上需要的尊严与荣誉。韩信封王后要衣锦还乡，项羽突出垓下重围后不肯过江东，都跟华夏族的社会性面子相关联。

这个"大众"，另有庶人、民众、人民、群众、平民、草民、老百姓等多个称呼。人民，是"大众"最通常的代称，在《水浒传》中王进落脚史家庄那一节就有了。人民的力量来自舆论、集会、造反，给领袖以面子，剥夺革命对象的面子。专制政府削夺的就是人民掌控面子的力量，通俗地说，就是耍政治流氓，逼人无耻。

总的说来，西欧、北欧、北美，人民的力量消融在公民权利中，受法制保障，有宪法与法律，就有力量。官员、军警是人民的公职人员。这就是欧美宪政。

人民的力量之一，是编笑话，尤其是职业型、政治型的笑话与冷笑话，以幽默或调侃的方式嘲讽暴君昏主、贪官污吏，例如古代的聊斋、现代的武侠小说等。

人生在世，无耻自讨笑话。大众笑官，是弄权者愚弄人民不成而反受其羞辱。

12. 真情实爱即幸福

从经验现象上看，物种进化论没有得到验证。但人的智力进化却如同上学已得到验证。人类社会进化过程中，只要婚姻是真情实爱，就是幸福。

因为男女授受不亲是伦理之必守。正当的爱情是五不限：

第一，不限年龄之差别。据传孔子母亲颜征在不到 20 岁时，嫁给 66 岁的父亲叔梁纥，两人年龄差别大约 40 岁，在鲁国的野邑陬地结合。史书没有直说两人的感情，但从孔父死后 14 年孔母艰难度日也未改嫁，可推两人十分恩爱。孔母也因此恪守妇道，教育孔子很成功，20 岁娶贵族之女，生子时鲁国君主送鲤鱼祝贺。

第二，不限民族之差别。上古时代中国虽有华夷之防，那是防止文明退化，却并没阻止通婚。晋文公的父母就是华夏人与西戎人的结合。汉朝与匈奴以和亲政策交好之后形成传统，留有昭君出塞的佳话，汉族与突厥、吐蕃、回纥等民族也都有婚姻。

第三，不限国籍之别。元朝以前华夷婚姻基本上都是异国婚姻，和亲政策之外有多少民间的自由恋爱，还未见有史书谈论。但从中华民国时期以来中国人与外国人自由恋爱通婚已非个案。苏曼殊的父亲、鲁迅的弟弟与日本人或同居，或成婚。

第四，不限文化程度之别。婚姻有如宗教，跟理性、知识等智力因素无关，主要还是情感、前世、世交等因缘的促成。胡适与没正式上过学的小脚女人江冬秀因父母之命、媒妁之言的传统成婚，在西风愈吹愈烈的背景下，情感生活越来越好。

第五，不限职业爱好之别。印度的种姓制度限定高等职业者与低等职业者通婚，中国大多数时候没有这种限定，即使有也是世家的规定，并非社会制度。明朝末年名妓柳如是与达官钱谦益不仅职业差异大，年龄也相差 36 岁，热恋成婚。

人类因性别、年龄、阶层等区别，男女有了多种差异，情感却不受任何差异阻隔。因缘聚合，真情实爱即幸福。

13. 个人五美德

无论东西方，都很强调个人美德，西方侧重正义、诚信，东方侧重仁爱、慈悲。一个人在中国，依照善的秉性所需要的五种美德是：温、良、恭、俭、让。

温，即温情。温情就字面的意思，指的是温顺的柔情，平和不猛烈，给人温馨真挚的感觉，令人感到温暖。这个词多用来描写女性，其实也适合很多男性。即使江湖豪杰也有温情的一面。一个人能给人温暖，使人心空晴朗，这多有魅力啊。天上最美是星星，人间最美是温情。世上最残酷的就是破坏温情，因激烈相斗。

良，即良好。良者，优也美也好也，就是美好。与性情良好的人相处，像河水流淌在宽阔的河道，十分舒畅。人心底善良，才能与人和睦友好相处。《诗经》有"琴瑟在御，莫不静好。""投我以木桃，报之以琼瑶。匪报也，永以为好也。"

恭，即恭敬。这是古人最为看重的优良品德之一，对尊长或宾客行大礼，男对女目不斜视，对长辈或名人谦恭。汉武帝时代县令见到才子司马相如都很恭敬。

俭，即俭朴。就字面意思，是指生活俭省朴实或品性节俭质朴。古代道家修道，修的就是使人情俭朴，时俗清和。俭朴省掉了排场，使物欲细水长流，所以古代社会总能持续发展，而现代社会则如同短跑冲刺。

让，即让人。儒家君子谦恭的重要特征就是礼让。不是小人般乱让，而是守礼谦让。在孔子看来，能以礼让治国，什么问题都能解决；不能以礼让治国，就会出问题。礼让是一种心法，让人自律，以礼节制民心，相让就不会有争执。是不是什么都要让呢？也不是，做君子，要当仁不让、义不容辞。

《吕氏春秋》说："富可润屋，德可润身。"小人最恨温、良、恭、俭、让，把这当奴性批斗，结果是邪恶横行。五种美德贯穿人生始终，才是最好的人生。

14. 从众为善不为过

从众，即跟随顺从大众的心理或思想意识，是人在婴幼儿、童

年时期的正常的必然状态，以哭笑造出悲欢情景，以众口一词、齐心协力造成舆论与势力。

人在青少年时期通常会比较逆反，尤其是男孩子，为显示自己是个大人了，反抗大人的过多干预与管制。逆反的个性会较叛逆，你说东他朝西。这样的一群人凑合在一起，便众说纷纭。君子群龙无首是好事，小人群龙无首便是一盘散沙。

个人在众口一词或步调一致的情形下，唱反调或标新立异，这或是因为天赋使命而崭露头角，或是因为仁义修养而坚守美德，在随波逐流的堕落环境中金鸡独立。古代如张良刺杀秦始皇，近代如王夫之隐居衡山不在清朝做官。

从众者在当今被批评为平庸、胆小。跟随顺从大众，如果是自发地去做好事，与人为善不图回报，但求心安理得，这就是好的。例如犯罪团伙或邪教成员认识到组织的犯罪性质或邪恶作为而脱离，两两成双、三五成群、成百上千甚至上万地反水，这是正义行为。从众为善不为过，绝非胆小平庸，而是良心择善而从、从善如流。

人从小养成心中有"众"，有成为人才、为社会公众服务的意识，或者说心中有众人之家、之国，时刻为家国着想，私心就会减少，私利就会献给社会。这就是常言说的好人。

这样的好人，有少女或孩子时代天性中较多的怜悯、羞恶之心，就会比较有仁心，有义气，如同《水浒传》中的宋江，善于团结他人，维护众人利益。从众为善的人顾全大局而胸怀宽广，目光视野自然就高瞻远瞩。

15. 国家行为趋利作恶

国家的强国意识是尊重强者，欺负弱者。个人的仁慈品性不这样。父母宠爱幼儿，通常是因为怜爱弱小，给予照顾。江湖豪侠打抱不平也是出于仁义情怀。国家却不是这样，国家通常是趋利，部族内部求公务实，民族对外则求私务实。

相对欧洲而言，亚非大陆的人在古代对整体利益比较看重，尤其是中土的中原古国，无论统一大国或分裂小国，都讲顾全大局，在个人与群体利益发生冲突的时候，都要求个人作出牺牲，包括牺牲爱情。

就国家而言，牺牲个人利益会解决众说纷纭的无决定、决议的散乱问题，会改变步调不一的无组织无纪律的散沙状态。南宋岳家军让金军感叹："撼山易，撼岳家军难"，因为岳飞领导的将士"冻死不拆屋，饿死不掳掠"，以牺牲个人的饱暖享乐，换来了百战百胜的战斗力。

具体地说希腊，雅典公民不肯作出这种牺牲，非要把女人嫁给自家人，允许舅舅娶外甥女，为了享乐不惜乱伦，打仗就不敌斯巴达。而斯巴达为了军力强大，生育力不强的男人可以让出妻子怀性功能强的男人的孩子。这样的斯巴达，雅典如何能在军事上赢？这样的希腊部族注定不能形成统一国家。

说到战国时代，齐、楚、燕、韩、魏、赵、秦七个国家，秦国之外的六国都因为贵族割舍不下"刑不上大夫"的特权，以至于李悝、吴起、申不害的变法都无法持续到底，魏、楚、韩等国最终被贵族的私利压制了庶民的公心。

而秦国则因为孝公坚定支持商鞅废井田、奖耕战，使平民可以分家增加国税，可以凭军功做将军而勇于公战，遏制住了私斗，进而秦国百年强盛，直到灭了六国。

近代史上国家趋利作恶，战争激烈。第二次世界大战中，日美双方在冲绳死伤惨重，但日本在战后还是因为利益跟美国继续合作。

国与国之间合作，基本上是趋利才合作，适合双方争取利益的目的，才会合作。

16. 难得辛劳

广东白话有"汗干钱散"一说，近似成语"不劳而获""渔人之利""坐享其成"。不劳而获，最早见于《孔子家语·入官》："所求于迩，故不劳而得也。"汗干钱散，不辛劳、不流汗却得到钱财，而这种占便宜得来的钱财，都难守住，容易散光。

这或许就是中国古代自然经济时代"士农工商"社会结构的正理：劳心者（士）治国（行政司法以管人），掌权者以仁义礼制行政，不贪恋钱财，形成人世清流；劳力者（农工商）被官管，获利农民为最，工匠其次，商人最低，所以重农抑商。

这就是古代邦国或帝国能够存活千年以上的原因。凡重商轻农之国三百年内必定衰微。一分耕耘，一分收获。多劳多得，少劳少得，不劳不得。辛劳得来钱财，心安理得。辛劳符合相生相克的理。通过勤劳所得，才觉得珍贵懂得珍惜。

懒惰者必无聊。无聊则没有幸福感。占便宜的人得寸进尺，贪污腐化而人心败坏，没有辛劳的幸福感，是走火入魔的散财人、败家子。

广东白话还有"无灵无难"一说。"无灵"的字面意思是没有心灵或没有灵魂，通常说的没心没肺，没脑子，没心计。俗话说"傻人自有傻福"。古代看似傻乎乎的人，虽穷而不凶不恶，所以官场能宽容。甚至白痴都能当上皇帝。宋朝以后，中国这样的人越来越不吃香了。

但凡这样啥事都无所谓（不往心里去）的人，活得很潇洒，不把批评当回事，笑罗汉似的承受一切磨难，活得额头上没有皱纹，心无烦闷，脑无邪念。从心理学上看，无灵的"傻人"能接纳自己和他人的缺点和错误，对各种负面评论一笑了之，正所谓"相逢一笑泯恩仇"。这样的人在朋党之争中能够脱颖而出。

无灵，没有隔夜的仇与愁，做事无执着，故而执着的人有的困难一概没有。

17. 有因必有果

因果，即原因和结果，是宗教、哲学、科学中经常被用到的两个或一对概念。正统道家讲清净无为、得道成仙，不求明了因果，难得糊涂。佛家，尤其佛教明确讲因果轮回，讲前世之因（例如被杀、受虐等，或行善、积德等）在今世转换为缘（家人、家畜、同学、同事等），形成的善果或恶果，劝人放下恩怨情仇。

人在世间求名利的成功，明了因果很重要，注意行事前后的善恶因果，听好师父、好父母的教诲以循规蹈矩，书生博览群书务必谨小慎微，以免一失足成千古恨。懂得因果与德行的关系，从小善待万物，长大莫管闲事，诸恶勿做，己所不欲勿施于人，善良受苦乐在道中。

常人很难说清因果，可能还会乱说，却一般都有对因果的正常感觉：善有善报，恶有恶报，时到得报。这种感觉上的因果，青少年经验少，情绪不稳，不太准确。中老年经验丰富，感觉老到，就比较准确。

中国有"天时地利人和"之说，就是对社会事物因果演变的模糊说法：天象变化引发地上和人事变化，因时因地制宜，因势利道才能成就大事。

所以老辈人总说：凡事尽人事，知天命，莫强求。这就有了民间说的种花得花、种瓜得瓜、种豆得豆、养鸡得鸡、养鸭得鸭、养犬得犬等生物种类不变之理。

从哲学理论上谈论因果，古代希腊的"四因说"（质料因、形式因、动力因、目的因）更有值得深究的学术意义：解析元素，透视形式，发现动因，寻觅目的（由小见大，由人间而天上）。

人想逞强和享乐时，会嘲弄民间经验、宗教教诲、科学理性、哲学理论，为感官快活或事业成功不惜折寿、伤残、送命，虽得逞一时，却最终被善恶因果规律嘲弄。

18. 择业很重要

关于人生行业问题，中国有句老话很经典：男怕入错行，女怕嫁错郎。

果敢文一字一意，说行业有时候指职业的类别，例如管治安的警察，管边防和平叛的军人。有时候指生产作业，史书说项羽性情中人，不求究竟，说曹操"任侠放荡，不治行业"，都不安于农、林、牧、渔等正道行业，成为乱世枭雄。《颜氏家训》说"以僧尼行业，多不精纯……"其中的"行业"指修持的道行的深浅。

中华古代太平治世的财富及发明是行业生产或促成行业发展。乱世之交的前朝末世，总有机敏多变、任侠放荡而不在正当行业中按部就班、求上进的人，德行在世人眼里不看好，却因不拘一格而天降大任，建成平叛功业。

刘邦、项羽、曹操等历史人物不为劳动行业而生。此外佛家、道家中的许多修炼人也不是劳动行业中人，却也能见到行业的说法，例如《大唐西域记》记载蓝摩国僧人"行业无纪"。这里的"行业"指的则是佛教徒恪守戒律的操行。

普遍来说，行业指的是人世间的生产作业的门类，如前所说农、林、牧、渔等，具体细化为职业类别，例如捕鱼行可分为捕鱼业、织网业等，医药行可分为医业、药业等，再分可为中医、西医及中药、西药等，笼统称为各行各业。

行业一旦形成，在一定的时候，就像道路天然就有了路基、宽长的区别、标准、级别一样，有了行业的交流和管理组织及相应的规章制度，如林业、汽车业、银行业等，各有各的行规业则。很少

有人轻易违犯而冒险做行业的耗子。

在世界上多数地区，农业长期比工商业更被看重，直到近代才反过来。农业生养同步可持续发展，工商业在某些方面极速毁坏自然资源不可持续。

人类选择高耗能的现代化，等于选择了开奔驰奔向悬崖。对于男女个人而言，是女人嫁给流氓赔上一生幸福。男人选错行业，犹如演说家端起冲锋枪去送命。

19. 城市与行会

行业在农村区分简单，就是庭外男耕，庭内女织及各项家务；细分则在城市，形成各行百业，城市文明与市井社会自然形成，有了聚族而居的家庭、遵守行规的行会、进行行政管理的政府，等等，社会就这样通过适应而发生组织的进化。

城市，是果敢文的"城"与"市"的合成词，表明城市两大作用：筑城防卫与进行交易。城墙之内居民集中居住，形成街区及市场，起初"日中为市"，逐渐衍生出早市、午市、夜市。城市因城墙坚固而安全，因交易兴旺而发达。

这样一来，城市自然就人口密集，工商业发达。一个城市与周围若干乡村，好像太阳与九大行星，自然就形成了一个地区系统，城市成了政治、经济、文化的中心。凡是自然演变的城市，基本都是从村庄到村镇，大镇建官府就成了县城。

通俗地说，城市是大森林，什么鸟都有。士农工商赶庙会似的来到县城，县城一多，划州管理，州又成了比县城更大的城市——管县城的上级。自然而然，除了边境，官吏、大农民（所谓地主或豪绅）、大商人都集中到城市，拖家带口，就有了社区、街道、诊所、学校、商场、会场、公园等。

行会最早就是古城的产物，有严密细致的章程，保证会员权利义务，对外实行垄断。例如手工业行会（匠人会所），还有商业行会（商人会所），作用是调解同业矛盾以协调相互关系，协调与官府的关系。同行由此不成为生死冤家。

行会在中国产生于隋唐两朝，随行就市（同街同店）而有了"行"的称呼，诸如"织锦行""金银行"等。宋代都市行会多达数十家，入行者成百上千。后来行会组织跟帮会搅和，到晚清更跟会党纠结。

行会在西欧出现的时期相当于中国南宋时期，主要为了团结抵抗城堡封建主乱收税，按照不同行业组织了行会：匠师带领帮工和学徒，学徒、帮工晋升得按行规。欧洲城市最初带着日耳曼人的农村公社的传统，就叫公社，市民即公民。

大致在中国元朝时期，西欧行会普遍发展，好似唐宋行会的历史涅槃。

20. 法制与权利

法制在中国承传家族、宗族的规矩，在欧洲则承传城邦、公社的规矩。起初都是由王者和贵族来组织社会，组建城市和国家；神道信仰和世间法律并用。

法制，由族规承传来的，家国一体没断脐带，族的位置高于个人；由邦规、社规而来，家的位置不重要，主要是国的居民点，个人的位置高于族。

个人的位置高于族，例如古代希腊城邦与罗马帝国，再如现代英国、美国、法国，法律制度就会把身份世袭看得如同个人的眼球和生命，起初维护王族与贵族的利益，遭遇持续的个人逃亡与组织起义，维持不下去了才转为共享。

中国因为族的位置高于个人，在古代从贵族到奴隶，都以家大族大为荣耀，为奋斗方向，故而普遍具有仁义的伦理职责和能够为

父母、家族、族国作出牺牲的精神。达官贵人做儿子时就学会了对父母的恭敬与对兄长的退让，故而有孔融七岁让梨的故事作为美谈。

但这并不意味个人权利在欧洲诸国比在祖国历朝多。实际的情况是，权势和货财等个人权利从春秋战国起就确定有了。荀子与后世史官用了"权利"这个词，相应地说，同时期的欧洲主要人口是被当牲口看待的奴隶，倒是没有普遍的个人权利，有个人权利的主要是贵族。在古代，欧洲贵族比中土官员自私。

这就形成了不同的权利获取的传统。中土历朝通过变法、改革，把原来属于世袭贵族或达官贵人的特权，自上而下的让给士农工商各阶层的大众共享。而欧洲则是通过从古希腊罗马，到中世纪各王国长达两千年之久的亡国灭种的征战，再到近现代的西、葡、意、荷、英、法、德、俄各国接力赛似的宪政法律制度。

中华民国时期，通过共和宪政与国民教育，欧洲争权夺利的意识得到普及。

中土从夏朝到清朝形成和承传的，从家庭到朝廷，由贵族到官员及父母，礼让特权的美德趋于消失，需要复兴，让铁索横江的船下海。

21. 资本与利润

看历史，由黄河到长江的"中土"历朝诸国，是最早涉及资本与利润问题，并有重大贡献的。欧洲在罗马帝国涉及商业的资本与利润，之后睡了一千年。

经济学说资本比较抽象，说白了就是经营工商业的本钱。读姜子牙经商的故事，就依稀可见商朝末年中土就懂经营本钱的道理了。果敢文字词多义模糊，从事工作的人可以将资本引申为出人头地的升官、从事工作的就业等的条件和本分之意。

成语"偷鸡蚀米""一本万利"，就模糊地包含了投入资本与获取利润的因果关系。古今中外，投资人与受雇者就形成了劳资关系，资本家有非常吝啬和贪婪的，雇工有非常懒惰和尖滑的。所谓"剥削剩余价值"的说法并不科学。

无论欧洲还是中土，投入资本而守礼或守法地撷取利润都是天经地义的。只是在社会急剧变革的时候，才有贪得无厌的人不顾劳工的利益进行剥削，才有好逸恶劳的人故意浪费或强夺雇主的钱财，把乱世当成强盗改变命运的时机。

商品的价值规律是：赚钱进，赔钱退。资本总是流向高利润行业。作为投资人，这样做是正常的、理性的，利己利人，因为代表生产力并付出高风险，收入最高既合情也合理。

工程师因为高技术获取高收入也是合理的。同理，普通工人的体力或智力投入包含的技术含量低于工程师很多，且不负担企业倒闭的风险，收入最低也是合理的。因此，雇佣工人"创造剩余价值"的说法基本属于空中楼阁。

反天理的事，是从欧洲出现、发展并传到中土来的。欧洲圈地运动"羊吃人"都几百年了，中华晚清与民国时期才有说商人"一本万利"的成语。

不通过商业交易与法制程序获得企业，是"无本万利"，抢资本夺超级红利。

22. 问题与社会

欧洲人盗匪似的"无本万利"由来已久，维基百科上可查英国圈地运动始于12世纪。这是当时贵族在国王追究不了的情况下发生的，后来因殖民而纵容。

从贵族以特权谋私到宪政下公民平均权利，形成"协商不成就打"的欧美科技文明以及推广建起的近现代社会，问题越来越多。

中土历朝的问题在太平治世是名分区别下的问与答，或者学校老师解释题目、解答问题等。官场有道而私心遏制，治世或盛世出现；无道而徇私舞弊，衰世或乱世出现，汉族农民义军的刀剑"扫帚"清扫不了积垢，胡人骑兵就来了。

欧美王国或民国的上不让下，到最后被迫成为平均公约数，美国爱默生以《问题》一诗作答：（相信上帝创世与救赎）的"信念创造了我们"，"《圣经》中列举的责任全都是从大自然的心中发生……"欧美的社会发展如同火山喷发。

果敢文说的"社会"，本意指特定土地上人的集会（自由结社），具体有春秋社日迎赛土神以表谢意的集会。唐朝有诗"未向燕台逢厚礼，幸因社会接馀欢。"后来，"社会"一词演变为结社形成的组织或团体，诸如同盟会、国民党等会党。

中土从崇尚君子到结成朋党的古代，再到组织造反的会党的近代，君子是"留下剩余力，建设天理国"。即使心智还不成熟的小人也"生当作人杰，死亦为鬼雄"，让女人能够为他一掬英雄泪。这种文化，现在没了。

现代人只注重研究物质及无人的自然界与个人缺席的社会以及人的身体，不注重研究连通宏观与微观的能量世界以及人的自由心灵，如同瞿秋白在《赤都心史》中所说："问题符号只在飞"，"还不知道怎样设问，怎样摆这符号，何况答案！"

面对问题欧洲古人合法地争，中土古人退避三舍才对阵，现代人则你死我活，宁为全瓦，不做碎玉。

23. 主义与战争

中土西化之前无主义，有哲理思想，无哲学理论。得理饶人，唯心论和唯物论通通不成体系。熙熙攘攘赶庙会不为名利，模模糊糊说问题只为安宁。这样，中土战争不追穷寇，任战败者生长或消

融，天意至上。

印度古代主义不兴，宗教却盛，婆罗门教绝处逢生后，最终赶佛教出了本土。欧洲古代哲学"爱智慧"而刨根问底，总有学生要超越老师，到了英国近代终于生育出霍布斯的机械唯物主义与黑格尔的理念唯心主义。推广这种精神就有了主动出击的庭审辩论与世界大战。

中华古代从华夏传说到三代的半传说、半信史，再到秦汉至明清的当时记载、隔代修史，形成三教共存共荣的文化：儒家信命，道家信道，佛家信佛，虽有争辩，却相互容得。

儒家之忍让、道家之真性、佛家之善愿，当成宗教未必最好，当成哲学说理不精确，却可以成为当今100多个国家或地区和平共处的契约原则。

茫茫宇宙的星球之间，肉眼看上去并肩或接踵，实际上区别巨大：不仅相距多少亿万光年，而且各自拥有的化学元素、物理规则真正是天壤之别。有的宇宙是独星，有的宇宙居然是银河金海。

我们把类似飞碟穿过时空隧道进入地球太空的事件叫做"穿越"。在当今地球世界，实现"活人穿越"还是任重道远，必须努力的事。但我们的思想现在就可以有穿越意识，不必等到死后。

据说，一对双胞胎相似度如同两个平行宇宙的相似度，但诞生在地球上的时间距离，在另外一个星球上计算，则可能相差一千年还不止。

真相究竟如何，我们及后来者，尽可能八仙过海，各显神通，但吕洞宾不跟张果老开战，曹国舅不跟何仙姑相亲。没有主义的执着，人的心灵之河是否更流动？

24. 流动决定价值

世间所有物质产品，都是从自然界原始材料按人的适应需要制造的，进入市场，能够流动卖钱的就红火，吸引更多工厂生产、公司推广；产品滞销，工厂、公司或者破产清算，或者退出转产。可谓流动决定价值。

流动指气体或液体在力的作用下引起的位置移动。火山、地震等特殊情况下还可引发泥石流、岩浆流等。位移的流动中物质能量保存多，价值就大；耗费大，价值就少。有空隙、空间、空洞、孔道等，就有风的流动，所谓"空穴来风"。

商品检验中抽样验货，少年性情不定所生的变化，作文下笔流畅，眼球转动灵活，也都叫流动。很难统一"流动"的定义。广义地说，气流、风流、水流、物流、人流、车流、诗流、文流，万事万物都可以因条件而流动。

稀缺为贵，多余廉价。价值高低由人决定。人作决定却是根据流动。百科名词解释决定，莫衷一是，单从商品交易上看，就是选不选，要不要。选要，就有价值，就有工厂生产，有公司推广；选不要，就没有工厂生产，没有公司推广。

人类群体或个体基于利益或立场（既定见解），衡量取舍某事物的词，被称作价值，要则有价值，不要则无价值。价值有多种形态，如社会价值、个人价值、经济价值、法律价值、名义价值等，真正的大小，取决于人的自由意志。

人丧失自由成了奴隶，某物或某观点强加于人，这个物品或思想就没有价值，成为人所不齿的狗粪。要想人吃狗粪，只有将人催眠，狂犬吠日似的生活。

人有尊严地活着，接受的物品和观点，是不违背人性和个性而自己要的，所谓社会、个人、经济、法律、名义等价值，才是真的。个人可以主动多向选择，不随波逐流，受人往高处走的价值观引导，才会形成真人流。

自由的人流市场是产生真善美价值的金蛹。价值归根结底就是要不要，如何要？物质或精神的品质与数量是不是由个人自由决定

要不要，要多少？物稀为贵，物多为贱，钱多为贱，钱少为贵，跟以物易物千差万别。

25. 遇事须静思

处世总要遇事，静思是碰上麻烦时的良方。例如儿子今天突然一句话惹得父亲大发雷霆。如果儿子立马回应，说："老爸去看心理医生吧。"父亲猛然上火，家庭就燃起战火。这时候如果儿子不语，静思："我这是咋了？"星火则一闪而过。

唐朝李白作诗："床前明月光，疑是地上霜。举头望明月，低头思故乡。"这是夜晚静思的作品。今人考证"床前"是井台，"床"又是凳子。这是干什么？不是静思，不去体悟一个游子月光下的思乡情怀，而是显示自己的一知半解。

人但凡有了显示心，就会惹是生非，父子也会开战。儒家礼教静思父子恩情，则会从"太阳大"，联想到"父母恩大"；知道"对父母要知恩，感恩，报恩"，就知道去安慰父亲，而不是去激怒。遇事静思，在家会孝顺，出门会行善。

静思的人会比较善于处事，从"君子量大"，联想到"小人气大"，选择与人为善做君子，定然遇事就会大事化小，小事化了。许多事情，原本就是庸人自扰。

人一旦有了静思，就会懂得一个显见的道理：原谅别人就是善待自己。正所谓忍一时风平浪静，退一步海阔天空。今人的误区是忍让是奴性，争强是个性。

人为什么会生气？细说原因，五花八门、千奇百怪，最重要的原因是浮躁，觉得没面子，或者得理不饶人。结果就是拿别人过失惩罚自己。

静思会发现，待人退一步，爱人宽一寸，就会很快乐。有钱人不静思，到处花钱去寻欢作乐，结果是遇事就浮躁生气。问心无愧心最安。

遇事静坐闭门思过，常思己过宽以待人。不静思，闲谈论人是非，无事也生非。静思而知己知彼，这是寻找解决问题的办法、压制冲动的路径。

26. 宽以待人道宽

宽容，即允许别人自由行动或判断。《不列颠百科全书》的解释是：耐心而毫无偏见地容忍与自己的观点或公认的观点不一致的意见。儒家称宽容为恕道。

儒家、道家，都一统在道上。道家求真性，以慈、俭、不争为路径；儒家求诚实，以仁、义、礼、让为路径。两条路都通往宽容，修炼忍性。庄子论天下，说："常宽容于物"；荀子教社会下层的少年，也是劝告引导其修习宽容原谅的功夫。

"大人不计小人过"，"宰相肚里能撑船"，说的宽大气量就是能容忍他人。欧洲的仇杀历史进展到两次世界大战后，才有坐在联合国讲理，听人批评的宽容。

中土从汉晋到隋唐形成儒道佛相互兼容的忍让传统，无论儒生、道士、和尚，凡真正有修为的人面临山崩地裂的危难处境，神色都能够宽舒从容、处变不惊。

宽以待人、大度容人，说来容易，要做到就必须修行。不通过接受他人一次次的冒犯、羞辱，犹如铁一样被千锤百炼敲打过，还真的难有大人的气量、宰相的肚量。近代有人将宽容当作软弱，贬为奴性，主张睚眦必报。心理学看这样的人就是自卑软弱，因而才记仇，不报复忍不住，极度难受。

小说《三国演义》推崇的刘备，《水浒传》中的宋江，武功平常却能够领导众多武功杰出的人，主观方面靠的就是罗贯中说的"宽以待人，柔能克刚"。

宽以待人、大度容人，这是心上的功夫。没有昆仑山一般崇高的心境，没有天空一样宽阔的胸怀，没有大海一样浩大深沉的修养，谁能做得到？宽容儿女容易，因为有爱；宽容仇敌难，因为恨难消。

仇恨难消而冤冤相报，东西南北结仇，家中也要打斗，没有敌人制造敌人，把人间当成地狱打造，脚下的路会越走越窄，最后是无路可走。学会宽容，是在修炼山一般的高度、气度和天空般的胸怀、大海般的承载。仁者心宽，处处是坦途。

27. 严阵以待路窄

严阵以待，最初是个军事备战用语，指打仗布阵，以整齐严正的阵势，厉兵秣马地等待来侵犯的敌人。

古代两军对阵，将士手拿刀、剑、盾，打起十二分精神。弓箭手弓在手箭在弦上随时发射。将军不懂阵势轻率出击，很可能一命呜呼，士气大挫而全军溃败。

宋朝司马光编《资治通鉴》，写汉光武帝建武三年的战争，就用了"严阵以待"这个词。明朝冯梦龙写《东周列国志》，多处以"严阵以待"描写战前准备。

现代战争跟古代战争军事手段上几乎有天翻地覆的变化，火药大量使用，枪炮替代了刀剑，将士作战不再穿笨重的盔甲，将领不再身先士卒在阵前厮杀，一开始就是两军战士相互开枪开炮的厮杀，血雨腥风更为酷烈。如此战争，战前依然要准备，需要挖战壕布阵，布置指挥所，同样有严阵以待的情势。

打仗严阵以待是必须的。轻率开战，不布阵设防，是拿命开玩笑。但有些国家和宗教，在马放南山、解甲归田的太平年月，仍然严阵以待。这就使社会人际关系演变成阶层对立。人与人形成阶级斗争，细微差异都被视为战争的火种。

和平时期的备战，在 20 世纪，演变出现敌我主义的意识形态，把人类在适应过程中出现的阶层和民族劳作、共同建构人类世界的努力破坏了，以种族或阶级的矛盾解释人与人的意见分歧、利益分配的差异以及冲突。

敌我斗争主义的思想文化教育，使敌我识别成了太平岁月里最重要的事，认为战争随时将发生或并没停止。人的自由意识与行为被当作敌视权力者的敌对手段，千方百计以制度进行防范，以人民名义予以铲除。

和平年代持"消灭敌人，自由属于人民"思想，掀动群众运动，以各种名义把人民之间的私怨化成批斗，睡觉都枕戈待旦地等待杀敌，可谓人生路越走越狭窄，窄到头碰头，眼对眼。

28. 邪道诽谤信谍

1933 年到 1945 年，欧洲曾经出现过希特勒领导的德国纳粹党专政。纳粹德国正式国名为德意志帝国和大德意志帝国，又称第三帝国，以纳粹党的独裁统治，把德国变成了一个严阵以待头、碰头的社会。

纳粹德国昂首阔步走在邪道上，言行激烈，经常骗人和打人，以编造谎言、肆意诽谤立国，名言是：谎言说一千遍就成了真理；崇尚暴力，肆意剥夺犹太人合法累积的财富，视犹太人、斯拉夫人为劣等民族，搞种族迫害，发动侵略战争。

邪道，字面本义是诽谤信谍的活法，另有旁门左道的妖术之意。左有笨的意思。其实只要与人为善，逆来顺受，说真话，笨不为邪，而是大智若愚。《礼记》论王制"执左道以乱政。"左道在这里是指"邪道"：不惜倾危国家。

古代名儒荀子说："虽穷困冻馁，必不以邪道为贪。"这是说人类在适应的过程中，即使穷途末路到快要冻死时，也不要动贪财的念头而骗抢。

邪道，并不只是社会下层的违法犯罪。社会上层，上至皇帝，不思勤政爱民，痴想吃长生不老丹，巧立名目搜刮民间钱财，建造堂皇宫殿用以享受，婚姻乱伦，都是邪道的做法，既无仁义情怀，也违背古礼。礼是正与邪的分水岭。

守礼言行正，非礼动邪念。但一正压百邪。近现代科技工业文明增长了人试图主宰宇宙的心愿，出现模糊正道与邪道边界的政治意识形态和文学艺术。

邪道喜爱诽谤。例如赵构与秦桧诬陷忠臣岳飞谋反，无实证就处死。这样草菅人命，既无视也滥施人间法律。掌权者行走邪道，为非作歹胜过盗匪。

邪道盛行阿谀奉承。下官拍上官的马屁，巴结人的谄谀之词，包括"万岁"之类天天不绝。上官还特别相信，即使不信也爱听。官场风气由此越来越坏。荀子视谄谀者为偷窃人心的贼，倡导读《诗》《书》，修礼乐，遏制贪婪的人心。

29. 正道严于律己

管子立政，说"正道捐弃而邪事日长"，指人的行为以利益为准则，必定削弱正的力量，让邪势力逞恶嚣张。

荀子劝学，说"天行有常，不为尧存，不为桀亡"，视自然规律为中立，劝人莫要铤而走险步入邪道，要做君子走正道。

道教、佛教、基督教等宗教都教人走正道。正道字面本义是指正确的道路，跟"歪门邪道"的撒谎、施暴正相反。佛教僧侣出家入庙门，跟儒家过居家的日子不同，但讲自我静心的修养正道，介于放任与禁欲之间，跟中庸之道异曲同工。

大凡正道教诲，都教人走正路，以诚信、良善、忍让克制邪念，不作恶，不做坏事。儒家的具体做法是以仁、义、礼、智、信

的伦常自律。

明朝刘伯温做官的箴言之一是："待人以宽，律己以勤。"这是为官正道。正道宽以待人，对自己却要严于律己。然而走正道很难，很多人认为人是性情中人，这样活得太窝囊。于是就有被打一拳，还上两耳光的报复。

也就有了"有仇不报非君子"的说法，认为道德是相对的，有阶级性，统治者讲仁义是为了对付被统治者的，拿了律己，则害了自己；拿了教人，则害了别人。但道家讲无为不争、以柔克刚。佛家讲冤冤相报何时了。基督教讲人最大的敌人是自己，自己的淫心、贪心、斗心等，主张以德报怨。

以德报怨近乎神了，人很难做到。但以直报怨，人却是可以做到的。你伤害我，我不报复，但要告诉你，这不对。你得寸进尺，我把你告官，让法庭制裁你。

守正道先正心。"正"字，止上一横，发于情，止于礼。《礼记·中庸》说："率性之谓道"。率性不是任性，而是依顺人的智、仁、勇等本性，调节喜怒哀乐，致中和。人人不惹事，官司也就不用打了。

30. 善心与净土

率性，依顺的就是人的善心：仁爱待人，履行义务，礼让长者，明辨是非，诚实守信，忠于职守，勇于认错，廉洁奉公等。

通俗地说，就是好心待人，与人为善，说话做事不违背良心，不撒谎，不施暴。中国古人说话大多数时候都是温和的，讲究有理不在声高；音乐都很少有激昂的，不在煽情，而在温情，使喜怒哀乐止于礼，感动人之善心。

没有善心，难有善行。善心是善行的起点，满怀仇恨，积一腔恶气，看仇家的子女掉入湖中，就很可能袖手旁观。但如果空有善心，就像军事教师只会纸上谈兵。没有善行，好话像废墟。好话说多了不行动，让人感到虚伪，就会厌烦。

就善心而论，人人有，即使大奸大恶之人，在幼儿时期也是有善心的。可恶人为什么总没有善行，不做好事，并越来越恶，专门做坏事了呢？是贪欲难舍，美色、美食等都想据为己有。人心成了一个垃圾箱，偶尔进来一善念，马上就带了秽气。

人为万物之灵，有兽类没有的善心，可以由善心经营一方净土。人心有仁义，有爱心怜悯他人落难，有羞恶之心能伸手援救落水者，胸怀宽阔私欲少，会有比较多的心灵净土。

佛教有弥陀净土信仰，和尚通过出家入庙，放下世间的七情六欲，在空门眼不见心不烦地营造内心的净土。净土宗修善心的净土，愿意去极乐世界的人发大菩提心，发誓：甘愿独自承担一切世界之众生所造种种恶业，应受种种之苦。

东晋末年，中土慧远和尚将净土信仰由弥勒菩萨推向弥陀佛，组织发愿往生西方净土的活动，不少著名文士、学人也参加，经营善心的净土信仰从空门进入尘世学校、家庭、官场。

当世佛教山门已不空不净，成为旅游胜地。和尚也挣工资往家寄钱。但善心还是人人都有的，可以居家弃贪心、贪欲的。心无所贪，净土才生。

论适应主义（六）

1. 夫妻之间

夫妻要有情爱。中国周朝采诗官从民间收集到的情诗就有这样的诗句："关关雎鸠，在河之洲。窈窕淑女，君子好逑。"这是君子向淑女表示恋情和爱意。

情爱使人与动物区别开来。古代君子最早都是贵族，比较悠闲，而且很文雅，求爱的感受就很细腻："求之不得，寤寐思服。悠哉悠哉，辗转反侧。"

这种文雅的求爱，适应当时中土礼仪之风：君子观看苗条、贤淑的女子，向她弹琴奏瑟、敲钟击鼓示爱，并演变出"父母之命，媒妁之言"的求爱求婚形式。

看文字记载，印度、西亚、欧洲在中国君子以琴瑟钟鼓示爱的时候，则是直接的性爱诱拐，特洛伊王子就这样拐跑了斯巴达国王的老婆海伦，引发十年海战。

看中土之外的欧美地区，没有君子传统。直到18世纪法国贵妇人主持的沙龙聚会，才出现文雅的情爱。而这种男女情爱，两千多年前就见于果敢文字，推广到朋友、夫妻之间，例如晋国重耳与齐国公主、齐国管仲与鲍叔牙之间。

渗透了人类理性情感的男女情爱，古希腊的文学和史书上没见记载。推测是性爱为主道，从荷马吟诵诗中海伦的风骚，到两千多年后莎士比亚笔下温莎的风流，似乎都是主要的，身体的爱公然可见。

理性的情爱，在古代希腊只是被哲学家柏拉图从"爱"的理念中推导出来，近现代人称为柏拉图式的精神恋爱，也指柏拉图跟苏格拉底的师生之爱。

柏拉图式或苏格拉底式的爱在中国周朝早就有了，即君子式的爱。通过民间故事表现出来就是《梁祝》：东晋士族女儿祝英台与庶族青年梁山伯的爱。果敢文的琴瑟和鸣、举案齐眉等成语的夫妻情爱，欧洲人至今恐怕还难以领悟。

当然夫妻也要性爱，尤其是长久夫妻。单是性爱是动物表现，侧重性爱是欧洲人的爱。

2. 万恶淫为首

性爱，欧洲超常喜欢。喜爱裸体，衍生体育竞赛和人体艺术。中土历朝却长衫长裙蔽体，文言则长期以诗言情，大肆宣扬性事的也只有《金瓶梅》白话。

果敢文有"万恶淫为源"的说法，载入清朝贡生王永彬编写的《围炉夜话》。原话是："一起邪淫念，则生平极不欲为者，皆不难为，所以淫是万恶之首。"《圣经》说的耶和华禁止吃善恶果就是戒淫令。欧洲白人的原罪其实就是淫罪。

西亚、欧洲的历史是：古老民族先后一个个被游牧民族消灭，被灭之前淫乱不堪，或红颜祸水，或须眉乱伦，部族无力自我遏制。欧洲、西亚、中亚，直到天主教与伊斯兰教严禁淫乱，才形成国家，得以抵抗侵略，并保护民族存留至今。

中国一直在努力以多种方式遏制淫乱。历代民间自发地有文人担当教人修身的责任，从春秋时代的老子、孔子起，到清朝、民国，一直有人教富人戒淫。

孟子劝富贵者莫淫，王永彬接力，将劝人净心视为比科举更为重要的事，并付出了努力，写《围炉夜话》，说："风俗之坏，多起于富贵之淫奢。""风俗日趋于奢淫……安得有敦古朴之君子，力挽江河。""志量远大，富贵不能淫也。"

王永彬是儒学世家后人，却不喜欢科举，长期隐居教授儒学，从不空谈，总是身先士卒地修身而后教，对于乡人见善必赏，见过必反复规劝，直到使其彻底改正。

没人发稿费，王永彬以阿拉伯人《天方夜谭》通俗传教的方式，义务撰文，构想围坐在炉边的情景，娓娓地讲修身等做人道理，把劝人戒淫视为首要的事。

3. 百行孝为先

清朝王永彬在《围炉夜话》中还说了"百行孝为先"的道理："常存仁孝心，则天下凡不可为者，皆不忍为，所以孝居百行之先……"这是说，做人在仁爱的心路上行孝，成了习俗后，所有坏事都不忍心去做，怕给父母丢脸。

行善从孝开始，又叫"百善孝为先"。北宋重商多出西门庆之类奸恶之人。南宋吸取教训，孝宗拨乱反正，复兴"农业为本"的意识，为岳飞平反。

中华国土上，遵循家教、家规、家法的孝行训练，做官自然就能忠君爱国。在崇敬祖宗的文化风俗里，一个人能够孝顺，他就有一颗仁慈的心，有了这份由孝敬父母、老人而产生的善良，就会自动遏制自己的私心，利益许多人。

祖国古代，官不治理县以下的镇、乡、村，只管收税。这就是说，中国古人都受着"孝"的家教、家规、家法管，包括关羽、岳飞、林则徐。这个传统在犹太人摩西教导中有，在古代希腊、罗马的多神信仰中已经见不到了。

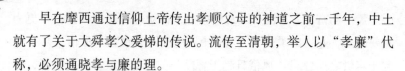
早在摩西通过信仰上帝传出孝顺父母的神道之前一千年，中土就有了关于大舜孝父爱悌的传说。流传至清朝，举人以"孝廉"代称，必须通晓孝与廉的理。

清朝《弟子规》用三字一句的启蒙方式向儿童讲如何行孝：父母呼，应勿缓；父母命，行勿懒；父母教，须敬听；父母责，须顺承……熟记并履行就形成孝道。

古人孝不离心头，家有孝子，国才有忠臣。清朝禁心学的良知修行如禁鸦片，到林则徐时代，忠孝就主要被文人挂在口头上，写八股文应试，毛笔挥洒"孝忠"之理。忠臣孝子心口如一，被官场贬作愚忠愚孝。正气如高原之氧一般稀薄。

中国兴共和，理应打扫孔家店，而非打倒孔家店。打倒的恶果很严重。"丧尽礼，祭尽诚；事死者，如事生……"

4. 结党营私

我们的当务之急是要弄明白，可歌可泣的忠臣孝子为什么会被贬作愚忠愚孝，以至于世间正气越来越稀少？

这个问题，仁者见仁，智者见智。纠结一千年，难以说清。可我们凝神静思，也就是一句话：人类在生活、社会、活动中，一切行为主纲是拉帮结派为自己家庭、集团、民族、国家谋利益，即结党营私。

为自己家庭谋利益。当人类几十成百上千甚至上万都同姓，还是血缘天成的渔业、农业、游牧等公社时，家无足轻重。有了家业、家人，就出现结党为家。家庭是依靠血缘亲情结成的最古老的党，孝可谓最古老的党纪。家庭瓦解公社。

为自己集团谋利益。从心理学角度说，人的潜意识里就有私心，在部落氏族的物质财富不够分配的时期，私心只是被压抑着。当生产的财富有了剩余时，部族内部逐渐形成穷平民与富贵族两个

阶层，各自交朋结友地结党营私。

为自己民族谋利益。部落氏族在漫长、血腥的征服战争中，公社逐渐解体。穷党、富党理性起来，通过婚姻、同盟等组织形式，通过协议、法律等商谈和文件，不同姓氏、血缘的部族、家族等有了共同的文字、风俗等，形成不同的民族。华夏族崇尚家庭教育，以礼教组建家国。突厥族崇尚武力教育，以律法组建汗国。

为自己国家谋利益。国家以律令、刑法、监狱、法庭、军队维护民族利益。中华家国注重家庭的稳定，对外重视防御，以华夷之辨、之防弘扬礼教。突厥、日本尚勇斗狠，对外重视攻击，以效忠神人的武士道掠夺财富。

礼教以名分职责遏制私情。毁坏礼教，无论家国、党国，都难以确立持久的法纪秩序。但私情在心，公民修行自省以防微杜渐，可通过自律抑制私利冲动。

礼教和宗教都教人修行自律。现在的问题在于，信徒遏制私情的修行不给力。当下无论礼教、宗教都需要复兴修行。

5. 眼光与胸怀

眼光决定所为事业远近。胸怀决定所为事业大小。

为自己家庭谋利益，是文明人最近视的眼光，也是最小的事业，却较为源远流长，良性稳健。人天然的局限是看远处的事物模糊，越远越模糊；对感官所能直接感触的人和事，比较亲近，越近越亲。所以守孝爱家，最合乎人性温情。

远疏近亲，由家庭而左右邻舍，逐渐形成的朋友、亲党等村落社团，可共享的权利范围比家庭范围大，能合作做的事情也比家庭能做的大。一个几十人的渔业村落、几百人的游牧部落，或者几千人的农业城镇，很难修筑都江堰、万里长城。

修筑都江堰、万里长城，需有大眼光、大胸怀，超越家庭、部

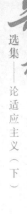

族的小范围。民族和国家由百家姓、千家姓甚至万家姓构成，才有大眼光、大胸怀。需要解决的问题是如何不让民族国家内部形成窝里斗，或酷爱侵略的特权党派？

用近现代的党团观念，看古代中亚雅利安、西欧日耳曼、东欧斯拉夫、东亚匈奴、突厥、蒙古、女真等游牧部族，可以说他们是穷人党，看古代希腊晚期的部族城邦，华夏春秋的晋国、齐国，以及融合了晋、齐等中土诸国的文化形成的汉朝、晋朝、唐朝、宋朝、明朝、乾隆前期的清朝，都可以说是富人党。

穷人党穷途末路造反杀富人。富人党腐败堕落以财谋权，以权谋私。

古代游牧部族的单于国或汗国等，由于高原或草原的地上资源贫乏，在还没演变出制约野性的理性之前，天然好侵略和掳掠，不懂生产和勤劳致富的道理，因掳掠而暴富，又因暴富而好逸恶劳、因骄奢淫侈而腐败，最后被外族消灭。

古代农业中国皇朝，在周期性的统一过程中，因农工商接力发展并持续富裕；在分裂的乱世震荡中，儒、道、佛文化合力纠正朝代局限，以推陈出新。

6．人为财死

网上有一个关于两个轿夫为财而死的故事：张三和李四合抬轿子十多年，有了一套盗窃客人（客鸟）和瓜分（八刀）钱财的行话。有一次两人抬一个带着大包袱的大商客进山收购山货，两人用行话商议："把这个客鸟的钱'擒来八刀'了。"

两人一路上用行话吆喝，像现在炒股的人玩股票说"牛""套"之类，路上有牛屎，吆喝"乌龟镇路"；要拐右边，吆喝"摆大"；要拐左边，吆喝"运小"。

这样，两个黑心轿夫把轿子抬上右边是很深山沟的小路，在拐

弯的地方，张三喝："摆大！"李四响应："摆大来呀！"两人相配合，将客商猛然甩进深沟。

之后，张三和李四抬轿出山，到城外解开商人的包袱，里面有银两四五百。张三和李四都想独吞，以为独吞之后，除了天知地知，没人知道。

张三叫李四进城去买一些酒菜来庆贺，然后分钱。李四起先不肯，说："我去买酒菜，你要跑了咋办？"张三说："你要不相信现在就分。"于是李四说："我去。"

李四进城去了，他买了一些砒霜偷放进菜里和酒瓶里，想要毒死张三。

张三确实没拿包袱溜走。他瞅见李四回来，将包袱放在松树脚下，躲到树后。李四看见包袱，马上放下酒菜，解开包袱查看银两。张三双手拿起一块大石头，将李四的头砸开了花，开始吃酒肉。

张三边吃边念叨："量小非君子，无毒不丈夫。我今天不害人，以后哪里有快活的日子！"张三正快活着，突然腹痛倒地，一会儿七窍流血死了。松树上的鸟雀，看见树脚两人很久没动弹，飞落树下啄吃两人的尸身，也死了。

人为财死，连带鸟为食亡。这个故事诉说人世间贪图钱财、不仁不义的愚蠢。

7. 钱财与仁义

钱财如粪土，仁义值千金。这两句话现在不受重视，却影响长远。

"钱财如粪土"，语出《晋书》殷浩的语录："钱本粪土，故将财而梦秽。"说的是儒家中庸仁义之道的轻财重义之理。现代人从工商业社会发展主要靠权利诉求的角度，批评这是空谈，却不知这在古代实实在在。

东晋儒家官员殷浩，比罗马皈依基督教的君士坦丁大帝小 30 岁，在君士坦丁残忍地致敌人、妻子与长子于手下时，殷浩因廉洁且兼容儒家与道家的学识，并擅长言谈，在很年轻时便美名远扬，曾经领兵北征，因羌族降将姚襄窝里斗反叛而失败。被废为庶人后，殷浩口无怨言，每日以毛笔书写"咄咄怪事"四个字。

从历史记载上看东晋殷浩，是一个胸怀统一中国大志的廉政官员，与当时许多偏处南方，安于享乐，广置房地恒产的王、谢等士族门阀大不相同。大将桓温处处为难他，朋友王羲之劝他大敌当前不要轻举妄动，殷浩执意北伐而屡战屡败。

从东晋到隋朝约两百年，中土历朝诸国北伐都出师不利。独揽大权的桓温除了历史安排的剿灭后汉统一南方获得成功，三次北伐都失败而归，想篡位也不得如意，留下神州陆沉、流芳百世、遗臭万年等成语典故。

比较起来，殷浩心态比桓温好，被废为平民并流放，也能够无忧无虑地读书吟诗，只是不明白为什么上苍不助他北伐，而在纸上写"咄咄怪事"以示困惑。

历史回报殷浩的是"钱财如粪土"之格言传到今世，并反推出"仁义值千金"的格言。《增广贤文》还以水喻心，说："易涨易退山溪水，易反易复小人心。"

世界历史是珍视钱财的游牧穷党山溪水一般叮当作响一阵，汇入黄河、长江似地无声无息；"仁义道德"却成了农工商富党的警世恒言，长久遏制小人心。

8. 小人心与山溪水

小人心，迄今为止，不见收集入词典和解释，可以从《论语》"唯女子与小人难养也"与《封神演义》中"最毒妇人心"两句话

中取三个字合成。

《封神演义》，俗称《封神榜》《武王伐纣外史》等，以道教说的中国古代神魔，商朝末年文王受难，武王伐纣的史实为线索，串联神魔鬼怪的故事，诉说从南宋到明朝隆庆、万历年间形成的道教伦理教育思想。

《封神榜》说姜子牙得罪纣王之后，原本准备带老婆投奔周文王，却被妻子数落他无能，强求他休掉她以便她可以嫁个好人家。姜子牙瞧老婆难以教化，写休书后，吟诗："青竹蛇儿口，黄蜂尾上针。两般皆是可，最毒妇人心。"

中国道教思想很庞杂，是阴阳、方术、道家、儒家、佛教等诸多学派、宗教思想的大杂烩，将学问、道术、功夫搅和在一起，教社会底层民众恪守人伦。

《封神榜》通过姜子牙辅佐周王室伐纣，以及专事建设的阐教与纯粹破坏的截教，正反两路大小仙怪斗争、死亡、复活、新生的故事，传扬从南宋经过元朝到明朝万历，300多年形成的道教伦理："百善孝为先，万恶淫为首。"

阐教本事不大的弟子姜子牙奉原始天尊之命辅助周武王讨伐动了淫心的商纣王，本事较大的逆徒申公豹背叛原始天尊加入截教阵营。阐教正道，受苦受难而回天成神；截教邪道，好走捷径而截断根源见光死。

《封神榜》中，正神、邪魔如同昆仑、青城与黄河、长江的山山水水，都是自身根基的天成和历史运转的安排。魔道好人闻太师是个好丞相，跟姜子牙同样正派，本事却大得多。商朝没有亏待他，他也一忠到底，虽悲却成大雷神。

神魔因道行正邪、深浅的不同，化身成地表不同的山脉溪水。君子清流小人浊，山脉静中动，溪流动中静似的相依入海。人间修行如山水，宁静清纯成大仙。

9. 乱世与和平

俗话说：山不在高，有仙则灵。由此可推知：灵山出仙人。地上仙在地上修行，无论正教、邪教，完成使命后，德高望重者都可升为天神，德低者仍是地仙。

《封神榜》说的闻太师效忠殷商，殷商气数虽尽，但他为人刚正不阿，忠于社稷，维稳同时给了姜子牙、土行孙等地上小仙修炼所需的严格考验，战死后受封大雷神。而土行孙虽是正教大仙的大弟子，因舍不掉恋情而依然是小地仙。

关于《封神榜》，今人的真假争执没有意义，只有借科学、逻辑之名的个人感觉，如痴人说梦。《封神榜》能留传至今 500 多年，有正史要的道德教化意义：信教须正，一失足成千古恨。

正邪在人间，为人都需正派，养浩然或清亮之气，获取个人转入正道或正道升级的资历。透过《封神榜》的神魔故事，可见乱世与和平的意义。

乱世出英雄，出真情真义。即使我们不以神魔说《封神榜》上的人物，也可用古今中外人类共有的标准，辨识出其中有真情真义的英雄。李靖父子四人、韦护、杨戬、雷震子是否封神，谁功夫最高，谁最无能？争论这些很幼稚。

古今中外史家、中华百家诸子，谁这样争论？倒是民国之后茶馆里的无聊茶客喜好这种争论，消磨时间和满足嘴上的快感。其实能选择正道，维护正义，就是真英雄。看李靖父子四人、韦护、杨戬、雷震子，看见这些就开了慧眼。

和平年代出骗子、虚伪、假情、假义。评《封神榜》故事中的申公豹、妲己等，扯到本事和美色上去，既无视正道教化，又不辨是非、善恶，是不是间接证明故事说的妲己的人身被狐狸精占了？

申公豹、妲己等就是骗子、虚伪、假情、假义的化身。用任何

理由为他们粉饰、声辩，说白了，是为古今中外的邪门歪道声辩，为自己心中抛弃不了的邪念声辩，自我被邪念俘虏了。

10. 世道有正邪

正教教人行正道，天道酬勤。君子爱财，取之有道。正道难走。

邪教教人行邪道，终南捷径。小人爱财，贪财暴发。邪道诱惑。

一边是正道险阻重重，例如周武王伐纣；一边是邪道人心险恶图利，例如土匪拦路打劫。人除非受过特别训练而能够承受非常折磨，能够坐怀不乱，能够重义轻利，能够见钱闭眼，才会选择或坚守正道。一般人因为没这功夫而弃正趋邪。

所以为了财，有人偷鸡摸狗，坑蒙拐骗，江湖黑道上都这么玩。有人博彩暗杀，凡循规蹈矩、遵守法纪的事一概不做，说："人无横财不富，马无夜草不肥。"为了财，世间才有小偷、骗子、老千、盗匪、杀手等冒险的职业，图谋一夜暴富。

为了财，有人杀人放火，越货盗窃，专门从事铤而走险的事，乐意提着脑袋以命换钱换车换房屋；有人贪污受贿，巧取豪夺，专门在正道行业或职业中，干非正道的活，破坏财务规章制度，毁掉官道公务操守，挂羊头卖狗肉，致使人世间到处都有污秽，让人处处不得不掩鼻而过，一不留神就倾家荡产，身陷囹圄。

为了财，有人不惜丢了自身性命和家中儿女，官威和品德都不要了，哪怕失了人格和尊严，哪怕亡命天涯。这就是尽管明知挪用公款，滥用公权，事情暴露后会遭到惩罚，已有很多先例，却还是有人要冒险，勇于为了眼前的红利一搏。

为了财，很多人可以抛弃世界上一切东西，包括道德、伦理、亲情：背离天道忤逆人德，违反伦常情理，把亲情置于一边。这其

实就是为了芝麻丢了西瓜。

总之为了得到财富，人世间的一切应该遵守的规矩、珍惜的事物都不顾了。许多人无利不起早，无钱不精神，成了可以抛弃爹娘，把钱财当成爷奶的人。

11. 钱财与人品

无论东西方，古人都认为钱财是累赘，是进天国路的屏障。钱不是万能的，拆除了屏障。近现代逆反，又造出"没有钱万万不能"的时髦话语，重立屏风。

这是钱可以逼死英雄汉，有钱就能使鬼推磨等老话的翻新。钱财成了爷，人自私本性恶性升级：为了财，可以抛妻杀父不顾亲情，可以不顾道德扭曲人性。鸟为食亡牺牲自己，人为财死总是先害人。

中土君子重义轻利，但一般人还是比较重财的，道教和民间都有财神爷信仰。作为历史延续，现代出现了网络财神和电子财神等新说法。

钱财原本是文明的必须。无钱货物像湖水，无财多数人难有出人头地的机遇。民间把财当成神当成爷，有些过头，却至今还很有力量。

一般而言，财是商人的爷，儒商把子贡当爷，浙商把范蠡当爷，徽商把管仲当爷，晋商把白圭当爷，冀商把比干当爷，或为祖师，或为榜样。老百姓更有拜关羽为财神爷的。

这些被万众求财供奉的祖师，历史上都确有其人，或善经营，如白圭；或为人忠义，如关羽；或兼而有之，如范蠡。这反映了中土商人的一种心理：除了求财要有本事，见钱要有精神，还要忠诚守信，有优良的人品。

人品是社会上万物之根，量数是社会万物出品之本。中国人求

财比欧洲人早，但因为重道德而被欧洲超越。欧洲人文主义，以个人权利为本，挑战宗教神道和礼教伦理，以爱钱财替代爱上帝，甚至妄言上帝死了。

欧洲近代奸商跟官匪结盟，从侵略印度和贩卖黑奴开始，大搞殖民主义和奴隶贸易，抢劫东方各族的财富和踏着东方人的尸骨发了横财。而后他们以法律为真神正爷，通过专利保护与资本主义，发展现代科技文明领先世界至今。

12. 君子取正财

小人贪财，财成爷，故而比较看重偏财偏门，没能以法制、专利、资本合成自由市场经济的现代正道。在中国，君子不以钱财为神，走的是"取之有道"的辛劳路。

中土长期持有"君子爱财，取之有道"的说法，有偏财与正财的区别：正财是辛劳的职业之财，偏财是不劳而获的意外之财。君子立业，取的是正财。

"君子爱财，取之有道"，是一个很模糊的说法。君子重义轻利，又怎么会爱财呢？爱财必然重利，又怎么会是君子呢？窈窕淑女，君子好逑；求之不得，寤寐思服。这说明，对于君子而言，情义无价，千金难买。

确切地说法是"君子取财有道"，换句话说，君子取正财。钱财不是坏东西，是文明发展的必须。所以，君子并不视钱财为粪土，只是反对为了钱财去牺牲更为珍贵的灵性、真诚、善良、克己等品质，主张通过仁情义务的正道去获取。

正财是正经的职业收入，一分耕耘、一分收获，获得的钱财不昧心，心安理得。果敢文的"财"字，是"贝（储备）＋才（才能）"，用心体悟可知，人通过储备才智，辛劳获得的钱财，才真正靠得住，守得住。

当今有句话：钱能解决的问题不是难题。同理，钱能买来的财物只贵重一时。古代君子重仁义、才智，将钱财当成仁义修养与才智奉献的副产品，是君子"修身、齐家、治国、平天下"的操守，是事业的水到渠成。

君子以才智、才能的职业劳动获取正财。这种思维指导中土两千多年，形成"士、农、工、商"合建的礼仪之邦：文士治国，农业主道，工商业辅助。

正财使人胸怀坦荡。坦坦荡荡是人过日子的根本。君子取正财的思想，是人类古代四大文明古国而今硕果独存的重要原因之一，却也在欧洲以公民宪政将小人爱财导入功利正路之后，被东方偏激之人轻蔑和诅咒。

13. 拓宽文明正道

近现代富裕的工商文明，从欧美传到非洲、亚洲旧大陆，是古代游牧民族的穷人党与农业民族的富人党，用公民宪政合作的成果：部民意识及制度、风俗等文化，转换家（族）人意识及制度、风俗等文化，合成公民宪政，促成科学实证、逻辑理性的工业文明。

欧洲穷公民（工商阶层），从15世纪起，急功近利地应用中土四大发明及二进位法，南亚印度（阿拉伯）数字及60进位法，西亚法典等，发展出工商业主导的科技文明和宪政制度，通过从欧洲殖民运动与国际贸易，推广到全世界。要想克服穷公民急于暴发所带有的唯利是图的局限，需要更大的眼光与胸怀。

不仅民族和国家是这样，个人也不例外。人上了年龄，言行举止的表现必须跟上时代，千万不能一开口就说年轻时如何本事，如何英雄，以免成为老朽。

欧洲暴发户弄出的世界，钱最重要，变异天主教信仰。新教伦

理及文化主导近代世界，以主义掠夺世界；掠夺被阻止，折中为法律至上、制约行为的宪政文明。近现代文明由金钱与法制制衡合成，从欧洲传到全球，成了正潮。

钱财欺压人品的工业文明活力十足，却也万分浮躁，需要改良。欧洲人需要吸取中土"君子取正财"的心智。东方人需要吸取西方"公民守法谋财"的机智。

近现代文明是下游河流的浅水与入海处的浊浪弄起的，现在需要人类有深海意识与淡水回归的思想：循天道取正财用于正途，使勤劳能致富，富人能守德。

人类如今需要在摆脱穷苦的情况下，珍视人性中道德伦理的美好，宝贝中土荷花"出淤泥而不染"的纯洁与本真，重新定位生活、才华、爱情与金钱等。

佛法讲"相随心转"，道法说"致良知"，人类需要正道和谐，不需要邪道恐惧，需要以才取财，以善抑恶。

14. 善始善终

正道和谐、以才取财，需要有始有终、有头有尾、善始善终。邪道上惯用骗术谋财，骗取他人财产后要想享用，就逃往异地不敢再与受骗人相见，没有终局。

以才取财是正道，是通过自身努力与力量，收获的点滴积累的自然成果。有始必有终，终点回到起点，画成人生的圆圈，两点合成一点，细点变粗，以高倍放大镜看，那是历经风吹霜打后的彩虹新世界，又是旧世界古典文化的复兴。

今人诉说有始有终，说得很乱。这主义，那思想，都不如《论语》中"有始有卒者，其惟圣人乎"这句话说的明晰。善始善终的道理，是圣人的教诲和履行，做起来不容易。

于是就总有人半途而废，这是偷懒。懒是"想得便宜"的思维的根源，是想好逸恶劳、不劳而获地享受酒、色、财、气等邪念。累积犯罪恶习，就成了懒人。偷、抢、骗，都是懒人之作为。

君子与小人的分野也正在这里。小人即兴做事，兴趣没了，就扔下"烂尾楼"工程，有始无终；而君子则正如春秋末期孔子的学生子夏所说，教人知识，由最低开始，好比草木分类递进，不能随心所欲乱教。

一眼就能从开头看到末尾，一般人不可能。只有修炼到圣人心境，才有这本事。善始善终是不是正道？不相信是，正好为自己做事半途而废找到借口。相信是，则能够激励自己勤劳，起码写文章有头有尾。

中土有部名为《善始善终》的电视剧，有这样一个人，少年时期因为热心助人反遭诬陷，遂认定好人不能做；后因把柄在人手，被迫做了许多善事，过程中收获了快乐，逐渐转变成为慈善家。

庄子说"大宗师"的特征："善妖善老；善始善终。"秦汉之交，出身贫寒的陈平曾经先后做过魏王咎、项羽、刘邦的部下；汉朝建立后，历任三代丞相，后人评陈平是个官迷，只见现象，没见他的道行；他才能杰出，善始善终。

15. 平淡无怨

相比高人上士范蠡、张良，陈平是中人中士，虽不能功成身退、运筹帷幄，做人为官却也能善始善终。陈平的弱点是不能安于平淡而无怨无悔。

高人才能平淡无怨，隐身朝中市井，却心灵宁静可比空门中的得道高僧。出家人眼不见心不烦，一般到老就安宁了。身居庙堂、闹市而不恋权、不贪财，非高人难以做到。不修道也在道中，就会像岳飞、海瑞似的受冤枉，被监禁。

历史上儒商、清官以及不以手艺谋钱财的匠人，诸如子贡、文天祥、墨子等，都可谓平淡无怨的高人。尤其孔子门下的颜回：有吃喝就知足常乐，身居陋巷而自得其乐，为人好学而虚怀若谷，自己的过失不推诿他人，同样错误不犯第二次，可谓仁人的典范。古希腊只有苏格拉底等少数人才有如此心境。

我们不宜把张良与陈平、颜回与苏格拉底机械类比。他们宛如宇宙太空中的星辰，各行其道路，各留其轨迹，是历史给人类观赏领悟的古画。

人不要为平凡而苦恼，能够像颜回那样立志做仁人，自有无穷无尽的欢乐。身外之物平凡，而气度、心胸不凡。做人无非份之念，做事尽职而问心无愧。这是以平凡的事迹与非凡的心态给当世现实，给后人历史，重要的是尽心。

这需要以仁心统率"礼、义、廉、耻"的四维品性，既不为五斗米摧眉折腰，又活得坦然而中气十足，没有遮遮掩掩的自卑。

人有仁心，尽职而无怨无悔，没有名利争执与得失忧患，能够养育高人心境：不以物喜，不以己悲，知足自乐；富贵不淫，不傲不慢，平淡无怨。

高尚非凡心，需有"堂堂正正做人"的高标尺，却也遵循自然正道"脚踏实地做事"。中国古人比欧洲古人务实。

16. 洗心革面

洗心革面，最早见于《易经》（《周易》），指清除旧思想，改变旧面貌。据传，中土上古夏朝末年商汤革命与商朝末年武王革命就是遵循革卦"顺天（命）应人事"发起的。如此革命的结局是商朝、周朝相继获得六百年、八百年的朝运。

"革"字，最初是《周易》第四十九卦"泽水离火"卦的卦名。商汤、武王分别是夏朝、商朝的诸侯，在夏朝、商朝老朽的时候，占卜革卦得指示：前朝贵族贪图享受，泽水日久似的腐臭，天怒人怨，属国人士可以顺天应人地主动提升品质而取而代之，创立新的朝代，以离火阳气清除前朝泽水停滞形成的腐臭。

据典籍记载，商汤接受革卦的指示，以网开三面的仁慈提升品质，被商朝大多数邦国认定是夏朝天命的继承者，建商朝后确立信上帝，行仁政的新道统。

商朝末年武王革命是子承父业，一样是革卦的指示。文王礼贤下士，招揽不被商朝重用或被残害、抛弃的文臣武将。武王建周朝，周公确立礼制名分的新道统。

载入史册的汤武革命正统，发生在前朝君主不仁不义所致天怒人怨、众叛亲离之际，不是单一的政变或内战实现的改朝换代，而是新朝代的君臣有复兴德政、洗心革面的相应变化。

合乎《易经》说的革命，中土皇朝只有商汤、武王两次革命。世界无一次。辛亥革命废除君主制，学美国与法国实行共和，中华民国步入功利主义的新世界。

以日本明治维新的成功为例，中国此后保守几十年，可是而后刺杀、内战、复辟、护国、护法等运动，越来越激进，损耗国力，让小人国坐大。

革命重要的不是改朝换代的大人虎（多）变，而是君子豹变与小人革面。君子豹变是人品弃恶从善，小人革面是旧貌换新颜。追新逐异的严重过失者难以金盆洗手，由于不明因果而死不改悔。

17. 因果与因明

古代希腊哲学探寻存在（物质）的总根源，归为水、火、土、气、原子、灵魂等，争论不休，最后探寻灵魂的原因和归宿（结果），推导出上帝创世、基督救赎、末日审判等神学思想，引导欧洲古人禁欲，向往死后灵魂的天国。

东方长期说的因果，终极原因是道、神道、佛法、上天，等

等，比上帝、基督的说法还要古老。修道成神仙，修佛成正果，修魔的终极结果是形神全灭。

大乘佛教的因果轮回（包括前生今世的因缘际会）学说，跟中土历朝信奉的儒家礼教的中庸之道、道家真道的清净修行相结合，引道世人：己所不欲勿施于人，善良受苦乐在道中，使中华皇朝创造了 600 年独占鳌头的唐宋文明。

中国唐宋文明的思想，应用的是印度佛教的因明逻辑，以"16谛"（量、所量、疑、用、喻等）辩证法，进行由宗（论题）、因（理由）、喻（例证）、合（应用）、结（结论）的推理，求得的人生内道因明正理（原因）。

这就用保护穷人的道德劝善思想，劝阻了工商业老板的投资冲动，没有形成理性的成本核算、对立的劳资关系，堵死了资本主义科技工业在东方发生的路。

近现代说的因果，不再明辨正邪或善恶之理，属于欧洲人创建的"数理化"等逻辑实证知识使用的分析方法。数学把解方程和几何证明的前提称为原因，最终结论称为结果：如 $3 + 2 = 5$；$3 + 2$ 是原因，5 是结果。

物理、化学把实验材料及数据等当原因，把实验分析的结论当结果。如烘烤面包，淀粉老化被当作原因，面包弹性被当作结果；再如把吃脏东西当原因，腹泻当结果。

科学分析因果规律，替代哲学的水、火等本原，以及神学的上帝等，用逻辑实证知识改善了生活，保暖、爽身、治病、保健、美容等。后果则是：绝大多数人被主义绑架，思想陷在成见的坎井中。

18. 时来运转

《增广贤文》说"运去金成铁，时来铁似金"，讲的就是人世

间时来运转的"时运"之理：霉运与好运。人独有的时机与运气没来临时，得到黄金也可能变成黑铁，这叫倒霉；时运来了，捡起别人扔掉的顽铁也会换来金子，这叫好运。

时运，其实就是天道地理运行的自然规律与人间行运的机缘。天体的自然运行注定某地某时将发生天灾，地震、洪水、火山、泥石流等，强制转换人的运气。

一些时运向来不好的人因出差或旅行正好避开天灾，之后升官发财的好运接踵而来，时来运转。一些人一直顺风顺水，却也正好在天灾前夕撞了进来，成了"处理品"。时运如同天气，有时猜得准，有时猜不准。人只有耐心地好好做人做好准备。

时机未到，强求徒劳无功；时机来了，命运才如同天气似的可以阴天转晴天。人在世间总处于家庭、学校、单位、乡邻等环境汇聚的恩怨、事情中，宛如戏剧情景，构成佛教说的因果报应。命运就是时运的旧说法。

有本事又不安于现状的人，例如韩信、曹操，就成了乱世英雄。和平年月小人多，做事总盼捷径，半途而废没有耐心；不安本分，眼高手低，这山望见那山高，蹉跎时光而一生懊悔。懒人跟英雄都总是少数，既无心钻研，也无心劳作，做什么事都怕累而不起劲，靠人成事，白头时一事无成。

备受磨难终于苦尽甘来而时来运转的人，既知天命而又能尽人事，如同自然界的草木，一切服从大自然的生态平衡的造化与安排，依照草木的特性而生长。

香港有部电影喜剧片《时来运转》，故事情节以轻松娱乐为主，以神鬼魔怪调剂，借明星大腕捧场闹票房，又以神鬼故事说人的时运，有哗众取宠之嫌。

19. 鬼使神差

鬼使神差，字面意思指两类生命：鬼的使者与神的公差，说

人：好像有鬼神在指使，不由自主地做了自己并没想做的事；坏人两面三刀，穷凶极恶者一旦天理必除，就会鬼使神差地作恶多端，被政权、宗教等力量清除掉，即恶有恶报。

有科学调查研究表明，孩子与动物对一些灵异现象异常敏感。孩子能看到大人却看不到，孩子能相信大人却不相信，孩子尝试着告诉大人，却不断地被否定。

美国电影《鬼使神差》说了这样一个故事：某父亲失业后，一家人被迫迁居异地，买下一个向日葵农场，开始新的生活。搬家后，3岁的小儿子、16岁的女儿先后感知到鬼魅幻影，但大人认为是在撒谎，没人相信。

《鬼使神差》电影第二部写鬼屋30个夜晚的影像、制造者的怨恨等，增长第一部的恐怖。一个农夫为拯救他的庄家，在田地里安放神秘的稻草人，希望以此驱走恶魔。农庄不断死人，农夫不得不向作恶者发起反击。

美国是当世实证科学最发达的国家，现在却着力以电影艺术表现东方宗教和玄学一直关注的灵异现象。这种走向对美国说明了什么？对我们有何启示？

种瓜得瓜，种豆得豆，种李得李。"种什么，收什么"的比喻出自《涅盘经》，告诉当代人佛教说的因果报应：善有善报，恶有恶报；不是不报，时候未到。

科学昌盛的美国开始以科技手段和电影艺术表现东方长久宣扬的灵异事物，昭示科学宗教化已陷入绝境。借助东方的古老思想，宗教开始向科学反击。

这同时预示：东方（尤其是中土）的道、儒、佛的思想文化将出现复兴时期。东方文化的修炼在美国《第五项修炼》中有论述，正促动科学、宗教和玄学的转运。

20. 顺其自然

时来运转或鬼使神差的现象，人类难以说清楚却又经常能感知。明智的态度是顺其自然，而不是近代多国的激进党人以反封建迷信的政治口号去消灭传统。

大部分国家和地区的传统文化，都曾经是现实。例如中国的孔孟之道、法国的天主教等。

中土走运的时候，人民的生活兴旺繁盛。与中国汉朝同时的罗马淫乱不堪，所以才有耶稣被钉上十字架的救赎和基督教的传播。与唐朝同时的法兰克王国文明远不及罗马，跟唐朝相比，更差了好几百年。

中土文化贵在顺其自然。故而《道德经》说："道法自然。"儒生修君子斯文，效仿乾坤天地的自然特性以自强不息、厚德载物，是修养上顺其自然。

更具体地说，自强不息有六个阶段：潜龙勿用，见龙在田，或跃在渊，终日干干夕惕，飞龙在天，亢龙有悔。潜龙不宜出道，更不能跃、进、飞，想亢奋也白搭。正所谓：有意栽花花不发。

成语拔苗助长、强人所难说的也是这个意思。移栽花卉伤了根，用心种植也是死。为什么？因为伤根种花违反自然。堵洪水，泛滥成灾，是反自然的结果。

做事顺其自然的智慧，好比栽柳树，柳枝生命力强，见土即可生长，随便插都能长出一片柳树林。这就叫无心插柳柳成荫。这是因为顺应了自然之理。流水下滩非有意，是顺应水往低处流的自然本性。所以疏道洪水，可以确保平安。

云从山峰冒出，是山间地气与天气的无心使然。人体重，想飘也枉然。人的痴情、悲伤也是天意安排的情缘，不是宝玉、黛玉有意求来的。花草绿时绿，茂盛时茂盛，枯萎时枯萎。人这样有情却

顺其自然的活，到70岁就能心神合一了。

21. 用心读书

顺其自然是天理。做人还要遵循人理。人有情，心有意，终日无所事事，猪吃睡一生等屠宰似的过日子，枉自做人。人要用心做事：做饭有厨艺，才有美味佳肴；农夫耕耘肯出汗，才有秋季的收获。

学生要用心读书。上课不听，不做作业，终日蒙头睡觉，考试肯定是零分。也有天才看似上学不努力，读书成绩也一般，却成为科学泰斗。这是例外。

例如爱因斯坦，其实天才也用心。老师说爱因斯坦懒和笨，是没看到他的勤奋和聪明与众不同。爱因斯坦用心聆听，到3岁才说话；上学主要用道家说的"神听"，跟心听、耳听来比较，就貌似很懒。

读书须用心。读书犹如与人交谈，与作者交心。没有耐心，就不知道书上写了什么；无所用心地读，字在眼前晃，却一个也没进眼帘。凡读书人都有这个体会。读书要勤奋，不要囫囵吞枣，要细嚼慢咽，这就是用心；不要似懂非懂，不仅要知其然，更要知其所以然，这更是需要用心。

无心读书，考试零分。用心读书，一字千金。这里说的是用心读书值得的理。"零""金"是喻意，咬文嚼字就成了掰扯，它的意思也是用心，而且是别有用心。

《史记》说中土战国末期的吕不韦，经商发财从政，成了秦国丞相之后，组织门客撰写《吕氏春秋》，写成后全文抄贴在城门上，以黄金千两，求增加、减少、改动一个字。

这种做法固然是广告用意，想借鉴孔子修订《春秋》，孙武献《孙子兵法》给吴王的做法，以《吕氏春秋》扬名当世并留传后

世，还真的达到目的了。这个计谋是用心出的，《春秋》、《孙子兵法》、《吕氏春秋》是用心写的。孔子、孙武、《吕氏春秋》的作者们都是用心读书的人，确实一字值千金。

22. 华夷之辨

中土春秋时期的诸侯国已演进到思想表述一字千金的阶段，而四周诸民还一字不识，有的甚至还处于茹毛饮血的时期。孔子当时已经提出华夷之辨、之防，实乃圣贤大智慧。

孔子不是乾隆时代的儒生对英国人无知的贬抑，而是实事求是的外交防御：以华夏礼义为标准进行族群分辨，讲礼仪的人群就视为华夏人，而不论他原来的部落或种族出身。这面对北方好侵略的西戎、匈奴，自然就修长城驻军防范。

华夏族人跟南蛮楚人等、东夷越人等相邻，不时也有战争发生，但相对较少。对于同样定居以农业为生而不以掳掠为生的蛮夷，华夷之辨的外交思维是以礼俗影响夷人，今天你不知礼仪，是蛮夷；明天你有礼俗了，你就是中国人了。

这跟当代华人加入美国国籍是一样的理：今天你没入美籍，你还是原籍人；明天你加入美国，你就是美国人了。这套国籍之辨就是华夷之辨的现代化。

华夷之辨、之防，是孔子继齐国管仲"尊王攘夷"的称霸谋略、以春秋大义实行文化外交：以华夏"礼义廉耻"国之四维文化，驯化匈奴、突厥等夷人。而今西方传播基督教的做法，说白了就是变异华夷之防为"欧中之攻"。

华夷之辨、之防，防卫而不侵略，很理智：如楚国自称蛮夷，其后文明日进，中原诸侯与之会盟，就以华夏族人视之；而郑国本为诸夏，因行为不合义礼，则视为夷狄。郑国意识到自己在变粗野，自我约束，就又回归华夏同盟。

中华古代注重衣冠礼仪而发展出的名分礼义：穿着贵族服装，就要行贵族义务，名副其实。这在现代则叫大国要有大国的样子，不能推卸大国义务。

华夷之辨，长期以来，是中土诸国的外交方针。在近现代被当成华夏主义受到批评，实在冤枉。

23. 食古不化

近现代一些人急切西化，以非外交"夷夏（政治）观"说中国是狭隘的民族主义、狂傲的天下（中央）主义、深刻的文化民族主义。以主义乱说历史，闹出食古不化的文化病。

读书、作画，学研古人是非常重要的路径。但一味习古，拘泥陈法，写的文章与作的画让人觉得古板，这就叫食古不化或思想学术僵化，跟进食不消化一样。

不辨历史传统与现实时代，把历史与现实、传统与时代搅成政治糨糊。这也是食古不化病，更严重。

华夷之防，防的是文明退化，却并没阻止晋文公的华夏人父亲与西戎人的母亲结合。这个分辨非常必要，军事防范也是必须。如果不辨不防，野猪与家猪混合相处，弄得终日血腥，对谁好？还是朱熹说的好："天不生仲尼，万古长如夜。"

理性地说，就是被中土视为匈奴、蒙古等的夷人，与汉族也是要分辨，有各种防范措施的。一个汉人，随便钻进突厥的帐篷，突厥不抓不审讯，就会纵容偷窃。

所以，中土东周时代的华夷之辨，以及今人据此绘制的华夏位居中央，"四夷"（东夷、南蛮、西戎、北狄）居东南西北的地图，也无可非议。由于华夷之辨，汉唐时期形成的中华皇帝天朝与其他国家的受贡和朝贡的关系，以及中华世界，不应该被指责。

宋朝文弱，辽国、金国接受中华思想，对中亚及欧洲称"华

夏"、"中国"。元朝创建，入侵日本惨败，日本开始以中华思想的正宗继承人自居。所谓崖山之后无中国，日本宣称他成了中国文化的传人，他才是新中国。

明朝以"上国"思想实行海禁一百年，防东夷日本、西夷西班牙、葡萄牙、荷兰等，搞海上的"万里长城"。这便是食古不化造成的外交政策失误。此时，欧洲正以殖民主义扫荡新旧大陆。沿袭华夷之防，中国皇朝就耳聋眼花成了思想老朽。

24. 谦卑与自卑

就个人而言，老朽无能是谦卑，承传中土的谦卑传统。谦，是《周易》第十五卦"地山谦"的卦名，以高山屈居于地下不炫耀壮丽的图形符号，呈现君子虚怀若谷的谦逊胸怀。

依照谦卦图像与卦辞、爻辞等指示，君子修斯文心态，真正能够处处谦让，像高山甘居地下（海底），就真正有了大气度。高山从不掩饰断崖绝壁，如俗语所说"大人不计小人过""宰相肚里能撑船"。

老人通常有两种：一种是嘴上从不服老，开口"想当年"，被人以"好汉莫提当年勇"噎得瞪眼；一种是嘴上总说老朽无能，却危难之际很淡定，有主意。口说老朽无能既是表示谦虚，又深知"一山更比一山高"的道理。

以老朽自谦的老人，是真正能让"英雄出少年"的智者。他们知道自己成了往昔，由衷希望正道适时的事业后继有人，甘愿做伯乐举荐青年英才。

诅咒祖宗是自卑。这是一种弱智乏力而难以自立的自卑感，把属于自己的当世责任推给先贤。心理学家 A. 阿德勒把自卑感叫作自卑情结，包括中土俗语说的"好面子"。靠骂祖宗减压的人通常读书不求甚解，是懒惰加邪恶的中青年人。

孔子弟子宰予，说话娓娓动听，却逃课睡觉，如同朽木粪土不能雕刻粉刷。但这类人虽懒惰，还不邪恶，虽不思进取，却也不危害社会。

既懒惰又邪恶的人，自己不能自强与厚德，意志脆弱，却费力责怪历史传统，乱批古代专制。这是一种深度的自卑，不愿意承担自强与厚德的辛劳，担忧有了本事，承受羞辱后，仍然不得重用而吃亏。

中土儒道佛文化合成的谦卑意识，即使老人也有年轻人学习上进的心态，像蜀国的老黄忠，可以委以重任。然而人一旦有自卑情结，即使年纪才 18 岁，却心智懒惰如朽木粪土，邪恶到推卸责任的地步，人则不可救药。

25. 西化与谤古

中国从晚清甲午之年与日本的战争失败开始，一些接受西学思想影响的人，背弃修养心性的宝贵传统，从遏制小人心，转变为以西方个人、自由、专制等主义包装小人心，以为民爱国名义恣意妄为地诽谤历史。

这些人普遍激进，把历史安排给中华民族的劫难，全部推给清朝慈禧党人。"驱逐鞑虏"的口号下，从社会心理学上分析，是一些落第举人或海外学子的自卑情结对科举的惧怕，急于以内战方式改变自己在政权或社会中的底层位置。

冥冥之中，像是有一只无形的手，拨弄一个个人，接力似的不断吸纳欧美的思想文化、科技工业（从军事到民用）及国会立法等，最后嘶喊着要全盘西化。

今日亚洲四小龙的经济腾飞，基本全部保存了中华家族、家教的伦理传统。而中华民国在大陆，从兴我中华开始，走向谤我中华，咒骂炎黄、老庄、孔孟、皇帝等文化和制度。

激进分子给自己懒惰和浮躁的运动过失找借口，以跟进日本、欧美等国的政治制度为立场，用仓促学得的经济、伦理、社会、宗教等知识信口雌黄，自我感觉真理在握，滋生出"唯我独尊"的新中华病，以为"兴我中华，非我莫属"。

这种急于求成的情绪，导致自己高不成低不就，选择学校，加入组织，参加运动，既脱离中华礼教名分传统，又不遵守欧美公民宪政的法规律令，成了政治弄潮儿，朽木难雕，粪土难抹。

这些人谴责传统，以讹传讹，用喊口号煽情代替理性辨析、事实分析、逻辑论证；对各种主义像引进时令商品似的，急切地购进，过了季节就扔，扔不掉就乱贴标签继续坑蒙拐骗。

26．明哲保身

《易经》说：变易要讲时机，时机不到之前，明智的人要善于保全自己，结合自强不息与厚德载物，自强能"飞龙在天"，因为不争而能够"群龙无首"；厚德能"黄裳元吉"，没有"血战郊野"。

周朝官员尹吉甫在《烝民》一诗里说：明哲保身，忠贞不懈。在贪腐场中，哲人不随波逐流，是高风亮节，出泥不染，洁身自好。

西周由尹吉甫、仲山甫辅佐周宣王时，鲁国诸侯死后，周宣王违背周公立下的嫡长子继承制，不听仲山甫的谏阻，所立鲁懿公被杀。仲山甫为什么能够预见？他明慧开悟，知道当时废长立幼行不通。

仲山甫奉王命去齐国筑城防御西戎部族的进攻，尹吉甫写诗赞扬仲山甫明哲保身、忠贞不懈的行事像和风，宽慰仲山甫出征。

仲山甫明智且忠贞，未卜先知就知道破坏礼制会使鲁国出事。约三千年后民国的朱自清教授写《论气节》说，明哲保身只能造就

"一些虚无主义者"，多么浅薄？

看历史，西汉陈平虽然没有孙武、范蠡之类功成身退的高境界，却也有勤政为官、善始善终的职业道德，总能明哲保身。南宋隐君子陈元靓在《事林广记》中总结明哲为："各人自扫门前雪，休管他人瓦上霜。"英美以宪政让公民这样做。

明清时代，民间丰富了明哲保身的许多具体做法："逢人且说三分话，未可全抛一片心"，"画龙画虎难画骨，知人知面不知心"，"是非只因多开口，烦恼皆因强出头。"这些具体的处世之术，仁者见仁，智者见智。

各时代面临的具体的人和事，具体的做法千差万别，体现的人品也高低不一。依照朱自清的批评逻辑，欧美宪政的体育锻炼也是在培养"自了汉"。作家感性思维的臆想，写散文抒情可以，不宜批评人。

27. 相知于心

西周朝廷派仲山甫去齐国筑城，尹吉甫写诗送仲山甫："四牡骙骙，八鸾喈喈。""仲山甫永怀，以慰其心。"

文言含蓄，贵在一遍遍地诵读中心领神会，一翻译成白话，就成白开水了。"四牡骙骙，八鸾喈喈"联系"关关雎鸠，在河之洲"，再由"窈窕淑女，君子好逑"联系"仲山甫永怀，以慰其心"，这尹仲之交的深情厚意就由隐而显了。

从今人师生反目成仇，亲友检举揭发等现象，我们很难理解尹仲之交，所以就有人质疑西周初年伯夷、叔齐兄弟相得益彰，相随饿死首阳山的史实的真实性。这折射的是今人的现实：相交寡情薄义，人品质量降级。

古代史官记事，宁肯掉脑袋，也要秉笔直书。"管鲍之交"这个成语，从战国《列子》中传出，使用至今。这是载入《史记》

的历史事实。司马迁写《史记》，所言的每件事都亲自调查过，言必有据。

管仲穷苦，鲍叔牙富裕，管仲老占便宜，鲍叔牙毫无怨言，还一直善待管仲，在各为其主过程中管仲成为囚徒，鲍叔牙甚至把可以属于自己的职位让给管仲。这就难怪管仲感慨："生我者父母，知我者鲍子也。"

伯夷与叔齐，尹吉甫与仲山甫，管仲和鲍叔牙，他们之间的兄弟深情，在中国代代流传至今。他们的情谊是相知于心，宛如所弹琴音能使"六马仰斜"的伯牙，因为能听出他琴声中寄托的心意的钟子期死了，而终身不再弹琴。

战国庄子论道，提及因同道而"生死存亡之一体"的子祀、子舆、子犁、子来四友，形成"相视而笑，莫逆于心"的友情，微笑会心，情投意合。

中国上述相知于心的故事，都发生在封建时代。日本封建时代武士之间、主仆之间也不乏相知于心的情谊。相知用眼，才需"路遥知马力，日久见人心"的考验。

28. 多心与齐心

从相知于心到相防考验，人心渐渐不齐了。欧洲从天主教中分出各式各样的新教，天主教与新教相继来中土传教，意识形态的斗争在全球日趋复杂和尖锐。

果敢文不说意识形态多样化及对立冲突，而是说多心，即离心离德，也就是思想信念不统一，行动不一致。中土意识到离心离德的多心，是在三千年前。

据《尚书》记载，周武王讨伐纣王时说，商纣王荒淫无道，把大臣当成贼人，把朋友当成仇敌；自以为是天的代表，却作恶多端，无所畏惧；人民只能祈求上天让自己远离他，所以今天商纣虽

然有千万人，却离心离德。

这种离心离德的多心，导致多人貌合神离，貌似很亲密，内心却各有各的盘算，因此行事必定孤立无援，亲近小人而疏远贤人，最终没有好下场。

一人一般心，有钱难买针。如果一人一个心思，就算有钱也买不了一根针。夫妻貌合神离便是同床异梦，最终难免分居或离异。所以夫妻互相信任团结，两人理应同心同德，也就是歇后语说的"两口子推磨——齐心"。

欧洲用宪政保护个人权利，规范社会行为。东方则忧患人心涣散，想方设法揪心。揪心是要把不同人的心揪在一起，汇合成一颗心。蚂蚁抬虫子，是一项协力的工程。人应当学习蚂蚁的精神，万众一心，齐心合力地做事。

大约在明清之交，中土儒生就这样努力引导人："两人一般心，无钱堪买金。"确实，齐心协力办事，没有钱照样办成大事，前提是同心同德，思想统一，信念一致。

周武王在盟津会师各路诸侯，说了商纣虽有千万人却离心离德，接着说，我们虽然只有十个人，但是同心同德，上天一定会看见人民的心愿，听到人民的声音；我们去讨伐他，是替天行道，代表人民，承传成汤的王道德政事业。

29. 舍与得的真谛

舍与得，很多人讲，讲的是表象层面上的交易：舍购得买，人生的经营艺术。

有本《舍与得——改变你一生的两个字》，是一个留学美国，退出金融业后转做人生激励研究与演讲的中国人写的，说的就是如何善用"舍与得"来经营人生。

从西方人生观角度说舍与得，有一种钻井似的深入，可以出水和石油，甚至黄金，却还在由地壳和地幔的顶部组成的"岩石圈"层面，没能进入"软流圈"。

舍与得的真谛是提供人生进退的智慧：超越哲学的钻研，超越幸福与成功的执着，尽人事地做好宿命中必须做的事，知天命地顺其自然，不患得患失，不经营人生，不拿天国做生意，不妄想主宰命运，顺着万物的天变轨迹行进。这种人生进退自然的智慧，小舍小得，大舍大得，体现了明朗大气的做事风格。

滚滚长江向东流，流入太平洋；雅鲁藏布江却向西流，流入印度洋；湘江北去，流入洞庭湖；昌江南下，流入鄱阳湖。人生如同江河水，不同人流向不同的去处，流水与石头合成波涛，水面有喧嚣，河底有静流。

大江大河的流水从来不是一直前进的，它时常后退迂回，进三退二或进五退三，这样包容了沿途更多的支流。人生就是这样江河水似的在进退中丰富生活的内容。舍得是一种境界，不计付出，舍己为人，体现出了胸怀宽广的做人高度。

舍得是一种心态，有取有弃，低调淡泊，体现了坦荡洒脱的人生追求。钻井似的深入，受阻"岩石圈"，钻头钝了，还要钻，撞了南墙也不回头。人生有舍得（取弃）的心态，硬钻不能进了，就软进，在心灵深处下功夫，反倒超越钻井，进入了人生的"软流圈"，大舍而获得比宰相胸怀还大的幽谷似的天地。

学会取舍的智慧，懂得进退的真谛，就能够去污秽而享受人生的美好！

30. 偶然与必然

人生充满偶然和变数。人升官发财，交朋友得配偶，很多时候是不确定的。命运在人的主观把握方面，幸福与不幸一念之差，写成小说、影视，情景扣人心弦。

　　某商人去北京做生意没做成，却在逃难中偶遇一江苏女子被救助。出于感恩的情怀，商人跟女子有了非生意的诸多交往，后来成就了一段美好姻缘。这是礼尚往来、感恩图报，由于珍惜善缘而获得的善报。

　　商人如果思想西方化，用数理化来计算，继续去不划算的原本不在经商计划中的地方，因而不去了，也没有过意不去的亏欠心理。这样因为无利可图而不珍惜，一段必然安排却偶然出现的姻缘也就擦肩而过。苏女也就成了父母安排的官员之妻。

　　人世间有许多事理，不在科学现象归纳的规律里。例如：某政府官员，根本不屑钻营，没有进入官场的升迁关系网，一般而言，他就要在科员的职位上终老，可是却从官场派系斗争的夹缝中偶然地脱颖而出。

　　上述商人得贤妻，科员升局长的偶然事件，从个人生涯过程的一般规律看并无直接关系，但从社会生活的复杂性与宗教说的因缘上看，又能解析出某种必然。

　　商人对苏女的好感，源于自身不太精细，有感恩的良好品质，合起来就有了无心插柳似的婚姻；官场派系之间不相让，科员人缘好，无派系，相结合就有了几派官员都能容得的升职机遇。

　　故而无论从事何种职业，首先不着眼技术，而在做人的德行正道上用心，就能珍惜偶然的相遇，能得到多助。技术上精明的人，千算不如老天一算。孙悟空似的小聪明，总也翻不出如来佛似的大智慧的手掌心。

　　中国 1937 年至 1945 年的八年战争，能持久就必然会获得最后胜利。这也宛如楚汉战争刘邦抗击项羽，坚持就是胜利。人的升官发财很多是偶然的。如果不珍惜现实和不务正业，最后失败往往是必然的。

唐一鸣

  我与朱粤椿先生是忘年交，相识纯属偶然，透析下又着实有着某种必然。他南腔北调，我南调北腔，相互之间能听懂对方国语的一半，思想却能百分百相通。

  朱先生热爱和平而论适应主义。主义，是指概念演绎的理论体系，这是从古希腊到近代英法逻辑实证方法建构的思想学说。

  朱先生走的不是这条路，而是我中华从春秋战国警句、格言、成语等在千言之内凝缩的解释。朱先生六集的思想文字可概括为一语：论适应以共生。

  论适应主义，或许会遭人非议，因为朱先生的思想并无长篇的理论阐述和体系打造。但说适应纲领，却比较准确：人生是个适应过程，共处生活趋于和平。

  读朱先生的六集之《人的根本》《实事求是》《性情与仁义》《三岁定向》《城市与行会》《偶然与必然》等，围绕适应，基本说了人类之林林总总的问题。

  人的根本是"五爱"："爱自己、爱家、爱事业、爱民族、爱祖国"；人生"两信"："处世靠诚信，做事靠自信"。

  人"行中庸"，书写自己的"一撇一捺"："文质彬彬有仁义，虽有野性能舍弃"；人生须"在心灵深处下功夫"，"去污秽而享受人生的美好"；"如果不珍惜现实和不务正业，最后失败往往是必然的"……

朱粤椿选集——论适应主义（下）

374

读朱粤椿先生的文集，宛如看一个女人试衣：出来，进去，再出来……读每篇短文，犹如提纲契领穿一件衣；耐心地读完六集 180 篇短文（包括序与后记），就犹如试过了 180 件衣，只要用心，过程中的体悟和喜悦都是自己的。

朱先生短文六集，思想涉及了个人与社会或者家国与天下；先生的名言是："我富有的时候像穷人的心态过日子；高官的时候像平民一样。"这句话可谓朱先生"论适应以共生"之纲领的最为精要的概述。

On Adaptation

(Vol.2)

On Adaptationism（Ⅳ）

(Kokang version)

1. Life is like a tree

It is known to all that a tree has a natural process of growth. Life is like a tree in the growth of quantitative change and quantitative difterence day after day. With the joining of a sperm and an egg, a person starts his journey inside his mother's body. As the seed developing its root under the ground, a person is growing from a tiny cell to a clear figure in those ten months of pregnancy. A baby was born like a seed breaking through the earth with its tender buds and undivided stems.

Before schooling, a person toddle through his childhood like a sapling waving and trembling in the rain. As storms always give way to the sun after going through hardness and difficulties, he realizes the truth of life. People study various subjects for developing individual thoughts. From three-year to five-year primary school, from junior to senior high school, from undergraduate to postgraduate, our grade advances like the stretching of the sapling influenced by the human environment, our thoughts accumulate in dribs and drabs, from the perceptual to the rational, intuitional to analytical.

People are like trees growing from young to old. Trees grow naturally with tick trunk deep root and flourishing leaves. It is the same with the growth of Human body and evolution of thoughts. Leaf grows more width, less thickness. Human body grows more height and width, less thickness. It is easy to be whimsical but medicated looking inside ourselves. Quantity can be increased by taking more experience and being diligence but thinking abstract analysis, summarized comprehensive, can only be developed step by step, as the leaves growing slowly.

Leaves absorb sunlight and assimilate carbon dioxide. The roots of a tree absorb water and minerals from the soil through the surface. Regardless of the root and leaf, enough area and volume can soil supplies enough nutrition. It goes the same with people. Whether in primary, secondary, university, we have stepped grade. It should have a certain number of students in the class to keep mutual promotion and make a balance. There also needs to be a certain number of schoolmates for affinity.

The perfect thinking ability needs not only different levels of trainings, but also competition and support from classmates and schoolmates. We are also in need of friends during the formation of our characters and qualities. As it's known to all that two heads are better than one. It is said that touch pitch and you will be defiled. Where your friend grow can have a big influence on his character.

Birds of a feather flock together. Trees and people can both be categorized. Good people should keep a distance with the bad one. A rat crossing the street is chased by all. Upright should be spoken out loud. Get rid of the bad before the rotten apple injures its neighbors. God helps those who help themselves. Don't hide your sickness for fear of treatment. Medicine can kill immortal illness. Buddha is predestined friends the human. Fool argues irrationally; thinking man is wise.

2. Genetic gene

The similarities between the previous and later generations should give credit to the transmission of genetic genes. Heredity is the characteristics passed on from dad-generation to son-generation through

genes. This so-called imitating means to copy human's DNA. However, according to the reasoning of Buddhist thought, the acquisition of human shape by dog is said to be that the genetic effect of dog's DNA works in life cycle among people.

Biogenetics requires the cautious observation and analysis, which are the necessities in biological experiments. A lot of knowledge relevant to genetics left by human culture is enough for us to understand why we should emphasis on blood ties or stress filial piety and ethics.

Si Maqian wrote biography for Bian Que (a famous doctor in ancient China) in *The Historical Records*. It said, "It's lucky for Huang Di and Bian Que to have ancestors' medical books, from which they can tell whether people are sick or not by observing the color of face." It means that the Bian Que's medical skill is not the results of his intelligence. However, it's the medical ancestors who handed down their contributions. To put it in another way, the medical knowledge was transmitted from masters to students. Many smart persons are always wrong-headed. If the window paste paper isn't pierced, the sunshine outside won't come in. Likewise, if there is no famous master to direct, one must be careful about the suggestion from experts. Thus it can be seen that complying with the ethical code is really important.

After drawn lessons by historians and comprehended by futurity for thousands of years, lots of remaining rumors get popularized gradually. Then they become the conventional culture. For example, after the approval and heritage by Han Dynasty, Qin Li Calligraphy turned into Han Li Calligraphy. The calligraphies passed down successively from one dynasty to the next in China, thus containing their preservation and evolution through inheritance from age to age. While the heritage of lyre-playing, chess, calligraphy, painting and many other artistries is the culture.

No matter the species or the human race, neither of them can cut off the transmission of DNA. Extinction means that there is no descendant of race. Supposing that the ancient Greek culture was separated by Teutonic military incursion and Christian, then there will be no persons influenced by heirs of the thoughts of Socrates, Plato or Aristotle in Greek. Therefore, this kind of tragedies talking above should be taken precautions against on our motherland.

Chinese people inherit our Chinese civilization. We should never underestimate our own capacities. Now that the Western learning has been introduced, it would be unlikely to give it back, merely not abandoning the cultural deposits that inherited by Lao, Zhuang, Confucius and Mencius. To be an excellent offspring equipped with sage's thought, and try creative efforts gradually.

3. Three-year old shows one's future

It is said that three-year old showed one's future and at the age of seven we could see what he like when grow old. In Jin Yong's novel, there was a man named Wei Xiaobao who lived in brothels till teenage. His habits of lust, cursing, lying and cheating, when gambling, have been already shown at the age of three.

The scientific basis of Three-year old showing one's future is that brain weight only 370 grams when the baby is born. At the age of 1, its weight almost approaches to 60% of adults'. At the age of two, it accounts for about 75% of adults' brain weight; At the age of three, it is almost the same weight with adults, brain weight 25% after dozens of years old.

The institute of psychiatry in London and King's College London made a survey and divided 1000 three years old children into five types in 1980: the self-confident, the adaptive, the silent, the self-discipline and the hyperactivity. In 2003, when the children were at the age of 26, the researchers visited them as well as their friends and relatives. The results showed that adult's personality has been accurately predicted at the age of three.

Investigators Professor Caspi gave a report in 2005 said that what a man experienced at the age of three would be absorbed like a sponge. This means that before the age of three, living environment will form people's corresponding character. That is to say, in Jin Yong's novel Huang Rong and Wei Xiaobao's character have been decided at three.

In India 1920, people found wolf child kamala at the age of seven, who walked like wolves on all fours, slept in the daytime and took evening activities. He was afraid of light, fire and water and ate only meat (tore on the ground with his teeth). He cannot talk and sleep immediately after eating and always shouted like a wolf. Kamala died at the age of 16, and his intelligence is only like four years old.

American scientists use positron emission computed tomography technology to scan infant brain. The research shows that after three years old, the complexity and richness of the brain has been basically shaped, and stops the new information communication. Then the structure of the brain has formed like computer, which hard disk is formatted, just waiting for the programming. That is to say, Huang Rong's interest as swordwoman and Wei Xiaobao's dream of being an official have been decided at the age of three.

American Davie Ding and Taiwan woman, Zhang Pingyi volunteered to be a teacher in poor areas of the motherland, out of the mechanism of taking pleasure in helping people formed at the age of three.

But many rural children are scolded by their parents at an early age. So when they grow up, all they want is to get out of the country life and go to a big city. Many people abused Confucius as a hatred of traditional mechanism, which may be formed at the age of three.

4. Reading opens minds

Going to school is basically the learning process a civilized society sets for children. Generally, there are elementary schools, junior high

schools, high schools and colleges. The contemporary national compulsory education covers the period from elementary school to junior high school or to high school.

There is a song saying that. Once there was a boy who carrying a bag and going to school everyday, not afraid of burning sun and heavy rain and strong wind. What really matter was the teacher's blaming of his laziness, and his parents' shame of his lack of knowledge. He studied neither for the official camer nor for fame, but to win credit for himself, and not to be bullied by others like cattle and sheep. When people read for such a purpose from the very beginning, they will learn from Confucius and Mencius to prosperous China eventually when they grow up.

Nowadays from elementary school, to middle school, people study with the focus on western knowledge, learning Chinese to read, learning mathematics for abstract thinking, learning English for xenophilia, and then the science, computer, art and music strengthening Chinese interest in western knowledge and ambition for getting more skills. In middle school, it divides science into segment for the analysis of physical phenomena, chemical change and evolution of biological species, and so on. Physics and chemistry are the strong point of learing. So if our country wants to be more connected to the world, we have to study western knowledge. In fact, Chinese are able to learn betfer.

Reading and studying, in general, must be taught by a teacher and the attitude is the key. Wen zi, a disciple of the sage Lao zi in Zhou dynasty, once divided study into the upper, middle and lower layers. He said that the upper study meant listening by soul; middle, by heart; lower, by ear. He advocated listening with concentration of spirit, at least by heart not only by ear.

The modern westernization movement advocated " traditional Chinese values aided with modern western management ", and opened the modern industry.

But we need to use the doctrine of the moderation to enlightenment and the kind heartedness to the humane and civilized courtesy, which should still be the dominant of Chinese cultural education.

This is precisely the responsibility we need to bear now. Don't let Zhuang Zi fight with Confucius out of your personal preference. Let those who take monkey as ancestors learn evolution by themselves. Let those who take fight as pleasure study conflict philosophy by themselves. Geography, history, politics, education are based on tradition. Teachers should take man's spiritual cultivation as essential and self-improvement and self discipline first.

5. *Cultivating morality with decisive action*

Derived from the truth of saying enlightenment in Zhouyi, cultivating morality with decisive action means that: as teachers, whose most important responsibility is to propagate doctrines of the ancient sages, that is, to cultivate the virtue of man.

What said above is the first step to tell one how to be a gentleman or a virtuous man. Actually, as a human, one will always seek for good and bless for himself. Yet, what is good, what is blessing? It is virtue and morality in fact. Maybe the answer sounds to be some conventional phrases, but it's not hackneyed tune. Provided that parents left their child with the vast wealth, while this child is virtueless or immorality, indulging himself in eating, drinking, gambling and frequenting the brothels. The result is quite clear that this person would dissipate the so-called fortune quickly, to make it worse, he would be killed.

As far as we are concerned, this world is mother who gives birth to everything, while only we human possess soul in this world. In fact, the two sentences imply the truth of cultivating morality with decisive action. Human, is the son/body of the world, or the spirit of the universe. Therefore, following the spirit of earth and heaven, the

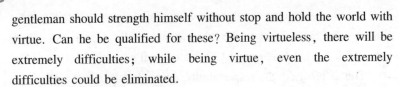

gentleman should strength himself without stop and hold the world with virtue. Can he be qualified for these? Being virtueless, there will be extremely difficulties; while being virtue, even the extremely difficulties could be eliminated.

Being teachers, the primary job is to deliver a sermon. Then as a student, what is his primary stuff? The answer is to perform the morality. Perhaps at the beginning of receiving instruction, students will always feel that the so-called "Dao (doctrine)" was wide of the mark, the major principle was useless. These soft things can not be better than the particular knowledge or the technology, etc, the calligraphy. However, being a great calligraphy teacher, what he should emphasize to his students is the virtue. If the one you followed is a man of ability, you will be aware of the truth.

The Dao (doctrine), if it comes from their teacher's mouth, students will think that sounds to be meaningless naturally. However, if the student performed what is said and turned it into subtle virtue one after another, he will find it useful, real and practical . Accompanied by morality all the time, he will be benefited from it through his life.

Begin every morning with "Good morning, dad and mom" when seeing your parents; At the elevator, say: "Madam, you first, please. " when meeting your neighbor; Offer your classmate a hand when coming across him carrying heavy loads…There was a professor in Japan, all the way he walked to school, who and then throw into the trash at the gate of school. Such teachers or students will worth the eye salutes and make friends everywhere. As we all know, it is difficult to do proper business, but as a person like this, it seems to be not so hard at all.

"Cultivating morality with decisive action" means that the morality focuses on performance. In the case of all social beings are conscious of fulfilling their moralities, the criminal law would be useless. Of course, this is the ideal case. However, according to historical records, there

were once ideal scenes indeed as no one pockets anything found on the road and no one in the prison during the periods of Wen-Jing (two Great emperors in Han Dynasty) and Zhenguan (a period time in Tang Dynasty).

Some people would think it appears to be reserved and old fashioned once saying virtue. But have a look at the Conservative Party in Britain. Are they old fashioned? No, they are real gentlemen. Human, nothing else than chaotic primarily, can he long for knowledge and enlightenment therefore. If he learned how to steal at first, his life is almost finished . That is why Socrates, the St Philosopher in Ancient Greek, always regarded: "Virtue is knowledge."

6. Devoted to Learning at the Age of 15

People know what they want at 3 through family education, read for inspiring the mind in primary school and form their own virtue. Walking on their way of education in life, they enter the stage of devoted to learn at the age of 15.

Our ancient education always left an impression that smart and active children had always been hit palm by other kids, standing as punishment or hitting hips by parents. That is either ignorant advocating or ruining school teacher on purpose.

The old-style private school started from Confucius. He taught students in accordance of their aptitude with no discriminations. How could there be rebuking and physical punishment. At his childhood, Confucius also played. What is wrong with playing? It is a pupil and kid's natural instincts to be active and naive. We shouldn't force him to sit a whole hour and do their homework till night. If he has an insatiable desire to learn, just learn or he should just play. Why do we need physical punishment?

Confucius said, "Since the age of 15, I have devoted myself to learning." "I'm not born to be wise. I just like traditional culture and

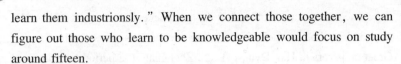

learn them industriously." When we connect those together, we can figure out those who learn to be knowledgeable would focus on study around fifteen.

Teenagers at the age of fifteen . Generally speaking, have strong mind and clear goal. So at that age, it's not difficult to devote to learning. People learn Confucianism at the age of fifteen, which is the time people go to college and learn classic work. We study the nature of things and cultivate moral character and manage the family's affairs well and rule the world, which make us devoted to learning. That is a feasible and chosen way.

The modern study merely focuses on classic works but on skills which basically lost the essence. Schools are almost western styled. But, western students have Baptist or go to church at very young, which is the western way of "cultivating morality with decisive action". If kids are forced to write in kindergarten and do homework till 11 o'clock even if in elementary school, how could that inspire mind? We must feel tired about this forced, exhausting and boring way of study, which leads students to fleeing away, let alone devoted to learning. At this time, children are looking forward to independence, which makes anti-study the beginning.

If a man can live longer than seventy years, when he makes it to devote himself to learning at the age of 15, he has been well established at 30, knowledgeable and no longer been confused at 40; the heaven-sent duty at 50, able to distinguish right from wrong in other people's words at 60, and able to do what he intends freely without breaking the rules at 70.

So it is important to devote to studying at the age of fifteen. Otherwise, you will confront unbearable difficulties one after another after 30.

7. *Get Married and Start Career*

In general, people get married and establish their career at the age of thirty. So Confucius said "Since 30, I have been well established". as for reading the book for rites then applying to practice, it refers to accomplish some certain goals, which proves that he can live independently by himself.

No matter ancient or modern, home or abroad, there are only a few people abounded everything and lived in seclusion in order to cultivate himself according to a religious doctrine and become a god or to learn from dharma for nirvana. Most people in the world are ordinary true men. They need to live with family, live for career and even live for fame. So marriage and career are two of the demands of most people. It is a stage of life when you reach it, you can feel a sense of achievement.

In ancient times, people got established at the age of thirty, usually succeded in the imperial examination as scholar Jinshi would obtained a grade level as county magistrate, which made them hold their heads high and glory on the face of their parents. As a scholar, that position perfectly meet their and parents' expectations. For impoverished students, that is the significance of reading. Reading helps us learn so much about beauty and truth that we can live a better life in our own ways.

Generally, those who are not devoted to learning are not living a life without hope. Farming, learning a craft, going out to do business, or put a fruit stands in situ, they also and have hopes to get married and have children at the age of 30.

At the age of 30, farmers who have more than ten acres of land, a small courtyard; craftsman who teaches the skill and has income; businessman who has experienced inventories, inspection, stocking up and shipping out the good and have a foothold at shopping malls, are

able to be a husband and father.

It must be admitted that everything has changed a lot compared with the ancient times. The imperial civil service examination has also been abolished; farmers are not stuck in the field. These past poor craftsmen and merchants have become the dominant of city civilization. Social occupational structure has changed from "scholar, farmer, artisan and merchant" to "artisan, merchant, scholar and farmer". The name "boss" makes people's heart fibrillating or itching. The unemployment of many graduates from college makes it hard to expect the gold room and gorgeous beauty.

The change of social structure causes the change of celebrities. Just like the poem said, "Those swallows which once lived in the eaves of rich people would finally fly back to the ordinary family." But getting married and owning a career at the age of 30 are still incentive hopes. If we ignored it, there will be a lot of quinquagenarian problems.

All in all, getting married and having a career can give everyone a goal in life. Then there are adult consciousnesses and sense of responsibility, which makes people not only focused on clothes, meals, work and sleep but also live with a goal.

8. Life Begins at Forty

There is a negative statement: everything comes to a dead end at the middle-aged. That is a compared saying with "At the age of 40, one has no doubts about the world."

The TV series to *At Forty* describes a psychiatrist husband and his wife as a director of ICU. Their life and love affair is full of twists and turns: after having a successful career at forty, they are not satisfied with their lives. His wife expects him to change his work in order to relieve the pressure of their household duties; the husband is diagnosed with cancer and almost dying. He confesses that he has fall in love with another woman. His wife keeps an eye closed to that woman.

What a tiring and troublesome life! There is no denying that they are living in a sandwich generation, but more importantly because they don't really understand what life is even at their forty.

Every one at forty reaches their best time. According to the law of nature, not only does his/her study enters a wise and clear stage, but his/her mind becomes mature. They know the do's and don't, what not to do and make a choice rationally .

Confucius said that when he was forty, he had no doubts about the world. This is not only an experience, but also the penetration and insight of the wise.

Hegel said the wise man of China was an archive-essay reason, which measured the wisdom of ancient Confucian sages in modern philosophers' ideas. If Confucius was a philosopher, he really should give the definition of "Forty" and "Unconfused" and then analyze in which case people feel confused and in which don't. However, Confucius is not such a person.

Hegel was a professor on theory research in 18 century. Period Confucius was the teacher of the Dukes and Princess and enjoying equality. He taught three thousand students, how to manage state affairs well and ensure national security as well as how to be empire's teacher. Hegel is not that cool. He is just a consultant for those feudal princes governors.

Actually, Confucius' aphorism is regarded as a academic saying with understanding of devoted to learning at 15, and well established at 30. At the age of fifteen one can sit quietly for three hours and read *The Book of Songs*, *The Book of Changes*, *The Spring and Autumn Annals* with interest, he would have the ability of self-improvement and self-discipline. At the age of thirty, if he can set a good example and not disturbed by others, then he will naturally become no doubts about the world.

Look at the psychiatrist mentioned above, he was busy with

college entrance examination at the age of fifteen without ambition and knowledge; at his thirty, he got job as a western doctor with the help of medical technology. Although he was married and established, he seemed to be showy and didn't have practical skills; at forty, he was told that he didn't have much time left, and listen to a young lady said "I love you". How can't he be dizzy?

9. Knowing the mandate of heaven at Fifty

At the age of 50, a teacher suddenly obsessed with stock. He was busy with observation of the stock market during the day and working on securities at night. At last, his teaching was delayed; then a bear market tied up all his money. He lived like a cat on hot bricks. This is became he did not know his duty at the age of 50.

Life means that you live and know what you live for. Since 50, people have known their heaven-sent duty and realized happiness consists in contentment. As a fifty-year-old teacher at a retirement age, if he wants to do pedagogy research, write books on his own experience theroties or improve the existing theory of pedagogy, then he has known his duty. If he begins to prepare for that, when he is retired he still owns a career. What a substantial life.

Confucius had known his heaven-sent duty in another kind of form around 50. Confucius became a school teacher under the time background of the ritual collapsed. He taught people to be benevolent and polite so that his disciples came like an endless stream. At the age of 50, he knew that teaching people was his life's mission, of which the most important was to teach Confucian scholar to be an official, to teach the king to restraint lusts and civilize people. So when he went into the official circle, he made great performance and promoted from a county magistrate to minister of justice.

Confucius was adept in managing the state affairs. At the age of 53, he made the State of Lu grow strong. But the emperor of Lu was

obsessed with singing and dancing and ignored state affairs. Although Confucius knew Lu (state) was not a good place to stay, and also knew that governors were all alike, he had to taught all these knowledge about benevolence and ritual to the governors. So he began to travel around those countries.

The governors loved him and in need of his vision, but couldn't accept his equality without a kowtow and his "noble" attitude as an emperor's teacher. That is to say, they can't afford his teaching. However, Confucius has to act like that to set an example to the scholars especially those who want to be official. So he worked as a consultant minister in other countries but without employment.

"Knowing one's heaven-sent duty" means to understand god's will. To know what the mission of one's life is. It doesn't mean people are old with low expectations and make no attempt to make progress. That's to say, if it is quite, stay quite; if it is meant to be active, be active.

Confucius lived in Lu (state) but his heart aid in every other courtry, knowing what governors should know but don't. So teaching what he knew to those ignorant warlords is his heaven-sent mission.

If Lu (state) gave Confucius a chance to make Lu into a powerful state, which attracted the governors came to visit, then he didn't have to travel. However, Lu (state) didn't give him the chance. It is doomed to take a long journey far away from home. To adopt or not is a matter of monarch, his mission is to inform them.

Now the 50-year-old teacher suddenly turned to stock, which was purely on a whim evoked by impetuous environment. So was he.

10. Man is the soul of the universe

Among all the living things in the earth, people are the only specie that can think smart: rational inspired, witty and resourceful in emergency cases.

This is indeed where we can separate human from animals and plants. Plant can rely on roots to grow up high. However, it is firmly stuck in the earth without making a move. Animals can move, fly, run and swim but their life was trapped by instinct. Even there is a stick around, they would never know borrowing it to knock and support for a lifetime. But human beings know.

Rational abstract analysis and summarizing ability changed people's instinctive behaviors, striding over the experience trap and using instrument can help people do things beyond their physical strength. So if you cannot get the fruits by jumping up high, you can use a stick to hit it or make a ladder so that you can climb up from underground. It enables human beings to have the intellect animals don't.

What makes human unusual is that they know what happens far away, what other people do and think, without sensory organs. How magic is it! In science, it is called far perception; in literary it is called inspiration thinking, the yogi called induction of the gods... The Han Dynasty official historian Ban Gu called the ability "psychic".

Human's ability of inspiration can't be understood by all but their sharp perception is widely recognized. Without a thermometer, some people can know the accurate temperature. Some people can measure the weight just by hand.

Sometimes when you feel baffled, then it gets inspired and finds its solution by what you see, hear, smell and touch.

Successful practice means when you hear the password "chicken ribs", you understand the army would retreat. Successful cultivator is really as Lao Zi said: you can know what happened around the world without going outdoors; you can understand the law of nature without looking outside of the window. Without personal experience, they can still make it.

Idiom "brainwave", "used his quick wits" contain the human's inspired thoughts. If there is no such thing as fabulous unspeakable

inspiration, how can people get sudden inspiration, quick mind and witty? Spirit sublimes emotion by correcting it from irrational way and domesticating its wildness.

Since 60, Confucius has been able to distinguish right from wrong in other people's words. But some people can't even when they are eighty or ninety. A lot of people reject good advice that hashes to the ears because they don't understand deep meaning between the words. On the surface, people are stubborn and unchangeable. But actually it is the lack of inspiration. Because of inspiration, people are suddenly awake as "Listening to a wise man's word equals reading for ten years." And they can see the essence from common sense; acquire logic and organized thoughts.

11. Fatigue and Rest

No matter thinking, talking or doing things, there is a time of fatigue and people need to have a rest. This is the law of nature.

On military attack, in addition to selecting the time when the enemy alleged laxity, we can also choose when they are lack of resistance because of fatigue. Once the government makes people fatigue, it will lead to all kinds of harassment. The officers become arrogant and their people get violence. Then the country began to collapse. Xianbei (an ancient nationality in China) and Mongolian exhausted all resources to build up their military power in history. However, they ended up nothing because both the officers and people were fatigue.

There is millions of blessing when a family lives in harmony. It helps to coordinate a harmonious relation so as to makes people free from tension and fatigue. In the state and society composed of sequence as scholar, farmer, artisan and merchant, controlling process of business competition is rhythmic, which put off fatigue. Nomadic tribe's military aggression is the easiest way to become fatigue and disintegration. When the wars ends, peace is coming by relaxation; when purging with ethos, officers and people feel scared.

Sediment increases and water slows down on downstream of the river. It is the exhaustion of the river. Mountains stretching from lofty to rage, sparse vegetation and erosion rock show their exhaustion. Dry and less elastic elderly skin is also fatigue.

Fatigue is a general state of nature and society. Shortness of breath, yawning, and stretching are the product of fatigue. Fatigue may evoke disease and patients get fatigue easily. So they need to have a rest in time.

The armies have a rest by freeing the horses in the mountain; people have a rest through sleeping in bed. Rest is a physiological mechanism all creatures have to alleviate fatigue and restore energy. When feeling tired, people can eliminate or relieve fatigue feeling and recover energy by reducing activity, doing exercise, listening to music or sleeping for a while. Good government, officials, should understand people's need to have a rest.

Tyranny means government uses power to strengthen people's labor, and deprived of their wealth. Those repeated labor makes the people resist in the end and the whole country becomes a total mess. These powerful weapons and wars make the country's wealth and civilization run out. Reducing the burden of taxation and cost or even duty-free is the ruling way coming out of Taoism to let people recuperate.

In the history of China, those in charge of Yao, Shun, Ping Zhang, Wen Jing, Zhen Guan knew how to let people rest without exploitation. In European history, the government understands this truth very late, generally after the Second World War.

To put it bluntly, The Confucian benevolent and moral politic is to let people rest and officer doesn't exploit people. In today's democratic constitutional government, it is actually benevolent governance by the

people.

12. Family and Career

Family has close relation not only with marriage but also with career.

A peaceful family will prosper everything; a harmonious country brings wealth in all sectors. This truth was mentioned in Yao and Shun's legend four thousand years ago. Yao didn't pass the throne to his son but gave it to Shun for the reason of Shun's virtue. Shun's father, stepmother, brother acted in collusion with each other and framed up Shun by fire, buried in the hole, etc. Shun handled these skillfully and made peace.

From Shun era, there came an interpersonal theory: There should be affection between fathers and sons, affiliation between monarchs and courtiers, distinction between husbands and wives, order between seniors and juniors, and trust amongst friends. This five teaching ethics ran through all peaceful time. If the family ethics exist, the country and world would not be disordered. In other words, the mess of the world can be solved.

In general, people will experience two stages in family. When they live with their parents, people learn about the most basic living experience and five teaching ethics. After marriage, they pass down what they get to children. That is the traditional culture and civilizations over the past thousand years.

Modern citizen was created by rich and poor people's revolution. First in Europe, then it spread to the whole world. However, the political theory of "world of justice" for the benefits of people spread from China to the whole world. In today's world, the family is one of the most basic social setting and the most important system of human being. It has the function of children's socialization, supporting the senior citizens, economic cooperation, and sexual pleasure for

community of human relationship.

A peaceful family will prosper everything; a harmonious country brings wealth in all sectors. The meanings of these two sentences have greater influence than gunpowder, paper, printing and the compass. Now, time will eventually prove everything.

The sentence "get married and start one's career" also pointed out the successful and happy road people can get. Almost everyone wants to have his own career, that is, entrepreneurship. Because of this, people were deluded by all kinds of advertising. However, when people were born, god only arranged for half of you, the other half need to find by marriage.

Family, to put it bluntly, is the first business for man and woman. A family is business. Be content without arguing for life can be happy for a long time. Both ancient and modern, Chinese and foreign, male and female, when the red candles were lighted up by these happy couple, career begins. Loving for each other, having children, growing old together is the main business. Wealth and reputation are just sideline.

The so-called career before marriage falls into a wrong path. *The Book of Changes* talked about career: Do what you love and help others; the divination Heng mentioned the golden law of family constancy and career success: When man does business outside, he should do like thunder; when woman deals with homework, she should do like a wind.

13. Work and Company

Homemaking women bring forth housework and home, and even household textile industry. Breadwinning men bring more jobs and industry.

Work is the social production of labor. For a long time, people repeatedly do a series of actions to create value. History in Han Dynasty

has recorded words such as "slave labor, work" etc. Then the word "work" is often refer to hard work, artisans, officer, history and institutions. And it usually refers to a man who is engaged in social affairs, working outside the home.

Those poets, scholars and litterateur who are not fastidious about words would prefer to take complicate with children, sports, perform tasks as work. So later, profession is also known as work. In Song Dynasty people even used "work" to describe craftsman who lived in goods store work.

Company in modern society is actually a labor organization developed from industry and commerce in Europe and American. It is a collective management in the form of board of directors for-profit and many people invest into shares.

The word "company (Gong Si)" was first originated from "List of Words", "Gong" means collecting a number of people's money; "Si" means operation. Zhuang Zi also said "company" is a public way of combining small things to big one. *The Book of Rites* said the history of the motherland is degradation. First, the world is harmonious society which people do for one; then became well-off society people do for their family; next comes to dominated society with destruction of principle. The literary intelligentsia's duty is to follow the saints' teachings, using the laws and courtesy to control the country and make all for one.

That is to say, in ancient China, "scholar, farmer, artisan and merchant" means corporate society, which uses the method of regulating the family and ruling the state by level of scholar to lead other classes. The substance is to make peace for country and safe for people instead of western company of wealth collecting company. To be clearer, in ancient time, family is small companies created by father and ruled by mother; country is a big company created by lords and managed by ministers.

Country is a kind of company created on "five teaching" ethics as affection, righteousness, difference, sequence and trust. Interpersonal affection comes first like blood is thicker than water; the distance between families was controlled by righteousness, which is dominated by ritual and assisted by law. This makes regime change but not far from Chinese Confucianism orthodoxy of the glory.

Millions of tribal died around the world but China enjoyed a long history and politic is out of control. What we need now is to tell home from nation and don't let the home affair destroy company's composition by intensifying the limited and unlimited liability.

Constitutionalism is the broadest and efficient economic organization form with the purpose of devising interests by setting of private resources to spread risk. It runs across the blood and geopolitical fast forward like bullet train and quickly dissipated energy of human beings. The global economic and political network like companies are mysteriously entered into a culture technology coveted human spiritual. Chinese public righteousness concept has a positive significance of detoxification.

14. The country is prosperous and the people live in peace

Wu Zimu, a Confucian scholar born in Song Dynasty but lived in Yuan Dynasty, was listed as "Stinking ninth category" —whose status was even humbler than prostitutes—by the Mongolian forcefully. From this, there is no wonder that he would deeply feel the darkness under the reign of Yuan Dynasty and recall the halcyon days in Lin'an—the capital of the Southern Song Dynasty. Thus, he accounted in his book *Meng Liang Record of Mountain God* (every thing recorded in this book seemed a fond dream today) like this: Every year once the sea tide overflowed, cities nearby would be swashed. Thus, governors would offer sacrifices to gods or ancestors all the year round. What's more,

they also ordered the Academy to compose Taoist Green Lyrics to pray for that the country is prosperous and the people live in peace. " This folk-custom described the Southern Song Dynasty's affinity to people: Pray the God to bless his country and the people.

When appreciating the ancient folk art in our motherland, we cannot see the people's hostility to the government, and there is no curse of "The evil old society". Say, in order to celebrate the country's prosperous and people's peaceful life, the Kylin Dance in central plains is mostly observed in the festivals or the day of jubilation.

In Hong Kong, villagers relying on fisheries and agricultures always use the grand ceremony — Bun festival — to thank God's Grace and pray for the country is prosperous and the people live in peace. Even if they were ruled by colonist, these villagers still hold that it's deities who brought them the piping times of peace.

So long as the Chinese are not involved in the movement and not oppressed, they always advocate that "Peace is to be cherished". This kind of wish is more popular in Taiwan. When each festival comes, no matter the local people who believe in Taoism or other adherents from everywhere, all of them are willing to go to some famous temples to offer incense to Buddha and pray for favorable weather or may the country be prosperous and the people at peace. Some of these famous temples are: The Jade Woman Temple of Guandu, Yong-Xing Temple in Daya District, Donglong Temple in Donggang, Chi Nan Temple.

If Dragon Boat Races were hold in Taiwan, two flags would be certainly inserted at the stern of dragon boat which belongs to the fishermen in Two-Dragon-Village: on one flag bears that "Favorable Weather"; the other one bears that "The country is prosperous and the people live in peace". This kind of National Peace Flag used to bless people live in peace also appears on the Miao People's Dragon Boat Festival in Guizhou Province. This proves that the culture, etiquette and custom are the same in Taiwan and inland. Thus, only our inland need

recover more and more traditional customs, can we win the hearts of Taiwan people's. Whether in the hearts or in the eyes of Taiwan people, the Canopus is a lucky star that symbols that the country is prosperous and the people live in peace.

There is a Mazu Temple located in Thailand's Ben Tou, on the gate's signboard belonging to the outer-hill bears "Guo Tai Min An (means the country is prosperous and the people live in peace)" these four Chinese Characters. Another example, Altar of Land and Grain located in South Korea's Seoul is used to sacrifice to God of land or God of Grain, and the important wishes promised by people are: May the country be prosperous and the people at peace, or may good weather for crops. Also in ancient time, the Jew put their faith in God and the main wisdom of their King's bestowed by heaven was to bless the people be strong and the country be affluent or may the country be prosperous and the people at peace when he managed state affairs.

Emperors in Qing Dynasty dared not to be hostile to Han Race publicly. Therefore, the Heaven Worshiping Ceremony in Qing Dynasty was a state fiesta, obviously it is a kind of state attitude, and so prayer as "The country is prosperous and the people live in peace" would be wished every year. Thus it can be seen that this kind of prayer is an integrative expression of Manchu and the Han's reflected on the aspect of our national culture.

It is said that Emperor Taizong of Tang who was of Turkic origin identified with "Rehabilitate" — a kind of Daoist idea worshiped in the political area by Ethnic Han — more positively, from this he created ZhenGuan Period (Golden Years) in which the country was prosperous and the people lived in peace. Such political pure brightness lasted to The Flourishing Kaiyuan Reign Period all long, everywhere presented the picture of the country was prosperous and the people lived in peace.

The idea of "The country is prosperous and the people live in

peace" is a significant content of feudal ethical code orthodoxy in our country, no matter officers or the public, their shard expectations are: The whole world is at peace or celebrating peace by singing and dancing or perfect tranquility under heaven. In view of those expectations, the people will approve the government as the state. While the national policy performed by the rulers is "temper justice with mercy".

15. Competition and Cooperation

In modern society, interest comes first and competition has become the first principle on one's way of being famous. This is an extreme way. When group organization relationship becomes rigidified and ethical relationship get selfish, the competition is necessary. It is more important in interpersonal relationships.

The Kokang Chinese has a tone for a word, a word for a meaning. The ancients said, "chasing together means 竞 (competition); arguing against means 争 (competition)." In modern times, when Chinese say the survival of the fittest in competition, it mainly refers to the action, especially in the field of military, political, and economic field. Modern market competition is intense. The enterprise thinks competition as the struggle for survival, human relationship is deteriorating as creatures.

The so-called competition in biology keeps the balance of nature's ecological. The essence is struggle. The cattle eat grass and so do sheep and rabbit; wolf and tiger eat meat and people also eat meat. Then there comes relationship between creatures and foods in biology. When the food is more and more nervous and finally intensified contradictions, there comes the biological struggle for life.

Theoretically speaking, competition was discussed when the motherland wasted imperial examination. Starting from the German law field, legal scholar Robert defined the concept "competition" clear as workplace of activities, just business community behavior between the supplies of similar goods. This definition of competition is very serious, which need to be separated among sports, entrance exam, presidential campaign, senators' debate.

Indeed, in the history of mankind disputes cannot fully solved by fuzzy competition. Religious belief organized "jihad" or political party launched a revolution or violence is unfavorable to express with competition in case of confusion. Commercial competition is a legal activity in modern constitutional government and social organizations and a game by contract. History jihad and war are often irrational bully struggle between countries and parties without contract.

If we separate competition from those fiercer, irrational and hard to reconcile combat, we can rationally find out that competition can be compatible with cooperation and become an interactive mode of business organization.

Competitive struggle or hegemony is an upgraded competition. There won't be really cooperation. It often is a life-or-death war. This one-must-die struggle will bring in new system in specific time. But it mainly contributed to the lost of human nature.

Cooperation or collaboration is the main interactive form in civilized human society, which brings the business competition to work together for common goals in republican society. So, market economic relations will gradually evolve into super fan of great ally of the interest groups, like the ancient family of China. But it is the world of ultra race, to great harmony society.

In fact, human beings have engaged in the activities such as co-creation, music production in accordance with laws and other cooperation. In Kokang language, there are some mottos like " When people are of one mind and heart, they can move Mt. Tai. ", " When the river rises, the boat floats high", " Husband and wife work, their sharpness can cut through metal " all tell the story of cooperation. If the intellectuals cooperate consciously, they can share knowledge and make

more discoveries.

16. On Comrade

Comrades came from the battles of modern times. The ancient harmonious China required colleagues.

Comrade is a westernized noun. It first appeared in the French revolution, then the period of revolutionary struggle, it became a common call between each other, which meant the politics point of view were same.

In recent times, "comrade" was first used by Emperor Guang Xu to call Kang Youwei, Liang Qichao, etc. Later the alliance and the nationalist party also used "comrade" to call people who participated in the revolutionary. Now the Kuomintang (KMT) is also using the term. Party members were asked to call Ma Ying-Jeou "Comrade Ma" when he was engaged in the campaign.

Now "comrade" is gradually less used with political meaning, and it's used even for gay.

In fact "Comrades" is not a trivial call; it contains challenges to the respect of tradition. Before Guang Xu said comrade, like-minded intellectuals called each other "colleague". Being different from "comrade", "colleague" is very tender, no political meanings. Colleague comes from the book of *The Book of Changes*, and "sky fire" is an analogy to describe collaborative gentlemen.

The gentleman do not advocate partisan struggle but they are affirmative to the harmony in differences. But there is something that a gentleman can not finish by himself, so there is a need to be of one heart and one mind in conjunction with the work of others. This is not organizational constraints, but like-minded. Do not attempt to work with people whose way is not your way.

Comrades clique by faith and discipline. A colleague is concentric with affinity to work united or go their separate ways. It is not a new

struggle and transformation of new society, new state, but a revolution just like a "fire day" picture: the fire in the sky shining, hanging over the domain; people belong unto it and everything is great.

Comrade is like a gust of wind, extreme person provokes the battle with heaven and earth and challenges to ethics. Colleagues gather together to make a difference and show their mutual respect to the heaven, make friends honestly. A harmonious society needs colleagues.

17. Dedication with all the efforts until death

"Dedication with all the efforts until death" is a Chinese idiom, and it means someone is diligent and dedicated to be a civil servant, to work to the last moment of life. This sentence is quoted from *Hou Chu Shi Biao*, an article of Zhuge Liang, who is from Shu country in the times of "the Three Kingdom", "I strive on till the end."

Zhuge Liang wasn't advertising himself. Historian Chen Shou from Xi Jin Dynasty reorganized Shu history, and put it down into the "history of Three Kingdoms". Some people questioned that is there any prime minister can be so dedicated. They may can not finish their own duty so to doubt others, or they just want to be peculiar; perhaps they may not think through.

Chen Shou was in the state of Wei, he should be close to Sima Yi. But as a historian with slightly integrity, he didn't. Because this is the history of Zhuge Liang. Liu Bei asked Zhuge Liang for 3 times repeatedly. After Zhuge Liang became the prime minister, he tried to fulfill the promise and he personally led troops to the northern expedition, but withdrawal led the first time. He faced with some officials' opposition when he was ready to launch the second Northern Expedition, Zhuge Liang wrote that article, and the word "dedicated" with faithful integrity moved people, and passed from generation to generation.

Example is always followed by people. This sentence is often

quoted when the loyal officials are trying to express their loyalty to the king.

"Dedicated" is used a lot afterwards to describe different people or things, but the common efforts is in recognition of diligence. We know there are not very many people who are really working hard.

Working hard needs great will and power. If life gets easy, we will be forgetful of our duties, and work carelessly. Pursuing quality is very difficult, it requires in every kind of vocation.

Once working hard become someone's working habit, it will not be easy if you ask him to be lazy or to have fun. If you entrust such a person to handle affairs, no memo is needed. He considers more than clients, works to the perfect, not only give people a replacement, but also for their own peace of mind. Hard working can make people go into a great state.

Efforts may also make people drop into "井" (well) if you take a look at the Chinese character of "进". People devote oneself heart and soul to work and they will be full with researching spirit, and it is the greatness of effort, but also, avoid by all means of being a "a person with a limited outlook".

18. Boundless as the Sea and Sky

As boundless as the sea and sky is similar to phases like all over the country, talk with eloquence, boundless, indulge in verbiage but is rather positive. Not exaggerated or practical, most of the times it refers to the vast, breadth of mind, cheerful personality, topic grand etc.

To watch the sea and fish swim to the center of sea further and further away, we wonder if it swims right way to the Dragon Palace. Looking at the sky, the eagle flies higher, farther and finally can't be seen, wondered if it flies right to heaven.

People in entire life have been to many places. People see well water or streams; see the sky as if climbing up at the top of the mountain, the hand can touch it. This is the remote villages, where people have nothing to pursue but going into the hole to learn about Zhuang Zi; see water as the Xijiang River estuary; see the sky hanging high above head; there are ranges of hills which make sky high. At this time, you really want to become fish and eagle to experience the mood as boundless as the sea and sky.

Speaking with fervor and assurance as boundless sea and sky, gives people an impression of great experience, plus taking it leisurely and unimpressively.

If we really want to realize something from "as boundless as the sea and sky", we need to think beyond the village between knowledge and discussion try to think and understand from adapting nature and society.

Some people have never been to many places, but never shy with stangers. In any place he is able to feel easy like in his own home. You could say he is rustic, but he is like mountains, inclusive of the whole forest.

This is in fact a kind of spirit! Enjoy my body. It belongs to me. In my mind it is the world. The performance of eloquence is not talking rapidly, but to show their world and universe outlook.

As boundless as the sea and sky is a state of mind. Never live in talking grand but in the adaptation to the nature and social life. On one side of the water, there are streams converge into the rivers then into the sea water; on the other side of the mountain is the mountain in a variety of attitude of confrontation, rolling, finally touch the sky.

The Book of Changes said stem hexagram: As heaven maintains vigor through movements, a gentleman should constantly strive for self-perfection. From the very beginning to the end, the process is an overcome of existing prejudice. As long as you don't believe there is such thing as limitation, you can see as boundless as the sea and sky.

19. At will within Bounds

Confucius talked about his achievement in *The Analects* at the age of 70: follow one's inclinations within bounds. This is a kind of independent state which is full of freedom but not beyond interpersonal ethics. This is hard to do both words and deeds, and it needs training for decades.

From age 15 to 70, 55 years is the most of our lives. The time is enough. Such as waving, 55 years waving everyday, up and down or left and right, circular, curve, wave... On the position of the unity of heart, what is action of cutting can be done, but not to touch. Why is that? Because the heart said no.

This is a journey with the goal of freedom. People make the identification and selection between two sides of warm and cold, tired and excited, good and evil, true and false, positive and negative. At the very beginning what comes is not what you want, you want to be passion but you become indifference, totally not happy. Then gradually, your dream comes true. Even if the gentleman constantly strives to become stronger, they can't be fully fulfilled. Sometimes they want to be a little lazy.

This needs adjustment and reduces the fatigue state of relaxation gradually. This process is really long. A wise man, from ignorance to choosing is probably few glimpse, or to try a few times. It takes half or a day to become skilled. But then "moment without boundary" is a long process and retention period is long and sometimes backwards.

Many people gave up on retention or back stage. If destiny isn't involved, we can take a step back and see bright future and new opportunities ahead. Although if destiny in this, but can not stand the rigors of the ill-fated or less, lose hope and back, not his own demons, then it vanishes. The later is not a chance.

Life is like a play being a human is so difficult. You don't know

where the real hero is. It seems to know the answer but not. Life is like a tree. You may be intoxicated in the root of a lot of young trees or green husk stage beauty, complacency and lose its completion.

What Confucius said is the process of the gentleman cultivation "righteousness, propriety, manners, wisdom and credit". Virtue means following one's inclinations when you are up to seventy. It is the same with personal cultivation in other field of life, such as high rank with flow out the dirt.

Confucius is very intelligent. From beginning he learnt in the right way. After passing thirty, forty, fifty and sixty, human and nature are connected mutually. Nature and human are combined together, which means there is nothing different between doing and doing nothing for nature and following one's inclinations without bounds for human.

20. The Weak and The strong

Economics research refers to the weak as the individual or organization that occupies a relatively small share of social resources. Ethics research perspective refers to the individual or organization that has the bad qualities as jealousy, showy, aggressive. We should combine economics research and ethics research together.

In ancient time, Zhuge Liang and Tao Qian were middle class according to economics, but they let the noble class like SiMa, Wang Xie felt shameful. They not only got some real knowledge, but also had a correct view of world inequality. They did not give a push to the moral degeneration of the world which was getting worse day by day. Officialdom was overrun like floods; Tao Qian considered the situation had way out timely. After Liu Bei repeatedly went to request Zhuge Liang to engage in politics, he kept the right that the wise man directs the brave man, which helped Shu (state) rule by law and eradicated the aristocratic family

The definition that the weak's need to be protected is not accurate.

In modern society, people need the government to protect property and patent. They are not protecting for the weak, but for human rights must be respected, and competition must be reasonable.

If wise men and brave men compete on a fair starting line, a lot of people could be distinguished lawyers, professors, entrepreneurs, businessmen... But they were cracked down as the poor and prisoners by a powerful combination of organization with power and money. These people are not real the weak in the sense of social, legal, economic aspects, but the strong was infringed by the organization of the weak.

Those who violate human rights are a lot of really strong people (including the wise and brave), with the power to hurt others. And then they are called the weak of society, law, economy and family. Then they use the name of so-called humanitarian aids to give the chance of corrupt officials to escape sanctions and getting glory. It is evil.

As the saying goes, a chopstick is easily to be broken, ten chopsticks are not. Now, those people in many places are like chopsticks. They use power-for-money deal to combine a group, like stick or mallet. Through the reason of ideology and some superficial reasons, people deliberately fabricate accusations which make the strong weak like tight steel wire. Then they beat them without stopping and torture those who would rather die than bending to the powerful. What's worse, they ask those who cannot bear the painful torture themselves and send flowers and pennants to them.

The call for law protection on women who are generally called as the weak, means the recognition of power trading in orgnizations, This is not the right way. The society is ought to be reconstructed.

In short, contemporary need Mencius' idea about sympathy and shame to renew legislation and make society peaceful and harmonious.

21. Maltreatment Makes People Mad

There is term "sadism" in psychology, referring in particular to sexual abuse. It is said that the number of men sadism is lager than that of women sadism. It is a matter that study of sexual abuse phenomenon in the field of psychology which can be done by experts or people who want to become experts. We should go beyond the field of psychology in which people make merry in abuse way and find out the reasons why born healthy people become weakness and atrophy in infants or childhood artificially from wider society.

Xiaoyu' er is the character written by Gu Long, who is forced into the wicked valley in childhood, then is trained to be abuser in the end. Rationally, Xiaoyu' er is much crazier than people who become sadists by reading contemporary fiction and watching films and TV programs. Gu Long describes Xiaoyu' er to be an immortal heroical swordsman surrealistically. These writing features are associated with the writer's environment and cognitive status.

Abuse is evil. Masochist will be forced into a crazy man when he suffers pain without dying. Reasonably speaking, Xiaoyu' er who is abused come out from the wicked valley, surely approving of the legitimacy of maltreatment and then become a master of sadism. As soon as he goes out of that valley, he begins to make mercy, spreading abusive virus malignantly.

In the contemporary era, a well-known man who is not satisfied with arranged marriage by his mother while is not willing to defy in case he suffers from unfilial infamy and loses study and play opportunity, etc. So that he hides the dissatisfaction in his heart and gets pleasure through torturing his wife in variety ways, revenging all authorities in abusive manner and showing his own power and conquest by writing abusive compositions. All of it is the fault of inferiority.

Austrian psychologist Adler has pointed out that due to

compensation of excessive inferiority, people compensate for their own inferiority complex through the pursuit of superiority. In the crowd of people of all ages and both sexes, there are some people hurting others as a result of inferiority complex.

Throughout the ages, peasants who takes "no matter rich or poor and noble or humble, all is equal" as a slogan and others in revolts kill the rich cruelly. Because of inferiority complex which breeds jealousy, display, and other adverse psychology that contribute to them becoming sadists in this world of turbulence, peasants seek satisfaction and pleasure with abusing people in beating, scolding and threat ways once they have killing power.

Sadists are willing to play dirty to flirt with and humiliate people who make them have a sense of inferiority. Meanwhile they see them kneel for mercy rather than let opponents die or suffer from physical pain. Maltreatment makes people mad and crazy so that it is significant to reconstruct a country of true gentleman.

22. Plead Guilty and Show Repentance

People can profoundly understand the principle of ruling the country after reading *The Book of Changes*, *Shang Shu* and *The Analects* with getting master of classical Chinese.

In *The Analects*, it recorded that Confucius counseled Wei Linggong that "Don't do to others what you don't want others to do to you". Zhu Xi added that "put you into others' shoes". Generally speaking, it also means that judging another person's feelings by one's own. If people don't want to suffer from beating, they had better not hit others.

During the Spring and Autumn Period, there was a story told about state of Qi. In one winter, the heavy snow was falling continuously for three days and nights. Qi Jinggong who hoped that snow would fall so many days that it could feast his eyes enjoyed the snow scene in the lounge wearing furred robe and talked with Yan Zi that " It is not cold because the spring comes. " Yan Zi was a gentleman and said bluntly that in ancient time when the gentleman was stuffed, he could consider that there are some people still hungry; when he wore warmly, he were able to care about people who were still cold; when he lived a comfortable life, he could be concerned with others who even worked hard. But how about you?" Jing gong felt embarrassed while was asked by Yan Zi.

At present, there is few people who are like Yan Zi and more people who are like Qi Jinggong that are not concerned with helping others who are in adversity when they are in prosperity. Many senior officials and wealthy people abuse power for personal gains and then commit crimes; however, they attribute it to bad luck.

In Western Zhou Dynasty, it was saying that "the noble cannot be punished", thus few noblemen was penalized and felt guilty of committing crimes. Until Tang Dynasty, there was a lot of etiquette which was broken. For example, people who drained away by escaping the punishment could not be tolerated by others who abided by common customs. This phenomenon is similar to that of Americans who treat fraudsters. In Wang Anshi political reform of Northern Song Dynasty, rulers forced the wealth and officials to get money from common people by cruel torture so that many wealthy businessmen ran away while there still were people not wanting to leave the evils to others. In Yuan Dynasty, integrity officials were tortured by crueler penalties and Han people were compelled to revolt.

After the Spring and Autumn period, more and more noble men who accept punishment come up and there are a lot of noble men who abide by rituals refusing to become treacherous ministers and traitors. The elders are ashamed and say that they lack power to rule it and bear the blame to the monarch.

Feudal Ethical Codes and Confucian Orthodoxies are based on rightness to cultivate the human sense of shame and regret. Therefore

Guan Yu of East Han Dynasty would rather be captured than escape with discarding relatives, Zhao Yun was very brave and versatile who would rather die in the turbulence than sell his soul to Cao Cao's camp for honor. Until Ming Dynasty, there existed many officials still having the feeling of gratitude and believing that drip grace, the smallest favor.

The traditional etiquette of political refers to cultivating families with ethics and governing countries with laws. Imperial authority makes people such as Song Jiang and others to plead guilty. Even if he was forced to go to Liangshan to keep alive, he did not relax and still hope to get the amnesty opportunity to be honored. Feudal Ethical Codes and Confucian Orthodoxies let Li Kui who had the feature of bandit and acted rashly feel guilty after making mistakes and show repentance sincerely without regard to losing his reputation.

23. What is meant to be famous?

Ordinary people want to be famous after having a warm family and establishing a promising career. A psychological research on hierarchy of needs said that people's needs can be concluded as five floors: survival, safety, love, respect and self-realization ranging from low and high. Being famous ranked the forth.

Most of people just follow their naive feelings regardless of reality. However, God seems to set some certain levels of need, such as bread, house, marriage, celebrity and angle. Those are metaphors corresponding to theories of hierarchy of needs.

As long as we are alive, we need bread and house out of natural choice. It fits the same with living things. Plants need water, sunlight and soil, etc and animals want food and place to live. It's a must for everything. What makes a man better than animal is that he is capable of using tools to make food and build houses or do furnishing instead of taking handout food.

Marriage is at the third level, which followed by the needs of bread and house and formed under the influence of surrounding environment. It also helps to form interpersonal environment including husband and wife, father and mother. That's a new journey of life called "marry and settle down". Ancients put family into priority and marriage was seen as family business. Personal will comes to next. (If not so, he might plan to be a hermit.) As for modern people, joy comes first. People enjoy two-person world. The coming of the age of civil society declares the fading of family.

Fame is the fourth floor during the journey of life. After marriage, people want to be extraordinary, expressive, and honor their ancestors. Then there will be a motivation for career: manor, fighting, gaining, and transforming society (or natural) ... No matter you fight against enemies to protect country or retired from decent job and come back to hometown, there is no denying that fame makes it.

Presenting a business card, is to get a title, even if it is a hollow reputation. It is vanity or face. Famous is not easy, not only could be targeted in the process, competition can also be objects, the envy of people slander, damage. Famous let people uneasy, worried about saying the wrong thing, do something wrong, afraid of being forgotten, and to fire myself...

Some people say that they prefer to remain in obscurity rather than be famous. This is just consolation after failure. Ordinary people get married and have their career at the age of 30. Rarely of them don't want to be famous, let alone their inner desire and family's expectation. Fame brings more than honor but benefits. As long as you are obsessed with demands, then stop being self-deception. Why do you struggle? Isn't it for fame? It's so silly watching a pig running without thinking own or eat it.

There is no fault of being famous unless you don't care about its scope and recognition. A good father or a good husband can be famous. Whatever the fame is, the size doesn't count and also beyond

our control. "Either makes or breaks it" can be seen as paranoid. Never troubles trouble until trouble troubles you. Fame is good or bad is the most important. Bad news travels fast. Short pleasure, long lament.

Obviously fame is meaningful. It is an affirmation praise and social trust of your life, work and career. After getting married and starting a career, fame just comes along——good parents, good husband and wife, a good chief, a good teacher... Those are truly belonging to you. What you get on purpose will finally turn out to be in vain. Fame is often accompanied by unhappiness.

24. What makes you miserable?

The reason of unhappiness has a wide diversity of opinions. However, the great saints think alike. Lao Zi said that unhappiness came from confliction. Buddha mentioned that unhappiness caused by taking illusions seriously. Confucius said no benevolence leads to unhappiness. Jesus said that unrighteous is the source of unhappiness.

Now when people talking about unhappiness, it touches the feeling at that moment: bitter, tired, hurt, depressed ... or inconsistencies: cool, unhappy; emotional, rational... Compared with the saints, these claims are too casual, like the clouds of sky, floating at ease.

In September 2006, NetEase made a survey on the topic of "If there is an afterlife, would you like to be Chinese?" There are 10234 people participating in the survey. 64% of them said no and among them, 37.5% of people said being Chinese "lack of human dignity"; 17.6% of people said that they can't afford to buy a house.

Confusion is the most superficial reason of unhappiness no matter which country people come from. When Blacks in the United States go back to Africa to find their roots they blame colonialism. Although they own big house and cars, they never say "I hate black Africa. Long live the colonial" but "I root in Africa. I love Africa." This is the clarity of thought.

When we see through the appearance to perceive the essence and take saints words as reference, we may find out that our unhappiness comes from being ungrateful not only between human but also nature. There is no good that we take daydream seriously or even forget who we are and where we come from. Being ungrateful inevitably leads to lack of benevolence and then unrighteousness. Here goes a saying that bites the hand that feed one. This idiom is clearer.

In history, many tribes were forced to dissolve into more compatible nations and culture, such as the Hittite, the Assyrians because of the lost temple after the conquest.

As an individual, if he speaks ill of his family every-day and complains about born in a wrong family, what do you think the unhappiness comes from?

Personal unhappiness should search for historical reasons and take history as a mirror. So we need to study history, read ancient books and listen to the saints' teachings.

25. Happy life

What is happiness? Tolstoy said that happy families are all alike, but he did not added that what is the alike happiness? But in *The Happiness of the Family* said, "The only reliable happiness in life is to live for others." Later in the *War and Peace* by Duke Maria's psychological activity, it said, "My vocation is to take another kind of happiness as happiness, which is to love and self sacrifice as happiness."

As Leo Tolstoy said, "Unhappy family is unhappy in its own way", each one have their own happiness or family happiness, especially celebrities. With famous celebrities, the answer of happiness is always fancy.

So, maybe it's wise to go back to Tolstoy point of view on family and personal happiness. The real enduring point of view tends to be come up by sages or thinkers. So back to Tolstoy, we can see the

perspective to Lao Zi's unseen strengths in being humble; form is emptiness of the Buddha; Confucius' benevolence means to love others; Jesus' love your enemies from what he said. What makes celebrity's view so attractive is because it makes sages pearl into the mask.

When people desire happy life, they always concentrate on fortune or material, such as money, car, woman, and flowers. On the way pursuing, they get complaints from parents, family breakdown, even a disease. It shows that the people do not understand what happiness is or happy life.

A lot of people spend more than half of their life like a blind man touching the elephant without knowing what he is doing. Tolstoy had such an experience, "As the past time, the past feelings can not be recalled. To chase it back is not only impossible, also depressively painful and unhappy." Tolstoy's marriage was a misfortune, even once a time "it feels so happy" had become a flash in the pan. In the novel, farmer Levin's wife does not belong to him.

The so-called the first half and the latter haft of one's life are just definitions in terms of time. Actually, people are living in the moment. But if you turn life into feeling, into stock trading, finally you must have a handful of waste paper. Every present time is attached to the past. Don't stubbornly cut off from tradition; every present time is also attached to the future. So you don't have to desperately make the decision of "to be or not to be". Don't make everything into gambling for gambling is a feeling of struggling for life, which will be charged by demons in your heart.

Happy life first is to come out from the self-centered, blind feeling and gambler desperate life . Have ego but not blind, always considerate others; Have feelings and clear goals, fight for the right thing. Think before act but not be timid. Don't be afraid of walking at the risk of stepped off cliffs. Think of another way.

So, happy life is to think and live wisely by following the teaching

of the sages and do your responsibility at present no matter how small things are in life, and always follows the call of spirit.

26. Go through the tunnel.

When pursuing happiness, people need to listen and follow the call of sprit or they will fall into the darkness of heart.

At the beginning of life, people won't do things that they have no feeling or no interest. Even if they are forced to do so, they can not stand for long. People prefer pleasant life. Good medicine always tastes bitter but good for health. It will be harmful to delay the cure of illness only because the bitter taste of medicine. Unpalatable advice benefits conduct. If they refused to follow the advice and fall into the trap, they deserved it.

Addicted to the Sweet taste will result in mouthful of decayed tooth. Indulged in dreamy pleasure will lead to drug addiction, which can't be got rid of easily. The sky of life collapsed and nothing can be done. Poisoned heart only regard drugs as the light.

On the road of pursuing happiness, people start from instinctive feeling. Once they can't sublime beyong that, people will be lost in the bread, houses, marrige and trapped; or if upgraded to be celebrity, they will be dizzy in greater vanity.

Therefore a lot of people make no progress around the age of thirty. They are struggling for survival, security and love. This is the majority of people. If people's feelings did not distillate to rational level, complaining "Oh my poor life, I can hardly afford food. "; "My house is too small, when can I have a house with three rooms and two halls?" Some people have got their wife and children, then they pause and ponder again, regreting of yesterday and wishing to make a new choice.

Successful people are stepping on the line of respect. At the age around forty, they don't need to worry about food or reputation; at this

time they really have to upgrade their needs without controlled by feelings and prejudice.

The ancients Fan Li retired in time after winning merit . It is said he lived at ease in fairy land of peach garden. Possessions and business became a space and time tunnel of Fan Li for a long time.

A colleague of Fan Li named Wen Zhong didn't understand to step back, which result in suicide. He was killed by dreaming of fame. There is no light in the darkness of fame. In that Spring and Autumn Period the road of justice was surrounded by oppression of the wicked. Gou Jian's heart is a hole which became the valley of darkness of Wen Zhong.

Bill Gates is the modern Fan Li in the United States. In June 2008, he and his wife donated their total wealth of 58 billion without heritage. "We want to feedback to society". From then on, he retired from enterprise management and threw himself into charity work, "I want to make positive contribution for the world". When he was fifty-two years old, he knew it was his time going back to Jesus.

27. Fear complex

Fear, means scared, referring to the panic which any living things have in the face of danger, or a state of emergency when we meet dislike things, such as the heart speeding up, blood pressure increasing, dilated pupils, screaming, night sweats, trembling, etc. It will get even more serious when cardiac arrest and shock happen. Someone is desperately afraid of wolves. When surrounded by wolves, he was scared to death before the wolves to the body.

Some fear come from facing reality. Such as a person standing on the edge of the cliff, being afraid of falling down will naturally produce muscle tension and physiological phenomena as people moving back. Other kinds of fear come out of imagination. Such as when test scores are not good, they are worried about going home with parents' blame.

They are hanging in the outside late and in the end they smash the window glass. Fear will lead to anxiety and hostility.

From personal cognition, the main psychological reason of fear is in heart. When something is identified as dangerous or nausea, this man will show a panic, abnormal status.

Newborn calves are not afraid of tigers, strength horns against fear of the Wolf. This saying means that fear is a psychological phenomenon. Experiments have shown that when all infants don't know what is dark, high water (buildings, aircraft), the central of water (ship), fire and other things initially, they have no fear; Some will laugh when looking at the wolf; They are not afraid to touch the maggots.

Later because of these experiences including being bitten by a wolf, or seeing the wounds by wolf, falling off from high, seeing people drowned, etc. People feel very uncomfortable and don't want to experience any more. So they have a psychological fear, physically strained and mutation status accordingly. Hence safeguards or isolation, but also avoids the danger.

Therefore, fear has the effect of self-preservation for people and animals. Be frightened to death happens when self-preservation mechanism is out of control. Generally speaking, fear is an instinctive behavior. Hence the defense or flight helps to avoid danger. When suddenly feeling the ground shaking, or finding masked men, people might escape the earthquake and hijacked by immediately fleeing away.

Psychological research said that even plants have fear. The psychologist used the polygraph experiment report as evidence.

Fear, anxiety and hostility, are normal states of psychology of everyone. Those who are afraid of nothing can be seen as abnormal or devil.

But when fear becomes a strong emotional entanglement, it will change into a phobia which becomes the pain of personal growth. It's

said to be not growing up. Many adults were controlled by the fear experience and psychological problems of the age of three. Those related hatred and hostile demons keep lingering in their mind, which lead to fear of social activities or some situations, people or events. What a loss of chances and fun in life.

28. Surpass fear

People are born with a physiological mechanism of fear; Fear is a psychological phenomenon that people have in common. This means that fear is an inevitable condition. For one thing people can be scared once, or even twice, but not the third times. People can not make it a heart disease. We need to overcome it.

Surpassing fear is the need of mental health. Whoever says "I am not afraid of anything", "I was born brave," is trying to satisfy his vanity when he cannot really afford to do so. It is a superior feeling comes from inferiority, but also a primary method to overcome fear.

In 1920, American psychologist Watson took "little Albert experiment" to prove that fear can be made by training. Originally bold young children who are not afraid of animals, heights, flowers or clouds began to show their fear by repeating related terrible phenomenon to him, accompanied by timid children who can expand fear.

Fear comes from the way of understanding: by repeating horrible things again and again can let fear spread. Bandits set up the authority in the way of "little Albert experiment". The hostage or villagers are forced to watch murder, peeling, etc. They also let the hostage beat and scold each other. When this entered into a state of hostility, bandits came to stop or even protected them. This is called Stockholm Syndrome—the hostages fell in love with the kidnappers.

That is to say people cannot see too many horrible things. If so, the interval time should be long enough and we should ask people who are not afraid (adult parents, experts and scholars, the brave, etc.) as a company and give the explanation and analysis. Fear can be changed. It shows the importance of Chinese family education, parents protect and educate children by love and wisdom.

There are some wrong tutoring ways need to be corrected. The most serious is parents blaming each other. Parents are a whole unit for a family, just like the left and right, up and down, front and back of the body, complement rather than repellent.

If father cannot be strict, then lef the mother do it. But they can't take this to slander each other in order to fight for love from child. Parents' hostile can make family a battlefield, which increases a child's fear. They don't want to go home or even scared to get married.

A strict father and a kind mother are a perfect match. A strict father make children fear so they would be obedient and observe law and discipline; Mother gives them forgiveness which helps children recollect confidence through difficulties and gives space and time for children to make mistakes.

Chinese parents ask their children to read *The Three Character Primer* and *Thousand Character Classic* for righteousness and wisdom, which are important to help infants overcome fear.

No matter what progress society makes or how much does value change, it is unable to change human's fear of plague, fires and floods. The force of nature is pretty huge that fundamentally catastrophe is offensive to the nature that people ask for. It is totally futile to change nature. The source of nightmares came from the waste land, dirty river, drought, etc. What can people really do is to improve moral character by understanding benevolence and righteousness, be courtly then try to distinguish right from wrong and follow the good deed.

29. On Being a Gentleman

In the Spring and Autumn period, the trouble time last for five hundred years. Our ancestor, those noble gentlemen came out of

retirement and gave advice to monarch. It was not the same understanding of depending on influential power in Republican period. They were the teacher of the king.

The so-called teacher of the king came out after Qin and Han Dynasty. Actually it was a misunderstanding of gentleman. The original meaning of gentleman is a man of noble character. We shouldn't learn the word by it literal meaning like "the son of the king" but "the teacher of the king".

The character "Zi" in the name of Lao Zi and Kong Zi (Confucius). It became the honorific title to master or teacher. Lao Zi means Master. Lao and Kong Zi means Master. Kong. What's more, the character "Zi" in Sun Zi, Mo Zi, Zhuang Zi and Han Feizi also was used as honorific title.

Han Feizi wrote the book *Statecraft* and dedicated to Qin Shihuang. As long as the later emperors learned it, they became the students of Han Feizi. Emperors in history who followed Confucianism are descendants of Confucius and Mencius. The difference only lied in the fact that some were competent and some were not. Han Feizi's statecraft belongs to the Legalism, which taught the emperor how to control courtiers. For a long time they just kept it for themselves.

After the *Statecraft* divulged to official circles, it was called as the golden rules for controlling subordinate, catering boss and being a government official. It was so insidious that Han Feizi came to a sticky end. Those kinds of statecrafts shared the certain background of history as Sun Bin's Military Science and Zhang Yi or Su Qin's sophistry which made Wei weak and Qin strong.

From then on any family of public officials wrote the summary similar to *Statecraft* would belong to invocations, which made it infamous and passed from mouth to mouth instead of writing a book. Ancient country, especially the gentleman would to do meditation and pranayama before reading. Taoist also pay particularly attention to hour:

from 11a. m. to 1p. m. , 11p. m. to 1a. m. , 5p. m. to 7p. m. , 5a. m. to 7a. m. they practice according to the clock. Europe and the United States didn't do that.

European and American's statecraft was based on Machiavelli "power principle", "unscrupulous", represented by the dual role. Machiavelli read and wrote for enlightened monarch. But he did not sit in meditation for his country.

Machiavelli's statecraft is mainly personal experience which has nothing to do with Jesus Shinto. Han Feizi and Li Si followed Xun Zi and believed in Feudal Code of Ethics and Confucianism. Being Qin Shihuang's teacher was performance of the gentleman's functions. But achieving unification by statecraft, changing the manner of discuss without doing, rival relationship between subject and object was called rebelling against orthodoxy in China, which was a betraying of their ancestor and misleading. Li Si had a miserable fate.

The orthodox Chinese must practice no matter the time and place. We should enhance our own cultivation and influence other people with virtue from home to abroad. That is the right way to conduct himself in society: God, Buddha, Natural Law and Nature...

30. Self-cultivation and Mental Repose, Be reasonable and Fair

Provided one cultivates himself according to a religious doctrine in a let-out way, then his guiding theory is to be: God, Buddha, Natural Law, Nature...But what is God? In ancient times, a king would be named as god by the populace if he was modest and did not strive for good and evil. Which did not mean the king was an immortal but his state reached in practicing Buddha or Taoism was very high.

Some of the Chinese parents are very patient. Their infants would be submissive to everything without being beat and scolded, which is similar to the situation like Christian are obedient to their God. If public

mind could not be quieted, the people would be sure to fight each other. Even-though in peacetime, the society cant' be peaceful, then the emperor would be blamed to incompetent.

No matter God or Buddha, actually, they are just different statements of different tribes by their people. But the same point is that their spirits mean the spiritual life that conform to the natural law, once this kind of spirit is fulfilled, miracles will be performed: bring back life to a patient, move heaven and earth, create the World and made People, etc.

However, no matter the emperor, gentleman, Taoist priest, Buddhist or Christian, they may not fly up in the air even if they cultivated themselves in a let-out way in the secular world. But the disciples with a high cultivation of Confucianism, Taoists, Buddhism or Christian are very reasonable and fair: their words stress reasoning, their deeds show kindness. Their being existence, play the role as the liaison between common people and god-man.

Be reasonable and fair means be considerate to understand and experience other person's feelings. This kind of ability enable to experience others' inner world is spoken of as "Thought Transferring" according to Buddhism or as "Mind Reading" according to psychology. But no matter what kind of parlances are, the person using this method to communicate with others must be very friendly, or debonair. What's more, his words and deeds are as mild as a drizzle and as gentle as a breeze, so people will be unguarded to open their minds.

If just depending on modern counselors' psychology knowledge and consulting skill training, this kind of ability said above could not come true. Consultation is a kind of method used to detect other person's inner emotions and thoughts from patients' behaviors. So compared to carpenters and doctors, the counselors are at the experience level in the same way. Some certain effects can be reached of course, obviously the more abundant the experience are and the more significant the effect

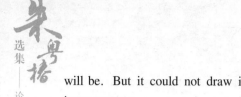

will be. But it could not draw inferences about other cases from one instance yet.

A person will quite be worldly-wise and mature after his experience and knowledge become plentiful at the same time, he will also know how to try to fathom other's minds very well. However, due to the fact that this person regarded the consultation as medical skill, he naturally turned into disease's enemy and got very strong resistance: Playing the game of "cat-and-mouse" mutually.

Magical power is not to conquer others with knowledge but is to move others by good will. While this kind of good will seems like baby's happy smiles without utility, guide, judgment, preach and so on, it's exactly the understanding persuasion; without quoting copiously from many source, there would be no many battlefields, actually magical power is just mention one example which serves for the rest in a psychic communion way: a case can simulated millions and millions ones.

Be reasonable and fair in Chinese traditional mode is to help others turelly. It makes the recipient feel kindness by saying one sentence like "Anything else". It can make him speak out his secrets with sincerity.

On Adaptationism（V）

(Kokang version)

1. Useless Means Good at Nothing

Good for nothing means not usefull or useless. The poet Huang Jingren in Qing Dynasty wrote in his poem *Random Thoughts* that, "Nine out of ten will suffer from being laughed at; intellectuals are good for nothing at all." This verse is even popular nowadays. However, it is not that reasonable.

Intellectual is the well learned person, and places five out of the Nine Classical Schools of Thought, having a higher status than artists who are good at music and chess and religious personages like monks, Taoist and nuns. As a intellectual, one has the chance to pass the Imperial Exams and become the governor, thus begin his official career. It is sarcastic to say intellectuals are good for nothing.

Good for nothing does not mean ignorance. A child can be ignorant, for they know nothing and fear nothing. This is extremely dangerous. However, an ignorant child can acquire knowledge from teachers and become a reasonable and useful man.

In other words, the useless can be changed through learning. Confucius once talked about the common people, he said, "freedom shall be given to the obedient man; teachings about danger shall be given to the reckless man to stop their fool hardy manners." Education is to make the ignorant wise.

Some people say that deep love is good for nothing. Deep love can

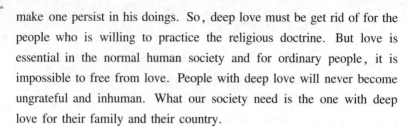

make one persist in his doings. So, deep love must be get rid of for the people who is willing to practice the religious doctrine. But love is essential in the normal human society and for ordinary people, it is impossible to free from love. People with deep love will never become ungrateful and inhuman. What our society need is the one with deep love for their family and their country.

Actually, good for nothing means good at nothing. The useless man is the one who is good at nothing. "人" (a Chinese charater meaning human), in its written form, is like a man standing upright with two feet on the earth. A man can be independent and support himself with two hands. A man with talent and skill is worthy and never depends on others for a living.

A man with the unique skill is always very popular. In other words, he who possesses the unique skill can lead a good life everywhere. A man's skill manifests his social value. For most people, they are have their own areas of expertise. A man should be the expert at one field rather than with broad knowledge but master of none. In ancient society, the intellectuals from the noble family needed not only to acquire knowledge through reading, but also to develop other skills including versify, calligraphy, music, shooting, driving and so on. In modern time, one go to university to get some techniques and skills with the hope to earn his living in the future.

Self-awareness is crucial for one to make the most of his techniques, and make fewer detours. A man with the knowledge of law shall be a lawyer rather than a farmer; with the knowledge of financial affairs shall be a accountant rather than a salesman. How silly it is for a cosmetologist to be a painter! It was Zhuge Liang' destiny to assist Liu Bei to become the king. Zhao Kuo and Ma Su were well known military advisers rather than heroes died on the battle field.

2. Life with Perception is Error-free

The Chinese character "Wu (悟)" has the meaning of understanding, comprehending and awakening. If we add another Chinese character in front of Wu, we can get other words or phrases such as perception, digestion, penetration, awareness, consciousness, thorough understanding, enlightenment, and so on. If a blind man touches an elephant's nose and assume it is a snake, and if a man reads a book but only knows one point of the author's ideas, we can say both of them are weak in understanding.

On his return of defeat Wen Tianxiang met an unusual man and was given a book called *The Methods of Grand Light*. Later he wrote a poem which said: "Who knows the real difficulty, I suddenly comprehended (Wu) the Grand Light. The sun rises and the cloud stays. The wind fades away and the lake calms down by itself. Scholarly honor or official rank can nearly kill a man's nature; loyalty to the emperor and filial piety should be a man's lifelong pursuits. I am the real hero in the world. And I will be an immortal right away." In his poem Wen Tianxiang said he has comprehended the Grand Light, which means he understood and became aware of The Methods of Grand Light.

The Wu of Wen Tianxiang is not the same as that of a common man. We can never know whether he became a celestial or not. The studies of Taoism, Confucianism, and Buddhism all have different comprehensions and commentaries, so we dare not say which one is right and which one is wrong. Our mind will be clear if we take all their advantages in.

With Wu we will not make a blunder in our life. To Wu the heart we will need a special ability of comprehending and analyzing. To Wu our ancestors we will understand Buddhism and sublimate our state of mind. To Wu happiness we will be happy for understanding. To Wu reasons we will perceive the reasons of studying Taoism. Studying Taoism and exploring philosophy, we may have the profound understanding of Wen Tianxiang's Wu of The Methods of Grand Light. To Wu an object, we will be granted the logic of the matter. To Wu the bright we will learn the true words. To Wu Buddhism we will comprehend the essence of Buddhism. To Wu the Chan we will acquire the marrow of Chan. That's why Wen Tianxiang can be most perfectly fulfilled both in humaneness and duty.

At the dawn of human's history there were many men who did self-torture. It is said that India's Brahmanism was started with the self-torture in the remote mountains. Later the practitioners in Hinduism insisted on self-torture but there appeared a kind of hedonism which is opposite to self-torture. The Buddhism takes a way just between them.

No matter what we study, Taoism, Buddhism, Confucianism or Christianity, as long as it is orthodoxy, we should know that they are all asking people to Wu the edifications of the sages. Because of common people's innocence of the essence of world and the truth of life, they indulge in pleasures and degenerations, and with Wu they can get rid of all the things.

The Tang-Dynasty-poet named Wang Wei said in his poem: "Having nothing is no doubt emptiness. But when pursuing emptiness, should we abandon the real existences? Can cleansing my soul get me rid of life and death? I am trying to Wu the Taoism but it seems I have missed my way. Because of infatuation we will actually get sick. Due to rapacity we will never be satisfied. Enjoyments and concupiscence are not the things I am wishfully thinking. Illusoriness is the thing I really wish." Wang Wei has another name called Mo Jie, and he is nicknamed The Poet of Buddhism in later ages. So we can know that the poems of Wang Wei are the Wu of a lay Buddhist who studies Buddhism. Wu is very important in both the study of Taoism and the study of Buddhism.

Studying Taoism or Buddhism should be a man's daily assignment. If we study rationally, abandon all the distracting thoughts and try to truly show our real soul, one day we will understand the Taoism, acquire the ability of Wu and delivering all living creatures from torment.

3. Cultivate One's Characters from Details

Character of a man can be seen from the trivial matters in daily life. Such actions as spitting and littering everywhere, using vulgar language and so on seem trifling would gradually develop into one's character.

It is not serious that once a person accidentally spits on the ground. Sometimes, there are no spittoon tissue or toilet near around. Once the bad habits like spitting at will are formed in his early age, one can hardly be a white collar in his adulthood. It can be said that merely by reading books cannot one become a white collar who must be careful and patient and cultivated through completing trivia.

The development and change of characters and events in novels, dramas, movies and serials all evolve detail by detail. It is an incredible story that the parents are killed by their baby immediately after it was born. Hui Man-keung in the TV series *The Bund* becomes the head gangster step by step. At first, he engage in student strike, fighting and playing with knife and gun. Gradually, he began to injure others and finally committed murder.

Ban Chao in Later Han Dynasty once said, "For anyone who has ambition, detail is less important." while actually every step in his life is full of details. Ban Chao was born in a historian family, yet he was not interested in liberal arts. He used to be the civilian in charge of the memorial to the throne and official document, and was dismissed due to the small fault.

Being the civilian, he admired Zhang Qian who was sent to the

Western Regions as the ambassador on the diplomatic mission. He was unhappy of merely being a civilian and hoped to be a hero. Encouraged by a fortune-teller, he finally decided to give up the civilian to join the army and became a military attache. Hardworking, eloquent, knowledgeable and with the ability to seize opportunities, he led an army to the north and won the war against the invading Huns. At last, he was dispatched to the Western Region and got tremendous diplomatic achievements.

Liu Bei once said to his son Liu Chan in the will, "Do not fail to do good even if it's small; do not engage in evil even if it's small. " He admonished his son of being virtuous. The king won support from his people not only by his imperial power, but by his virtue and morality.

It is in conformity with the laws of development that the good deed comes from the minor matters and the great career is developed and accumulated from the small jobs. The philanthropist must start his charity career in small scale. Small beneficence continuously adds up to large. As he becomes rich, he final has the capability to carry out the charitable undertakings for the whole society. Rome was not built in a day. No one was born a sinister gangster, but the cumulative result of the small evils.

One's character is cultivated from the detail. The smallest good, like doing a favor by pushing the cart, shall be done; the smallest bad, even stealing a needle, shall not be done. There would be a peaceful world if everyone could cultivate his character from the smallest good.

4. Preventing Illness from Food and Troubles from Speech

Restraint is necessary for the people. It is certain that anybody who tries to do all the things he wants and behave unscrupulously would do harm to himself as well the others. One may get sick or poisoned if he doesn't choose food with care.

Fu Xuan in the Western Jin Dynasty wrote in *On Mouth*, "illness comes from food and trouble from speech." Fu Xuan had served successively as county magistrate, canton governor, regional guard officer and royal guard officer. He was removed from his position when getting old due to the political reasons. However, he was particular ahout the diet and enjoyed his later years at home.

Illness comes from food. It is recorded in *The Analects* of Confucius that uncooked food should not be eaten. In *Compendium of Materia Medica*, it is clearly pointed out that man could be killed instantly if he is not abstemious in eating and drinking. People can have better health and prolonged life is illness could be prevented from food。 Just as the old saying goes, "eating less in super and one will live till 99". It has been a medical common sense that illness comes from food in modern society and children are told about it from their parents and relatives.

Trouble comes from speech. He who talks much errs much. That is to say, careless speech may cause the unexpected accident. In China, talking is more of an kind of art. According to Confucianism, a gentleman should speak frankly and bluntly to repay enmity with justice; meanwhile, he also should be prudent in speech.

Talking at venture mighty cause trouble. If the careless speech is offensive to others and violate taboos, a beat and scold, even a fatal disaster would come out, which is nothing new in history and in real life. Careless talk is especially taboo in business. Arbitrary promise such as prolonging the warranty period and covering all the losses would encourage customers' desire to get more and abet them to escape from the responsibility on their part.

It would go wrong if the mouth serves as the only channel of information exchange and energy supplement. Meanwhile, other ways of communication, like letter, facial appearance and gesture, would leave unused.

Enough is enough. Things will develop in the opposite direction when they become extreme. Hands would lie waste if not used at all. Say what should be said and never say what shouldn't. To know what should be said and what shouldn't is as significant as the floodgate in the embankment. It can keep one safe. If a man take the responsibility that he couldn't afford to out of a false sense of pride, he must break his promise, and his long established reputation would be destroyed in a moment.

Illness comes from food and trouble from speech. Mouth should be used wisely.

5. Importance shall be attached to "格"

"格", a Chinese character, means grid literally. Children are afraid of learning to write Chinese characters, because they have to be written in grids which make them feel that they are fenced in.

"格" can be used to make a lot of collocations. One character added behind comes 格范 (paradigm), 格尺 (ruler), 格令 (grain), 格法 (law), 格条 (lattice bar), 格样 (standard), 格调 (style), etc.; and one character added in front comes 人格 (personality), 品格 (morals), 官格 (official creed), 国格 (national dignity), etc.

Personality is more commonly known as one's whole character and nature. People all live in an invisible grid in which his character, style and manner are formed, just like the freeze-frames in a movie. The grids are different, so the personality varies from one man to another, manifested as the differentiation of being introverted or extroverted, good or bad, restrained or publicized, thrift or extravagant, broad-minded or narrow-minded. Confucius said about a man that "At fifteen his mind was set on learning. At thirty he established his stand. At forty he had no more perplexities. At fifty he knew the mandate of Heaven. At sixty his ear was attuned." It can be understood that man's personality may change according to the different ages.

Morals refer to the virtue in the personality, the noble character. Nobody can be born good or evil. However, goodness and wickedness co-reside within one's mind. Along with the influence of surroundings in the environment, one has his own inclination of being a good man or evil one.

Official creed is the beliefs, principles, and opinions on how to be an official. According to Confucianism, the official is just like the chamberlain. The citizens should be regarded as their own children with both love and reason. In this way, the good official must be upright and incorruptible; while the bad official must be venal and corrupt. According to Legalists, what the official should follow is nothing but the legislation, which is the same with the local magistrates in Europe and America. The citizens are treated equally both in politics and legislation. In this way, the good official must perform his duties according to the law; while the bad official must be corrupt through misuse of law.

Different from personality or official creed, national dignity is the state or quality of being a separate and independent nation. In other words, it is the unique features on nationality, people, customs, language and script, which make one country distinguishable from the others. A country without its national dignity is not a real country.

In one word, the so-called "grid" here is the norms, the morals and virtues of being a perfect man, the standard in finishing a job, the regulations and laws a government should obey. A man will process his own personality with the norms in heart. Only by this can one be a gracious man with good manners.

Grid (格), "口" as its form, would become "國 (a traditional Chinese character, meaning the country)" when putting "或" inside; "国 (a simplified Chinese character, meaning the country)" when "玉" inside; "囚 (prisoner)" when "人" inside; and "固 (solid)" when "古" inside. The country won't last long if the government values the present more than the past and its people must live in unrest, feeling dizzy like sitting in the roller coaster. On the contrary, the country will be stable and prosperous if the government could learn lessons from the past and apply them to the current development.

6. No Blame attaches to the Unconscious Doer of Wrong, More Blame Attaches to the Conscious Doer of Wrong.

"Unconscious" here particularly refers to the the state of being an infant who is lack of knowledge and common sense, or ignorant. It doesn't mean be in a coma. It is humble for an adult to admit his ignorance that there are so many things he doesn't know. According to Confucianism, he who is ignorant is an inferior man, has conscience a worthy man, and believes in the heresy an evil man.

People, born unconsciousness yet with the ability to learn, are endowed with intelligence. Being unconscious is the normal state of an infant, and is also the motive force for an adult to learn. The young people are so innocent and frank that they always tell the truth. It's not their fault, rather the essence for a man to survive. One the contrary, the omniscient and omnipotent superman is unable to stay on the earth at all.

Because of ignorance, people have the sentiments of admiration and loyalty and have the pursuit of religious faith. The great scientists and truth seekers are more likely to admit their ignorance and never persist in their prejudice so as to approach to the truth. Newton and Einstein were great scientists of this kind.

What a man fear most is not the ignorance, but the state of an arrogant youngster that considers the illiteracy as wisdom, the fallacy as truth and the heresy as science. The arrogant people would talk nonsense, overflow with vanity and self-conceit, and behave willfully and wildly. Their peacockish behavior would sow the seeds of crime

sooner or later.

The arrogant people are unlearned and incapable. Their hearts are just like deserts with not even a blade of grass grows and the kerosene lamp lacking of fuel, which is more dangerous than being ignorant and impoverished. Ignorance can be changed through learning. The arrogant people dare to to do all kinds of evils, just like one-winged stormy petrel flapping and crying in the storm. The ignorant are blind, while the arrogant are mad.

As the English saying goes, Knowledge is the light, and ignorance is the dark. And in Italian, there is a famous saying reads, "Ignorance is the night of wisdom. " From this it is clear that if the people don't acquire knowledge through learning, their hearts will be covered by darkness and deluded by fallacy. And they may become the dangerous people or terrorists who lust for the crime.

Out of ignorance, people are afraid of God's punishment and devil's harassment. And then they will avoid the evil doings. It is a good thing. The worst misfortune of life is that a man is controlled by such evils as being unscrupulous and being without the bottom line. If so, the people would become mercenary, lust for rights, control the armies with the heresy, force the masses to violate the virtue and morality and commit crime in public.

Socrates once said, "One thing I know, that is I know nothing". All his life, he was trying to guide the youth to come back with the belief "virtue is knowledge", and taught them to be more patriotic and devout. In one word, no blame should be attached to the ignorant baby; adults who commit a crime should be executed; and more blames should be attached to the conscious doer of wrong.

7. Karma and its Positive or Negative Side

Chinese people believe in fate. Buddhism believes in Karma, Confucianism believes in predestined affection, and Taoism believes in lucky chance.

In the field of philosophy, Karma refers to the chain of cause and effect, both direct and indirect. Karma, meaning the cause-effect relation in Buddhism which is not as broad as its definition in philosophy, is the belief that one's actions in this life affect all his future lives.

Karma is frequently used by Buddhist to explain the relations in current life; that is to say, the reason why people could get together is that they already had some kind of relationship in their previous life. To make it simple, Mr. A slapped Mr. B in the previous life, that's why Mr. B slaps Mr. A back in this life. In the Buddhist legend, Sakyamuni in his previous life was the Wholesome King (the king of the deer) who was kind to King Brahmadatta (the king ruling in Benares). And in this life, Sakyamuni becomes the master of the previous King Brahmadatta.

In Confucianism and Taoism, predestined affection and lucky chance have the same meaning with Karma, although different in wording. There are some lyrics, "Love is always short and simple. But why the people have to leave when the music is over? If there is the next life, is the promise of this life still to keep? Since the love of this life is hard to come by, please don't give it up rashly with regret."

Good match, meaning the positive Karma, is the reward in this or next life gained from the good deeds one did previously. In Chinese Tang poetry, it reads, "New friendship is decried by the secular and frivolous world, worse still, the old friends have been long lost and no affinity can be found." Good match includes finding a good job, admitted by a ideal school, having a happy marriage and having a kind mother-in-law, etc.

Bad luck, meaning the negative Karma, is the evil result in this or next life due to one's previous wrong doings. It is stated in Buddhism that "Six evils around prevent one from pure heart." and "The inner

vexation may result in external evils", etc. According to the doctrine of the Buddhism, it is the Karma that brings about the good job, retardation in scholar, broken up family and so on.

The TV serial *All Men Are Mortal* narrates about the stories four people in their previous life and this life. In 1930s. The playboy Su Yunfei (in previous life), Bund Triad member, fell in love with Qin Wanying, girl of a rich family. Su revenged Qin by killing the head gangster Pan Siye, murderer of Qin's father. At the same time, he had relations with Duan Xiaoyu, Pan's concubine. After the death of Pan, Su died unnaturally, too. In the year 1990, Su Yunfei (in this life) met the restaurant waitress Shen Xiaohui, the reincarnation of Qin Wanying. Su didn't fall in love with Shen in this life, but got to know Xiang Lan, the reincarnation of Duan Xiaoyu, through her. At last, Su lost his heart on Xiang and married her. In this life, Su was terribly afflicted by his boss, Chen, the reincarnation of Pan Siye. It was Karma that brought Su, Qin, Duan and Pan together in two lives. In this life, the Karma among Su, Qin and Duan was positive, while negative between Su and Pan.

It is mysterious about Karma, and its positive/negative sides. Although hard to believe, it conceives the idea that people should perform benevolent actions. So, it helps to make a better world to believe in Karma.

8. On the Impasse of Life

The impasse of life can be described with two Chinese idioms-ambush from ten sides and Chu song from four sides-both refer to the desperate final hours of Xiangyu, surrounded by enemies, isolated and without help. This is what one fear most in his life.

Dated back to the Western Jin Dynasty, Chen Shou, a historiographer, noted down in the *History of the Three Kingdoms*, "Xiang Yu fell into the ambush and killed by Emperor Kao Tsu of the

Han Dynasty". This concerns about the ending of the War Between Chu and Han. XiangYu, a brave, arrogant and ever-victorious hero, was totally defeated by Liu Bang and Han Xin and committed suicide. Xian Yu used to despise Liu Bang and abandon Han Xin, and finally fell into the hopeless situation.

In Yuan verse and *The Romance of the Three Kingdoms*, the idiom "ambush from ten sides" were often be used in the war stories to describe the heavy besieges. XiangYu was ambushed on all sides in military impasse. In the night, Xiang Yu heart the Chu song all around and mistaken that the Han army had taken his position. He thought it was the will of God that he must die. Thus he lost his morale and bade his final farewell to his beloved Yuji. Xiang Yu broke the siege and withdrew to the Wujiang River, with only 28 soldiers left. Then, he refused to cross the river and make a comeback. At last, he killed himself at the riverside.

Xiang Yu, as a man, is unparalleled in history. However, there are so many people are in the hard situation which is similar to Xiang Yu. Once there was boss who was so successful and influential in business that everyone knows about his. As the saying goes, business is as fierce as war and competition is cutthroat. Finally he went into bankruptcy. He tried to find a job and in vain. In addition, his case was placed on file for investigation and prosecution. He might be put into prison because of bribery. At the same time, the drug dealer of whom his daughter, a drug addict, fell foul asked him for money. Besides, his wife left him. Even his lover wanted to get him into troubles when her failed to asked for dally money. He wanted to kill himself, but ending up with the disability.

As the paragon of the whole creation, humans will eventually survive if there is the spirituality. In other words, the hardship will never last. If a man could take the natural course, he will feel hopeful in predicament sooner or later.

The so-called impasse or predicament of life are mostly caused by the people's radical action and irrationality.

It's the most unfortunate that humans beings have evolved from the four-legged animal to the creature standing on two feet. Once the people dwelt under the vine and fig tree. Gradually, they became completive and engaged in the endless war. Once the monkey is believed to be humans' ancestor, the doctrine of adaption would become the doctrine of war. And everybody would become Xiang Yu finally. If humans are defined as the political animal, they will be pushed into a brute urban battlefield.

So don't be Xiang Yu who was full of glories through his life, but totally defeated at last, even impossible to acquire a peaceful end.

9. Laughters in Married Life

Marriage is the a blessing in one's life, yet the source of many annoyance. So marriage brings about both happiness and sorrow.

The couples laugh the most when they are young. For the character and temperament are less stable in youth. The young get married for love. Without mutual interference from parents, not being burdened by children, if the job is not bad, due to attraction of opposite and similar tastes, thus resonance between lovers come. The couples can't help laughing out. Generally, young couples laugh more often and loud.

Man and wife laugh even more in wedding celebration. Certainly, there are exceptions. For someone who is forced to get married would be frowning at marriage celebration, however, this is rarely seen. In general, the day for wedding is full of joyfulness. The two start from mutual attraction and affection to entrusting and committing each other for lifetime. The hardships they experienced would be like the mellow and fine scent in wine production. No matter the couples are young or not, they are all brimming with smiles at the wedding party, especially the elder ones who could not get married for various reasons when in

youth.

All couples wish to enjoy merry laughter forever. It is natural and normal to hunt for happiness and keep away from sorrow. So it is the same as couples get along with each other. *The Infinite Life Sutra* reads, "The pleasant words and a joyful face won't lead to disharmony". That means husband and wife should get on with each other with all smiles and sweetness, so as not to influenced by crabby and vinegarish temperament which possibly results in quarrel, fight, even divorce. The earlier laughter became the self-mockery: how silly we were at that time!

The family establishment will bring about responsibilities as well, such as who wins the bread and who does the housework, etc. In ancient times, men work outside and women took more household labor. The family is similar to a limited liability company and each one has distinct duties. Thus the marriage lasts for a long time. So the analogy of the lute and psaltery played in harmony as the wedded bliss and the stories of husband and wife treating each other with respect and courtesy were well spread. However, great changes have taken place in modern families. Both the husband and wife work outside and do housework together to support the family. Duties are no longer as clear as the waters of the Jing River and the Wei River, thus disputes and contradictions inevitably come.

It may not be that bad to have arguments and conflicts. It is just as the water running along mountains, sometimes the high waves slapping against the cliffs. The co-existence between man and wife has an ever-lasting influence. It is like a long river runs among high mountains. Sometimes a small brook warbles over its rocky bed, weaving into the winding stream. It glides through the valley gently with a murmur. In narrow channel, the flow rushes while in wide it moves slowly. Only a few good matches could be regarded as Darby and Joan, the majority are like frying pan and its slice which fight for whole life but never be

apart.

Where there is a frying pan, there is a slice. Husband and wife fall out only at the very beginning. As long as the pan and slice are not smashed, the couples would grow old together.

Man and wife are willing to laugh together with days going on. As *The Book of Songs* goes, "To hold your hand, to grow old with you", and this is the finest smile.

10. Marriages are not Shackles

Once the spousal relationship was settled down, the marriage and family will come into being. Usually, the family form of a husband and a wife, a house and a yard is mostly in Europe and America. And that of a husband and several wives and multiple rooms and yards was mainly in Asia and Africa. Phenomenally, the families display a function of offspring reproduction, venereal diseases precaution, healthy childbirth and labor division, etc.

The family is the social cell instead of a jail. Thus marriage couldn't be developed as fetters to shackle the normal life of men and women. Given that men and women don't share spouse relationship and name and completely shut family out of life, the tribe wouldn't be different from whorehouse. Obscene matters such as fornication, homosexuals would emerge in endlessly, leading to country destruction. The cultivation development of nomadic tribes is the same as family forming and stabilizing which makes the marital status and responsibility clear.

It is said there are two originations for the name of "zhangfu" (husband). The husband feared his wife's unfaithfulness and heeled behind her one zhang (ten feet) away. The other saying is the women hope to be protected, thus to find ten-feet high giants as husbands to avoid being robbed as wife by others by force. The historiographers will tell the truth, but what we are sure is, at least, marriage and family

have the dual functions of giving birth to healthy babies and stabilizing the society.

And what we almost certainly is, at the beginning, marriage doesn't involve too much love. It is mainly for stabilizing the whole tribe and preventing wives snatching, also for meeting the demand for women themselves which was implied by the partial "女（woman）" of Chinese characters "婚姻"（marriage）

Seemingly, the process of how marriage and family are developed is simple. However, for orangutans and monkeys, probably they won't have marriage and family like the human beings even after they naturally evolve for 100 hundred million years. Logically we mean it is providence. And the historical legends confirm that "man is the soul of the universe".

From the Chinese bible, *the Book of Changes*, we know "Men tend to work more outside the home, while women take on more of the household labor." It is the principle for stable conjugal relations. Thus glory, responsibility and faithfulness come into being. However, the fall out and divorces also exist.

From the historical recordings, the dissolute affairs between human beings were increasingly severe. The Europe, West Asia and North Africa didn't manage to stop the licentious affairs, leading to thousand of civilized nations being demised or self-destruction. The establishment of the doctrines of Confucius and Mencius in China helps the country last to 1911. A. D. , the end of Qing Dynasty. Women were not allowed to get adultery but remarried.

In Earlier Song Dynasty, Fan Zhongyan's mother got remarried for bringing about her son, not for impulse, passion and chaos in private emotional life. The husbands should be faithful and loyal and the wives should be chaste and pure.

11. "Face" is Given by the Public

"Face" is a kind of glory relevant to one's status in the eastern interpersonal relationship. It is hard to give a clear and affirmative definition to "Face". Generally speaking, it refers to the esteem needed by the members of a family, a party or a country according to the traditional customs. It is some kind of significance rather than contempt, mockery or drollery.

"For the sake of one's face" is frequently said by the Chinese. In the Kokang language, there are similar wordings, such as "save one's face", "give the face" and so on. The "face" here refers to the spiritual and ideological needs, including honor, fame and respect, etc., i. e. the humans' social features put forward by the scholars.

The social requirements determine the needs of face. Men care about their official position. Women care about their family background. The post is classified into different ranks. Such needs as the disparity are all related to the "face". Importance is attached to the social features by the easterners who have a strong sense of "face". For men taking a concubine and women committing adultery, "face" matters. Few of such people can be found as have not even the slightest sense of "face". The concept of "Face" also exists among the westerners, much weaker than the easterners.

It can be seen that "face", a kind of dignity and honor out of psychological need, is given by the public. It was relevant to the Chinese social "face" that Han Xin retired and returned home after conferred the title of King and Xiang Yu felt too ashamed to go back home after breaking out the encirclement of the Battle of Gaixia.

The so-called public are also named as the masses, the common people, the people, the crowd, the folk, the civilian and so on, among which "the people" is most widely used and can be traced back to the story Wang Jin settled down in Shijiazhuang in the book *Water Margin*.

The people's power comes from the public opinion, assembly and revolt. They save the "face" of their own leader's, and strip of the "face" of the revolted. What the tyrannical governments do is to deprive of its people's right to have the "face". To make it simple, they play political games and press the people to become shameless.

To sum up, in Western Europe, Scandinavia, and Northern America, the people's power merges into the civil rights, which are under the protection of law. According to the constitutional system in Europe and America, the officials and the polices are all public servants. Where there is the Constitution and the law, there is the power.

As one of the people's weapons, satire, especially the jokes and anti-humors on jobs and politics, is used to mock the fatuous and tyrannical rulers, for instance, Strange stories from a Chinese Studio in ancient China and the Modern Wuxia.

In the world, a man without any sense of shame is doomed to be mocked. The ruler that tries to fool its people will eventually outsmart oneself and lose face in front of its people.

12. Real Happiness Comes from True Love

Judging from the appearance outwardly, Human beings have not evolved according to Darwin's theory of evolution. Yet, the development of human intelligence has vividly verified his theory. Through the evolution of human society, where there is the true love in marriage, there is the real happiness.

It is Chinese traditional moral principle that there should be no communication between man and woman before getting married, which must be complied with strictly. The true love is beyond "Five Differences".

Firstly, beyond the difference in age. Reportedly, Yan Zheng, Confucius' mother, married 66-year-old Shu Lianghe, his father, when

she was less than 20 years old. They got married at Yeyi in the ancient state of Lu (Shangdong Province), and the father was 40 years older than the mother. There is no historical report about their affection, but it can be reasoned that they loved other so much that the mother didn't remarry for 14 years since the death of the father, even life was hard. Confucius's mother is well known for scrupulously keeping the woman's virtue. Mother's morality influenced Confucius a lot and he finally became a man of noble character. He married the daughter of a noble family at the age of 20. King of the State of Lu congratulated them on the birth of their child.

Secondly, beyond the difference of ethnic group. In ancient China, defenses were set up against the foreign people only for the sake of protecting its civilization, yet the intermarriage was allowed. Parents of Duke Wen of Jin were intermarried between Chinese people and Xirong people. In Han Dynasty, it was a diplomatic convention that the Chinese people and Huns people were intermarried through which the relation between the two nations were cemented. "Zhaojun Goes Beyond the Great Wall as a Bride" is a much-told story in Chinese history with wide popularity. Han Dynasty also carried out the policy of "connection through marriage" in Han Dynasty were also carried out with Turkic, Tubo, Huihe and other ethnic groups.

Thirdly, beyond the difference of nationality. Before Yuan Dynasty, almost all of the intermarriages between China and other nations were for political and diplomatic reasons. There is no historical record about the free courtship in non-governmental circles. However, it was commonly seen that a Chinese married a foreigner since the Republic of China. For example, Su Manshu's father lived together with a Japanese woman and Lu Xun's younger brother married a Japanese wife.

Fourth, beyond the difference of education background. As religion, Marriage has nothing to do with intellectual factors like rationality and knowledge, but with love, prelife, family and relations, etc. which contribute to the chance to get married. Hu Shi married Jiang Dongxiu, a bound-feet woman without formal education, due to the tradition of arranged marriage. Even though, their emotional life was getting better in the social unrest.

Fifth, beyond the difference of profession. In India, marriage between the people with the profession of high-grade and of low-grade is forbidden due to the caste mark. In China, such discrimination does not exist for most of the time. Even there is, it is just the family provision rather than the social system. At the end of Ming Dynasty, Liu Rushi, a famous prostitute, was married by Qian Qianyi, a high-ranking official. 36-year-old difference in age, the couple had the entirely different professions, yet fell in love and got married.

Owning to the diversity of sex, age and stratum, there are variety of differences between man and woman. However, there is no disparity exists in love. All in all, real happiness comes from true love.

13. Five Types of Virtue of Individuals

Both Oriental and Western culture stress on individual virtues. Among all kinds of virtues, justice and credibility are characteristic for westerners while the Oriental are inclined to benevolence and mercifulness. The five types of virtues a man should be equipped in China, in the light of goodness, namely are "温" (temperateness), "良" (kindness), "恭" (respect), "俭" (frugality) and "让" (courtesy).

"温" means warmth. The concept of warmth literally indicates tender feelings, expressing soothing mildness and sincerity. This is usually more of a feminine phrase but also fits in many masculine context. Even a heroic swordman has a self of warmth and tenderness. What a charm it is when one can spread warmth to others to make them emotionally worry-free! The shining star is most phenomenal in the

night sky, so it is warmth in the human world. The shining star is most phenomenal in the night sky, so is is warmth in the human world. Nothing is crueler than the radical attempt that make warmth dispersed.

"良" is the state of fineness, specifically meaning excellent and beautiful. Staying with men of fine temperament is like river running smoothly through a broad watercourse. Coming in good terms with others require a man to have a kind heart. One proof is what is said in *the Book of Odes*："With such harmonious love, all will be happy and peaceful. " and "a quince she threw to me, a jade pendant I gave her in return. This is no a requital, but to show that I'd love her forever. "

"恭" means respect, which is one of the most valued quality in ancient times. Taking solemn salute to the respectable senior and guest, men looking straight at women and showing respect to the elderly and personage is the practice of "恭". In the time of Emperor Wu Di of the Han Dynasty, even the county magistrate treated the gifted scholar Sima Xiangru with high regards.

"俭" literally means frugality in terms of being economical in expense and modest in temperament. Our ancestors cultivate morality just for make social relationship and convention simple and clear. Restraint and frugality disperses ostentation and extravagance, limiting material desire to a trickle that runs long. That explains why ancient society developed in a sustainable manner while the modern world dashes like in a sprint.

"让" means give precedence to others and it's the most important feature of the Confucian gentleman's magnanimity. Other than the pretentious declining to accept, gentlemen give precedence with rules and modesty. In the eyes of Confucius, ruling the country with magnanimity can solve any problems it may encounter, otherwise magnanimity will be in disorder itself. Magnanimity is a mental rule that leads to self-discipline. Guiding the people with courtesy and there would be no conflict. So does magnanimity applies to everything? Not

really. A gentleman should be duty-bound and take boldly on what justice is called for.

In *Lv's Commentaries of History* it says "Wealth elevates the decoration of a room and virtues elevate one's morality." Hypocrites hatred the five virtues, criticizing them as a symbol of slavery, which only results in prevalence of wickedness. One's life will be complete and happy only when the five virtues are carried and practiced all the way.

14. Conform to the Good Conscience Rather Than the Bad

Conformity refers to the psychology or ideology of following the public behavior and opinions. It is a normal and inevitable state at the time of baby and childhood, in which joys and sorrows are expressed by crying and smiling; the public opinion and forces are brought out by the unanimous voice and the unite efforts.

People usually experience the rebellious phase in adolescence, especially for boys, who is eager to show that they are already adults through the struggle against the grown-ups' excessive intervention and control. Someone with the rebellious personality is liable to rebel. People of this kind are less apt to listen to each other. If they get together, they would have divided opinions. It is a good thing for a group of superior men to be leaderless for each of them can make their own contribution. However, for the inferior men, they would fall into the state of disunity like a sheet of loose sand.

In the situation that all the people unanimously comply with conventions, one may become a maverick or expresses an opposing view due to the reasons of standing out conspicuously for the sake of certain responsibility (e. g. Zhuang Liang who assassinated Emperor Qinshihuang in ancient China) or to stick the virtue and morality while others degenerate (e. g. Wang Fuzhi who became a hermit in Mt

Heng in the Qing Dynasty)

Those who follow others are criticized as being mediocre and timid. However, it is righteous for a man to follow the crowd if he does the good deed spontaneously and help the others without the intention to be repaid to feel at ease and justified. For example, a member of the criminal organization or cult renounce his bad cause and join the camp of justice and the others follow him one by one. By no means is it timid and mediocre that people conform to the good conscience rather than the bad. It is kindness and righteousness that our hearts follow.

Only the concept of "public", or the consciousness of serve the people and the society, or the idea of keeping family and country in the mind, could one always take into account the national interests with less selfishness and more dedication the society. Those are the good people as we always praised.

The good people, who are with the sense of compassion and shame as exit in the nature of girls and kids, apt to be benevolent and chivalrous, like Song Jiang in *Water Margin*, who is good at working together with others and maintaining their benefits. Those who conform to the good conscience are broad-minded and work for the benefits of all. Then can take a broad and long-term view.

15. National Behaviors Draw on Advantages and Avoid Disadvantages

National power consciousness is to respect the strong and bully the weak. That does not apply to the personal benevolent character. Parents show special love to their kids and take good care of them usually because they are young and vulnerable. It is also benevolence that propels the chivalric to be keen for righteousness as well. However, it is another case when it comes to a nation for its drawing on advantages. The nation always pursues the pragmatism. Fairness would be advocated in the domestic affairs, while benefit for the nation itself

would be put in the first place pertaining to the external ones.

In comparison with Europe, importance were attached on the overall interests among the ancient people in Asia and Africa continents, especially those ancient nations in the Central plain, both the united nations and small divided ones. when conflicting with the benefits of the whole, people were asked to sacrifice their own interests, even their love.

By sacrificing the individual interests, a nation is able to address problems among divergent opinions and chaotic indecisions. The nation would stick together and be more powerful. Yuejia army of the Southern Song Dynasty really impressed the Jin's counterpart by making them realize that "it is easy to move a mountain but difficult to hinder the Yuejia army". Yuefei as the leader, the Yuejia army consistently stuck to the belief that "they will never occupy the peasants' houses because of frigidity, never rob them anything because of starvation". For them, the personal enjoyment was sacrificed and transformed into the power of defeating the enemies.

Taking the citizens of Athens Greece as an example, they would not make such sacrifices. For enjoyment, they allowed one to marry his niece at incest and inevitably encountered Waterloo in Sparta war. In order to power their army, women in Sparta were allowed to conceive the baby of other men with better fertility instead of their husbands. Consequently, Sparta could never be defeated by Greece, and Greece could never be a united nation.

In terms of the seven nations Qi, Chu, Yan, Han, Zhao, Wei, Qin in the Warring States Period, because the upper class in six of the states except for Qin could not disclaim their privileges, some political reforms conducted by Li Li, Wu Qi, Shen Buhai all failed at last. And for Wei, Chu, Han, the devotion to plebeians' fairness and interests was actually stifled by the self-importance of the upper class.

With the determined support of Qin Xiaogong, the political reforms

carried out by ShangYang including abolishing the well-field system and encouraging cultivating lands, distributing national taxes to all walks, promoting those who fought hard and bravely for the nation to the army general. Thought these reforms, interpersonal conflicts were suppressed. Qin had enjoyed its prosperity for one century and eventually conquered others.

In modern times, Some countries started the brutal wars in order to their own advantages. In World War Ⅱ, America and Japan both suffered heavy losses in Okinawa war, but they entered into alliance with each other again due to the common interests.

Collaborations among countries can only be carried out when there exist the common interests.

16. Toil is Bliss

There is a Guangdong vernacular which goes: Hanganqiansan. It is the synonymous with the idioms that " Get something for nothing,", "profit at other's expense", or "sit idle and enjoy the fruits of other's work ". "Get something for nothing" was firstly recorded in the book *The Sayings of Confucius-Take Office*, "to get the things needed from the nearest, one may get it without much efforts." Hangaqiansan, literally, means that the money obtained without hard work is hard to keep and easy to be used.

It probably explained the rationale of the social structure with the intellectual, the farmer, the artisan and the merchant in the ancient Chinese natural economy era. The head-worker (the intellectuals) managed the country. The ruler administrated with benevolence, righteousness and courtesy and without greed, establishing a bright society. The labor-worker (the farmers, the artisans and the merchants) were the managed. The Policy Emphasizing Agriculture at the Expense of Commerce was implemented because at the time, the farmer could get the most profits, the artisans get the medium and the

merchants get the less.

This is the reason why the ancient Chinese empires could exist and survive for thousands of years. Those dynasties which had overemphasized business and underestimated agriculture all inevitably declined within 300 years. One will get what he has sowed. More work means more gains and same is true with less work and no work at all. Making money by means of legal acts gives people a peaceful mind and conscience. The rule of mutual promotion and restraint among things can also be applied to hard work. One will only treasure what they attained through hard work.

The lazybones and bummers are inevitably bored. And being bored means the absence of happiness mentally. Freeloaders are not satisfied with what he has already get and always want more. To gratify his desire, they would resort to the illegal way which impair the human nature. They can never experience the happiness of hard work and will degenerated into the incorrigible spendthrift.

There is another Guangdong vernacular saying "无灵无难". "无灵" (Wuling) literally means being without soul and heart, or more commonly, brainless and naive. There is a Chinese idiom goes, " God sends good fortune to fools". In ancient China, the naive people would always survive in the officialdom, for they were mild even though without much money. Thus, an idiot would have the chance to be an emperor. However, such kind of people have gradually lost their influence ever since the Song Dynasty.

People who don't take things too much to heart can lead a elegant unstrained life. They don't care others' critiques and face the hardships with laughters. Without annoyance and wicked idea, they are full of the vigor of youth from a psychological point of view, the Wuling "fools" can be tolerant to the shortcomings of themselves as well as the others. They can let go of any negative critiques with a smile, just as a Chinese proverb goes "problems can be solved with a smile". Such people are

capable of standing out in the competition of official circles.

There are no such animosities or worries that can last over one night. Being Wuling will make a persevering man who can conquer all the difficulties.

17. Cause and Effect

Cause and effect, or reasons and consequences, is a pair of concepts which is frequently used in religious, philosophical and scientific fields. Orthodox Taoism stresses pure inaction and immortal. Where ignorance is bliss, it is folly to be wise. Buddhist, especially Buddhism explicitly discussed karma, believes that previous life events (for example, being killed, being abused, etc., or doing good things and performing good virtues, etc.) will all be converted into the corresponding good results or evil consequences in current life through certain connections (family, livestock, classmates, colleagues etc.).

The rule of cause and effect really matters when it comes to the pursuit of fame and fortune. As the old saying goes, "One false step brings everlasting grief", to avoid such mistakes, one should listen to the instructions of masters and parents and abide by their rules, and a student should take read books with cautions. With a clear idea of the connections among behaviors and results, one shall treat everything with kindness, refrain from doing evil deed and not meddle in other's business. Do unto others as you would be done. One would enjoy the hidden happiness out of suffering.

It is difficult for an ordinary people to explain the rule of cause and effect. One may have a feeling that good will be rewarded with good, and evil with evil when the time comes. However, this explanation about cause and effect is based on the feel and not that precise, especially for a youngster because of their inexperience and unstable emotion. As for the elder with more experience, the understanding would be much better.

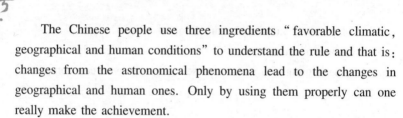

The Chinese people use three ingredients "favorable climatic, geographical and human conditions" to understand the rule and that is: changes from the astronomical phenomena lead to the changes in geographical and human ones. Only by using them properly can one really make the achievement.

So the old normally hold the view that one should always try his best and leave the rest to God's will. And that also brings the truth that what one sows he reaps and the everlasting law in the animal world about their reproduction.

"Four Causes Theory" (material cause, formal cause, efficient cause, purpose cause) of the ancient Greek carries a more deep academic gravity when approached from the philosophical angle which represents analyzing elements, developing an insight into forms, finding out motivation, seeking for purposes (from micro to macro world, from the mankind to destiny).

Folk experience, religious instructions, scientific rationality and rationality theories will be looked down upon when one is indulged in presuming to be brave and creature comforts. But he will be mocked by the rule although he seems to have achieved enjoyments and career success at the cost of losing health, hurting people and even their life.

18. Choosing a Right Profession

As for choosing a profession, there is an old Chinese saying goes, "Men are afraid of the wrong choice of profession, and women the wrong choice of husband".

"Profession" in KoKang is polysemous. It can be used to refer to the classification of jobs, such as the police who is in charge of public security, and the soldier who is responsible for garrisoning and pacifying the rebellion. Or it refers to certain industries. In historical records,, Xiang Yu who always fellow his heart and Cao Cao who was chivalrous and accommodating, yet not worked for particular line of

business both were heroes in trouble times and didn't engaged in such industry as agriculture, forestry, animal husbandry and fishery. In *Family instructions of Master Yan*, "In the monks and nuns profession, most of them are not pure..." Profession here means professional skill and standard.

In the peace and prosperous times of ancient China, wealth and inventions had promoted the industry development. However, there are always some people who are wise and chivalrous at the turning point in the era. They didn't work for the industries talked above, and were not thought highly of, only to stick to the career they chose and achieve great accomplishment.

Liu Bang, Xiang Yu, Cao Cao and so on were not born for work related with manual labor, so were many Buddhists and Taoists, yet they also concern with some professions. For example, in *Report of the Regions West of Great Tang*, it read that the monks in Lan Mo kingdom had no achievement in profession. Profession here refers to the Buddhists' doctrines and principles to follow.

In general, profession means the categories of the productive operation, such as agriculture, forestry, animal husbandry and fishery and so on. To be specific, it can be regarded as the categories of jobs. For example, fishery can be divided into fishing industry and fishnet manufacturing industry, etc., Medicine can be divided into medical industry (which is subdivided into traditional Chinese medical science and western medical science) and Pharmaceutical industry (which is subdivided into Chinese herbal medicine and Western medicine). In one word, profession here means all walks of life.

Just like the road has the properties of roadbed, length, width, standard and grade, once the profession was formed, the corresponding rules and regulations about the communication and management will be formed. The industry of forestry, automobile and banking, etc. all have their own regulations. A few people may try to break the

profession regulation.

In most parts of the world, agriculture had overweighted industry and commerce for a long time. Until recent times, the situation has reversed. Agricultural production is a sustainable development, while industry and commerce will destroy the natural resources and never restore.

Humans develop their modern society with high energy consumption, which amounts to drive a Benz towards a cliff at a high speed. For the individuals, a woman who marries a bad guy will suffer a life-time. A man following a wrong career, just like a public speaking using a machine gun on the battle field, will achieve nothing.

19. City and Guild

The division of work is quite simple in rural area. Man goes out to work for bread and wife is responsible for household duties. On the contrary, in the city, the trades are subdivided clearly into many different industries. The urban culture and civic society are formed naturally, in which the families are gathered in community, the guilds operate under certain regulations, and government administrate the public affairs, etc. Thus, the whole society adaptively changed its organization.

"城市", meaning the city, is a compound by two KoKang words "城" and "市", standing for two major functions of the city-defense and trade. Inside the city walls, the residents live together. Streets and markets are formed. At first, people "traded in the market during daytime". Later, the morning market, noon market, and night Market were gradually developed. The solid wall ensured security of the city, and the market made it prosperous.

Therefore, the city becomes densely populated and flourished with the developed industry and commerce. A city and its surrounding villages, just like the sun and its nine planets, naturally establish an

regional system, and the city gradually become the center of politics, economy and culture. For any naturally developed city, it mainly started from the village to the town, and the county after building its government.

Commonly speaking, the city is just like the large forest which is to all kinds of birds, and the intellectuals, farmers, artisans and merchants all gather in the county. With the the increase of counties, the State which is larger in scale than and exercise the jurisdiction over the county came into being. Naturally, the government officials, the landlords, the principal merchants all went to cities with their families except for the borders. Gradually, the living areas, the streets, the clinics, the schools, the markets, the palaces, the parks and so on were formed.

Guild was originally derived from the ancient city. It had the rigorous regulations to ensured the members' rights and responsibilities, as well as maintained its industrial monopoly. Two major kinds of the guild that the handicraft industry guild (craftsman chamber) and the commercial guild (merchant chamber) were established to coordinate the relationships and conflicts in the same industry and between the industry and government. Therefore, people in the same industry would not become the irreconcilable enemies.

In ancient China, guild was born in the Sui and Tang Dynasties. In the Chinese idiom " Sale of products according to trade demand and price changes", "trade" refers to a particular business or industry, or trade guild. there are " the brocade trade" and " the gold and silver Trade", etc In Song dynasty, the number of guilds in the big cities were over ten, and the hundreds and thousands of people had participated in these guilds. Later, the guilds were mixed with the underworld gangs, and intertwined with the secret societies in the late Qing Dynasty.

Guild emerged in Western Europe at the same period of the

Southern Song Dynasty of China, with a aim to resist arbitrary taxation of the feudal lords. Various kinds of guild were established according to the different trades. The craftsman worded with his assistants and apprentices. Regulations and rules were stipulated on how to promote the assistant and apprentice to a real craftsman. European cities were born with the commune character which came from the Germanic rural tradition. The people live in a city was called the citizen.

Guilds in western Europe flourished at the time of China's Yuan Dynasty, as if the history of the guild in the Tang and Song Dynasties recurred.

20. Law and Rights

The law evolved from the regulations of family and clan in China, while from the rules of city-state and commune in Europe. If the law came from the clan regulation, the family would closely link with the clan. In this circumstance, the clan must have a superior position over the individual.

If the law originated from the rules of city-states and commune, the family which only functions as the place to live would have a relatively low status. In this case, individuals must be superior to the State.

In the country with the individual over the clan such as the ancient Greek, Roman Empire and some modern countries like the United Kingdom, America and France, the individual identity and hereditary title, treated as valuable as one's life, are strictly stipulated in the law. The law were initially made to maintain the rights and interests of the loyal and noble family. Such privilege infuriated the masses and they began to escape and rise up to resist. Finally, there came the law for all the individuals.

In China, the clan has a higher positior than the individual. In ancient days, all social strata from nobles to slaves took great pride in

having a large family, which was also the goal they were striving for. Therefore, people generally stress the moral principles of being humane and righteous and would sacrifice themselves for their parents, families and nation. The nobleman learned to treat his parents with great respect and brothers with courtesy as a child. The story that Kong Rong gave up his rights and gave away the bigger pears at the age of 7 has been passed down from generation to generation with great compliment.

However, It doesn't mean that people could enjoy more individual rights in the European countries than in all the dynasties of Chinese history. In fact, people enjoyed the individual rights, such as the personal power and property ever since the Spring and Autumn and Warring States Periods. The word " 权利 (rights)" was invented by Xun Zi and continue to be used by the subsequent historiographers. During the same period, the majority of the population in Europe were the maltreated slaves. It was the nobles who had individual rights. In ancient times, the European nobles were much more selfish than the Chinese officials.

Two different kinds of traditions to obtain rights were formed. In China, the rights and privileges which originally belonged to the noble families or the officials were deprived of and distributed to the masses, that is, to all the social strata including the intellectual, the farmer, the artisan and the merchant. Yet in Europe, the rights were obtained through struggle and stipulated in the constitutional legal system which is established in the long run of history, from the ancient Greece and Rome, the medieval warfare which lasted for over 2000 years, till Spain, Portugal, Italy, Netherlands, the UK, France, Germany and Russia in modern times.

In the Republic of China, the consciousness of rights struggle had been popularized through the republican constitution and national education.

It is Chinese traditional virtue that to give away privileges with courtesy. It had been cultivated from the Xia Dynasty to the Qing

Dynasty and applied to different ranks and classes, whether in family or in public. Yet it is going to disappear nowadays and in urgent need of revival.

21. Capital and profits

Looking back into Chinese history, the countries, located at Central Plains between Yellow River and Yangtze River, had been the first to consider and contributed a lot to the problems of capital and profits. While Europe is through ancient Greece and Rome, the medieval kingdoms of up to two thousand years of subjugation and genocide campaign, to the modern and contemporary Spanish, Portuguese, Italian, Dutch, English, French, German, Russian country relay race.

Capital is relatively abstract in economics. To make it plain, capital is the capitalized cost in industrial or commercial operation. From the story of Jiang Ziya doing business, the preliminary thought of operating capital had already appeared in the Central Plains at the late Shang Dynasty. Some words in Kokang are ambiguous. The meaning of capital can be extended into the factors and status that be used to one's own advantage like getting promoted and find a good job.

The idioms "going for wool and coming home shorn" and "gaining enormous profits of a small capital investment" have vaguely shown the causality between investing capital and obtaining profits. At all times and in all countries, the investors and employees have formed the labor-capital relationship. Some capitalists are very stingy and greedy, and some employees are extremely lazy and cunning. It is not scientific and reasonable to say "exploitation of surplus value".

No matter in Europe or the Central Plains, it is perfectly justified that the investors invest capital and obtain profits according to the propriety and laws. Just in time of dramatic social change, some insatiable people would exploit the labors disregarding their benefits,

and some indolent people would intent to waste or rob money from their employers. These bad guys just regarded the troubled time as the opportunity to change their fate.

The law of value operation in commodity exchange is that more capital would be put in if more profits could be get, and vice versa. Capital always flows to high-profit industries. It is normal and rational for an investor to do so, and it is beneficial to all. All in all, it is reasonable and fair for the investors who are on behalf of the productivity and undertaking the high risk to get the highest profits.

It is justified for the engineer to have a high income due to his high-tech skills. Similarly, it is reasonable for the ordinary workers to earn less. Because they take the jobs with less techniques and don't need to bear any risk in case his company goes into bankruptcy. Therefore, the concept of hiring workers "to create surplus value" is just a illusion like a castle in the air.

Such fallacious concept was born and developed in Europe and spreaded to the Central Plains. It had been a few hundred year since the phenomenon of "sheep eating people" in European Enclosure Movement. While in China, the idiom to describe a businessman that "gaining enormous profits from a small capital investment" didn't appear until the late Qing Dynasty and the Republic of China.

"High profits without investing" refers to getting profits not through commercial transactions and legal procedures. They just grab capital and win super bonus.

22. Problem and Society

The robber-style "High profits without investing" had been so far quite some time like in Europe. In Wikipedia, the Enclosure Movement in England can be trace back to the 12th century. The Enclosure Movement was initiated by the new aristocracy who were not under the control of the king, and was connived with the England opening its

colonies overseas.

From the aristocratic privilege to the equal rights for all under the constitutional government, what finally came was the European and American technological civilization with the feature that "by negotiation or by violence". Modern society were established based on this civilization and more and more problems have been encountered.

In the peacetime of Chinese history, questions were asked by a person and answered by another from a different status, for example the school teachers answer questions from the students. If the officials are upright and unselfish, the time of peace and prosperity would appear. On the contrary, if officials play favoritism and commit irregularities, the time unrest and decadence would come. In the era of disorder, the problems must be solve by force. In the Ming and Qing Dynasties, what the domestic peasant uprising couldn't settle would eventually solve by the cavalries from Manchus.

In European and American countries or in the Republic of China, the privileges of the upper class were never enjoyed together with the lower class, and eventual forced to split to the rights for all. Emerson, an American poet, tried to answer this question in the poem *Question*, "faith (believing in God Creation and Redemption) created us", "The ancient 'Bible' enumeration of the responsibility/All of nature from what happens in the heart..." The European and American society developed vigorously like the volcanic eruption.

The original meaning of "社会 (society)" in Kokang is the people's assembly (to form an association freely) in a specific place. In particular, it refers to the assembly (会) in spring and autumn to offer sacrifices to the God of Land (社) and give thanks. The word "Society" can be found in the Tang Poem with the meaning that people come together and offer sacrifices. Then, "society" was developed into the organizations or groups with the certain guideline, such as the Tung Meng Hui, the Kuomintang and other parties.

In ancient China, reverence was shown to people of noble character at first and then to the people of the coterie. And in modern China, secret societies were form to against the oppression or persecution. At that time, the capable people strove to make a better world. Even the ordinary people would practice the doctrine of "alive, be man of men; dead, be soul of souls". How heroic an how touching they were! Nowadays, this culture is no longer there any more.

What the modern people focus is merely the material world including the nature, the society and human body, rather the spiritual world like people's mind and energy. Qu Qiubai once wrote in *Thoughts in Red Capital*, "the question symbols are flying in the sky", "How one can come to the conclusion without knowing what the question is?"

To solve a problem, people in ancient European would resort to the legislation and in ancient China with a strategic withdrawal. In modern times people become the irreconcilable adversaries and each sticks to his own version.

23. Doctrine and War

No doctrine had ever existed before western ideologies come into Chinese culture. In Chinese culture, there are only the philosophical thoughts, but no philosophical theories. Chinese people carry out the doctrine of being reasonable and forgiving, of being subjective, or of being objective. However, none of the above thoughts have been developed into a theory. They go to the boisterous temple fair not merely for making profits; they talk in a moderate and tactful way with the hope not offending others. Thus, in Chinese war philosophy, it is the art of warfare that leave an outlet free for the losers and let them take their course.

Rather than the doctrine, religions were flourishing in ancient India. After the survival from a desperate situation, the Brahmanism

（Hinduism later）successfully surpassed the Buddhism and finally stifled it. In European ancient philosophy, The spirit of "love of wisdom" and inquiring into the root of the matter were highly praised. Students would always outstrip their teachers. Eventually, mechanical materialism of Hobbes and Hegel's philosophy of idealism came into being in modern England. To some extent, both the court debate and the World War were promoted by the spread of this spirit.

The three religions（Confucianism, Taoism and Buddhism）survived, developed and flourished together within the process of Chinese long history, from the prehistoric legend, to the semi-legend and semi-recorded history in the Xia-Shang-Zhou Dynasties, till the history records and record revisions from the Qin and Han Dynasties to the Ming and Qing Dynasties. With different beliefs that the Confucianism believes in fate, Taoism in Tao and Buddhism in Buddha, three religions argues, yet tolerate each other.

It is not necessarily the best to classify the three doctrine that being tolerant in Confucianism, taking the natural course in Taoism and good Karma in Buddhism into religion, and it is not exact to regard them as the philosophical theories. However, it is definitely the compact principles of peaceful co-existence for over 100 countries and regions in the world today.

Seeing with the people's naked eyes, two stars in the vast universe seems quite near, but the fact is another story. Hundreds of millions of light years away from each other, they are composed with entirely different chemical elements and physical structures. For example, some stars are composed with mere stone while some are rich in natural resources.

That the aircraft like the UFO enters the earth space through the Time Tunnel is called "Time and Space Travel" On the earth today, much more efforts are needed to realize the "Time Travel". Luckily, our mind can travel through different ideologies at present without any

wait.

It is said that the similarity of two parallel universes is the same as that of the twins. But it might be more than one thousand years if the time spanning of the birth on the earth is calculated in another planet.

To discover the truth, we and our successors have to demonstrate all of our prowess and spare no effort on it. In that process, some principles must be observed. Try to think, Will people's mind be more active if no ism is upheld?

24. Flow Determines the Value

All the material goods in the world are manufactured from the raw material in nature by man's adaption needs. Of these goods, some can flow in the market, which make profits and more factories and companies would began to produce and promote. While the others cannot be sold, so the factories and produce them would go bankrupt or stop producing them. It can be said that flow determines the value.

Flow refers to the movement of gas or liquid under the applied force. The flows in volcano and earthquake are manifested as the magma eruption and mudslide. In the flow, that can save more material and energy has greater values, and that with more consumption has less values. In Chinese, a proverb goes, "an empty hole invites the wind" whit the meaning that the wind will flow where there is the gap, space, cavity or hole and so on.

Flow also involve the sampling inspection of goods, the change of a teenager's character, as well as that one write a composition very fast and the eyes move very quickly. So, it is difficult to standardize to definition of "flow". In a broad sense, all the things, the gas, the wind, the water, the goods, the people, the vehicle, the poem, the scholar, etc. , can flow under certain circumstances.

A thing is valued if it is rare. The value of a thing is determine by a man according to its flow. Looking up in a dictionary, it is hard to decide how to explain the meaning of "determination" here. From the perspective of commodity exchange, the customer's choice will determine the value of the goods. The chosen have value and the factory will produce and promote, and vice versa.

Based on the interests and standpoint, the community or the individual make their choice to accept or reject. People call it the value. The accepted is of value, and the rejected is of no value. Values are classified in to various categories, such as the social value, the personal value, the economic value, the legal value, the nominal value and so on. What decide how much the value should be is people's free will.

A man deprived of freedom becomes the slave. The imposed things or thoughts are utterly worthless. The man with the imposed ideas is just like a walking dead, with no value.

To live with dignity, one must accept the things and thoughts out of his humanity and personality, and pursue the real values, i. e. the six kinds of value illustrated before. A man can make his own decision autonomously. A great man is guided by the noble value and never falls by the wayside.

The value of truth, goodness and beauty would be incubated in the market with the flow of free people. The value, on earth, lies in whether to choose and how to choose. Is it right that the material and spiritual value be decided by man's free will? When a thing is scarce, it takes more value. All in all, flow determines the value, which is quite different from the barter exchange.

25. Be a Man with Reflection

When encountering troubles, reflection would help solve the problem. A son makes his father furious in a word. Then, the son said immediately, "Dad, you need to see a psychiatrist." The father will get mad suddenly, and the family will come to the war. If the son could

stop saying anything and reflect about the words he just said, "what had I said?" There would be no more conflict between the father and the son.

Li Bai, the poet in the Tang Dynasty, versified : "I descry bright moonlight in front of my bed. I suspect it to be hoary frost on the floor. I watch the bright moon, as I tilt back my head. I yearn, while stooping, for my homeland more." This poem was entitle with *A Quiet Night Thought*. According to research, "In front of my bed " there was a well. The "bed" actually referred to a stool. The question is, is it meaningful to do such research? As a matter of fact, they couldn't realize nostalgia of a man residing far away from home, which just showed their superficial knowledge.

He who likes showing off would stir up troubles. Even between the father and the son, a war would be aroused. Confucianism teaches a man to reflect the love between parents and children. Like the sun gives out to all the lives, parent devote the selfless love to their children. So, the children should be thankful and express their gratitude to the parents. Knowing this, what a man should do is to comfort his parents rather than make them angry. With the habit of reflection, one shall fulfill the filial piety at home and do kind deeds outside.

A man with reflection will deal with things properly. As the old saying goes, the gentleman is broad-minded and the inferior man is narrow-minded. To be a gentleman and be kind to others, the problem encountered will be reduced less serious and then to nothing at all. There's not too many troubles in the world, only the unenlightened people agitate it.

A man with reflection is surely understand that to forgive others is in fact being kind to oneself. As the saying goes, endure for a while and things will be calm and tranquil; take a step back and you will see a new horizon. However, there is a misconception nowadays that being tolerant means slavishness, and fighting for personal interests is

Why do people get angry? There are variety of reasons among which the most important are that people are impatient and impetuous with the feeling of "losing face", or they argue a point to death. As a result, they have to punish themselves with others' faults.

Through reflection, one may find that happiness will come if he could treat others with tolerance, and love others more. Some rich men spend money for fun. They cause trouble frequently and get angry easily but never learn to reflect. A man with a clear conscience can gain peace of mind.

It is good for a man to reflect on one's misdeeds in private and be lenient with others. The man who talks of people behind their backs will make troublle out of nothing. By reflection, one can know his own situation and that of the others. It is the key to solve problems and restrain impulse.

26. Tolerance Leads to a Wide Road

Tolerance is allowing others to do things and make judgment freely. In *Encyclopedia Britannica*, it is explained as the willingness to accept the behavior and beliefs which are different from one's own or from the public patiently and without bias. Confucianism regards tolerance as the the principle of forgiveness.

Confucianists and Taoists are all unified by the Tao. Taoism strives for the human nature by the way of mercy, thrift and without importunity. Confucianism is striving for honesty by the ways of humanity, righteousness and courtliness. Both of the two ways are leading to the tolerance and build up ones tolerance. Zhuang Zi talked about the world and said, "People should always be tolerant to everything." The content of Hsun Tzu used to be the teacher of the youth in the lower class and guided them to be tolerant and forgiving.

The broad-minded people who have the tolerance to others are

described with the following two Chinese idioms that "A great man will not remember the faults of little men. " and "a prime minister's heart is big enough to pole a boat in. " The vendettas in Europe lasted until the end of the World War Ⅱ, when the United Nations established as the organization to solve the international disputes and tolerate the argument and critiques from different nations.

In China, it have been the tradition for Confucianism, Taoism and Buddhism to practice the doctrine of tolerance and forbearance, which has been formed and developed ever since the Han and Jin Dynasties to the Sui and Tang dynasty. Confucianists or Taoists or Buddhist monk, he who really practices the moral teachings could solve the problems with ease when facing troubles and hardship.

It is easier to be said than done that being tolerant and lenient towards others. The moral teachings must be practiced if one wants to achive this. Only by withstanding others' offense and humiliation time after time, can one be forgiving and tolerant. In modern times, someone regards tolerance as weakness, and degrades it as servility. They even advocate to seek revenge for the smallest grievance. From the psychological point of view, such people are self-abased and interiorly weak. Therefore, they bear the malice and couldn't help seeking revenge. Otherwise, they would feel uncomfortable.

Liu Bei, the leading character in the novel *Romance of the Three Kingdoms* and Song Jiang, the leading character in the novel *Water Margin* were both not good at kung fu, but there were quite a number of martial-art masters under their leadership. Subjectively, the reason is that they were "tolerant to others and dealt with problems in a soft and subtle approach " (a saying from Luo Guanzhong).

Being tolerant and lenient towards others is about one's mental state. How could one form his moral state as great and tolerant as the deep ocean without the noble and broad mind like the high mountain and wide sky? Owing to love, it is easy to be tolerant to children.

Owing to hatred, it is hard to be tolerate to enemies.

Seeking revenge for unsettled enmity makes one the enemy of his surroundings, even with his family. He turned the world into a hell of resentment, posing obstacles along his life path until it is finally and completely blocked by hostility. Acquiring the ability to forgive is to forge one's state of mind and bearings to the mountain high and ocean deep. He who is benevolent has a broad mind and will walk on the broad road in his life.

27. Embattling Leads to a Narrow Road

Embattle, originally used in military preparations, refers to having the troop in full battle array to get ready for invading enemy.

In ancient days, once on the battlefield, officers and soldiers held sword and shield, plucking up courage. Archers were standing by, with everything ready. If the officer launched a reckless attack without the full understanding the enemy's formation, he was more than likely to be killed immediately. And his soldiers would be demoralized and the troop might be totally defeated.

The word "embattle" was used in the book *History as a Mirror* compiled by Sima Guang, a Chinese historian of the Song Dynasty, when recording the war, which took place in 27 B. C when the Eastern Han Dynasty Emperor Liu Hsiu reigned. This word can also be seen in portraying the preparations before war more than once in book *A History of the Various Kingdoms in the Eastern Zhou Dynasty*, written by Feng Menglong of the Ming Dynasty.

Compared with the ancient warfare, the modern war has changed dramatically in military equipments and means. As the gunpowder is used extensively, gun has taken the place of sword. The soldiers are no longer wear the heavy armor and the officers would not charge at the head in the battle any more. On the contrary, at the very beginning of the battle is the heavy bombardment, which makes the war even gorier.

Even in such a modern war, it is still necessary to get fully prepared, that is, to dig the trenches, arrange the command post and so forth, which serves the same purpose as embattling.

When it comes to the war, to embattle is a must. It can be regarded to risk the life to start a war without arraying the troops for battle and setting up the fortifications. However, there were some countries and religions embattling even in the times of peace and prosperity, which resulted in the evolution from interpersonal conflicts to the antagonism between social strata. And then class collision appeared, even slight differences would make the situation boil over and result in war.

In the 20th century, the ideology of Friend-or-Foe derived from the preparation for war in peace time, which strongly influenced the social development. It not only destroys the strata and nation's labor which were formed in humans' adaptation to the society, but also does harm to the efforts to build the human world collectively. In this circumstance, people are inclined to impute the disagreement and the conflict over the unequal distribution of interests to races and classes.

With the education about the fight against enemy getting intensified, the identification of friend and foe becomes a matter of prime importance in peace time. It is generally accepted that the war will break out at any time and have never stopped. In this case, people's consciousness and behavior of pursuing freedom would be regarded as hostile means to against the authority. To eliminate it, the authority takes the strict precautions by law and regulation and finally uproot it in the name of people.

In peace time, the thought that "wiping out all enemy and freedom belonging to the people" is held to stir up the masses movement. The private hatred are vilified into the impersonal criticisms. In such a society, people have to be alert to every sound and movement all the time in case the enemy. Consequently, the road of life was getting narrower and narrower, even head to head, eye to eye.

28. Slander and Flatter-the Wickedness

From 1933 to 1945, the Europe was under the dictatorship of Nazi government of Germany leaded by Hitler. Nazi Germany, German Empire or Great German Empire as its formal name, is known as the Third Reich. It changed Germany into a combat-ready society by the the Nazi Party's dictatorship and the ideology of National Socialism.

The Nazi Germany fell into the evil way. They injured the civilians and slandered to establish a new country. As their notorious saying goes, the rumor said for thousand times becomes the truth. Under the rule of Nazism, war and violence advocated the legal property of the Jews . The Jews and the Slavs were regarded as the inferior races. Race persecution was taken place. War of aggression was started.

The evil way, literally, is the way of living filling with slander and flatter. It also refers to the heterodox way. Heterodoxy here can be understood as being stupid. Actually, he who cannot play the fool is not a wise man. It is wise to be honest and accept the inevitable. In *The Book of Rites* on the king's rule, it reads, "to rule in the evil way will bring unrest to the society". Heterodox way in this case refers to the behavior of disregard the national security.

Xun Zi, a famous scholar in ancient China, once said, "Don't gain money in improper ways even when in desperate poverty". That is to say, adapting to the society, one should never get money by fraud and robbery, even if he is impoverished and cannot afford the clothes.

Evil way is not exclusively refer to the criminal acts committed by the under class. The upper class, up to the emperor, is delinquent in their duty and not solicitous of his people. The fatuous and self-indulgent rulers were dreaming of being immortal all day long. They obtained money from the people by cheating or forcible means and built

splendor palace to live in. Their marriages were associated with incest...All the above are evil doings, which are neither humane, nor courteous.

One would be a good man when conducting himself with propriety; a evil man without propriety. No matter what, the good will always prevail over the evil. With the development of modern science, technology and industry. Humans are ambitious to rule the whole universe more than ever. The political ideologies and literary arts which blur the boundary of being good or being evil begin to exist.

Slander is featured in the evil way. For example, Zhao Gou and Qin Hui maliciously accused Yue Fei as a traitor and executed him without any evidence. Such action as trampling human life as wild grass is the disregard of legislation and the abuse to law. When the rulers fall into the evil path, the influence is much worse than the bandits.

Flatter prevail in the evil way. The petty official fawns on his superiors. Words of flattery, including "wish a long life", can be heard everywhere. At the same time, the flattered believes in such words deeply. They like these words at least even not believing. By and by, the bureaucratic culture is getting worse. Xun Zi treated the people who flatter as the thief stealing heart. In his opinion, *The Book of Poetry* and *The Book of History* shall be read and system of rites and music be learned to curb people's greedy heart.

29. Pardon All Men, But Never Thyself-the Goodness

Guan Zu talked about politics. He said, "more evils would come if the legitimacy was abolished". To make it plain, when the interests becomes the only norms to guide man's behavior, the righteousness will be weakened and wickedness will become overwhelming.

Hsun Tzu talked about education. He said, "Nature operates based on its own law. It will not come into existence for the emperor Yao,

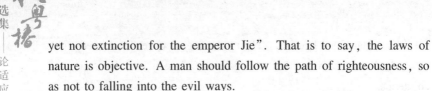

yet not extinction for the emperor Jie". That is to say, the laws of nature is objective. A man should follow the path of righteousness, so as not to falling into the evil ways.

Taking the middle path is the doctrine that preached by the Buddhism, Taoism and Christianity. Middle path, in religion, refers to the correct path in its literal meaning, and is the contrary to crooked ways like the lie and violence. Leading a different life from the the Confucians who live at their home, the Buddhist monks go to the temple and pursue the middle way in between the indulgence and asceticism, which is similar to the Golden Mean.

All of the teachings about the middle way guide people to the correct path. The wickedness shall be overwhelmed by the kindness, goodness and tolerance. Evils shall never be done. In the field of Confucianism, the five cardinal virtues of benevolence, righteousness, propriety, wisdom, and faithfulness are promoted for self-discipline.

In Ming Dynasty, Liu Bowen set one of his official motto as "Pardon all men, but never thyself", which is the correct path of being an official. It is the truth that one is strict with himself and lenient towards others. However, it is not easy to pursue this truth. Many people think that it is nebbishy for a man, who was born with love and hatred, to follow the above maxim. Thus and so, like for like, one punch come and two slaps back for retaliation.

As a result, it has been a popular saying that "he who not revenge is not a real man". According to this, morality is relative and stratified. The ruler advocate benevolence and righteousness is for the sake of appeasing the ruled. In this case, the fulfilling of such maxim would be harmful. Different from this, the Taoism believes in that things should take their own course and that softness can overcome strength. the Buddhism teaches that there's no end to revenge. The Christianity preaches that the biggest enemy one should conquer is himself, including his lust, greedy and aggression.

It asks people to requite evil with good, which, nevertheless, is difficult to carry out for the mortal and is almost only can be dong by God. However, what can be done is to meet resentment with justice. I would not revenge your harm to me, but I must tell you that what you've done is wrong. If you don't stop hurting me. I will appeal to the court and your will be punished by the law.

To take the correct path, one must possess a righteous heart. "正", a Chinese Character, means correctness. In from, "一 (a horizen stroke)" lies above "止 (stop)" with the meaning of stopping before going too far. In *The Book of Rites-Doctrine Of the Mean*, it reads, "One should behave or conduct by his instinct". By instinct does not mean be willful. On the contrary, one should adjust himself to the best condition by the nature of human wisdom, benevolence, courage and so on. There would be no lawsuits as long as all the people are self-disciplined.

30. *Kind Heart and Pure Land*

A man with the kind heart is straightforward and obedient. Such traits could be found around them as loving others, being responsible, being courteous to the elderly, righteous, honest and trustworthy, dedication to his work, having the courage to admit a fault and integrity, etc.

Or more commonly known as they are kindly and friendly; they are honest and never tell a lie or resort to violence. In ancient times, the Chinese were gentle and moderate most of the time when talking, low in voice while sound in reason. The music was rarely impassioned with more warmth than incitement, People were well mannered and their kind hearts aroused.

Goodness can hardly be done without the kindness. Goodness comes from kindness. If a man without kindness and full of hatred would look on indifferently when seeing the enemy's children falling

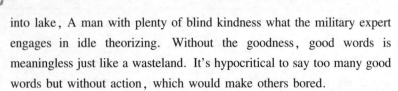

into lake, A man with plenty of blind kindness what the military expert engages in idle theorizing. Without the goodness, good words is meaningless just like a wasteland. It's hypocritical to say too many good words but without action, which would make others bored.

We all possess a kind heart. Even the wicked person, in his early childhood, is kind-hearted. But why they become more and more wicked and commit the evildoings rather being kind and do good deed? Because he is so greedy that want to keep all the good things for himself. People with the evil heart is just like the dustbin. Even occasionally come in a good intention, it will immediately take a bad smell.

As the paragon of animals, human own the kind heart which other animals don't possess. A man with kind heart is able to create the pure land. A man with kindness and morality has more pure land in his heart. He is with love and show mercy to the miserable; with the feeling of shame and dislike and rescue the drawning; with a broad mind and less desire.

Buddhist believes in the Amitabha Buddha and the pure land. Monks leave their families and practice the religious belief, trying to get rid of human's sentiments and passions. With peace, they are building the inner Pure Land by Buddhism. Buddhas are trying to create the pure land for kindness, the Nirvana where the people with kind heart will finally enter. They make an oath that they are willing to bear alone the bad karma and subject to all the pain caused by the earthlings.

At the end of the Eastern Jin Dynasty, Hui Yuan, a famous monk, from central mainland preached the doctrines of pure land from Maitreya Buddha to Amitabha Buddha. He had organized the activity that people make a pledge to do good deed with the hope to go to the Pure Land, in which quite a few intellectuals and scholars also participated. Afterwards, the doctrine of Pure Land had spread from Buddhism to school, family and officialdom in people's daily life.

At present, the Buddhism temple has become the tourist attraction. It is now longer the pure land. The monks begin to earn salary and send the money home. No matter what, everybody still owns the kind heart, thus abandon the greed and live in the inner peace. The pure land can emerge only from the kind heart.

On Adaptationism（Ⅵ）

(Kokang version)

1. Love between the Couples

What in between the couple is love. In the Zhou Dynasty, officials were sent to collect poems from the public. In one of those love poems, it reads, "Guan! Guan! Cry the fish hawks on sandbars in the river: a mild-mannered good girl, fine match for the gentleman. A ragged fringe is the floating-heart, left and right we trail it: that mild-mannered good girl, awake, asleep, I search for her." Through these verses, a gentleman expresses his affection to his beloved girl.

It is love that distinguish the human beings from the animals. In ancient China, the gentlemen were all from noble families. They were carefree and elegant, thus they were sensitive when paying court to a woman, as depicted in the love poem: "I search but cannot find her, awake, asleep, thinking of her, endlessly, endlessly, turning, tossing from side to side."

This kind of graceful courtship agreed to the Chinese etiquette at that time. When coming across a pretty and mild-mannered girl, the gentleman would play the se (a twenty-five-stringed plucked instrument, somewhat similar to the zither), ring the chimes and beat the drum as a token of his love, from which the arranged marriage came into being.

According to the written records, during the same period in India, Western Asia, and Europe, the direct sexual absorption rather than the

elegant courtship were seen. Helen, Queen of Sparta Kingdom, was seduced by the Trojan prince, causing the naval warfare which lasted for a decade.

Quite different from China, such tradition as to woo in a gentle way never had be found in Europe and America. The graceful affection had not appeared in those regions until the 18 century in the salons and parties held by the French noblewoman. Yet this affection between the friends and couples were recorded in Kokang language over 2000 years ago. For instance, the affections between Chong'er in Jin State and the Princess in Qi State as well as between Guan Zhong and Bao Shuya in Qi State both belonged to this kind.

No records have been found in ancient Greek literature and history books about the love between men and women full of human rational affection. It is deduced that sex dominated love. Homer depicted Helen's coquette in his epic poems and over 2000 year later, Shakespeare wrote *The Merry Wives of Windsor*. It is obvious that what mattered was the lust of flesh.

The idea of rational love was originally derived from the concept of "love" by Plato, ancient Greek Philosopher. In modern world, this kind of love is know as the unearthly Platonic Love, which also refers to the love between Socrates, the teacher and Plato, the student.

In China, the so-called Platonic love or Socratic love came into exis as early as in the Zhou Dynasty. And people call it the gentleman's love. *Butterfly Lovers*, a Chinese folk story about the gentleman's love, narrates the love between Zhu Yingtai, daughter of a noble family and Liang Shanbo, son of a poor family in the Eastern Jin Dynasty. In Kokang language, idioms like "The lute and psaltery are in harmony" and "husband and wife treating each other with courtesy" are used to modify the love and felicity of husband and wife, which is hard for the Europeans to understand even nowadays.

Sex, of course, is essential between the couples, especially the

permanent ones. Only for sex is the reflection of the animals and emphasizing on sex is the love of Europeans.

2. Lewdness is the Worst of All Vices

The Europeans are especially keen on Sexual Love. The sports tournament and body art were derived from the fond of nude. In Chinese history, people wear conservatively. In traditional Chinese language, abstruse poems were composed to express people's affection. Only in *The Golden Lotus* (*vernacular*), the sexual affairs narrated undisguisedly.

In KoKang language, it is said that " Lewdness is the origin of all vices", which was recorded in the book *The Fireside Chat* written by Wang Yongbin. The original quotation is "Lustful thoughts will tempt people into wrong doings that he would never do in daily life. So, Lewdness is the origin of all vices". In Bible, the forbidden fruit actually refers to the lewdness. The original sin of the white European is actually lust.

The history of Southwest Asia and Europe can be concluded as the old nations were conquered by the nomadic nations one after another. Before the conquest, the lewdness, lust and incest were so prevalent that these nations were not able to restrain. Thanks to the the doctrines of Catholicism and Islam which prohibit the lewdness, the countries in Europe, Southwest Asia and Central Asia were established and developed so as to resist aggression and are still in existence.

In China, unremitting efforts have been make to restrain the lewdness. Through the ages, some nongovernmental learned people had taken the responsibility of teaching the virtue and morality. From Lao zi and Confucius in the Spring and Autumn Period, to the Qing Dynasty and the Republic of China, the rich were taught to get rid of lewdness.

Mencius persuade the rich and the powerful not to be lewd. Wang Yongbin developed Mencius' thought and place the virtue and morality

over the official rank getting from the imperial examinations. He had made great contributions on this and wrote *The Fireside Chat*, saying "The deterioration of social conduct mostly originates from the lewdness of the rich and the powerful". "The lewdness makes the social conduct deteriorative ... the virtuous people are in urgent need to save the world". "To set a far-reaching ambition and be impervious to the temptation of wealth and high position."

Although Wang Yongbin was born in a Confucian family, he wasn't interested in getting an official rank through passing the imperial examinations. Long being a hermit, he taught the Confucianism and never gave empty talks. He always practiced what he preached before teaching others. He would praise the fellow villagers who practiced virtue and admonish a wrong doer to correct his bad deeds.

Without any payment, Wang Yongbin rendered the Arabic work *One Thousand and One Nights* into popular language. He told the stories in that book to teach people how to be a virtuous person and persuade people get rid of the lewdness to the priority.

Ever since 1950, country gentleman like Wang Yongbin has hardly been found. During that period, China had suffered from poverty. "Lewdness" was exclusively for the rich and the powerful underground which had not corrupted the public morals. The reform and opening also brings in the popularity of "lewdness". Without the examples of the virtuous man, the rich followed the trend of lewdness. The personal and social conduct were totally ruined.

3. Filial Piety is the Best of All Virtues

In the Qing Dynasty, the principle that "Filial piety is the foundation of all virtues" had been posed by Wang Yongbin in his book *The Fireside Chat*, "a man with filial piety would not commit any wrong doings, so the filial piety should be put the first place among all virtues."

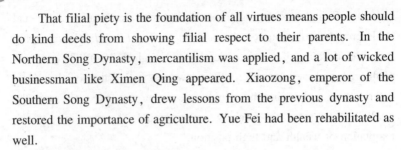

That filial piety is the foundation of all virtues means people should do kind deeds from showing filial respect to their parents. In the Northern Song Dynasty, mercantilism was applied, and a lot of wicked businessman like Ximen Qing appeared. Xiaozong, emperor of the Southern Song Dynasty, drew lessons from the previous dynasty and restored the importance of agriculture. Yue Fei had been rehabilitated as well.

In China, an official who follows the teachings of filial piety from his domestic discipline and rules would be patriotic and loyal to the throne. In the culture that ancestors are worshiped, a man with filial piety must be benevolent. The kindness originated from the esteem to the parents would overwhelm the selfishness and benefit the others.

In ancient China, the officials were only responsible for the taxation. They were not in charge of the administrative areas lower than counties, i. e. the town, the countryside and the village. In other words, the ancient Chinese, including Guan Yu, Yue Fei and Lin Zexu, all observed the domestic discipline and rules to which the importance of filial piety were attached. This tradition can be found in Judaic Law of Moses, but couldn't been seen in the polytheism of ancient Greece and Rome.

The Chinese legend that Da Shun shows filial piety and respect to his father and takes good care of his bothers was 1000 years earlier than the Mosaic Commandment to honor one's father and mother in the name of God. During the Qing Dynasty, the civil officers, with the alternative name "Xiaolian", must know well how to be filial and incorrupt.

In the Qing Dynasty, children were taught the filial piety though the enlightened reading material *Standards for Being a Good Student and Child* in the understandable wordings, "When your parents call you, answer them right away. When they command you to do something, do it quickly. When your parents instruct you, listen

respectfully. When your parents reproach you, obey and accept their reproach, try hard to change and improve yourself, and start anew..." The children were asked to memorize their principles and practice the filial piety.

The filial piety was deeply rooted in the people's heart in ancient China. It is believed that the dutiful at home makes the official loyal to his sovereign. In the Qing Dynasty, the subjective idealist philosophy was banned by the government. To the time of Lin Zexu who had stamped out the opium trade, the loyalty and filial piety were just be used as the lip-service for the literati and written in the eight-legged essay for passing the imperial examination. At that time, righteousness was not valued any more. Being loyal to one's country and filial to one's parents were regarded as the blind devotion to his lord and parents.

To develop republicanism in China, the dregs of Confucianism should be discarded. However, what people had done was to overthrow its whole system, which has lead to bad consequences. In the Qing Dynasty, the Confucianism teachings that observe the proper etiquette in arranging their funerals. Hold the memorial ceremony and commemorate the anniversaries with your utmost sincerity. Serve your departed parents as if they were still alive..." was well understood by the children. However, nowadays in China, the adult could not comprehend its meaning unless being translated.

4. On Form a Clique to Pursue Selfish Interests

It is an urgent matter to make it clear that why being loyal to one's country and filial to one's parents were regarded as the blind devotion to his lord and parents and why righteousness was no longer valued?

Different people have different views on this question. So it is really difficult to answer. After reflection, the conclusion is arrived at that in human life, society and activities, people would join together to

gain interests for his family, group and nation. In other words, people would form a clique to pursue selfish interests.

People pursue interests for their family. The concept of family meant nothing in the clan where numerous people were of the same surname or in the commune of fishery, agriculture and animal husbandry which were naturally formed by the blood relationship. Family came into exist when family property and family members assembled. The family, established with the bond of blood is the earliest clique and the filial piety is regarded as the earliest clique discipline. The existence of family crumbled the commune.

People pursue interests for their group. From the psychological point of view, there is the selfishness lying in people's subconsciousness. In the clannish society where there was not enough materials to allocate, the selfish interests was suppressed. With the development of productivity, the surplus wealth was produced. The clan had classified into two groups, the plebeian who was poor and the aristocracy who was rich. And each group would work together for their own interests.

People pursue interests for their nation. The clannish society gradually broke down after the endless bloody tribal wars. The rich and poor groups became rational. Intermarriage was permitted and alliance was established between the two groups. Agreement and laws were stipulated. The languages and customs from the tribes and clans of different surnames and blood were unified. And finally, the nationality was formed. The Chinese nationality attached importance to family education and establish their country on the base of Confucian code of ethics. While the Turkic nationality upheld military force and ruled the Khanate with laws and decrees.

People pursue interests for their country. The country would take such measures as regulation, law, prison, court and army to safeguard the national interests. In China, the domestic stability and external

defense are stressed. The ethical code is carried forward as the distinction between the civilized Chinese and the barbarians. On the contrary, in Turkic Khanate and Japan, military force and external aggression are advocated. They are guided by the Samurai spirit and plunder wealth from other countries to satisfy their own needs.

According to the ethical code, the titles and duties are applied to curb the selfish interests. Family or country, once the ethical code is breached, its law and order could not last long. Born with the selfishness, one should always engage in introspection and self-discipline so as to suppress the selfish interest.

Self-disciplinary was taught in the Confucian code of ethics and religious doctrines. Unfortunately, their follower aren't able to practice the teachings efficiently and inhibit the selfish interests. Nowadays, practice the moral teachings are in urgent need to be revived and practiced, whether Confucianism or religions.

5. On Vision and Ambition

Vision determines how far one's career could go; and ambition determines how great one's career could be.

It is the shorted vision and smallest career for civilized man to work in the interests of his own family, yet it has been long standing and help to keep the family steady and stable. Man is born with the limitations that they couldn't see the things far from them clearly, the farther, the vaguer and that they tend to get close to the people and things which they could touch and feel directly, the nearer, the more intimate. Thus it can be seen that he who practices the filial piety and love the family well reflects the human warmth and tenderness.

In the village and civic organizations established by friends and relatives that come from different families and neighborhoods, people will enjoy more rights and interest and can make bigger accomplishment than the family does. It is impossible to build the Dujiang Weir and the

Great Wall by the village with ten villagers, or by the nomadic tribe with hundreds of members, or the agro-town with thousands of residents.

Only with the long-term vision and great ambition which are beyond the scope of the family and the clan, could Chinese people build the Dujiang Weir and the Great Wall. All in all, it is the nation and the country, composed of numerous different families, that have the above to qualities. The problems need to solve are how to avoid the internal conflict or even fratricidal strife with the country? And how to prevent the formation of the aggressive privileged parties?

According to the modern clique concept, people in ancient times can be divided into the groups, the poor and the rich. The former group consisted of the Aryan people in Central Asia, the Germanic people in Western Europe, the Slavic people in Eastern Europe and the East Asian nomads like the Huns, the Turkic people, the Mongolian, the Jurchen people and so on. The latter included the city-states of the late ancient Greece, the State of Jin and the State of Qi in Chinese Spring and Autumn Period, the Han Dynasty which combined the culture of the states in Central Plains like Jin and Qi, the Jin Dynasty, the Tang Dynasty, the Song Dynasty, the Ming Dynasty as well as the early Qian Long Times in the Qing Dynasty.

The poor, if standing at bay, would rise up and kill the rich, being corrupt and rotten, who gain power with bribery and abuse power for personal gain.

Before the civilization was evolve to enlighten their savagery, the Chanyu Countries or Khanates of ancient nomadic tribes naturally depended on invasion and pillage due to resource shortage in the plateau and grassland. Without knowing the production technique and becoming better off through the labor, those nomads, getting rich quick through pillage, became indolent and voluptuous, and eventually were conquered by other countries.

Although experiencing the cyclical unifications, the ancient China had enjoyed the lasting prosperity owning to the sustained development of agriculture, industry and commerce. In the period of national disunity and chaos, the Confucianism, Taoism and Buddhism had collaborated to break through limitation of the age so as to weed out the old and bring in the new era.

6. People Die for Money

A story on the Internet goes that two sedan carriers died for money. Tom and Dick had worked together to carry a sedan chair for more than ten years. They invented such jargons as "foreign bird" to rob their customers and "eight slices" to divide up the booty. One day, they were hired by a merchant with a large piece of baggage, who was going to purchase mountain products. They discussed in their jargon, "Let's make the foreign bird's money eight slices."

They shouted with their jargon on the way, just like the stockholders using "bull" and "lock" in stock market nowadays. When there was some cow dung in the way, they shouted that "The tortoise press down the road". When it was time to turn right, "Make a big turn", and conversely, "Make a small turn" to the left.

In this way, the two bad porters carried the sedan chair to a pathway with a deep gully on the right. At the turning, Tom shouted, "Make a big turn." "A big turn is coming!" Dick responded. Then they collaborate to pitch the merchant down to the gully.

After that, Tom and Dick went out of the mountain with the baggage left on the sedan chair. Going out of town, they unwrapped the baggage and found four or five hundred tael of silver in it. Both of them wanted to pocket all the silver, thinking no one would know his evil.

Tom asked Dick to get some dishes and liquor to celebrate the fortune they got, after which they would divide the money. Dick, disagreed at first, said "what if you run off with the money?" Tom

reassure Dick, "We can divide it right now, if you don't trust me."
Then Dick said: "I will go."

Dick went to town and got some arsenic. He put it into the dishes
and liquor so as to poison Tom to death.

Instead of running off with the money, Tom put the baggage under
a pine tree and hid behind the tree when Dick came back. On seeing the
baggage, Dick laid down the food at once and went to check the silver.
Just then Tom lifted a big rock and smash Dick's head. Dick died
immediately. After throwing away Dick's body and the sedan chair,
Tom started to enjoy the dishes and liquor.

Tom mumbled as he ate, "A magnanimous man is honorable and a
ruthless one is a real man. If I didn't kill him, how the hell can my
paradise come?" While Tom was enjoying his happy time, he suddenly
fell to the ground with fierce abdominal pains and very soon died a
painful death. After seeing them laying still for a long time, a bird on
the pine flew down to eat their bodies and died too.

People died for money, simultaneously, birds died for food. This
story is about are telling the absurdness of people's greed for money and
being wickedly selfish in the world.

7. On Money and Virtue

Nowadays, little importance has been attached to the idiom
"Money counts for nothing while virtue is most valuable". However, it
had great influence in Chinese culture for nearly two thousand years.

"Money counts for nothing" originated from *History of the Jin
dynasty*. It reads, "Money is just like the dung and dirt. One would get
rich if he sees the dirty in a dream". It is about the golden mean of the
Confucian school which stresses virtue and belittles money. In modern
times, it has been criticized as empty talk from the perspective of the
development of commercial society which mainly appeals for the rights,
nevertheless the examples based on such thoughts could be found in

ancient China.

Yin Hao, a Confucian official in the Eastern Jin Dynasty, was 30 years younger than Constantine the Great who was a Roman Christian. While Constantine the Great treated his enemies, wife and elder son brutally, the young Yin Hao had already won good reputation. He was equipped with the learnings of Confucianism and Taoism. As an incorruptible official, he used to lead troops to march north. Unfortunately, he failed at last due to the betrayal of Yao Xiang, the submissive General from the Qiang nationality. Demoted as a commoner, he never complained, but write the four words "What a queer story!" with a writing brush every day.

From the historical records, Yin Hao was an honest and upright official of the ambition to unify the motherland. He was quite different from the lords and distinguished families who lived in the remote south with the only aim to enjoy the luxurious life and get large quantity of property and estate. Although he had got warnings form Huan Wen, the General, and advices from Wang Xizhi, his friend, that he should not take military actions with the formidable enemy right in the front, Yin Hao insisted on march north and was totally defeated.

Yin Hao was not in real power and his being defeated was only exclusive. During the 200 years between the Eastern Jin Dynasty and the Sui Dynasty, all of the North Marches from Chinese dynasties were thwarted in the first battles. Huan Wen, who was in real power, successfully conquered the Later Han and unified the South China. He also led the north march for three time but in vain. Besides, he planned to usurp the throne but failed. Some Chinese idioms came from Huan Wen, such as "perishing of the territory of motherland", "to leave a good name for a hundred generations", "to leave a stink for ten thousand years" and so on.

In comparison with Huan Wen, Yin Hao had a better attitude towards life. Being demoted and banished, he wrote and read without sorrow and anxiety. Only one thing he couldn't understand that why God didn't help him win the north march. However, what he could do to express his confusion was just write "What a queer story!" on the paper with a writing brush everyday.

What history responses is that his quote that "money and wealth are pure emptiness" has passed down to modern times. And there also comes the saying that "humanity and justice are truly priceless". In *Popular Collection of Traditional Chinese Wise* sayings, mind is metaphorically regarded as water. It goes like that, "A mountain stream easily raises and lowers its water. A small mind frequently changes its ideas".

In the world history, the impoverished nomadic peoples struggled for a while and were finally overwhelmed by the powerful countries, just like the gurgling or bubbling mountain stream would finally flow into the Yellow River and the Yang-Tze River and become tranquil. However, the "humanity and justice" will live forever to guide people's behavior and restrain the small mind.

8. The Small Mind the the Mountain Stream

So far the "small mind" are not included in any dictionary. It can be traced from "Only women and men with small mind are difficult to get along with" in *The Analects of Confucius*, and "The woman with small mind is the most dangerous" in *Fengshen Yanyi*.

Fengshen Yanyi, known as *The Investiture of the Gods* or *Romance of King Wu of Zhou overthrowing tyrant Zhou of Shang*, from the perspective of Taoism, narrates the Chinese ancient gods or demons. The historical facts that King Wen of Zhou took the responsibility to save common people who were suffering from the tyrannical rule and King Wu of Zhou overthrew tyrant Zhou of Shang were chosen as the main thread of the book. The stories of gods and demons were interwoven. The Taoism ethics formed from the Southern Song Dynasty

to the Longqing and Wanli period of the Ming Dynasty is expounded.

In *The Investiture of the Gods*, Jiang Ziya planned to seek shelter from King Wen of Zhou with his wife after offending Zhou of Shang. His wife scolded him for good-for-nothing and force him to get divorced so as to marry a better man. Knowing it is difficult to change his wife's mind, Jiang Ziya wrote the bill of divorcement and said, " In comparison with the poisonous snake and wasp, The woman with small mind is the most dangerous".

Chinese Taoism is an enormously complex system. It covers the concepts of Yin-Yang, metaphysics, Taoism philosophy, Confucianism philosophy, Confucian ethics, Buddhism and so on. Combining the knowledge, Taoist magic arts and Kung Fu, Taoism teaches the people at the bottom of society to abide by the principles of human relations.

In *The Investiture of the Gods*, through the plot that Jiang Ziya assisted King Wu of Zhou to overthrow the tyrant Zhou of Shang, and the stories about the fighting, death, resurrection and rebirth happened between the Church of Chan in the name of construction and the Church of Jie in the name of destruction, the Taoism philosophy which were formed in over 300 years from the Southern Song Dynasty to the Yuan Dynasty and to the Wanli period of the Ming Dynasty was propagated that "Filial piety is best of all virtues, and lewdness is the worst of all vices".

In the church of Chan, Jiang Ziya, the follower with litter ability, received orders from Primeval Lord of Heaven to assist King Wu of Zhou to overthrow the tyrant Zhou of Shang. While Shen Gongbao, the follower with great ability, betrayed Primeval Lord of Heaven to joint in the Church of Jie. The church of Chan stuck to the right way and its followers final became God of Heaven after sufferings. One the contrary, the Church of Jie was a cult and its followers were doomed to a tragic end in take the short cut.

In *The Investiture of the Gods*, the god of heaven and the evil

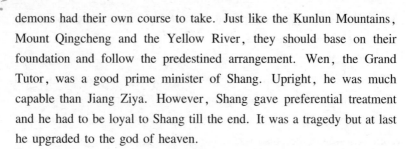

demons had their own course to take. Just like the Kunlun Mountains, Mount Qingcheng and the Yellow River, they should base on their foundation and follow the predestined arrangement. Wen, the Grand Tutor, was a good prime minister of Shang. Upright, he was much capable than Jiang Ziya. However, Shang gave preferential treatment and he had to be loyal to Shang till the end. It was a tragedy but at last he upgraded to the god of heaven.

Streams on the earth are the incarnation of gods and demons. Due to their different moral conduct, the streams vary a lot. The gentleman is the clear stream while a base person is the muddy one. The most beautiful landscape must be the natural and peaceful one. Conduct the self-cultivation wholeheartedly, one would be a real great man.

9. *On Troubled Times and Peacetime*

These is an old saying, "A mountain has a fame not for its height, but for a deity being in it." from which it can be inferred that the gods come from the high mountains. Gods of earth practice moral and religious teachings on the earth, orthodoxy or cult. After that, the ones of high moral standing will be invested to the gods of heaven, while the rest remain the gods of earth.

In *The Investiture of the Gods*, the Grand Tutor Wen vowed loyalty and devotion to the declining Shang Dynasty. He was righteous and loyal. While maintaining the stability of the country, he gave harsh trials to the little god of earth like Jiang Ziya and Tu Xingsun and so on. At last, Wen was invested to the Grand God of Thunder after died on the battlefield. However, Tu Xingsun, although the first disciple of the god of heaven orthodoxy, remained little god of earth because he couldn't give up the romantic love.

It is meaningless for the people at present to distinguish whether the stories in *The Investiture of the Gods* is true and false. Only some individual remarks in the name of science and logic are like the lunatic

ravings. *The Investiture of the Gods* has been passed down for 500 years, because it functions the virtue moralization significance which the Standard History requires. That is, one should follow the orthodoxy, or else his one false choice may bring the everlasting grief.

Right and wrong coexist in the world. A man should be upright. With the awe-inspiring righteousness, one could go to the right path or go further in the right way. From the fable of *The Investiture of the Gods*, the significance of troubled time and peacetime is manifested.

Hero of loyalty and affection would be born in the troubled times. Disregarding the rank of the characters in *The Investiture of the Gods*, true heroes can be judged according to the common standard at all times and in all countries. Taking Li Jing together with his three sons, wei Hu, Yang Jian and Lei Zhenzi for example, it is really naive to ask the following questions, did they invest to the gods of heaven? Who was the best in martial arts? And who was the the most incompetent?

Have such questions been argued by any of the historians in ancient and modern time at home and abroad and different schools of thinkers during the period from pre-Qin times to the early years of the Han Dynasty in China? On the contrary, since the Republic of China, the bored customers in the teahouse of preferred the debate on these issues so as to kill their time and satisfy the chatter pleasure. As a matter of fact, he who chooses and defends the right is a true hero, just like the characters mentioned above.

Deception, hypocrisy, falsity and pretense emerge in peacetime. In *The Investiture of the Gods*, Shen Gongbao and Daji, etc. are such examples. As to their ability and good looks, they neither valued the virtue and morality in the right way, nor made a distinction between right and wrong, good and evil, which is an indirect proof that the body of Daji was acquired by the fox spirit in the story, isn't it?

Shen Gongbao and Daji, etc. were the very embodiment of deception, hypocrisy, falsity and pretense. Any excuse to whitewash or

justify their wrong deeds are the apologists of the evil practice. He who protests for the wicked idea is captured by the evil.

10. On the Rightness and Wickedness in the Society

The orthodoxy teaches people to pursue the rightness. And it is believed that hard work makes great success. A gentleman makes money proper ways. However, it is not easy to stick to the proper ways.

The cult misleads people to take the wickedness. A Chinese idiom goes like "Mt Zhongnan is a shortcut to a ministerial job" which means to take a shortcut to promotion. A inferior man makes money through improper ways. Yet the improper ways are alway alluring.

Facing the choices of the two absolute opposite ways, the rightness which King Wu took to overthrow tyrant Zhou and the wickedness which the bandits took to commit robbery on the road, how would one choose? The people who could choose and stick to the rightness must have noble personalities. After some special discipline, they are able to endure the extreme hardship. Valuing honor above material gains. They do not lust after woman and money. However, for most of people, they would forsake the rightness for the wickedness.

For the sake of money, the outlaws steal and swindle. They gamble and assassinate to gain money, but never try to get legitimate jobs, because they believed that only the ill-gotten wealth can make them rich. Thus, with the hope to be rich over night, some people choose to be a thief, swindler, gambler, bandit, killer and so on at all hazards.

For the sake of money, someone desperately commit murder, arson, theft and robbery. They risk their lives to get money, car and house. Someone engage in embezzlement and take bribes. Having the decent and legitimate job, they violate the financial regulations and ruin the professional ethics. As a result, they would end up in prison and

lose all their belongings just because of a slight oversight.

Someone even get money at the cost of their own lives, their children, social status, morality, and dignity. For the sake of money, they are not hesitate to be a fugitive. There have been many cases that people got punishment after the exposure of their misappropriation of public funds and abuse of authority. In spite of this, some people still take risk to obtain a profit.

For the sake of money, many people can forsake everything in the world, including virtue, ethic and family love. They must suffer a big loss for a little gain.

All in all, people would disregard all the regulations to be followed and the things to cherish merely for the sake of money. So many people never do things without proper benefit. To gain money, they can even abandon their parents.

11. On Money and Virtue

Ancient people, both in western and eastern countries, regarded money as the burden and the hindrance to enter the heaven. Since money cannot be used to do everything, people used to take actions to get rid of this hindrance. However, nowadays people tend to say "It cannot be without money" and begin to set up such hindrance again.

It is the recondition of the concepts that money talks. Being the slave of money, one would have the selfishness in his nature even worse. For the sake of money, one would abandon his family even kill his beloved people, distort humanity, breach the law and commit sins. A bird would kill itself for food, while a man would harm others in order to gain money.

In China, the great man values honor above money. Nevertheless, the ordinary people value money a lot. The God of Wealth is worshiped both in Taoism and among the people. And nowadays, the Network God of Wealth and Electronic God of Wealth emerge as the continuation

of the history.

Money, in essence, is a must for civilization. Without money, goods would be worthless and most of the ordinary people would never stand out. The money worship among the people is radical yet somewhat powerful even at present.

In general, the businessmen all worship the God of Wealth and the businessmen from different regions also have their own founders to revere or examples to follow. For instance, the Zigong worship from Confucian businessmen, the Fan Li worship from Zhejiang businessmen, the Kuan Chung worship from Huizhou businessmen, the Bai Gui worship from Shanxi businessmen, the Bi Gan worship from Hebei businessmen. Some ordinary people even honor Guan Yu as the God of Wealth.

Those founders worshiped by the people in the hope of getting rich were really in history. Among them, Bai Gui was good at management; Guan Yu was loyal and righteous, and Fan Li was an all-round man. It reflects the Chinese businessman's attitude towards making money that if one want to get rich, besides his capability, he also should be courageous, faithful and virtuous.

Moral standing is the root of our society, and wealth is the base of economic progress. China started its ecomonic development earlier than Europe, yet was surpassed by the latter because in China moral standing is stressed. In European humanism, people challenge the religion and moral principles by individual rights. They have exchanged the God worship for money worship. It is absurd for them to proclaim that God is dead.

In modern times, the European profiteers colluded with the government. The invasion to India and the black people trade as the beginning, they carried out colonialism and slave trade. They got rich suddenly by plundering wealth from the orient. After that, they set law as the only criterion. Through patent protection and capitalism, they

develop the modern technology and take the lead in the world.

12. *The Honorable Man Makes Money in the Right Way*

The petty man is greed for money and regards money as his God, so he would always try to get more in the unscrupulous methods, rather than obeying the laws that operate in a free-market economy which is composed of legality, patent, and capital. In China, the honorable man isn't crazy for wealth. They earn money "in proper ways" through the hard work.

It has been long cherished by the Chinese people that "money is covetable for an honorable man who is good at making it". Money falls into two types according to the ways of getting it, the hard-earned money and the easy money. The money made by the honest hard work belongs to the former, and conversely, the unearned windfall belongs to the latter. The honorable man makes his fortune legitimately.

Actually, it is paradoxical to say that money is covetable for an honorable man who is good at making it. How could an honorable man, who values honor above material gains, loves money? How could a man be honorable, if he lays too much stress on money? For a real honorable man, affection is invaluable, just as the poem reads, "A mild-mannered good girl is the fine match for the gentleman who search but cannot find her, would be awake, asleep, and think of her."

To be exact, an honorable man obtains money in proper ways, namely, through honest hard work. Money is not evil but a must for the development of civilization. From this perspective, instead of despising riches, an honorable man is just opposed to sacrificing valuable qualities, such as spirituality, sincerity, kindness and self-denial, to make a fortune. Moreover, he would adhere to the right money-making ways which are based on kindness and obligation.

No pains, no gains. A man would feel at ease and justified if he

earns his living by the sweat of his brow. In Kokang language, the character "财（money）" is compounded by "贝（reserve）" and "才（wits）". From the word formation, it is can be concluded that only the money obtained by reserving wits and hard work is credible and tenable.

It is said nowadays that the problem which can be solved by money is not a difficult one. Similarly, the things could be bought with money are just precious for a while. In ancient times, the honorable man thought highly of kindness, righteousness and wits. Money was regarded as the by-product of virtue cultivation and wisdom dedication, as the honorable man's conduct of self-cultivating, family-regulating, state-ordering and world-governing, and as a natural success of the career.

The thought that the gentleman obtains money through labor which is based upon wit and talent had guided China for over two thousand years, and made China the became a land of propriety, with the effort of all the social strata including the scholar, the farmer, the artisan and the merchant: civil officials administered the country, agriculture held the leading post, while industry and commerce played a supplementary role.

To get money in the right way puts people at ease, which is the foundation of living. Although the thought that the gentleman obtains money in the right way is one of the most important reasons for the great achievements of four civilized ancient countries to survive, it was also scorned and cursed by eastern extremists, after civil constitutionalism led petty person's greed for money to the utility right way.

13. On Promoting the Civilization

Modern affluent industrial and commercial civilization has spread from Europe and the America to Africa and the old continent of Asia. It

is an achievement made by the poor party of the ancient nomadic people and the rich party of agricultural nations under Citizens' constitutional cooperation, which includes the culture of tribe consciousness, converting family consciousness, system and customs then in turn facilitates industrial civilization with scientific proof, logic and ration.

From the 15th century, the European poor citizens (Industrial and commercial class), had eagerly put the Four great inventions of China, binary method, Arabic numerals, Sixty Carry Law and Josiah code into use in order to develop technological civilization and the system of constitutional government which were leading by industry and commerce. They popularized these inventions to the world by European colonial movement and international trade. To overcome the mercenary limits exiting in poor citizens who are eager to get rich quickly, they should be broad-minded.

Nation and country is the same, and people are without exception. When you get old, what you say and how you behave should catch up with the time instead of boasting about prideful experiences at your early years. Try to leave any impressions but old and useless.

In the world of European overnight millionaires, money is the most important, which can change the belief of Catholicism, Protestant ethic and culture dominated and plundered the modern world. When the plunder meets difficulties, they compromised to constitutional civilization with the principle that law is supreme to governing the action. Modern civilization is a synthesis of money and the rule of law in a balanced way. It became a main stream after being spread from Europe to the world.

The industrial civilization is energetic as well as fickle, in which world money is more important than moral quality. It needs to be improved. Europeans are required to absorb the idea that a gentleman makes money through honorable means in Central Plains. Easterners need to learn westerners' wisdom that citizens should take money

abiding by the law.

Modern civilization appeared due to the shallow water of downstream and muddy waves at the mouths of rivers. However, we can't follow the same thoughts anymore. What we should do is to make lawful money and use in the right way. Only in that way can diligence makes people rich and the rich keep morality.

Nowadays, humans need to cherish the good ethics of human nature in the case of getting rid of poverty and value the purity and truth like the lotus in Central Plains which rise unsullied from mud. What's more, humans need to rediscover life, talent, love and money.

In the Buddhist doctrine, there is a saying that your appearance can be changed by mind. And Taoism points out people need to have conscience. What people need is harmony and righteousness but not fear of depraved life and they should make money with talent and use good to control evil.

14. To Start Well and End Well

Doing well from the start to the end is required for us to follow the right path, harmonize with the surroundings and make money by capability. While deceitful tricks are consistently used by swindlers, who have to run away elsewhere to enjoy the illicit money so as to avoid the meeting with the victims. They would be in a constant state of anxiety all the life.

Making money by self-capability is praised, which is a natural outcome of self-effort as well as the accumulation of strength and knowledge. To finish what you have start is a complete circle of life, with the starting point joining the terminal point. When putting it in a historical perspective, we have a brand new world like the bright rainbow after a fierce storm as well as the renaissance of classical culture in the old world.

Modern people give too many explanations to the idiom that to start

well and end well. Yet all of them are inferior to the one provided in the book *The Analects of Confucius*, saying that "only sages can do well from the beginning to the end". Indeed, it is the sages' edification and performance which is not easy for us to achieve.

Consequently, there are always some people giving up halfway, which is regarded as laziness. Laziness is the root of the thought of getting money through unscrupulous methods, as well as the evil idea of getting windfall to lead a life of luxury with wine, sex, money and power. The accumulation of the vices leads to laziness, which further results in theft, robbery and cheat.

Whether a man is honorable or petty depends on this to a great extent: the petty man would just suit themselves but lack perseverance. When losing interest in the idea, he would just drop out, leaving the unfinished business to no end. While the honorable man, just like what Zi Xia, one of Confucius' students at the end of the Spring and Autumn Period, said, would impart knowledge according to the learners' level, starting from foundation and advancing step by step, like the growth of vegetation in stages.

It's impossible for ordinary people to predict the outcome. Only sages can make it. Is doing well from the start to the end the right path? For those who have a negative opinion, it is just an excuse for them to leave their work half done. While for those who have a positive attitude, it serves as a powerful motivator for them to be diligent, at least to stimulate them to finish a complete essay.

There is a TV series in China, named *All's Well, Ends Well*. It narrates a kind-hearted man was framed up, so he supposed that the good would always been injured. Afterwards, he was blackmailed and forced to engage in quite a few charitable deeds. In the process of doing good deeds, he got joy and became a philanthropist gradually.

Zhuangzi once described the main characteristic of great masters- "Do well from the beginning to the end." At the turn of the Qin and

Han Dynasties, Chen Ping, born in a poor family, sequentially became the subordinate of King Jiu of Wei, Xiang Yu and Liu Bang. After the establishment of the Han Dynasty, he served as the prime minister for three successive generations. The judgment of Chen Ping as an office seeker in the later generations is superficial and partial. Those people haven't been aware of Chen's merits yet – preeminent capability and doing well from the beginning to the end.

15. Live an Ordinary and Complaint-free Life

In comparison with Fan Li and Zhang Liang who were masters, Chen Ping could only be classified as the ordinary people. Although he was not able to map out strategies and leave the officialdom undefeated, he started well and ended well as being a man and being an official. Chen Ping's weak point is that he couldn't live an ordinary and complaint-free life.

It is the master that is ready to live in seclusion, being ordinary and without any complaint. They live with the inner peace just like the accomplished monk does. Being a monk, one live his whole life peacefully in his own world and would not see to other's life. However, it is difficult for the ordinary people to get rid of the rights and money when he is engaged in the officialdom. On the contrary, if one tries to pursue the uprightness among the injustice, he would be treated unjustly and even imprisoned. Examples are Yue Fei and Hai Rui.

In history, master includes the learned businessmen, incorruptible officials and the none-profiteering artisans. Tzu Kung, Wen Tian Xiang and Mozi, etc. are of this kind of people who could lead an ordinary and complaint free life. Yan Hui, disciple of Confucius, was especially well known for this. As an example of the benevolent people, he felt contented with the most basic livelihood like the simple food, drink and shabby house, he was extremely modest and studious, he never blamed his own mistakes to the others or commit the same mistake for a second

time. In ancient Greece, only Socrates and other few people could have such state of mind.

Actually, it is not proper to make a mechanical analogy between Chen Ping, Yan Hui and Socrates. Like the stars in the cosmic space, each of them has their unique features and lifestyle, which would be comprehend and commented by those who live after them.

It's unnecessary to be distressed for being ordinary. If one could make up his mind to be a benevolent person as Yan Hui, he could also enjoy the inexhaustible joy. Such people may pay no attention to the external things, yet they are certain to have a big mind, that is, they conduct themselves asking for no more than their due and fulfill their duty with a clear conscience. Their ordinary deeds and unordinary mind enlighten people in those days as well as nowadays about the importance of being responsible and conscientious.

To reach this state of peace, it needs sense of propriety, justice, honesty and honor, which has to be led by a big mind. Only in this way can one lead an easeful life with righteousness and assertiveness.

If one fulfills his duty without any complaint and regret, there will be no conflict over fame and gains, no anxiety about losses. And it is exactly what it takes to develop the mind of the great: not pleased by external gains, not saddened by personal losses, and contenting himself with what he has. Neither riches nor honors can corrupt him. He will keep peace in mind and modest attitude forever.

Being noble is uneasy, because there's a high standard of being righteous. Yet it also takes a down-to-earth attitude. In one word, ancient Chinese were more pragmatic than ancient European.

16. To Turn Over a New Leaf

First appeared in *I Ching* (*The Book of Changes*), the idiom "to turn over a new leaf" means to eliminate the old ideas and to renew the old image. It is said that the Shang Tang Revolution in the late years of

the Xia Dynasty and the King Wu Revolution in the late years of the Shang Dynasty raised abiding by the Ko Hexagram that "To do man's best and leave all else to God". Those two revolutions endowed the Shang Dynasty with a history of 600 years and the Zhou Dynasty of 800 years.

49 "Ko (Revolution or Molting)", as its origin, is the title of Chapter 49 of *The Book of Changes* that "Tui, the joyous, lake is over; Li, the clinging, fire". Shang Tang and King Wu used to be the feudal vassals in the Xia and Shang Dynasties respectively. In the era of the declining Xia and Shang Dynasties, they got the apocalypse through the divination of Ko Hexagram that the corrupt life of the upper class in the previous dynasty had aroused the widespread indignation and discontent. They two should follow the mandate of heaven and comply with the popular wishes of the people to overthrow the rotten society and establish the new era.

According to historical records, guided by the Ko Hexagram, Shang Tang who was benevolent gave the wrongdoer a way out and was made the successor of the emperor of the Xia Dynasty by most of the states in the Shang Dynasty. After the foundation of the Shang Dynasty, the new Confucian orthodoxy that believing in God and carrying out the policy of benevolence was established.

King Wu, also guided by the Ko Hexagram, followed in his father, King Wen's footstep and launched the revolution in the end of the Shang Dynasty. King Wen was courteous and condescending to the wise government officials who were discarded or cruelly injured in the Shang Dynasty. After the establishment of the Zhou Dynasty, King Wu founded the new Confucian orthodoxy about the system of rites and personal status.

Written into the annals of history, the revolutions of Tang and Wu happened on the occasion that the tyranny in previous dynasty enraged its people. It was not a simple change of regime through the coup or

civil war, rather it was the revival of the totally new benevolent government.

In Chinese imperial revolutionary history, only two that the Shang Tang and King Wu Revolutions confirmed to "Ko" in *The Book of Changes*. And there was none of such revolutions in the other places of the world. The Revolution of 1911 overthrew the Chinese monarchy. Following the examples of the US and France, the Republic of China implemented the republicanism and entered the brand new utilitarian world.

The success of Meiji Restoration had brought Japan the rapid development. But for the decades after the Chinese bourgeois democratic revolution, the successive radical movements, such as assassination, civil war, Monarch Restoration, National Protection, Constitution Protection and so on, consumed the national power and gave the change for the vile man to take advantages.

What matters in the revolution is not the overthrow and change of dynasties, it should bring in a brilliant regime and a brand new society. For 38 years, the Republic of China had taken anti-tradition actions in Chinese mainland. it was the Westernization in essence. The blind pursuit of newly-emerged things would lead to serious misconducts. People would never repent if people couldn't be clear with its causation.

17. The Karma and the Classical Indian Logic

The ancient Greek philosophers tried to explore the origin of every existing substance, and counted them as water, fire, soil, gas, atom, spirit and so on. After the endless argument and through finding the origin and the conclusion of the spirit, the Theology of Genesis, Jesus Christ salvation and the Last Judgment, etc. was created to introduce the abstinence among European ancients and make them long for heaven after death.

Long heard in the orient, the Karma has its ultimate grounds as

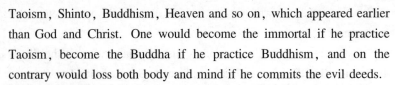

Taoism, Shinto, Buddhism, Heaven and so on, which appeared earlier than God and Christ. One would become the immortal if he practice Taoism, become the Buddha if he practice Buddhism, and on the contrary would loss both body and mind if he commits the evil deeds.

The Karma and transmigration (of the pre-life and this life) doctrine in Mahayana Buddhism, together with the golden mean in Confucianism and the inaction in Taoism, preaches the teachings that one should do unto others as he would be done and one would enjoy the hidden happiness out of suffering. Based on this, the civilization of the Tang and Song Dynasties had been in the leading position for 600 years all over the world.

The civilizing thought of Chinese Tang and Song Dynasties adopted the Classical Logic of Indian Buddhism. According to the "16 categories (prameya, Saaya, prayojana, etc.)" of dialectics, the proposition, reason, example, application and conclusion are applied to deduct the origin of human life.

In this case, the rational cost accounting and opposite labor relations were not able to be established thus prevented the development of the bourgeois science, technology and industry in Orient.

In the modern theory of cause and effect, good and bad or benign and evil are longer distinguished. Instead, it belongs to analytic method which is used by the European-established logical positivism knowledge like mathematics, physics and chemistry, etc. In mathematics, the premise of equation and geometric proof are called the cause and the solutions are called the effect. Take $3+2=5$ for example, $3+2=5$ is the cause and 5 is the conclusion.

In physics and chemistry, the experimental materials and data are regarded as the cause and the experimental results are the effect. For instance, when baking bread, the starch retrogradation is the cause and the elasticity of the bread is the effect. Another example is that the cause of eating unclean food will make the effect of diarrhea.

The scientific analysis of cause and effect regulation replaced the origin elements of water and fire in philosophy and God in theology. The logical positivism knowledge changes people's life, bring in heating, body cleansing, medical treatment, health care and cosmetology, etc. The consequence is that most people are dominated by the isms and their own thoughts are trapped by the preconceived ideas.

18. Every Dog has His Day

In Popular *Collection of Traditional Chinese Wise sayings*, a saying goes as "Good luck makes iron like gold, and bad luck makes gold like iron." It is about the luck that would change from good to bad in the world and vice versa. It is the bad luck that one may have the gold changed into iron if his fate is unfavorable. And it is the good luck that one may pick up a piece of scrap iron and exchange it to gold once the fate is in favor of him.

Luck, to its essence, is the lucky chance operates between the natural law and worldly events. The movement of the earth would inevitably cause the natural disaster at some time and in somewhere, like the earthquake, flood, volcanic eruption, debris flow and so on which would enforce people with bad luck.

Someone who is always out of luck happens to escape from the disaster because of business trip or travel out. Then he win promotion and get rich, enjoying successive good lucks. Just as the old saying goes that every dog has his day. There are also some people used to have everything goes well with them but come to the place right before the disaster accidentally and become the "sacrificial lamb". Luck, just like the weather, sometimes can be foretasted while sometimes cannot. What can be done is just wait with patient and be a good man.

A futile attempt would be made if it is not in the right time. But when the occasion presented itself, good luck would suddenly appear as the cloudy day turns into the sunny one. When man lives in this world, he has to be engaged in the complex relationship among the families, schools, workplace and neighborhoods which is quite similar to the plot of dramatic works. All of the relations above construct the Karma in the buddhistic concept. From this aspect, Karma is the old term for luck.

The people who is capable yet not content with his lot, for example Han Xin and Cao Cao, becomes the hero in the time of misfortune. More unsuccessful men would come into being in peacetime. They always try to find the short cuts and leave things unfinished without patience. They have great ambition but little talent and not willing to devote to their duties. To them, the grass is greener on the other side of the fence. They waste the time and rue it bitterly all their life. Like heroes, the absolute dawdlers are also belong to the minority. They are neither bother to toady for personal gain nor willing to work hard. They try to avoid the difficult and tiring job and always depend on others. Eventually, they are getting old with nothing accomplished.

There is a kind of people who have suffered a lot. When bitterness is finished, sweetness begins. Taking the natural cause, they can do their best and leave all else to God. Just like the plants in nature, they grow in compliance with their biological features and the natural environment.

In the Hong Kong comedy movie *Those Merry Souls*, the plots are light and entertaining, in which the demons and ghosts are interwoven. In this movie, luck is discussed through the ghost stories, which is really confusing.

Is the accidental death really accidental in this world? In the world, competitions exist everywhere. The American is advanced in science and technology, meanwhile it has the movie *Batteries Not Included* which is about luck and has it retaken. What kind of information does it convey?

19. *Emissary of Ghost and God*

Emissary of Ghost and God, literally, refers to two kinds of creature, messenger of the ghost and envoy of god. It used to describe the people who have done the unintentional things unconsciously as if controlled by ghost and god. The bad guys are double faced and the utterly evil man would commit all sorts of evil with devilish impulse. As the saying goes like evil will be recompensed with evil. They would be eliminated by the political power and religious force.

Scientific research shows that children and animals are extremely sensitive to some supernatural phenomena. Child can see and believe the things and phenomena which adult cannot. So, when they try to tell the adults about the strange things they have seen, they are always not believed.

The American movie *Batteries Not Included* narrates that a family was forced to move to other place after the father lost his job. They then bought a sunflowers ranch and started the new life. After moving to the new house, the 3-year-old son and 16-year-old daughter perceived the phantom of ghost one after another. However, none of the adults believed them and thought they told a lie.

In *Batteries Not Included* 2, the scenes of 30 night and the resentment of the evil producer are depicted, which make it more horrible than the previous episode. To save the crops, a farmer set the mysterious scarecrows in his field with the hope to find the demons. With more and more people losing their lives in the farmland, the farmer finally strikes back to the evil.

America is the country with the most advanced positivistic science, yet puts forth effort to present in its movies the supernatural phenomena which have long been the interests of the oriental religion and metaphysics. What does this trend mean to America? Does it convey any message to us?

If a man plants melons, he will reap melons; if he sows beans, he will reap beans; if he plants plum, he will reap plum. "One would reap what he has sown" originates from *Nirvana Sutra*. It teaches people in modern time about the Karma in Buddhism that good will be rewarded with good, and evil with evil. When the time arrives, one will get all the rewards he deserves.

In the scientifically advanced America, the supernatural phenomena begin to be shown via scientific techniques and cinematics. It is the manifestation that the religion evolution of science has gone to a dead end. The religion begins to make a counterattack to science in the name of the ancient oriental thinking.

Meanwhile, it predicts that the revival of the Taoism, Confucianism and Buddhism thinking and culture in Orient (especially in China) will come. The oriental doctrines are discussed in the American book *The Fifth Discipline*, which are now promoting the development science and the revival of religion and metaphysics.

20. Doing What Comes Naturally

Being perceptible, it is hard for human beings to explain why the luck may turn from bad to good and why there are unexpected happenings or curious coincidence. Facing such occasions, it is wise to take the natural cause rather to eliminate them in the name of against the feudalistic superstition as the radical people in many countries have done in recent times.

The inconceivable traditions in any countries and regions all came from the reality by lucky chance. For instance, the doctrine of Confucius and Mencius and the Catholicism in France. China has experienced some obstacles in the development in the recent century and good people may run into ill-luck. As a matter of fact, it is the inevitable result from abusing Chinese traditional culture and setting artificial cultural trap.

In Chinese lucky time, people in the Han and Tang Dynasties led the best life all over the world. By contrast, the parallel Rome of the Han Dynasty underwent a licentious society, which brought about the salvation that Jesus was crucified on the cross and the spread of Christianity. The parallel Frankish Kingdom of the Tang Dynasty was even worse than Rome, whose civilization lagged behind the Tang Dynasty for hundreds of years.

In Chinese culture, the idea is treasured that to let things take their own course. Therefore, in *Tao Te Ching*, it goes as "The Tao way follows the nature". The intellectuals behave well as the gentleman. They obey the order of the universe to make unremitting efforts to improve themselves and to fulfill their social commitment. They take the course of self-cultivation.

To be more specific, to achieve the full self-improvement, 6 phases are necessary that to conceal the talent and wait for the right time; to learn from great man; to take actions according to circumstances; to work hard and be careful and discreet; to make accomplishment and be successful; and never be conceited or arrogant. If one could not be fully prepared in the first phase, he would never upgrade to the following stages. Just as the saying goes, "things do not always turn out as one would expect".

Some Chinese idioms have the same meaning. For example, "to help the shoots grow by pulling them upward" and "to force someone to do something against his will". However careful it is, the flower would be dead if its root is damaged during transplant. Why? Because to make the flower with root damaged alive is against the law of nature. When the law of nature is violated, people will get punishment. To block the flood will result in flood disaster.

The wisdom of taking natural course can be compared to plant the vigorous willow. You poke a willow stick in the mud and it grows into a tree, even the willow woods. That is to say the well-laid plans may fail,

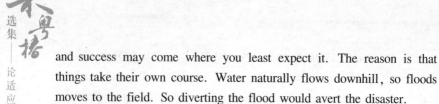

and success may come where you least expect it. The reason is that things take their own course. Water naturally flows downhill, so floods moves to the field. So diverting the flood would avert the disaster.

Due to the meteorologic and geographical conditions, the mountain peaks are wrapped by the clouds. Humans are not able to fly by themselves due to their biological features. Even human emotions including the blind passion and sorrow also have this natural rules and regulations, but cannot be demanded by people. To everything there is a season and a time to every purpose under heaven. He who let things take their own course will have the peaceful state of mind when he gets old.

21. Learning with Your Heart

It is the justice of nature that we should let things take its course. Humans also have their own laws to obey. A person can never be called a person without a heart or lead a pig's life waiting for being slaughtered someday. Things that are worth doing are supposed to be done with a positive heart: good cooking techniques can make a delicious dish, a good harvest can only be got by sweating and working hard.

A student should read books with heart. If he does not listen to the lecture and finish the homework carefully, but just sleep days away, it is definitely a zero score that he will get in an exam. Chances are that some talented students who don't work hard and can only get an average score may be the leading scholar in scientific field. It is an exception.

For instance, Einstein worked pretty hard despite his innate talent. He was described as lazy and an slow, but still his unique diligence and intelligence were ignored by his teachers. He had been listening with heart before he started to talk at age of three. He had unintentionally followed the rule of listening with soul brought up by Chinese Taoism, which is kind of lazy compared with listening with ears.

When reading we should use our heart. Reading is like

communicating and exchanging ideas with the author. We can't understand even one single word if we do not have patience and do not use heart, which is an experience of all readers. One must be diligent when reading and absorb everything with heart. Not only should he know what it is but also why it is so.

One can get nothing in an exam unless he learns by heart. He can obtain quite a lot of treasure if he learns by heart. "Nothing" and "treasure" are used metaphorically, which is not logical at all if understood literally by someone intentionally.

Lv Buwei, in the ancient book *Historical Records* at the end of the Warring States Period, stepped into political area after doing business for a while. Becoming the Prime minister of the Qin dynasty, he started to gather many scholars to compile the book named *Spring and Autumn Annals of Mister Lv*. After the book was finished, all the contents were carved into the gate. And a thousand pieces of gold would be bestowed to whoever can add to even one change of word to the article.

That may sound pretty shrewd and like an advertisement. With the hope to make the book famous and hand it down to later generations, Lv Buwei followed the examples of Confucius revising *Spring and Autumn Annals* and Sun Wu offering *The Art of War* to King Wu. As a result, his aim was reached. This plan was designed with care. *Spring and Autumn Annals*, *The Art of War* and *Spring and Autumn Annals of Mister Lv* were all written with heart. Confucius, Sun Wu and the authors of *Spring and Autumn Annals of Mister Lv* were the people who read and learned with heart and their every character understood is worth a thousand pieces of gold.

22. *The Differentiation between Cathay and Barbarians*

During Spring and Autumn Period, thoughts expressions was worth a thousand pieces of gold in Chinese vassal states. However, people

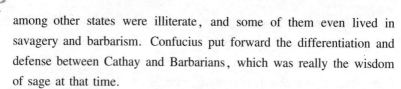

among other states were illiterate, and some of them even lived in savagery and barbarism. Confucius put forward the differentiation and defense between Cathay and Barbarians, which was really the wisdom of sage at that time.

Different from Confucian scholars at Qianglong Era who depreciated Englishmen ignorantly, Confucius made diplomatic defense based on the reality. He made the differentiation according to the Chinese etiquette. Those who abode by the etiquette was regarded as the Chinese Hua Xia people, in whichever tribe or race he used to be. As to aggressive Western Tributaries and Hun, the Great Wall was constructed to defend their invasion.

China was adjacent to Chu State in the Eastern Tributaries and Yue State in the Southern Tributaries. China had conflicts with them every now and then, but much less frequently than with the western and northern tributaries. As to the barbarous tribes who made a living by agriculture instead of looting, China would influence them with Chinese etiquette according to the diplomatic thinking of the differentiation between Cathay and Barbarians. Those who didn't know the etiquette were barbarians, and those who knew were Chinese.

It is the same that the Chinese become the American citizen nowadays. If one is not naturalized in America, he still belong to his original nation. Once he is naturalized in America, he is an American. The nationality system is actually the modern version of the the differentiation between Cathay and Barbarians.

The differentiation and defense between Cathay and Barbarians was a kind of cultural diplomacy based on the Chinese civilization in the Spring and Autumn Period. It was a dominant strategy of Confucius since Guan Zhong of Qi State proposed the theory of "honor the king and drive off the Barbarians". They domesticate Hun and Turkic with the sense of propriety, justice, honesty and honor. In fact, that the western countries spread Christianity in China can be regarded as the

"influence of Europe to China".

In the differentiation and defense between Cathay and Barbarians, it was rational and wise that the aim was to keep guard instead of invasion. The barbarous Chu State developed its culture by day and made alliance with the states in the Central Plains, so it was treated as a Chinese nation. The Zheng State, originally belonged to China, didn't comply with Chinese etiquette. As a result, it was considered as a barbarous tribe. When Zheng State realized that they were degrading to be barbarian and became self-restraint, they returned to the China alliance.

Importance was attached on the dress and etiquette in ancient China, from which the social status and propriety were developed. Those who are dressed with aristocratic clothing should perform the duty of aristocrats. The dress should match the status. In modern times, it is called that the great power must be worthy of its name and cannot shirk the assumed responsibility.

The differentiation between Cathay and Barbarians had long been the diplomatic realism of many states in central mainland in Chinese history. However, it is criticized as Chinese nationalism in modern times.

23. On Be Slave to the Ancients

In modern China, some people were eager to pursue the westernization. They mistook the political idea that "the differentiation between Cathay and Barbarians" as three isms, namely, the narrow nationalism, the arrogant centralism and the deep cultural nationalism. To make irresponsible remarks on history with isms would lead to the problem that the culture being slave to the ancients.

It is important to study the ancient culture via reading and writing. However, being stereotypical and pedantic blindly, one would become old-fashioned and inflexible after reading the ancient books and articles.

Thus, he could become the slave to the ancient, just like swallowing the food but without digest it.

It would be even worse if one could not differentiate the historical tradition and modern trend, and confuse the history and reality, tradition and tendency as political issue.

In ancient China, defenses were set up against the foreign people only for the sake of protecting its civilization, yet the intermarriage was still allowed. Father of Duke Wen of Jin was a Chinese man while his mother came from the western tributary. Such distinction was of significance, so was the military protection. If no distinction or protection were set up, everything would be mixed up and the society would fall into disorder, which would do no good to anybody. What Zhu Xi once said is quite reasonable that "If Confucius has never come, the world would remain uncivilized region forever. "

To be rational, some foreign countries like the Huns and Mongolia should also differentiate themselves with Chinese people. They also needed various distinction and protection. For example, if a Chinese thief was found to sneak into a tent in Turkic but not caught and put on trial. As a result, the theft would be connived.

So, the differentiation between Cathay and Barbarians in the Eastern Zhou Dynasty was reasonable, and it was blameless to make the map with Chinese territory in the central and four uncivilized Tributaries (Eastern Tributaries, Southern Tributaries, Southern Tributaries and Northern Tributaries) around according to that differentiation. Also, no blame should be given to the tribute relationship in the Han and Tang Dynasties. Due to that differentiation, China, as the central of the world, received tribute from other countries.

The Song Dynasty was less powerful. The Liao and Jin Dynasty accepted Chinese culture and called themselves as "China" to central Asia and Europe. According to Japanese point of way, China was no longer there after the Southern Song Dynasty lost the Yanshan Battle.

The Yuan Dynasty used to invade Japan and was defeated. Since then, Japan claim itself as the authentic successor of Chinese culture.

In the Ming Dynasty, guided by the thought that "China is superior to all the others", maritime trade was banned. The maritime "Great Wall" was constructed to cut the connection with Japan in the east and Spain, Portugal, and Netherlands in the west for over 100 years. Actually, it was a failed diplomatic policy caused by sticking blindly and stubbornly to old. At that time, the European colonialism had been developing and influencing the Old and New worlds. While what the Ming Dynasty had done was only to follow the old. And the imperial government had been doomed to decline.

24. Humility and Inferiority

Personally, the elderly, who are able to regard themselves as incompetents, are humble and carry forward the Chinese tradition of humility. Humility is the name of the fifteenth trigram in the *Book of Changes*, in which the image of the high mountains, rising below the sea level and never showing off its stunning spectacle, symbolizes the honorable man's humble mind.

According to the indication of the images and text in Humility Trigram, the honorable men conduct themselves with grace and courtesy at every moment, like the high mountains rising below the sea level, peacefully and unassumingly. Furthermore, the real honorable men would always keep an open mind, just like high mountains never disguising the cliffs. And we have so many proverbs related to it in China, such as "The wise always tolerate other's defect" and "A great person is large-hearted or magnanimous."

Generally, the elderly fall into two categories: One category never yield to age and would always linger lovingly over the account of his exploits. Yet their words would usually be stuck in throat in others' disdain – "Yesterday's sun can't dry today's clothes." Conversely, the other category ordinarily belittle themselves. But when in trouble, they remain calm and independent. Calling themselves the incompetent shows not only their humility, but also a deep understanding of the proverb- "However strong you are, there is always someone stronger. "

The elderly who self-abase themselves the incompetent are the real sages, and can encourage the youth fulfill their promise. Knowing that they time has gone, the elderly are willing to recommend the young talents and sincerely hope the young generation can follow their upright track.

Cursing ancestors is a sign of inferiority, implying incapability and dependence. Those people just try to shift the responsibility onto the ancestors. The sense of inferiority is also called as inferiority complex by Psychologist A · Adler, which shares the same meaning with a Chinese proverb- "Being too conscious of face". The lazy and wicked people, middle-aged or young, who relieve their stress through cursing ancestors, would always be content with superficial understanding when reading.

Zai Yu, one of Confucius' students, was s good speaker. Yet he would skip classes to sleep, just like a rotten wood undeserving of delicate carving. Nevertheless, these shiftless and lazy guys would not endanger our society.

Those indolent evildoers, who never ask for self-improvement and iron will, would always put all the blame on the historical tradition and the autocracy in ancient times. It is an intense sense of inferiority: They don't want to take the trouble to obtain self-improvement. What's more, these people always have an unwarranted anxiety that even if they have gone through hardships and been qualified for the position, they won't be thought highly of.

The culture of Confucianism, Taoism and Buddhism composed the consciousness of humility in China. The elderly could be also charged with an important mission, if they keep a beginner's mind, just like

Huang Zhong, a general of the Shu Han dynasty during the Three Kingdoms. However, once a man is trapped in the inferiority complex, he will be indolent and stoop to shifting off responsibility, which is incurable.

25. On Westernization and Defamation of History

Since the defeat of the Sino-Japanese War in the late Qing Dynasty, some of Chinese people who were influenced by the Western learning had renounced the valuable tradition of self-cultivation. On the contrary, they began to disguise the long-restrained evil thought with the western individualism, freedom and despotism, and slandered the history unscrupulously in the name of people's benefit and patriotism.

Those people were generally radical and blamed all the sufferings in Chinese history on Ci Xi and her adherents indiscriminately. From the social psychological analysis, their slogan of "overthrowing the feudal rule" was the embodiment of the inferiority complex of some candidates who failed the imperial exams and overseas Chinese students. Because they were fear of imperial examinations and were eager to enhance their political and social status through the civil way.

After the Opium War, two old-style teachers in village combined the belief of Jesus Salvation and peasants' revolt. They created the religion of Worshiping God which in their followers believed and established the Taiping Heavenly Kingdom in the area of Hubei, Hu'nan, Jiangxi, Jiangsu and Anhui Provinces. There they demolished the ancestral temple and the memorial tablet of Confucius and Mencius. That was the beginning of the defamation of history and the malediction of ancestors.

As if there is an invisible hand, people were endlessly pushed to take in the western ideology and culture, technology and industry (from military purpose to home use), and congressional legislation, etc. And at last, they asked for the overall westernization.

Nowadays, in the economic takeoff of the Four Asian Tigers, almost all the ethical traditions of Chinese family system and family discipline were preserved. On the contrary, in the mainland, the birthplace of Chinese culture, people began to defame its culture and tradition including their ancestors, Taoism, Confucianism, emperors and so on.

The radicals looked for pretexts for the failure of movements caused by their indolence and impulsiveness. They upheld the Japanese and western political system, make irresponsible remarks with the shallow-understood economic, ethical, social, and religious knowledge. They thought they had already grasp the truth and became extremely conceited, saying "we are the chosen one to invigorate China."

Their demand of instant success made them neither fish nor fowl. As to the choosing school, joining in organizations, participating in movements, they neither follow Chinese tradition and morality nor obey the western constitutional laws. They finally ended up as a band of incorrigible political pioneers.

Those people condemned traditions and transmitted errors. What they had done were merely agitating, replacing the rational discrimination, factual analysis, and logical argument. They were anxious to bring in all sorts of the isms. They would discard the isms which were no longer prevalent and influential, or just change their names and continue to blind people if they couldn't get rid of.

26. Wise self-protection

According to *The Book of Changes*, changing demands right timing. Before the timing, wise men should be skillful in protecting themselves from incurring troubles through self-discipline and social commitment. On the one hand, self-discipline can "let the Dragon fly in the air" since non-competition brings about "a multitude of dragons without a leader". On the other hand, social commitment can "bring

good luck and prosperity" and "avoid outbreaks of fierce wars in battlefield".

Yin Jifu, a minister in Western Zhou Dynasty, expressed the idea of keeping away from troubles wisely and staying faithful to his duty unremittingly in his poem *The People*. In the official circles, wise men never follow the tide blindly but show a sharp sense of integrity; they get immersed in the corrupt system but still keep their moral integrity.

Upon the death of Emperor of Lu, King Xuan of Western Zhou Dynasty abolished the lineal primogeniture system established by Duke Zhou and killed the legal king Duke Yi of Lu without taking the assisting ministers Yin Jifu and Zhong Shanfu's suggestions. How could Zhong Shanfu anticipate the result of this move? Zhong Shanfu was intelligent enough to realize that removing the elder to set the younger on the throne could not work at that time.

By King's order, Zhong Shanfu went to build city walls in the kingdom of Qi in order to defend the attacks from Xirong tribes. Yin Jifu highly commended the behaviors of Zhong Shanfu in a poem and offered him great consolation for his expedition.

Zhong Shanfu was wise and loyal enough to foretell that destroying the succession system could cause troubles to the Kingdom of Lu. About 3 000 years later in the period of the Republic of China, Professor Zhu Ziqing claimed that wise self-protection from troubles could only create "some nihilists" in his essay of *On Integrity*. Such a shallow argument!

In history, Chen Ping of Western Han Dynasty has not achieved as distinguished career as Sun Wu and Fan Li have on retirement, but he is devoted and dutiful as a minister all his life and he is always wise enough to keep out of trouble by discretion. Chen Yuanliang, a hermit in Southern Song Dynasty, once summarized a wise man as someone that "concentrates on sweeping the snow from his own doorstep and doesn't bother about the frost on his neighbor's roof" in *Vast Records of*

Daily Matters (Shilin Guangji). Britain and America encourage ordinary citizens to do so by constitutional system.

In Ming and Qing Dynasties, the concept of wise self-protection was enriched. For example, "when you are acquainted with someone, you do not need to show genuine intimacy but limit your behaviors to daily greetings"; "In drawing a tiger or a dragon, you show its skin, but not its bones; In knowing a man, you may know his face, but not his heart"; "Disputes usually come out of tattle, and troubles usually arise from recklessness". Opinions on these philosophies of life may differ from one person to another. Different people have different views on this question.

When dealing with different matters in different times, people may adopt different ways and show different characters. According to Zhu Ziqing's logic of criticism, the practice of constitutional system in western countries is aimed to produce " citizens who concentrate on protecting their own interest while paying little attention to the public welfare". However, by imaginations and fancies, an author can write prose works to express his emotions but he may not be apt at writing critics.

27. Soul mates

When Zhong Shanfu of Western Zhou Dynasty went to build city walls for the state of Qi, Yin Jifu wrote a poem to send him off saying, "His steeds are galloping unremittingly, Eight bells of each steed are tinkling on. " "My heart will be always with Zhong Shanfu, I wish his task be well done. "

His words are restrained, but if you read it over and over again its meaning becomes self-evident. The poem can not be translated into a prose for the sake of beauty of language. From " His steeds are galloping unremittingly. Eight bells of each steed are tinkling on. " to "Merrily the ospreys cry, On the islet in the stream. ", and from

"Gentle and graceful is the girl, A fit wife for the gentleman." to "My heart will be always with Zhong Shanfu, I wish his task be well done.", the deep and firm friendship between Yin and Zhong becomes obvious.

In view of the current phenomena such as hostility between teachers and students and accusation from relatives or friends, we may probably hardly understand Yin and Zhong's friendship. Some of us even question the truth that the famous two brothers Bo Yi and Shu Qi of Western Zhou Dynasty supported and helped each other and later starved to death together on Mount Shouyang. It reflects the sad reality at present: people are usually cold and indifferent to each other, and moral degradation becomes widespread.

In ancient times, historians insisted on recording the true history at the risk of being killed. The phrase "the friendship of Guan Zhong and Bao Shuya" first appeared in Lie Zi of the Warring States Period and it is used till now. This story is recorded in *The Records of Grand Historian*. This book is based on the true stories which are all investigated on the spot by the author Sima Qian.

Guan Zhong from poor background always took advantage of Bao Shuya of rich family, but Bao did not bear any grudge but show genuine friendliness towards Guan. After serving different heads, Guan Zhong became prisoner of Bao Shuya, but Bao made Guan in place of his position. Guan Zhong concluded, "It's my parents who gave me my life, and it is Baozi who knows me."

The deep friendship between Bo Yi and Shuqi, Yin Jifu and Zhong Shanfu, as well as Guan Zhong and Bao Shuya passes on from generation to generation. They know each other from heart as Bo Ya who played the guqin well enough to "compel the admiration from six horses" ceased to play on hearing the news of his soul mate Zhong Ziqi's death.

Zhuang Zi of Warring States Period commented on the four friends

Zi Si, Zi Yu, Zi Li and Zi Lai as people with common ideals who "linked their lives together" and "smiled at each other with complete sincerity".

The stories of genuine friends above all happened in Warring States Period in China. In the same period of Japan, the mutual trust among warriors and masters and servants were also not unusual. The friends you know on the surface need to be tested as the old saying goes "As distance tests a horse's strength, so time reveals a person's heart."

28. To Be at Odds and of One Mind

People are gradually at odd from knowing each other to guarding to each other. Various reformed churches are separated from Catholic Church. When Catholic Church and reformed churches came to China to preach, and the ideological struggle became more complicated and acute.

In KoKang language, different from ideological diversification and conflict, people say be at odds or dissension and discord-unable to reach agreement and act in unison. The Chinese people had realized this dissension and discord three thousand years ago.

It is reported in *Book of History* that when King Wu of Zhou overthrew the tyrant Zhou of Shang, he said "Licentious King Zhou treated chancellors as thieves and friends as enemies. Thinking himself as the representative of the God, he did all kinds of evil and was fearless. People only prayed to be away from him. So even though King Zhou had millions of people, he suffered the dissension and discord."

Dissension and discord results in the fact that many people appear united outwardly but divided at heart. So they are doomed to be isolated and helpless. Being close to the villain but keeping distance from the wise man, they would come to a bad end.

If people are of different minds, they even cannot make the

decision to buy a needle even though they have money. The couple sleep in the same bed but dream different dreams. Each of them has his own plan. As a result, they would live apart or get divorced. So couples should trust each other and act in unison. Just as the Xiehouyu (two-part allegorical saying) goes, a couple makes the millstone go— cooperation.

In Europe, the constitutional governments are established to protect the private rights and regulate the social behaviors. In Orient, what are concerned is that people are of different minds. So, means are always tried to unify the different people and made them of one mind. It is a cooperative project for ants to carry insects. People should learn from ants and act in a concerted effort.

At the turn of the Ming and Qing Dynasty, scholars in China once taught people that with the unified mind, people can get everything even if they don't have money. Indeed, if people can cooperate and nothing cannot be accomplished without money. The precondition is cooperation. People are of the same mind and belief.

When King Wu of Zhou joint forces with local officials at Mengjin, he said that even though Zhou had millions of people, but he had dissension and discord. Although they only had ten people, they were of one mind. God would surely know people's wish and hear their voices. The punitive expedition aimed to act for God and exercise morality for the people in the world so as to continue benevolent government established by King Tang of Shang.

29. The True Meaning of to Give and to Get

To give and to get are talked by many people. What has been talked is about trade that "to give" can buy "to get". This is the management art of life.

A book, *To Give and to Get-Those Two Words Changing Your Life*, is about how to manage the life with the method of "to give and to get". The author is a Chinese. He studied abroad in America. After retiring from financial industry, he devoted himself to the researches and speeches on life inspiration.

In western outlook on life, they are not able to have a deep comprehension on to give and to get like. Their understanding is just like drilling. Getting water, oil, and even gold, they are still in the lithosphere (consisting of crust and the mantle), not moving on to the asthenosphere.

The true meaning of giving and getting is about the choice in one's life. People should take the natural cause. One makes study transcending philosophy, and is persevering more than be happy and successful. He does his best and obeys the laws of nature. He doesn't worry about personal gains and losses or tries to operate the life. He never attempts to do business with God and dominate his own destiny. This kind of wisdom makes he proceed and step back freely. Knowing that the more one give, the more he will get, one would be clear and generous when doing something.

The Yangtze River flows eastward into Pacific; the Brahmaputra River flows westward into Indian Ocean; the Xiang River flows northward into Dongting Lake; and the Chang River flows southward into Poyang Lake. Life, as the rivers, will proceed to various directions. Flowing water strikes the rocks to form waves. Noisy in the water surface, it is tranquil in the river bottom.

Never do the great rivers move forward continuously. Sometimes, they go back and detour, including more branches on the way. Like the flow of rivers, one's life is enriched during the procedure of advancing and backing. Willing to give up is a kind of quality. A man's broad mind is embodied by his noble behavior like to help others without seeking any rewards and sacrifice his own interests for the sake of others.

Willing to give up is a state of mind. Being wise to make choices,

being low-profile, and being indifferent to fame and wealth, one would lead a magnanimous and natural life. In the process of drilling, the drill may be blocked by the hard stone in lithosphere. If continue, the drill will become blunt even be broken down. With the mind of giving up, one would make changes when encountering the obstacles. Learn to contemplate, one would surpass the difficulties and enter the "asthenosphere" of life. In this case, to give up will bring in enormous space for development.

One should learn to obtain the wisdom of giving and getting as well as to know the truth of advancing and backing. Only be this can one enjoy his life without any bad influence.

30. On Eventuality and Inevitability

Life is full of eventuality and change. Most of the time, it is by chance that people get promoted and rich, make friends and fall in love. Destiny depends on people's subjective grasp. A momentary slip may turn the happiness to the opposite, which must be a cliffhanger in the novel of the movie.

A businessman was failed in his business in Beijing. In the difficult position, he received help from a girl whose hometown was in Jiangsu Province by chance. Out of gratitude, the businessman had a lot of none-business contact with woman and later they were blessed with a happy marriage. Good will is rewarded with good. One will get good returns if he is grateful and cherish the good opportunity.

If the businessman's thinking was westernized. He would made a precise calculation and found the business in Beijing may not profitable. As a result, he would cancel his plan in Beijing and he would never show his gratitude to the Jiangsu girl. Thus, to give up the unprofitable business means to miss the marriage which is the inevitability in the eventuality. The Jiangsu girl would follow her parents' arrangement, and be the wife of an official.

Many phenomena in the world cannot be explained from the scientific point of view. For example, there is a government clerk who disdains to be a sycophant and doesn't have the resources to secure the official position and get promoted. Usually, he would be the clerk all his life. However, he is eminent in the factional strife and becomes the director of the bureau.

Such chance occurrences illustrated above as the businessman married a good wife and the clerk promoted to the director cannot be directly connected with the general law in one's life. However, it can be regarded as certain inevitability from the points of the complexity of social life and the religious karma theory.

Taking the instance of the businessman, he had favorable impression on the Jiangsu girl. Although suffering the loss in business, he was grateful, so he could engaged in the unintentional marriage. For that clerk, he had nothing to do with the factional strife. He was neutral and had good relationships with everyone, so his promotion could be tolerated by any of the fractions.

Whatever job to take, only a man becomes a man before being a qualified employee, can he cherish the fortuitous opportunities and gain much help. He who is too cunning in his will not get a good result. If one always play the Sun Wukong-style petty tricks, he will never gain the ultimate success.

China finally won the Second Sino-Japanese War (which lasted for eight years from 1937 to 1945) owing to Chinese people's perseverance. As Liu Bang defeated Xiang Yu in the war between Han and Chu, perseverance is victory. On many occasions, people get promotion and rich by chance. One will be doomed to failure if he doesn't cherish what he has already got and not fulfill his duties.

Postscript

Tang Yiming

Mr. Zhu Yuechun and I are good friends despite great difference in age. We met by chance, yet there were some inevitability that brought us together. Although we have different mother tongues and can understand only half of each other's language, we hold identical views.

Loving peace, Mr. Zhu expresses his opinion on Adaptationism. Ism refers to the theoretical system of conceptional deduction. It is a kind of thought and theory based on the logical and empirical methods ever from the ancient Greece to modern British and French.

Quite differently, Mr. Zhu opens a new path. He concisely elucidates the Chinese maxims, aphorisms, idioms, etc. within one thousand words. Mr. Zhu's thoughts in the six volumes can be concluded as to live together in supreme harmony with Adaptationism.

It may cause some criticism to entitle the books as On Adaptationism, because there is lack of long theoretical exposition and system in Mr. Zhu's thoughts of adaptationism. Yet it is precise to regard it as the guiding principle of adaptationism that life is a process of adaptation and people tend to live together in harmony.

Adaptationism as the topic, articles including "Foundation for Mankind", "Seek truth from facts", "Temperament and Virtue",

"Three-year Old Shows One's Future", "City and Guild", "Happenchance and Inevitability" and so on in the six volume covers various problems a man may encounter in his life.

A man lives on "Five Loves" that one should "love oneself, one's family, career, nation and motherland" and two "qualities" that one should act in good faith and with self-confidence.

It is good for a man to "walk in the middle" to lead a good life- "being graceful and sympathetic, and knowing when should give up even in wild eagerness". One should "put effort in cultivating a strong soul", "enjoy our life without bad influence"; "One will be doomed to failure if he doesn't cherish what he has already got and not fulfill his duties" …

To read Mr. Zhu's collection, it is be more or less the same as to see a lady trying on the new clothes-they come out of the fitting room and enter it and come out again…Each article is just like a fitting and to read the 180 articles (preface and postscript included) in the six volumes means to try on 180 clothes. There are full of enlightenment and joy in the process if to feel with the heart.

In Mr. Zhu's collection, the topics cover the aspects of the individual, the society, the nation or the world. He once said that "I would conduct a life with the attitude as if I am poor when I am rich, and with the attitude as if I am a common people when I am with a high official post". And this can be regarded as the most essential interpretation of the guiding line of Mr. Zhu's thoughts that "to live together in supreme harmony with Adaptationism".